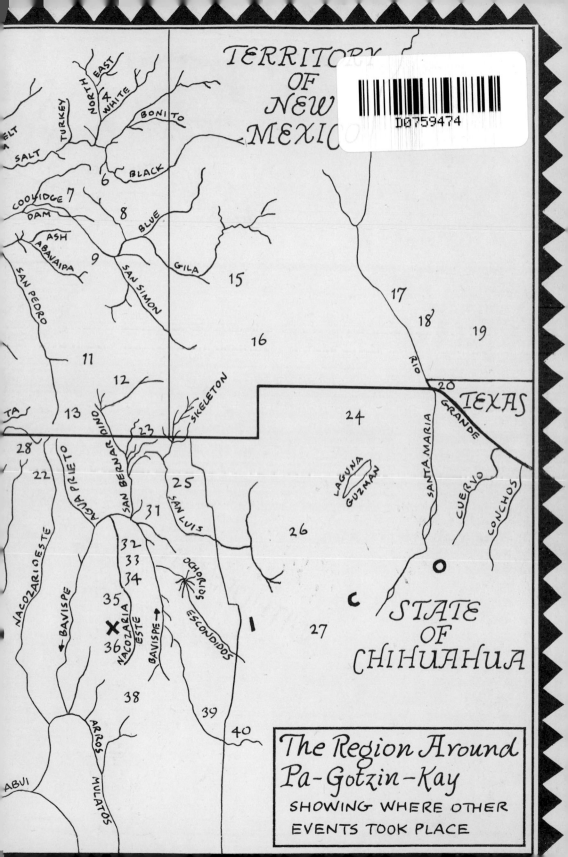

The Region Around
Pa-Gotzin-Kay
SHOWING WHERE OTHER
EVENTS TOOK PLACE

THE FIRST
HUNDRED YEARS
OF
Niño Cochise

THE FIRST
HUNDRED YEARS
OF
Niño Cochise

The Untold Story
of an Apache Indian Chief

AS TOLD BY

Ciyé "Niño" Cochise

TO

A. Kinney Griffith

ABELARD-SCHUMAN

LONDON   NEW YORK   TORONTO

Copyright © 1971 by Ciyé (Niño) Cochise
and A. Kinney Griffith
First published by Abelard-Schuman Limited 1971
All rights reserved

Library of Congress Catalog Card Number: 70-157-980
ISBN: 0-200-71830-4

LONDON	NEW YORK	TORONTO
Abelard-Schuman	Abelard-Schuman	Abelard-Schuman
Limited	Limited	Canada Limited
8 King St. WC2	257 Park Avenue So.	228 Yorkland Blvd.

An Intext Publisher

Printed in the United States of America

Contents

THE FIRST
HUNDRED YEARS
OF
Niño Cochise

Prologue   1872-1876

I WAS BORN in the Dragoon Stronghold, Chiricahua Reservation, Territory of Arizona, on February 20, 1874. My grandfather, Chief Cochise, died there of old age on June 7, 1874. My father, Tahza, the eldest son of Cochise, died in the whiteman's citadel of peace, Washington, D.C., on November 15, 1876.

A peace treaty had been created by Thomas J. Jeffords,[1] Chief Cochise, and General Oliver O. Howard on October 14, 1872. There was to be no more war between the Apache and the whiteman. The Chiricahua Reservation was established on December 14, 1872, by Executive Order: 3,100 square miles in the center of Apacheria. President Grant appointed Tom Jeffords the Agent of this vast domain with its 2,500 population. History records that U.S. Indian Agent John Philip Clum came with scouts and cavalry in the summer of 1876 to force us Chiricahui[2] to vacate our reservation and march to his adjacent San Carlos Reservation.

History further records that Clum's vainglorious effort succeeded in moving only 831 Chiricahua Apaches (212 from scattered clans followed later) to San Carlos, as more than 1,000 others had vanished. It does not record, however, that my father, Tahza,[3] the hereditary chieftain, with something of an

1. An outstanding frontiersman, Jeffords became Blood Brother of Chief Cochise in a sacred ceremony in 1870.
2. Chiricahui is plural, Chiricahua is singular; their formal name is Chi-hui-ca-hui and means "We The People." AKG.
3. Clum spelled it Tah-zay in San Carlos records. AKG.

omniscient mind, foresaw dark days ahead for his people and, although he led his tribe to San Carlos—so that the Chiricahui could not be blamed for breaking the treaty—he adroitly arranged for his own clan of thirty-eight to disappear enroute. Under the leadership of his young wife, Nod-Ah-Sti[4] (who took in the group me, their only son (*ciyé*), Niño Cochise, and the aging *shaman*—medicine man—Dee-O-Det), the family clan escaped and fled south into Sonora, Mexico, disappearing into legendry. They were never again entered on any reservation list.

Since our names had never been entered in military records, none of our clan were ever tagged or tattooed. We had been listed on our original Chiricahua Reservation, but these records disappeared when Taglito[5] resigned in protest over the arrogant breaking of the J-C-H treaty. And Taglito, our beloved Agent, who spoke Apache fluently and knew us all by our true names, would not tell. He promptly dubbed us "The Nameless Ones."[6]

For years our clanspeople laughingly referred to themselves as "the missing ones." The military did not know—or would not admit—that any Chiricahui had escaped while being herded to other reservations.[7]

Two months after the relocation, Clum took a delegation of twenty Apaches, headed by Chief Tahza, to Washington to be interviewed by President Grant. While in Washington, Tahza caught pneumonia and died. He was promptly buried in Congressional Cemetery in an unmarked grave.[8]

4. Tom Jeffords fondly called her Niome and the name stuck.

5. *Taglito* was the name given Jeffords by the Chiricahui collectively and means "Redbeard"; his Blood Brother, Chief Cochise, called him *Chi-ca-Say* (my brother).

6. To this day the names of Tahza's clanspeople do not appear on the rolls of the San Carlos, Fort Apache, or Mescalero Reservations. Officialdom did not, and does not, recognize their existence. Only an occasional Indian visitor's pass would reveal a strange name that harks back to Pinery Canyon, Ajo Caliente, and Chiricahua Reservation days. Not until 1914, when the few still living (who had been railroaded first to Florida, then to Fort Sill, Oklahoma) and their descendants were finally permitted to live on the Mescalero Reservation in New Mexico, were some "Nameless Ones" identified, but not officially. AKG.

7. For data on all reservations see pp. 565–568 of *History of Arizona and New Mexico, 1530–1888,* by Hubert Howe Bancroft, San Francisco, 1889. AKG.

8. In 1960 the Society of Arizona Pioneers erected a headstone over the grave with proper inscription and epitaph. AKG.

Prologue

When Clum returned to San Carlos and told of the unfortunate death of Tahza, my uncle, Naiche, youngest son of Cochise, flew into a violent rage. With other chieftains later to become prominent, he bolted the San Carlos Reservation and rode the war trails, beginning the "Geronimo Wars" that did not end until September, 1886.

Much has been written about those embittered warriors and their families, who so violently objected to the whiteman's perfidy and fought a losing battle to the bitter end, but the pages of history are singularly blank regarding one segment of Apache life:

What happened to those thirty-eight "Nameless Ones" who escaped the whiteman's rule that fateful day in 1876?

And now I, Niño Cochise, pen these lines from memory and from tales told to me by my mother, by my *shaman,* and others who lived and died in that bygone period. I have survived the transition from the days when the whiteman used horse cavalry to fight us, to the present when he uses air cavalry to fight other wars. Yet I find it impossible to pinpoint the time and place where myths and realities merge and where legends die and life goes on regardless.

Chapter 1   1876-1886

Pa-Gotzin-Kay

I WAS only two years old at the time of the hegira, but my mother said I rode behind her on the saddle, or in front of her, depending on which position was best at the time. Naturally I cannot recall it myself.

I do remember our new stronghold in the Sierra Madre for I lived there a long time. It was situated on a shelf of red earth about one kilometer wide and four kilometers long, curving north and south. The western side was a sheer drop-off into Nacozari Canyon. The eastern side flanked an amber escarpment that stretched to the forested, snow-capped range which is the backbone of the Mother Mountains, dividing the incredible Bavispe Barranca from the headwaters of the awesome Yaqui River.

Only an eagle could fly in or a bighorn sheep might safely enter from either side where the shelf was pinched off by a wonderland of rocks. Our horsemen had to creep through narrow, winding clefts at either end, and even this was a perpetual risk as the trails wound around sheer ramparts and a misstep could bring a disastrous fall. It was a natural fortress.

On the shelf were abundant water, trees, fertile red land, and a world of solitude. We had plenty of living room and privacy as well as security. We called it Pa-Gotzin-Kay[1]—in

1. See *An Apache Campaign in the Sierra Madre,* by John G. Bourke, Captain 3rd Cavalry, U.S. Army, Scribners, New York, 1886. Also *On the Border with Crook,* by Captain John G. Bourke, Scribners, New York, 1891. AKG. Pa-Gotzin-Kay was one of about ten seasonal strongholds my ancestors maintained in our *Cima-silkq* (Mother Mountains, or Sierra Madre) long before the Conquistadores came; we also knew the gold, silver, copper ledges such as El Tigre, Tayopa, Las Chipas, Sno-Ta-Hae, and El Cobre.

English, "Stronghold Mountain of Paradise."

Although Indians are supposed to have long memories, events up to the time I was six are vague to me. I must depend mainly on what my mother, our *shaman* (medicine man), and others told me from time to time.

Enroute to Pa-Gotzin-Kay we had lived mostly on cactus fruit, and we fed cactus pulp to our horses. Climbing into the highlands we ate pine nuts, acorns, even skunk cabbage roots. When we arrived at Pa-Gotzin-Kay we were worn down to the rags on our backs and the scrawny horses we rode. We set up a circular camp and began what was undoubtedly the most primitive existence imaginable. We had no guns, though most of the men had belt knives; now they made lances, clubs, traps, bows and arrows—boys became experts at throwing stones—and we managed to kill small animals for our first meals. We used sharp-edged stones as tools to shape the materials that nature provided and built dome-shaped wikiups. We used stones to strike sparks, and once a fire started we seldom let it die out.

There was plenty of deer, bear, burros, cougar, rabbits, jaguar, bighorns, wolves, skunks, squirrels, coatis, and moles; there were also turkeys and an occasional hawk or eagle. Men took turns hunting, day and night. Inherent skill and patience prevailed, and we had meat on the fire and furs and hides for clothes and *kabuns* (moccasins). The chill of autumn came to the mountains, then rain, then snow. The wild animals disappeared. As I think back now, it seems being cold and hungry was our lot in life. Sometimes we called ourselves "the hungry ones."

Our existence was at its lowest point when a Chiricahua brave named Zele galloped in and told Mother that her husband had died in Washington; in her way of thinking he had been killed by the whiteman, and she went into black-face mourning.

❧ ❧ ❧

DURING the next few years other wild-riding braves would show up unexpectedly and tell us of the awful conditions our people were living under in the American reservations. Many people had broken free only to be recaptured by the cavalry led by Apache scouts!

The message bearers would disappear as suddenly as they had arrived—instinctively on the run—and before long larger and more frequent groups of escapees would show up at our hideout to rest up. Always Mother would somehow feed them, although we were no prime examples of well-being other than that we were free.

In the summer of 1880, when I was in my seventh year, an event occurred I'll never forget. Over 300 well-mounted warriors and about 200 of their women, with a long line of laden pack mules burst in like a wild storm. Having broken out of the Warm Springs (Ajo Caliente subagency) and the San Carlos Reservations, they were led by my father's brother, Naiche, and included were my mother's brother, Golthlay, along with Zele, Nanay, Beduiat, Loco, Ponce, Juh, Gar, Gordo, Hal-Say, Mangas, Chatto, Chappo, Perico, Nolge, Chi-hau-hua, Benito, Chuntz, Poin-sen-ay, and Kaah-Tenny.

I will never forget the uproarious activity as they proceeded to unload the mules and butcher several of them, and by nightfall everyone on the rancheria for a change had enough to eat. We ate with both hands, for the first time in memory I satisfied my appetite. The new arrivals went on to tell how enraged they were over reservation life. Although most of them had previously escaped, only to be surrounded and returned, this time they had broken out for good and vowed never to be returned. They were now committed to the *Netdahe* life.[2]

Led by Indian scouts, the American cavalry had been hard on their trail but here they were secure for the Americans could not cross the international border. To show their esteem the wild ones gave us packsaddle-loads of cooking utensils, clothes, blankets, food, grain, saddles, some firearms, and other items—

2. The term *Netdahe* means "death to all intruders." It dates back to the original Spaniards under Coronado and those who followed in their rapacious efforts to conquer Apacheria. The Apache brave took the *Netdahe* oath upon reaching manhood and lived by it the rest of his life. Early in the 19th century the vow was amended to mean "kill all whitemen."

all of which was welcomed, especially as it was loot from ranches and haciendas they had raided on the way south.

After about a week of resting, feasting, boasting, and getting roaring drunk, Nanay took a small group and worked in Sno-Ta-Hae, our gold mine just a few kilometers from camp. Other warriors would form into bands of about forty and ride out; a week or so later they would return, sometimes laden with booty. Sometimes braves were missing while others were bloody with wounds.

I was thrilled with their comings and goings—stalwart braves riding forth to battle with the hated Nakai-Ye[3] and the despised Pinda-Lick-O-Ye[4] in distant places. When they returned, I would creep close to their council meetings and listen to tales of daring exploits and savage battles.

I distinctly remember that Beduiat (commonly called Victorio), a chief of the Warm Springs *iya-aiye*[5] of the Mimbreno Apaches, who now had a stronghold in Miguel Canyon a day's ride northeast from us, stopped off once to rest before riding on to his rancheria. He was running low on rifles and ammunition, and had proposed a treaty with the Mexicans at Vado d'Santa Maria.

Old Nanay, a subchief under Beduiat, hoped that this agreement would bear fruit as they needed the weapons to fight the Americans in the New Mexico and Arizona Territories. Golthlay was away on a raid at the time so Beduiat sent Nanay and another man to make the arrangement. Nanay returned and said the Mexicans had agreed to supply weapons for gold and would prepare a great fiesta with plenty of tequila for all.

Beduiat sent Nanay and four men to fetch the gold which they had cached at his rancheria. Meanwhile, urged by the promise of much tequila, Beduiat and his main band of about ninety warriors got restless and rode on ahead, east toward Santa Maria, a four days' ride, there to await Nanay and the gold.

When Beduiat arrived at Santa Maria the fiesta was already in full sway. He was greeted by the alcalde, Colonel Garcia. Beduiat explained that the gold would be there soon. Garcia

3. Nakai-Ye: Mexicans; Nakai is singular—pronounced *Nockavdi*.
4. Pinda-Lick-O-Ye: White-Eyes, Pale-Eyes.
5. Clans.

seemed pleased and told Beduiat to gather his men in the plaza where the young Mexican women would serve them food and drink. The warriors tied their horses to hitch rails and joined the local people; but the señoritas suddenly dropped their *botellas* and gourds and ran away.

Then Beduiat saw that he and his men were ambushed— surrounded by Mexican *soldatos de cuera* (leather-shirt soldiers). He shouted an order and the warriors ran for their horses. The first volley cut down a score of them but the remaining Apaches made their escape on the horses. The *soldatos* followed, and a running battle lasted through the night. Dawn found them in the Sabinal Hills (Galena) near Lake Guzman. At sunrise, Garcia's soldiers were reinforced by General Terrazas and a regiment of red-shirt cavalrymen. But the Apaches were equally mobile and the fight lasted into the next day. They fought until they were completely out of ammunition. While fighting with only lances for weapons, Beduiat (Victorio) was shot out of the saddle. Only six braves escaped, and all were wounded; they were rallied by a war-chief named Mangas, son of the late Mangas Coloradas.

Old Nanay, on his way to Santa Maria, met Mangas and the wounded men and brought them to Pa-Gotzin-Kay, where Golthlay heard about Beduiat's defeat.[6]

While at that time the U.S. Army was not allowed to cross the border, this ban said nothing about Indian scouts. Shortly after Beduiat's force was destroyed, information sifted in to Golthlay that Sergeant Mickey Free of the Apache Scouts had sent word to Garcia that Beduiat would be in Vado d'Santa Maria to trade for guns. Free, it was also believed, had apprised Terrazas of the whereabouts of Beduiat's war party.

Mangas told Naiche and Golthlay (who now was known as Geronimo) how the ambush and subsequent battle were carried out. Golthlay immediately called his men and made plans for vengeance. He notified Chi-hau-hau, Juh, and Chatto, who now had rancherias in nearby canyons.

In the meanwhile Apache outriders had reported on Ter-

6. This account of Victorio's last battle differs from the reports made by U.S. Army Scout Mickey Free and recorded by Lieutenants Thomas Cruse and Charles B. Gatewood in the *Scouts Journals* at Fort Bowie and Fort Cummings, but the time, place, and results are the same. AKG.

razas' return route through the mountains. The chieftains mapped out battle tactics, splitting their forces of over 200 warriors into four groups. In the up-Bavispe River Canyon they caught the Apache-hater in an ambush from which he barely escaped alive.

Quoting the Old Ones of our tribe, I want to state here—regardless of what contemporary historians say or think—that Golthlay (Geronimo) was not the world's smartest man, not even by Apache tribal standards. When he was drunk or suffering with a hangover, which was frequently the case, he was either an absolute dullard or a ferocious beast. When cold sober, he was a bombastic speaker. He was a dreamer type but, if given time, would come up with some cunning way to organize a fight or a raid. This drew the average warrior to him and many idolized him, but when it came down to urgent, on-the-spot decisions in battle, my Uncle Naiche was the hero *every* time.

❦ ❦ ❦

THE *Netdahe* war party returned with sixty horses and ten pack mules loaded with many Mexican rifles and much ammunition, along with crates and bags of edible spoils. This plunder was divided between participating warriors and their families. There was a great feast in Pa-Gotzin-Kay that night, and Golthlay became the orator:

"We lost three men," he began, then named them. "They were brave men." (Their names were never mentioned again; that is Apache law.) "We left many Nakai-Ye *gusanos* to the crows. We gained many *besh-shea-gar,*[7] and many good *chelee.*[8] But that is not enough. We will ride to Santa Maria and punish others who murdered Beduiat and his brave warriors. He was our greatest chief—next to Chies-Co-Chise[9] and Mangas Coloradas!"[10]

Nanay and Mangas stood up simultaneously and shouted that

7. Iron-that-shoots.
8. Horse (s).
9. The formal name of Chief Cochise.
10. Red (bloody) Sleeves, also called Roan Shirt. AKG.

they craved vengeance on Santa Maria; Chief Naiche roared the same sentiments and said they would ride in the morning. There were shouts of agreement from all sides.

That night in our wikiup I could hear Mother sobbing. In the morning before dawn I heard her speaking by our fire with Dee-O-Det, Naiche, and Golthlay. What was said I do not know —no mere boy was allowed to come near them—but I caught something about Pa-Gotzin-Kay . . . "a peaceful place" . . . and "for The People to keep it that way."

After daybreak the war party rode out of our stronghold in single file, down the treacherous trail to Tesorabi, a small pueblo that had never recovered from a raid in which Beduiat had wrecked it. They by-passed Basaranca, a larger village on the flats of the Bavispe Bend, near where they had ambushed Terrazas three days before.

Cutting straight east to Santa Maria, a barrio of about 100 people, they had one purpose in mind: to destroy our enemies. The townspeople saw the Apaches coming and took to the hills, leaving only a few to resist. They were quickly overcome and killed. Golthlay (Geronimo) burned two men in the small church, while Nanay and Mangas set fire to the town. Most of the buildings were of adobe but had brush roofs that burned easily. The warriors rode into the canyons to hunt down those that hid there and killed them without mercy.

The *Netdahe* gathered up about 100 head of cattle and goats, a few horses and mules, and captured about twenty women and children, all of whom were descendants of Indian mothers and Mexican slave masters. The people and the loot, Golthlay gave to Chief Juh, who had the smallest band, having lost most of his clan at Janos over twenty years before and never having regained a good following.[11]

11. Back in 1858, Chief Juh, with his followers, a wild mixture of all the Apache tribes, including Golthlay and his young clan, had camped near Janos. They had traded turquoise stones for some food and pulque and were celebrating. A Mexican colonel named Carasco, with a troop of Chihuahueno cavalry, surprised the Apache camp and massacred most of the women and siblings, including Golthlay's mother, his first wife, Alope (nee Juh), and their two small children. The enraged Golthlay and Juh rallied their drunken men and killed over half of the *soldatos* and routed the rest—earning for himself the Mexican name: Geronimo. *I Fought with Geronimo* by Jason Betzinez, The Stackpole Company, Harrisburg, 1959. AKG.

Back in our rancheria my mother again protested so vehemently about her brother's savage raids—"you will bring the whole Mexican army down on us"—that Golthlay moved out of Pa-Gotzin-Kay and set up a permanent camp in Cienega Canyon near Chi-hua-hua's rancheria twenty kilometers nearer the border. From there he made frequent raids into the New Mexico and Arizona territories, as well as in the states of Chihuahua and Sonora.

During a drinking spree after one of these raids, Golthlay (Geronimo) was surrounded by American troops and forced to surrender his whole following. They were herded into the San Carlos and the Whiteriver (Fort Apache) Reservations, and for a few years there was peace and quiet in Pa-Gotzin-Kay.

🌱 🌱 🌱

THEN one day in 1884, Golthlay and a large band of *Netdahe* suddenly arrived back at our peaceful rancheria. Mother was greatly disturbed, but could do little about it.

Golthlay brought me a fine pinto mustang and told me to take good care of it. I was grateful, but tried to hide my pleasure. Then Naiche gave me a silver-mounted saddle and a bridle with hand-wrought silver headstall.

"You are both my best uncles!" I exclaimed. "*A-co-'d.*"[12]

I always admired Naiche. Everyone said he was like his father, my grandfather, Chief Cochise. Now, at the age of ten, I was soon to be a warrior—or so I thought.

There were six other boys about my age in our clan and for the past few years our main job had been to hunt for meat. We meat hunters always used bow and arrows and traps, as in the olden days. Mother would not let us use firearms; she said the sounds of shooting might betray our hiding place. No dogs were allowed in the rancheria for the sounds of their barking could have been heard for great distances, especially at night. Now, at Naiche's suggestion, Mother named me chief of the hunters. I went around walking on clouds. Was I not a chief? Even though only Hunting Chief, I was proud of the title.

12. "Thank you!"—an expression seldom used.

This was *maba* (bear) hunting time—the season when he was fat and lazy—and our people needed more bear grease. While we were ranging the hills after bruin, deer and rabbits invaded our field of half-grown corn. We turned our attention there and soon our stock of dried venison grew, with fourteen deer killed the first week, and an uncounted number of coatis, squirrels, turkeys, and brush rabbits. Soon the deer and other animals left our garden and field, but those pesky rabbits never did learn. However, as long as we could grow things, we had no critical food shortage. Even our small herd of horses that had been found unfit by the warriors, and about thirty head of cattle left from the raiding days were increasing in numbers; all we needed now was a normal amount of luck.

The warriors, however, well-fed and rested, went back to their old habits of mysteriously going and coming, and one evening Golthlay stood at the council fire and in a strong voice told how he had raided a White-Eyes ranch along Sonoita Creek and burned the house and barn and driven off the cattle and horses. Then soldiers of *Los Goddammies* had come, and in the fight he killed many of them, but four of his warriors were killed, including subchief Poin-sen-ay.

On these sad occasions, the wives and children disappeared to some private retreat to grieve for their loved ones. During the period of mourning, the widows cut their hair short and rubbed mud and ashes on their faces. I shared the grief of Poin-sen-ay's widow and her son Kasale, who was my youngest and newest hunter.

After Kasale concluded his keening, I asked him if he would like to have several boys for hunters and act as their chief. He was elated and seemed to forget his grief. There was a bit of ritual attached to this, so I led him to my mother's wikiup.

I asked for permission to enter with a friend, and when she gave us permission, we went in and sat cross-legged on the floor. She brought us some meat and ashcakes. After eating I said:

"I think we need more hunters to keep the camp in meat."

"Then get them," Mother said. "You are chief of all the hunters."

"I will need another chief to lead the new party."

"Then make a new chief. That is the law."

"I will name Kasale to be my new chief."

Kasale and I recruited hunters and put them to work making arrows. I rounded up four old horses. At dawn the boys rode out and, as luck would have it, the first canyon below the south rampart had deer in it and each hunter soon had his *venado*.

The Apache wasted nothing: the entrails were not removed on the spot of the kill. Whitemen, I have been told, called us "gut-eaters." We did eat some of the gut if we were very hungry, but usually made the gut into thread for sewing, thongs for tying, bags for carrying water and food. Some blood was lost in the on-the-spot cleaning of the deer, however, and that was when trouble started for our novice hunters.

Kasale had brought his horse close to load his deer, but the horse balked at the smell of blood. It reared and kicked, spooking the others, and they all bolted. A horse will always return to his home corral and these ran true to form.

I was home at the time and saw the four riderless horses, saddles flapping, come galloping into camp, two abreast. Golthlay, Naiche, and Dee-O-Det were strolling our way when the horses ran by. Golthlay and Naiche stepped nimbly aside, but the old *shaman* was not so quick. A flapping stirrup caught him a glancing blow and knocked him down. He growled something about this crazy place as he struggled back up. Golthlay shot me a look and we hurried over to the corral and examined the horses.

"These are the horses of my new hunters," I said. "Kasale, Boa Juan, Kersus, and Peridot. Maybe they rode into trouble with some Mexicans."

"No. This is deer hair, and there is blood low on the side of the saddle. If a man was shot while in the saddle, the blood would be on top, running down. These *chelee* did not run far; they are not blowing. Come, Niño, you are the hunting chief, bring the *chelee* and we will find your hunters."

He and Naiche mounted their horses. We had back-tracked only a short distance beyond the south rampart when we saw the boys trudging up the canyon trail. Glad to see their runaways, they led us back to where their deer were down. We dismounted, and Golthlay told Kasale to bring his horse close. The horse shied, but Naiche grabbed one deer carcass and dragged it close to the skittish animal. Golthlay, holding his own mount, jerked a limb from an old log and with his free hand whacked the horse between the ears. The animal staggered. As it recovered, Golthlay whacked it again, and this time dropped it to its knees. Naiche then tossed the deer across the saddle. The horse staggered to its feet on shaky legs and stood still while Naiche roped the carcass across the saddle. The other horses also got rough handling, but from that time on most anything could have been loaded on them.

❦❦❦

THE day came when the warriors brought back Uncle Golthlay (Geronimo) wounded. He had stopped a pistol ball in the fleshy part of his left thigh and the slug was lodged against the bone. He could walk on it, but limped badly. Mother helped Dee-O-Det dress the wound with herbs, and the *shaman* also dusted it with *hodenten*,[13] but it kept on swelling and turning blue. It was obvious that Golthlay needed better help; otherwise he would either lose the leg or die.

While returning from their most recent foray, Golthlay's men had rescued a boy fleeing from two vaqueros who wanted to kill him for stealing a calf. The vaqueros fought back and Golthlay was wounded. The *Netdahe* killed the Mexicans and brought the boy along to the rancheria. He looked like an Indian, but it turned out he too was a Mexican. He was about sixteen and because his Mexican name was hard to pronounce we named him Nakai, and the name stuck. Nakai soon proved himself to be a good Apache; in his gratitude for having been rescued, he offered to fetch a *médico* for the wounded Golthlay.

The situation was discussed; then Nakai, Chief Naiche, and I were elected to ride to Magdalena. We all spoke some Mexican-Spanish, but only Nakai knew the doctor. When we arrived at Magdalena, Naiche and I hid ourselves outside the village. It was not long before Nakai came with the doctor in tow. After they passed us and were well beyond the village, Naiche and I caught up with them. At gun point Naiche told the doctor to dismount; then he blindfolded him, so as not to reveal the route

13. Made from ground tule pollen and/or pollen from poppies; made sacred by the *shaman's* incantations.

to Pa-Gotzin-Kay. Nakai introduced the *médico* as Pablo Gutierrez; he had told him that a rock-scratcher (prospector) had broken a leg and blood poisoning had set in. The doctor, not in the least fooled, asked Nakai in Spanish: "What do these Apache want of me?"

"We have a wounded warrior and we want you to heal him."

We rode silently most of the way back to the rancheria. The doctor's blindfold was removed and he could see the women peering out of their wikiups. He also noted the armed men.

Naiche led the doctor to the wikiup where the patient was lying on a bed of skins. Dee-O-Det knelt nearby, chanting, and doing something with his *hodenten* bag. Doctor Gutierrez ignored him and got down to work. He examined the wound and located the bullet. Golthlay grunted; Dee-O-Det cackled; I watched, fascinated. Gutierrez probed for the bullet and extracted it. Golthlay sighed with relief. Then the doctor poured some smelly stuff into the festering wound, and Golthlay let out a bellow that could have been heard clear across the canyon.

Doctor Gutierrez proceeded to bandage the leg with white cloth, and the patient began to relax. The doctor then asked if he was free to go. Golthlay said he would be escorted back, but he must first eat and drink, as it was a long ride to Magdalena.

Mother and another woman brought chunks of roasted mule meat and corn on the cob and served both doctor and patient. When they finished eating Golthlay got out a small ovendi bag counted out two gold pieces (I think about $100.00), gave them to the doctor, and asked if that was enough. The doctor smiled and said it was more than enough, and if he was ever needed again to send for him.

❦ ❦ ❦

GOLTHLAY got well and he and his followers left. My mother was glad because, although a *Netdahe's* daughter, she now dreaded the warrior clans as they always presaged trouble. Yet she would not even dream of denying them a haven in Pa-Gotzin-Kay.

Autumn came to the high sierra, and frost was in the air. We hunters began our annual deer, bear, and elk hunt, so we would

have meat to eat and skins to keep us warm all winter. We
hunted the first day in the mountain meadows south of Lookout
Peak and did not see any deer, not even their spoor. Then we
saw the reason—the tracks of a huge cougar. We tracked the cat
until dark, then made camp. We spent a restless night—every
now and then the cougar would scream nearby, as if defying
us.

About noon the next day we met Kasale and his hunters resting beside the stream in a small canyon. We dismounted and
drank, and while our horses drank, we talked about the cougar.
Getting restless, I walked up along the creek a bit and suddenly
saw the clear outline of a cougar's pugs. As I studied the track,
to my amazement a blade of grass that had been crushed
beneath the cat's paw sprang to an upright position. Now I
knew the cougar was close enough to be watching me!

Excited, I waved to the others of the combined party to come
and see what I had found. They brought the horses and we
spread out. I had never killed a big cat, but I knew of their
power to fight when cornered. I had not gone far up the trail
when a movement above caught my eye. It was the big cougar,
slinking toward the top of the rimrock.

Kasale joined me and I apprised him of the situation. He
circled back to climb the rimrock, while I worked along the
bottom of the brushy canyon. The cougar, sighting Kasale,
promptly hit for higher ground, climbing to the backbone of the
ledge where there were many caves. When the other hunters
joined me, we eased our mounts toward the top. This was a
natural place for a cat to lie in wait for anyone stalking it. We
dismounted and led our horses, cautiously watching the terrain. Some of the caves in the sandstone ledges were big enough
for a cougar den, others so large they had once housed families
of Yamparika Indians. Now there was spoor all around, with a
set of fresh tracks leading into one cave.

While our hunters ground-hitched our horses a short distance below, Kasale and I held council on the small shelf in
front of the cave. We decided that if we all came close to that
dark hole and kept our best arrows aimed on taut bows, we
could put eight shafts into the cat as it came out.

On impulse, I grabbed the dirtiest, sweatiest headband
within reach—Kersus'—and threw it into the cave. It brought

prompt results. The cougar bounded out, roaring, followed by two squealing kittens. Six of us fired arrows as planned; two missed—the bowmen had froze with "buck fever."

The snarling cougar sprang into the air and tumbled head over tail down the rocky slope off the shelf. As she struggled, several of us loosed second arrows. One arrow penetrated the cat's open mouth. During her death throes we calmed down a little and it became apparent whose arrow was stuck down in the beast's gullet. Mine. Boa Juan and Kasale caught and killed the kits.

It was then that we discovered that all of our horses had stampeded during the commotion. Sadly, but wiser, we rigged a tote-pole and four of us took turns carrying the cougar about three kilometers back to the rancheria, arriving long after moonrise. We then had to skin the lioness and her kits. Later the kits' skins became excellent arrow quivers. The old cougar's hide was tanned and I slept on it for many years.

❦ ❦ ❦

AS the rancheria was quieting down one night, the cry of a night bird was relayed from the north ramparts. Our vedette said people were coming. Soon Golthlay and about thirty Wild Ones galloped into the compound, herding six of the scrawniest mules I had ever seen. The commotion rousted everybody out of the wikiups, but there were few cheers of welcome, only acceptance. Some of us boys drove the mules into a corral, others took care of the warriors' horses; then we all hurried over to the fires to hear what they had to say.

Golthlay sat cross-legged, as if in deep thought, but Naiche held the center of attention, telling of their sweep through the Santa Cruz Valley, Arizona. As they neared the Don Pedro (Pete Kitchen) ranch, they carefully scouted the area. Seeing no one, they approached the nearest barn and attempted to force the door which was barred from inside.

A beehive nearby was upset when a warrior picked up a fence post with which to ram the barn door. The bees came swarming forth and the invaders were routed. Along Portrero Creek they encountered the six old mules. They took them, but not without mishap. A ranch hand hiding along the creek bank foolishly fired his ever-ready muzzle-loader at the Apaches, and the *Netdahe* promptly killed him. Three men in the fields beyond the creek heard the shots and closed in to give battle. The warriors killed them and left, with no casualties, but with booty of only six rawboned mules. Mulemeat, however, is good meat.

After Naiche ended his tale of the raid, Golthlay stood up and told of seeing and avoiding a large column of American cavalry riding the San Bernardino Springs trail, but of being seen by a pair of their Indian scouts. One scout wounded Loco, and Kaah-Tenny shot the scout. But Golthlay had one of his "feelings" that the White-Eyes were closing in on him. Golthlay was known to have a sixth sense, a prescient mind.

Once again Nakai and I were told to go fetch the doctor. Recently Doctor Gutierrez had moved his office to Basaranca; this was a more prosperous mining, farming, and cattle town than sleepy little Magdalena, and only about twenty kilometers from Pa-Gotzin-Kay. The doctor actually seemed glad to see us, maybe because he knew he would be well paid. We did not blindfold him, and he was talkative, asking how Geronimo was —using the Mexican name for Golthlay—and adding sarcastically that if current rumors were true he must be doing fine.

We arrived at the rancheria just as the sun was rising beyond the mountain, coloring a sweep of amber mare's-tail clouds that made one think half the sky was on fire. We led the doctor directly to the big communal kiva. Inside several women were busy with hot water, tending the wounds of two men, with Dee-O-Det helping. The doctor went right to work.

Old Loco had a bad wound, the Apache scout's bullet having entered his right side and torn up several ribs. Golthlay came in and greeted Gutierrez:

"*Cómo l'va, Médico?*"

"*Muy bien,*" the doctor grunted as he glanced up. Obviously intent on his surgery and unable to speak any but his native tongue, he nevertheless found time to give Golthlay a piece of his mind, telling him that he had incurred the renewed wrath of the Mexican government and that the *soldatos* were hunting him with renewed vigor. He advised Golthlay to surrender to the Americans, as the way he was behaving was bringing destruction down on all Mansos.[14]

Golthlay just bragged about how he had destroyed many Mexicans and their towns, would destroy more, and that he did not want anything to do with *Los Goddammie* Pinda-Lick-O-Ye.

"Pinda-Lick-O-Ye or Nakai-Ye, gringos or greasers, papists, or *Los Goddammies"* he once said, "I often wonder which I hate the most." Both had, of course, repeatedly betrayed him. Golthlay was a hard man to understand.

Later in our wikiup I found him talking with my mother:

"I will send Pa-Nays-Tishin to San Carlos to find Tzoe," I heard him say. "Tzoe is a stupid Tonto, but is the favorite Apache scout for General Crook. Tzoe is also his eyes and ears on the reservation. The *Innaa* call him 'Peaches.' He workes for both sides, for the yellow iron. He will get Pa-Nays-Tishin to join the scouts. The scouts are all over Arizona and Sonora looking for me. Pa-Nays-Tishin and Tzoe will decoy them to the lower rancherias where they will realize we could easily destroy them. Then Crook will talk peace."

"You make any kind of peace you want, my brother, but do not surrender me or anyone who wants to stay with me."

"Ha! Do you want to stay and fight the Mexicans?"

"No!" Mother snapped. "I can live in peace here in Pa-Gotzin-Kay. Only those will stay who do not believe in war."

"You will starve. What will you eat for meat?"

"You forget our boys are hunters. With no wars, they will have time to hunt more. Also our cattle will have calves if they are not eaten by your men before they have time to breed."

❧ ❧ ❧

THE next morning Golthlay and his warriors were gone, except for the few wounded. About ten days later he and Naiche returned with some loot and distributed it. I got a Hamilton gold

14. P. Tomás Manso, kindly curator and *procurador* of New Mexico for Spain from 1630 to 1655, had a notable influence on the Chiricahua, Mimbreno, and Mescalero tribes. AKG.

watch, which I still have. Mules were butchered and a fill-up feast was had by all. Then a council meeting was called.

Golthlay wanted to talk. He told of going to Casas Grande to see the Mexicans about a peace treaty, and the Nakai-Ye were good to them, giving them much tequila. Many warriors became very drunk and fell asleep, and the Mexicans slaughtered four who could not wake up. It was the same old story; a trap baited with liquor for the Apaches. Golthlay walked into this trap all his adult life.

He became boastful, telling how they fought their way clear, and when riding back to his rancheria in Cienega Canyon, he saw a camp of American soldiers which he promptly surrounded, taking many horses and mules. He did not lose a man there. Now, as they had invaded Mexico, he was at war with the Americans, and he was at war with *all* Mexicans except those who lived in Basaranca.

Golthlay emptied a bottle with a long drink. Then, waving it above his head, he let out a fierce Apache war cry:

"Cat-ra-ra atà un' Innaa ǹ un' Nakai-Ye!" (Curses and destruction on all whitemen and Mexicans!)

The celebration lasted until the tequila and mescal ran out in about two days, with everybody feeling fighting mean. Golthlay, Naiche, Juh, Chi-hua-hua, Kaah-Tenny, Nanay, Mangas, and Benito, with their respective clans, planned another raid. As it was winter, they chose the warm desert lowlands of Sonora.

After attacking several ranches, they took time out to eat and drink all the spoils before attacking the village of Galenta. Here the Mexican military was bivouaced. The *Netdahe* killed at least thirty *soldatos* and escaped with twelve braves lost.

They returned to Pa-Gotzin-Kay two months later, and again Golthlay became the schemer and orator.

"Now all listen to me! The Americans have scouts all over the hills. Many are Apaches; they spoke to us. We are all going to move down to Chi-hua-hua's rancheria . . . the Americans will be there and we will talk peace. We cannot forever hold out against both the Mexicans and the Americans. We cannot make a treaty with the Mexicans—they stab us in the back every time! But the whiteman—maybe . . . " Golthlay stared at the many faces before him.

"It is not that I want peace, neither do I want Big Sleep. I do not care for myself, but I care for our families. When our enemies get together it will be only a matter of time; they are too many for us. Our bones will lie white in the mountains, the canyons, the deserts. Then we will be no more—*enju!*"

The council quickly voted for peace, but Naiche stood up. However, Dee-O-Det, our canny old *shaman*,[15] had dismissed the council knowing Naiche did not want to surrender; he was a *Netdahe* who would fight both Americans and Mexicans to the end. Golthlay, possessing a keener imagination (or intuition) would surrender if he foresaw advantage in doing so. Besides, Tzoe (Peaches)[16] had brought word that General Crook had promised Golthlay would be reunited with his family at San Carlos. Golthlay was a persuasive talker, as was his warrior son Chappo, and his half-brother Perico. After the meeting ended, the trio took Naiche to one side with a jug of pulque and by the time the jug was empty they had won him over.

The next morning both Naiche and Golthlay came to our wikiup in a hangover mood. Golthlay intended to bait Mother into moving our clan to San Carlos with him. Mother flatly refused. Naiche suggested she could move south into Yaqueria. Both said Pa-Gotzin-Kay was no longer safe. She maintained that we would be safe here if the *Netdahe* would move out and do their fighting elsewhere. She blamed our troubles on all whitemen—from the Spaniards on down to *Los Goddammies* with their craving for yellow iron and white iron. Only Taglito (Tom Jeffords) was exempted: "He does not speak with a forked tongue," she maintained.

The two chieftains turned to leave, having lost the battle with this shrewd woman. I was squatted just outside the low door as they came through, Naiche first. With boyish impishness I thrust an arrow between Golthlay's legs, and he tripped and fell to his knees. I leaped up, was off and running. I knew I was fleet of foot, but he was soon gaining on me. In terror of being caught, I stopped abruptly and dropped to all fours. He came

15. The tribal *shaman,* or medicine man, always had the last word.
16. In later years at Fort Apache, his son Teddy Peaches gave this collaborator much information on the life and times in Pa-Gotzin-Kay during the 1880's. AKG.

thundering like a charging stallion, tripped over me, and went skidding on his elbows. I made my second mistake by laughing at him.

He grabbed me by the belt of my *himper* and the scruff of my neck and tossed me high into a young pine tree. Just when I thought I was safe up there, although hanging precariously, he shook the tree, roaring with rage, and when I came tumbling down, he walked away, laughing with maniacal glee.

🌺 🌺 🌺

SOON came the day when there was a sudden exodus from Pa-Gotzin-Kay. Where there had been over 300 lean and hungry Apaches of all ages yesterday, today there were but forty-five, including the wounded. About half were youngsters of various sizes. Only six people in the prime of life were left, among them my mother and her sister Nadina.[17] The rest were old people, including our *shaman,* Dee-O-Det.

I took my hunters out to scour the hills, and we soon found that General Crook's cavalry and scouts were combing the region. We had doubts that Golthlay's peace-treaty plan would work, so Mother ordered us to take no chances. Our clan prepared to slip away from the rancheria and hide in the Bavispe Canyon caves until we were sure.

Tzoe, the "sympathetic" Apache scout with the cavalry, arrived one night and told us that Crook's forces had made the hazardous march to the Sierra Madre to accept the surrender of Golthlay and all his Apaches, a surrender that Golthlay had well planned. Nothing was known about us Pa-Gotzin-Kay Apaches.

Crook's march through the rugged terrain had indeed been a tremendous military campaign. Following the old Apache trails, his forces had toiled up the sheer canyon-wall trail with its many switchbacks, and criss-crossed the mighty Bavispe Barranca and its many tributaries to the headwater canyons of

17. Nadina had been captured several years earlier with Chatto's band after the McComas killing and had been penned on the Mescalero Reservation. After a time she and her half-grown son, Alchise, jumped the reservation and found their way to Pa-Gotzin-Kay.

24

the Yaqui gorge. Soldiers who had "crossed the canyon" had accomplished what they considered one of life's great adventures, but to Apaches it was just another crossing.

Tzoe, Pa-Nays-Tishin, Mickey Free, Kay-I-Tah, and Martiné had performed an admirable feat; they had led the other scouts as well as the troopers away from Pa-Gotzin-Kay, El Tigre, and Tayopa, yet had so effectively covered the Sierra Madre range that the Wild Ones and their families were gradually moved north toward the border. They rendezvoused at Chief Chi-hua-hua's rancheria located in a small glade outside *Cañon de los Embudos* (Fraud Canyon). Chi-hua-hua came out to greet them, saying he was ready to surrender and that Golthlay and his bands would be in later.

Actually Golthlay and his braves were already behind boulders on the rimrock above the box-canyon, ready for any sign of treachery from the white cavalry. Even some of the Apache scouts Crook had with him were fooled. The scouts had gone into the canyon in advance of the troops. When they had scouted the rancheria, they reported back to Crook that the position in the canyon was dangerous, but for the time being it was clear. Had fighting broken out, Crook could not have retreated; the trail ended in the glade hard by an unscalable wall, which is why it was called Fraud Canyon. On the single-file trail, the *Netdahe* would pin them in a deadly cross-fire, as Golthlay pointed out later to the dauntless general.

When the wily old Chi-hua-hua was satisfied that peace would be made with Crook, he sent word up to Golthlay, who took a round-dance trail down to the rancheria.

They all sat down to talk; the officers on one side, the Apaches on the other, the interpreters in the middle. This was the spring of 1885. Crook had even brought a photographer along to record the event. They talked on and on into the night. In the meanwhile the cavalry cooks were preparing a big meal of several of Crook's pack mules that had fallen off the switchbacks of the sheer canyon trail. These carcasses were brought into camp and roasted, and Crook's Indian scouts and the Wild Ones joined in a friendly feast.

The next day Crook agreed to make peace with Geronimo— as that doughty officer insisted on calling Golthlay. Naiche, Chi-hua-hua, Kaah-Tenny, and other chiefs (with all their peo-

brushy tule basin—a perfect hiding place in case of necessity. Arrangements were made for parleying between Crook and his aides and Golthlay, Naiche, and Chi-hua-hua the next morning.

An illicit trader named Jean Tribollet, hovering on the outskirts that night, saw his chance and traded Golthlay several jugs of rotgut for a tote bag full of Mexican jewelry that the men had acquired on recent raids. The Wild Ones soon were roaring drunk and, in drunken exuberance, Naiche fired his gun into the air.

Golthlay, hearing the shot in the dark, thought fighting had broken out with the soldiers; he let out the fierce *Netdahe* war cry. He and Naiche and about forty of their closest followers stampeded (with great glee, I was told later) and headed for the mountains. When the dust settled only about 100 Apaches remained for Crook's custody.

From the military point of view this was a disaster, and General Crook was soon replaced by General Nelson A. Miles, on whose staff was Lieutenant Charles B. Gatewood. Golthlay knew Gatewood and trusted him—somewhat. The next contact was again made by scouts led by Mickey Free, in September, 1886. Golthlay refused to have anything to do with Free, but agreed to surrender to Gatewood—at Skeleton Canyon in the Territory of New Mexico. He and his band of Wild Ones were now treated as prisoners of war, and were promptly convoyed to Fort Bowie, Arizona, and put on a train to Florida, never again to return to their homelands in Arizona.

Chapter 2 1887-1889

Transition

PEACE, we all felt, had definitely come to Pa-Gotzin-Kay and everyone pitched in to make our rancheria an even better place in which to live. We cleaned up the shelf from the eastern cliff-face to the western drop-off, from the north rampart to the southern barrier of rocks. Recovery crews combed the area for anything usable that had been abandoned in the hectic days gone by, piling items in a big central kiva—odds and ends of clothing, blankets, furs, pots, pans, saddles, horseshoes and hoof boots, Colt pistols and Remington rifles, most of the guns needing repairs. One group worked at picking up debris—dead trees were chopped into firewood, brush would make kindling, trash was either burned or thrown over the rimrock at a place where it would not be seen. We dismantled ramshackle wikiups and built new ones around an enlarged compound. We built a large corral of brush and two smaller ones of rails. Our hunters kept us supplied with meat; young women foraged in the hills for nuts and berries. We improved our fields and carefully attended our livestock.

We reopened our gold mine; this was the Spanish gold vein Nanay had discovered years before, and the Wild Ones had worked at times. Now that they were gone, we worked it, calling it "Sno-Ta-Hae." ("Just lying there")

When *Chawn-Chissy* (winter) next walked the mountains, we settled down to doing only necessary chores, with time out for ceremonials and the holding of council by the Old Ones.

A committee of three had, unsuspected by me at least, been

keeping a sharp eye on the behavior of the older boys. Three of us were told to present ourselves dressed in best garb at the next autumnal full tribal council: I, Niño Cochise, Young Chi-hua-hua, and Nakai—the Mexican waif who looked like an Apache and acted like one, yet possessed the aggressive canniness of some distant Spanish forebear. A report was then made before the council by the three people who had secretly observed our behavior during the two years just passed. Our virtues were extolled and shortcomings evaluated, with the result that I was elected chief of our whole hodgepodge tribe. Nakai was elected my subchief, and young Chi-hua-hua was appointed my assistant or whatever title I wished to give him now that I was the chieftain. I was going on fifteen. My mother had been and remained the "Queen Bee" and of course old Dee-O-Det remained as tribal *shaman.*

A prolonged cheer went up to confirm the selections. I was choked with emotion as Mother brought me forth dressed in a long buckskin jerkin trimmed with squirrel tails and embroidered with beads, shells, and a gold swastika. My *himper* was of wool. My *kabuns* were hip-high and fringed, and their turned-up toes tinkled with tiny silver bells. My headdress was a white turban of woven eagle-breast feathers.

The people began to chant:

> *Who does she bring?*
> *Who does she bring?*

The high-pitched voice of Dee-O-Det replied:

> *Our young chief she brings!*
> *She gave him life and now she gives him to us!*

He sprinkled *hodenten* first on my face, then to the east, then to the west, the north, the south, and finally on the fire. As he placed a necklace of cougar claws—a powerful charm—around my neck, Mother said:

"I also have a present for our young chief. His father gives it through me."

She hung the turquoise Thunderbird Emblem that was the badge of High Chief of the Chiricahui around my neck. Tears came to my eyes; I could not stop them. I walked quickly toward our wikiup as though I sought something, but it was really to hide the tears. I was able to get control of myself finally and went back to the council fire, where Mother sat at my right and Nakai at my left. Food was brought and a rousing feast got under way. Someone had made *tulepa* (beer), but there wasn't much, as we had very little grain from which to brew it.

Mother had promised to tell me about my father when I became a man and she now sat and talked about him until long after the others had gone to their wikiups. I remained silent, listening, thinking. I had heard stories about my father, Tahza, and how, along with Uncle Naiche, they had promised their dying father Cochise that they would keep the peace.[1] Now I understood a lot more about my ancestors.

❧ ❧ ❧

APRIL, 1889, came. I was now going on sixteen, tall and slender. We were living off nature, as was our tribal custom, but this year I determined to make a greater effort to obtain things that my uncles had told me about. I said to Mother:

"When Golthlay and Naiche were with us they brought us many things, things they said they bought at Sasabe. Now we no longer have *tudishishun* (coffee), *ikon* (flour), *inchi* (salt). I think I will go to Sasabe to see what we can buy."

Mother agreed but asked why not go to Basaranca, since it was nearer. I said:

"I will go to Sasabe; it is an American town. Golthlay has told me about it; also he said Basaranca was a thieving Mexican town. I will go to the Pueblo Siscohnill, where the Papagos, who are our friends, will take us in to Sasabe to trade. We will take three pokes of gold—with our yellow iron, anybody will trade."

I noticed she seemed a little excited. I told her she and Nadina should get ready to go, and that we would be gone one half-moon. I believed a party of twelve would be best now that

1. The peace treaty made at Treaty Rocks in the Cochise Stronghold, Dragoon Mountains, by Chief Cochise, General Oliver O. Howard, and Thomas J. Jeffords in August, 1872, resulting in the formation of the Chiricahua Reservation. Permitting the fierce Chiricahui to remain in their native land, the reservation extended east from the San Pedro River to the Animas Range, thus covering the southeast corner of Arizona and the southwest corner of New Mexico, a primitive area of nearly 2,000 square miles. AKG.

all Apaches were supposed to be on reservations. A larger party would arouse the White-Eyes suspicions, I reasoned. We could travel unnoticed, but if we were attacked, we'd scatter, and if pursued, fight in the traditional manner. I would leave Dee-O-Det home to take care of things.

I chose nine men, including Alchise to help his mother and mine do the buying, Nakai as interpreter, and Boa Juan as our farrier. We spent the day getting ready for the trip, everyone happy with anticipation. We picked twelve horses and three pack mules, and all pitched in to ready camp supplies, saddles, *aparejos, modulas, and armas.*[2]

Two days later we rode out just as the sun came over the peaks. We made good time and paused for a midday spell and to water our animals at Cienega Canyon. That night we camped on the bank of Cottonwood Creek. Just before coming to the campsite Alchise had dropped a small white-tailed deer with bow and arrow; we roasted that good meat on spits hanging over a dry-cedar fire.

The second day found us down in semi-desert hills where one blanket was enough to keep you warm at night. Kasale was the first one up every morning. He got the fire going, and Mother soon had a pot of *kinnikinick* tea boiling. Venison and Nadina's ashcakes with the strong black tea made one think of the days when Apaches were always on the trail.

As we rode on there was an abundance of coatis in the mesquite and pyracantha brush, and we spooked a large herd of javelina in a cactus grove. Kasale dropped a fat sow with one arrow and quickly removed the musk sac. We roasted that pig late in the evening and it was good; it was easy to live off the land in this region. Only once did we see other riders in the brushy hills—I judged them to be Opatas, but they were too far away to worry about. After three more days of steady riding, we were in Papagueria.

On the sixth day several Papago Indian men hailed us at a

2. These were our modifications of the Mexican "leather-shirt cavalry" equipment: a *modula* is of tanned horsehide to protect the legs of both horse and rider from high cacti and other tall brush. The *armas* are a pair of blanket-sized soft calf-leather skirts that protect the rider's legs, feet, and the undersides of his horse. An *aparejo* is a fully equipped packsaddle. Mules need no special protection—nature seems to provide for them.

water hole and told us in sign language that their chief, Don
Pedro, bid us welcome. I spoke to them in Apache, and they
shook their heads. So I changed to Mexican, and they understood. Nakai stood by in case an interpreter was needed. I told
them we came in peace and wished to trade with the merchants
of Sasabe and the Papago people.

Sasabe was a short ride from there, but I figured we had
covered at least as much distance[3] since leaving our rancheria
as an old-time Apache party would have. We were trail-weary.
Nakai and Eugene, dressed somewhat like vaqueros, rode in
first and the rest of us made camp on the edge of the little
Sonora-Arizona border town.

They came back to report that the people were mostly Nakai-
Ye with some *blancos* (whites) who didn't seem to care about
a few Apaches. Everyone they talked with seemed eager to
trade for yellow iron. I got Mother and Nadina, and along with
Eugene, Kasale, and Nakai, we walked into the village. Nakai
was our cashier. The first place we entered was a general merchandise store. Mother spotted coffee beans in a huge bag. She
asked for two bags.

Nadina caught sight of a stack of calico cloth. She bought five
bolts of varied designs, then two of blue serge and one of denim.
When the storekeeper showed her wool yarn, she was delighted. Nadina liked to weave and sew, crafts she had learned
on the reservation. They also bought 600 pounds of white flour,
100 pounds of sugar, and 100 pounds of salt.

The flour alone made a heavy load for our three pack mules.
When I asked if there were any mules for sale, Miller, the
storekeeper, said he had four mules with packsaddles for sale
for $200. Nakai, interpreting while helping himself at the
candy barrel, said he thought they cost too much, but since we
needed the extra animals to pack all our purchases back to
Pa-Gotzin-Kay we might as well buy them.

I told him to buy them and to pay for whatever my mother
wanted. Outside, Kasale and Eugene were standing guard.
There were people watching us; they seemed honest although
curious, but somehow I did not trust any of them. I told Eugene

3. Sasabe is 250 (airline) kilometers from Pa-Gotzin-Kay at 294°. Allowing
about a fourth as many more for trail ups and downs and twists and turns, it
was a ride of about 310 kilometers or 180 statute miles. AKG.

and Kasale to go with Nakai to fetch the four extra mules and I stood watch.

Mother, all out of breath, called to me. The storekeeper had given her a sample of hard candy and she was bubbling with delight. I tried it and told her we would buy some for our people. Back outside, I looked up and down the main road of Sasabe. There were a dozen or so buildings on both sides, including a saloon, a blacksmith shop, a large red house. There were wagons and carts and saddled horses at the hitching racks. Dogs, goats, and burros wandered around.

Hi-okee, Boa Juan, and others brought our original mules to the store, leaving two men to guard our horses and camp. They tied the animals to the hitch rail, and I dug out our other poke of gold from my saddlebag. I went into the store and asked Miller what more we owed him. He muttered something in bastard Spanish that I did not quite understand, so I pinched the poke at the halfway mark and handed it to him. He weighed it and said that was just right. Nakai, Kasale, and Eugene came with the four new pack animals and tied their hackamores to the hitch rail.

Mother was really pleased. She and Nadina had quite an assortment of items to load. Mother had never been inside a general store and this was a great treat for her. It seemed she had bought everything in sight.

❦ ❦ ❦

WE were headed home by late afternoon. I rode at the head of the column, as was my proper place, and when the trail permitted we rode two abreast, with Nakai at my right. The two women rode at the rear, as was Apache custom.

I saw a dust cloud to the left front and knew that the Papagos had spotted us and were riding to meet us. As the cloud grew larger, I counted twenty men. I told my men to see that their rifles were loaded and ready—just in case.

The Papagos were carrying a white flag, but I was leery. They rode very much as we did, two abreast. As they came closer, the chief, a big, fat man, held one hand palm forward and said:

34

"I am called Don Pedro. Welcome, Mansos, to Sischonill."
I felt much easier.
"I am Niño of the Chiricahui. I come to bring presents to our Papago cousins."
He turned his horse and motioned to us.

We rode on for several kilometers, then entered a mesquite forest. I had never seen mesquite so dense and was happy we had good *armas* and *modulas* for protection. This was flat, fertile, red earth. Suddenly we came to a clearing with many round huts of woven grass, which made them look like huge baskets turned upside-down.

We dismounted, and boys came to watch our horses. I told my men to unload our pack mules and remain on guard. Don Pedro stood by, eyeing every move, his curiosity having got the better of him. I opened a box of red-striped hard candy and nodded to him. I never saw a man so fat move so fast as he grabbed the candy.

Soon his women served us food. These people were farmers. They served us white potatoes, carrots, turnips, tomatoes, beets, and cabbage. No meat. My mother asked a lot of questions about the food. Don Pedro had his women give her a supply of seeds.

The Papagos were so kindly to us that I got uneasy. There were only nine of us men, but about fifty men in their village. Such odds never fazed an Apache; the worry was how many more were hiding out, watching and waiting to ambush us. Some of them were drinking something—they did not offer us any—and they were getting boisterous. I quietly talked with my men, and they voted unanimously that we move out. We loaded up and left like thieves in the night. Perhaps it was only the Apache's inborn mistrust of strangers, but, we had all agreed to go.

Because of our visit with the Papagos, our trail home was by a different route from that we had pioneered to Sasabe. This one, through Coyote Springs, was shorter but more hilly. Part of it was along the route used by Apache raiders for the past several centuries; I recognized it from descriptions given me by Naiche and Golthlay.

When we rode into our rancheria, having been gone thirteen days, we found a very curious clan waiting to see what we had brought. Mother was busy giving orders to those unpacking the mules, and trying to tell of the trip at the same time. She told them everyone would share, that her son, their chief, had brought presents for all.

The people began to sing, *"She gave him life and then she gave him to us . . . her ciyé is ours . . . he belongs to us."*

At that moment I would have died for any one of them. I vowed to myself that I would never let them down as long as I drew breath.

Dee-O-Det, the *shaman,* appeared out of nowhere, saying, "I see all went well with you."

"Everything went well, praise to your charms." This made him smile, and I added, "I have a present here for all, but you will be the first to taste it."

I handed a box of candy to him. He smelled it, then took a tooth-cracking bite.

"Yee-yoouuh!" He hustled off and soon returned with empty hands; he had hidden the candy for future use—*shamans* are that way.

"You are old and wise," I said. "I notice you are spry. What have you been up to, my *shaman?"*

"While you were gone I ate my annual bowl of *shaman's* soup."

Every year or so this *"shaman's* soup" magic had popped up, a subject known only to a chosen few. This time he chose to enlighten me:

"One must hunt and kill the oldest, biggest, boniest buck in the hills. He must be so old he has a gray beard or he is not good. Then he must be thrown whole into a kettle of boiling water— hide, hoofs, and horns. He must be boiled down to a bowlful. Then one must eat that—it is a powerful potion, and lasts a man a year."

I thought that over for a while with Dee-O-Det eyeing me. I decided to change the subject.

"You know," I said confidentially, "I think I realize why the yellow iron is so important to the Pinda-Lick-O-Ye. It has great influence on them. It has great magic. It has great power . . . with it in our possession the White-Eyes even smile at us Apaches."

Old Dee-O-Det, expressionless, said, "You are learning."

Holos (the sun) had made its journey across the endless sky and neared its western retreat as we talked on. The night fires were burning brightly and food was being served.

While my people were crunching candy, I told of the trip to Sasabe and how on the return trip we had to unload the pack mules at narrow places on canyon trails and lead them up, carrying the packs on our own backs. Then I went into detail about how Dee-O-Det and I had discovered what gives the whiteman the many things that he has—his secret of yellow iron, and how he makes it work for him.

The *shaman* jumped to his feet and in his high-pitched voice said:

"It was *ciyé* who found the secret, our young chief. It was he who made the first tests of the yellow iron."

Again the people began to sing, *"She gave him life and gave him to us . . . her ciyé is ours . . . no one shall take him from us."*

Mother asked to be heard, and when all was quiet, she explained that we had brought back many good things such as pots and pans, knives and forks and spoons, new kinds of food and drink, and seeds to plant and grow. There would be cloth to make clothes such as the Americans wore, white-iron needles with which to sew garments, and thread that is thin and long.

When the excitement quieted down, Dee-O-Det led us men in a discussion of the powers of the whiteman's yellow iron, his white iron, the combination of which could start wars. But could it *stop* wars?

🌱 🌱 🌱

SEVERAL days later Nakai came to our wikiup with a stranger. Our guard at the lower rampart had intercepted him. He was an Apache and appeared several years older than I.

"I am called Mangas-Chee," the stranger said, eyeing me closely. "I am the son of Mangas, who is the son of the greatest chief of the Mimbreno, who was father of Nali-Kay-Deya, one wife of the greatest chief of the Chiricahui, who was father of your father . . ."

"So, I suppose that makes you my cousin!" I interrupted with a laugh.

"I greet you, my cousin!" he responded quickly, and from that day on we often called each other cousin. "When my father surrendered with Golthlay and was sent to Florida, my mother and I hid out; then we went to San Carlos and lived with her mother. We did not like San Carlos so we escaped."

I looked toward Mother.

"Yes," she said, "he is a Tudairvia. I think he is Mangas-Chee."

I told Chee he was welcome here, and he told me more of his troubles until Mother brought food. He shut up then and ate. That young Apache was quite an eater!

I thought over what he had told me. He wanted to live with us, but he had left his mother, Neo-Deya, at their last camp two mountains north in a black canyon. She had been shot and wounded by Mexican soldiers who had given up the pursuit when night came. To make matters worse, he said they had left her mother to starve in the big canyon (Bavispe) when they came to the mountains and the feeble old woman could travel no more. I was quite put out by this revelation, even though what he had done was common Apache custom in days gone by. But we at Pa-Gotzin-Kay did not abandon our Old Ones.

I turned to Nakai and told him to fetch saddled horses and another man and the four of us would go bring the two women in. Chee looked at me as though he thought I had been touched by a *ló-kohí-muhté*.[4] Nakai soon came with Klan-O-Tay and four horses, and we set out on a hard and fast ride.

Chee's mother, Neo-Deya, recognized me at once, or at least said so, but she did not look familiar to me. When she tried to walk, she couldn't quite make it. She showed me the wound in her hip and it was festered. We bundled her up on Klan-O-Tay's horse, and I told him and Nakai to take her in to Doctor Gutierrez in Basaranca.

Chee and I then rode on to find Anasta, his grandmother. It was a hard ride down into the side canyon below the Big Bend and it was dark when we found her. She was more dead than alive. Partly covered with leaves and small branches, only her

4. Crazy owl.

eyes showed life. I told her who I was, gave her some water and a strip of jerky. While Chee helped her, I cut a couple of long poles, laced them together with the ropes all our saddles were equipped with, and laid a blanket across them. By then the moon was up.

We got an early morning start, and dragged and carried the old woman safely up to Basaranca. When we arrived, Doctor Gutierrez had extracted the bullet from Neo-Deya's hip. Upon seeing me, he said:

"Seems you Apaches are always getting shot . . ."

I refrained from mentioning that Mexican soldiers did the shooting. A nurse prepared a bed for Anasta. The thin, gray-haired woman lay there like a corpse. The doctor bent over her, and after the examination, he said:

"Give her good food, and lots of it, and she will be as well as ever."

With that opening I told him we were in need of a plow, harrow, harness for a team of horses, hoes, rakes, and shovels. He nodded, eager to help, and said he was sure I could buy those implements in Basaranca. We Apaches had reason to suspect the integrity of the Basaranca citizens, however, and I told him so. He agreed. We discussed the situation and he stated he would personally escort us around town and see that we received good treatment.

We bundled up the two women for a slow ride up to our rancheria. I paid him his fee, thinking that some men acted like friends while others wanted to make war on us. I was remembering the recent past.

❦ ❦ ❦

THE next day I took my ten best trail men—Nakai, Mangas-Chee, Klan-O-Tay, Alchise, Boa Juan, Kersus, Kasale, Eugene, Hi-okee and Peridot—and headed back to Basaranca. We were armed but tried not to show it. I'd left Young Chi-hua-hua at home to help Dee-O-Det and Mother; he was a good all-around man but lacked something when it came to handling horses. We were riding our best horses and leading our pack mules.

We arrived in Basaranca when the sun was overhead and

met Doctor Gutierrez. True to his word, he escorted us, and in the two main stores we bought all the farming implements we wanted, paying for them in raw gold. The merchants treated us civilly, probably in deference to the doctor, and the only sign of dishonesty came when the gold was weighed and figured into pesos, reales, and dollars. Outside we talked that over with the doctor and he said we needed a gold scale to tell the value of gold that is not in coins. He took us to his *casa,* gave us a scale, and instructed us in its use.

Meanwhile my men had loaded our purchases and were ready to travel. We arrived at the rancheria as twilight was cloaking the escarpment.

That night I went to bed worried. Had I done right by going into that Mexican stronghold—and by trusting Doctor Gutierrez? After all he was a Mexican! Would they come swarming in here for our gold?

Sometime later I awakened screaming from a nightmare. The Mexicans had me tied to a stake and were lighting fires to make me reveal the place where I found the gold. In the dream I was torn between giving up our way of living or dying. I had chosen death, and they lit the brush piled around me. I felt horrendous burns before my screams awakened me.[5]

"What is it, Ciyé?" I heard Mother call.

"A ghost bothers me," I answered.

I didn't sleep any more that night. I got up and went to Dee-O-Det's wikiup, intending to awaken him. He was squatted outside on the keystone of his ring of sacred stones around the wikiup.

"I have been expecting you," he said. And after a pause, "That which bothers you, will not be."

"Do you know what bothers me?"

"A *shaman* knows many things," was his quick reply. "In some tribes a *shaman* must know these things or he will not be *shaman* very long." He paused for a moment. "Your trouble is you gave the Mexicans yellow iron. Now you think they will tell others and they will come and make war on you. But they will not. The doctor likes you as he would his own son. He will see to it that his people do right to you."

5. The Apache believes dreams are a harbinger of either good or evil if properly interpreted.

Very much relieved, I never questioned how old Dee-O-Det knew all this—I just believed him.

At dawn, everybody able was out and ready to work our fields. It was now that Chee showed his versatility; he had learned about farming on the San Carlos Reservation. I made him a subchief and agricultural leader of our clan. He was also a fast worker in more ways than one. He had not been at Pa-Gotzin-Kay more than two weeks when he married Ealae, one of our two marriageable maidens.

We had some trouble modifying the harness to fit our two biggest horses before we could plow. In previous years we had scratched the ground with pointed sticks that a man or woman pulled. It broke up the ground a little, but this plow really did the work and we harrowed the land smooth. It was late May and just right for sowing the Papago vegetable seeds. Our first full-scale farming and gardening venture was a success under the guidance of Mother and Chee.

🌷🌷🌷

AUGUST, 1889, came and the corn was man high. We had stationed guards around the fields both day and night to keep the rabbits and deer away. The tomato vines were loaded with green fruit that would soon ripen.

Then one day Doctor Gutierrez came up the trail on his plodding old horse. We were all glad to see him. I took him over to the creek that flowed from our main spring and through dozens of small canals which watered our garden. There we had planted many vegetables, including melons and potatoes. There were doing very well. On a higher slope of the red earth we had planted about an acre of pinto beans, and the stalks were bearing heavily. Before long they would be ready to harvest.

"This is good land," the doctor sighed. "One would never guess that such a place existed here in the High Sierra, and it is so peaceful and balmy in the summer."

"My people like it here. We will fight to stay here until *Holos* grows cold. But now, let us go back to the compound and Mother will give us something to eat. I am hungry."

Mother served us venison stew with mesquite beans and flour

bread. While we were eating the doctor told us that Basaranca was growing with new people, mostly miners. He was building a large house which he hoped to be able to equip with ten beds for his patients. He called it a hospital. And he added, "But many of my patients are so poor that I cannot save enough to finish it this year."

I questioned him about his project and learned he needed 1,000 pesos gold to complete it. I told him he would have it and that we might need that hospital some day.

My thoughts raced back to the time when I gave this man raw gold and then was afraid I had done the wrong thing, and how Dee-O-Det had said there was no need for worry. My respect for the old *shaman* rose. I reached for the gold scales and weighed out one thousand pesos.

While he was preparing to leave, I asked him if he thought it would be wise for us to come to Basaranca again.

"*Segura!* These new people do not know an Apache from an Aztec, and do not care. The local people, as long as they are kept satisfied under the belt and below the belt, are prone to be lazy and forgetful. Your only trouble, if any, Niño, would be with American prospectors if they come to Basaranca."

Doctor Gutierrez rode back to Basaranca.

Nakai went back to overseeing our tanning crew; Chee remained foreman of the farm and garden; Kasale and Eugene were with the mining crew; and I lent a hand to some oldsters who were building a communal bakeoven. Summer wore on and our crops were ripening in the fields. When the crops were in, I promised my people, we would have a good old-fashioned Apache celebration.

In Arizona or New Mexico it might have been a different story. We have to go back to the cause of those Indian troubles in the beginning. In those days, we *Teneh Chockonen* (Apaches) had the same peaceful existence, with plenty of room to move around in and time enough to enjoy our wonderful world and life. We lived very well on what nature provided. Then one day invaders came—the conquistadores, like monsters in shining armor. We vanquished them and maintained our old life. The padres came and were rejected. They called us Apaches "The Common Enemy." A swarm of hybirds—Nakai-Ye—surrounded us. We fought them off.

Then came the Pinda-Lick-O-Ye—the mountain men—trapping our streams for fur animals. These were followed by *tecs'oti*—rock-scratchers. Then a stagecoach line cut through our mountains; the soldiers came and chased the wild animals away. Next they tried to chase us away. We fought back. And that foretold our doom.

Now, at Pa-Gotzin-Kay, the rock-scratchers were the bane of our existence. All Apaches called the prospectors by that epithet because, when they first came to Apacheria, a watching brave said that the White-Eyes must be scratching the rocks because they itched. He did not yet know that they were scratching the rocks for the yellow iron and white iron in our beloved hills. Would they come here to Pa-Gotzin-Kay? This was the last place for us. We had fled from America because of them, so naturally we would fight to protect our last stronghold. To this end, I resolved, I must prepare my people

❦ ❦ ❦

ONE crisp autumn morning a trail guard appeared and said that Doctor Gutierrez was approaching the north rampart. I saddled a horse and rode out to him. We met at the spring where he was watering his horse.

"How, Doctor!" I greeted him.

"Glad to see you, Niño! I came to tell you that if you want to buy Mexican or American clothes, you had better come and do so. Basaranca sees many strangers these days; prospectors and cheaters are all over. Everybody grabs for what the other man has. They have been panning the Bavispe to the Big Bend until the waters run mud. They have been prospecting all summer, and I do not think the whole crowd has found as much gold as you gave me the last time I was here."

"I hope they will go away, because I do not want to fight, but that is what will happen if rock-scratchers come here."

When our horses were through drinking and had grabbed a few mouthfuls of grass around the pool, we rode up the trail to the communal compound. I called the people together for a brief council; the outcome was that the twelve of us of warrior caliber mounted and returned to Basaranca with the doctor.

He took us direct to the main store, and we had a hilarious time as we each chose two pairs of pants—some liked linsey-woolsey, others chose Strode's corduroy. We each took our pick of bright-colored velveteen shirts and jumpers. Some also bought curve-brimmed Borsalino hats, and we all got a pair of boots.

Everything went well until we tried to walk in the boots. Those high heels were a bit tricky. I was first to get them on, and when the men saw me trying to walk, they really laughed.

When Nakai showed up fully dressed they had more reason to laugh. I laughed too. He had on a white Borsalino, a red-white-and-blue silk shirt, green pants, and yellow boots. We sized each other up, walking around each other like two fighting cocks, each laughing at the other.

As though reading my mind, the doctor explained that the high heel kept one's foot from slipping through the stirrup and also was helpful when roping a horse or cow; you could dig the heels into the ground and hold the struggling animal better. But I did not like the way they made me stand—it seemed all my weight was on the front and I felt that I was falling forward.

Although the doctor counseled us to wear them a little each day until we got used to them, I sat down and pulled mine off and got back into my *kabuns*.

We all wore these Apache moccasins—actually soft leather boots. You could roll them down below your knees in the summer time; and in the winter, or when working through thorny brush, you could roll them up as far as the hips. After paying for all the items, we rode back to the rancheria. We were learning, making progress. Soon, I thought, we would be like the whiteman. Maybe this was one of his many secrets—perhaps clothing made us different. I was very wrong and I was soon to find this out.

Back at the rancheria we had a gay celebration that lasted far into the night. While we were gone, our women had worked together and prepared a sumptuous feast and the stay-home men had constructed several large tables along lines suggested by the doctor. Heretofore we had sat on well-placed logs, or squatted, eating in the old manner by piling food on the smooth side of a piece of dry bark or on a curved stone, or we ate off the knife or from the fingers. Now we had cooking and serving utensils.

Transition

This evening meal was a special event, consisting of two fat does, roasted whole. The entrails cavities had been stuffed with potatoes, onions, garlic, pinto beans, and corn. Cooked together they gave the meat a grand flavor. Our long and somewhat hectic day had given us all wolf-sized appetites. However, there was enough for all. For the time being we were no longer "the hungry ones."

After the meal was finished, the men played cards—a game much like Mexican monte. The Apache loves to gamble, often betting everything he owns on the turn of one card. It wasn't long before some of us had lost our new pants.

Losers switched to our popular old game called *Wap*. A hoop, made of a pliable limb bent into a circle, was lashed into position with a rawhide thong. A long slender pole was made with notches spaced at certain lengths toward the butt of the pole. The object was to use the pole as a lance. The men stood around in a sort of circle. The hoop was set to rolling, and as it passed each man, he tried to throw his pole through the hoop. If the pole knocked down the hoop, the nearest notch where it hit the rawhide of the hoop was counted as points for that man. Of course the one who threw the pole farthest before the hoop fell, would get the most points for the least number of notches. If a man could throw his pole all the way through without knocking the hoop down, he won the game, shouting, "Wap!"

Tonight I soon lost interest in *Wap*. Whether I had eaten too much or the long day had brought too many things to my mind, I had drifted into a black mood, so I sought out old Dee-O-Det.

"You want to know what the future holds for the Apache, don't you?" he asked, as if reading my mind.

"Yes, my *shaman*. What do you think?"

"I think that one day the Apache will become friends with the White-Eyes. Then the white man will marry Indian woman and Apache will marry white woman, and soon no more Apache. We will be in white man's blood and then White-Eyes will have won—destroyed the Apache forever."

That hit me hard. But it was logical, there was no denying it.

I walked out of that old *shaman's* hut determined to upset his predictions. I would teach my people not to mix our blood with any other race. I wanted to preserve us as a people.

45

Chapter 3 1889-1890

Words of Wisdom

I RETURNED to our wikiup and went to bed, my mind in a turmoil. I heard mother snoring softly in her bed; why couldn't I sleep?

The *shaman* had put a disturbing thought into my mind: racial intermarriage! If we let the White-Eyes come among us their young men will take our young women, and our men will take their women; then where will the Apache go?

I must have fallen off because wild dreams began infiltrating my mind. The Apache will never trust *Los Goddammies* and they will never trust us gut-eaters. We must always live apart. In my dreams I was trying to convince a large group of White-Eyes that I meant to live and work with them. They pretended to believe me. I finally escaped from them in a storm of bullets, waking in a cold sweat.

In the morning I again went to see the *shaman* but he apparently had left early for his morning walk, as was his custom. Hearing a commotion from beyond the compound, I went to investigate.

Asa, one of our entrance guards had a prisoner: an *Innaa!* Asa, a headstrong son of the late Chief Juh, told me this *blanco* was caught sneaking into the rancheria with the intention of slaying the *shaman.* The whiteman was a little taller than I and about ten years older, bare-headed with shaggy brown hair and a short beard; his leather garb was crudely made and dirty. I spoke to him in Spanish, asking what he wanted and why he was here.

He replied in Spanish and pointed to the rampart which was the south entrance. "I am looking for Tayopa."

"This man says you came to kill our *shaman.*" I nodded toward Asa as I said this.

"I came to kill no one," the stranger denied. "I am lost."

Asa said, "I have sent two men to bring the body of our *shaman.*"

Two men came with Dee-O-Det, but he was very much alive. I asked him if this stranger had tried to kill him and he shook his head.

The stranger then said he had seen the *shaman* but avoided him. I questioned him further, and he admitted "he had been in a fight with some greasers near Magdalena" two weeks previously and had run to hide in the mountains. I asked him about pursuers, and he said he had not seen any after the first day. He seemed sincere so in Apache I told Asa to give the man his weapons; Asa returned his belt gun, a carbine, and a knife.

"I am called Jim Ticer." The man smiled a little. "James Allen Ticer."

"I am called Niño." He reached out and we shook hands. Some of the *shaman's* words of wisdom popped into my mind: "The last person who talks to you seems to influence you and sway you his way." In view of my thoughts and dreams of the night just past and the good impression this whiteman made on me now, I wavered with conflicting thoughts and was surprised when I heard myself say, "You are welcome to stop here and rest."

He thanked me and explained he had hidden his horse down along a red ledge, and I told Asa to go with him and bring his outfit here. They returned shortly and there was no doubt he was something of a long rider, judging from the scuffed saddle, frayed lariat, and trail-worn appearance.

I pointed to a big cedar nearby. He hitched his footsore horse and opened his blanket roll. Mother gave me some boiled venison, corncakes, coffee, and sugar to take to him.

"You Indians are kind," Ticer said with a faraway look in his light eyes. "I don't seem to get along with the Mexicans, and I can't stay with the Americans. What tribe are you?"

I said abruptly, "Apache," but refrained from telling him that now he was here we would not let him leave. I asked him why

47

he could not stay with the Americans. He seemed to pale a little but replied in a firm voice:

"I was a soldier in the American army, stationed at Fort Huachuca. Well, I got a ten-day furlough and went to Tucson.[1] I won at the faro table and met a woman. We went on a party and it lasted for at least a month. When I sobered up, I was a deserter. That was a year ago. So I decided to try prospecting out in the hills. One day two men tried to arrest me. They said I was an American outlaw and we fought—with guns. Now I am also 'wanted' in Mexico."

I informed him that he would be safe here if he obeyed our laws. I gave him an outline of things to do and not to do, and added that we were farmers and miners, no longer warriors. He then said he had an education, understood farming and mining, and would be glad to help us. I asked him how long it took him to learn to speak Spanish, and he said it was easy. He used to be a schoolteacher, he told me, and offered to teach me English if I'd teach him Apache. I told him I'd think about it, and that he was to camp right there for the night.

I entered our wikiup knowing Mother had been eavesdropping.

"So," she said, "you have made friends of this White-Eyes."

I told her the man's name and that he had offered to teach me to talk like a *blanco;* I explained that this could be a good thing as I could learn their secrets and then I'd know how to get along with them—which was a heap more than Golthlay could do.

"My son, sometimes when you talk this way, you make me think of Chi-hen-nes. He was a great *shaman*. He said that all great chiefs who were gone would come back to us again and lead us to victory. He raised up Ponce who had fallen on the field of battle, and old Ponce is living with us now."

"Our *shaman* is great, too, my mother."

"Chi-hen-nes was his father. That is why Dee-O-Det is great."

"I think I will have a talk with the son of Chi-hen-nes," I said and left for the *shaman's* wikiup.

"Ha!" said our *shaman* as he invited me in. "You wish to ask about my father! Sit down and I will tell you about him. He had great power. Sometimes he called back people from the Spirit

1. The Morning Report of Hdq. Troop, 4th Cav., Col. C. E. Compton, Cmdr., Fort Huachuca, A.T., April 8, 1888, lists Cpl. J. A. Ticer, furlough expired. AKG.

World and they walked the earth. Sometimes they came back in pale skin. Sometimes I think Taglito is one of them. Do you think this Pinda-Lick-O-Ye is one of them?"

"Do *you* think so, my *shaman?*"

Dee-O-Det nodded and I believed him. Although I thought that our *shaman* had the power to bring people back from the Spirit World, if there was an all-powerful reason for it, there was yet some doubt in my mind.

Back near our wikiup Jim Ticer was making himself a stick-and-canvas wikiup and all the siblings in camp were watching him. I gave him a hand, then asked him to take a walk with me. He was agreeable and we had a long talk. Thereafter we spent many days together, until I was able to grasp the rudiments of vocal expression in English. I gave him the comparative in Apache. Since we were both able to speak Spanish, Mexican style, we were making a start toward becoming trilingual.

Ticer said Pa-Gotzin-Kay was a paradise and he read about another paradise from what he called the Good Book. He had a knack for fixing things, so I got him to repair the pile of salvaged rifles and belt guns in our big kiva. He also taught me how to wind, set, and tell time by the Hamilton watch Naiche had given me years before.[2]

One day I suggested that if he would teach all among us who wished to learn his language, I would pay him in gold. He agreed. Thus was started the first English school in the Mother Mountains, with all Indian students. The youngsters were especially eager, and knowing the Apache's natural penchant for gambling, Ticer made a game of studying—with prizes!

We held class every morning and every evening and by the time winter passed we had a tribe of English-speaking Apaches, and, I might add, our teacher now spoke passable Apache. At one council meeting I outlined a resolution that our people should speak English at all times, on the theory that practice makes perfect.

---

2. I carried that watch many years and it worked perfectly until recently. Modern technology cannot make a new hairspring for it, so it is a museum piece.

❦ ❦ ❦

SPRING came and as usual we were out of coffee and other staples. I decided it was too risky to go to Basaranca to trade since those rock-scratchers would get too curious about where we Mansos got our gold. At the council meeting I announced we would go to Sasabe, taking three pack-train men and "Ticher Ticer" for a quick trip. Of course Mother wanted to go and so did Nadina. That made seven in all—two women and five men —with six pack mules and seven horses.

The canella and red mountain range was streaked with green at this time of the year. Blossoms of all kinds were everywhere and it was warm. We rode the west slope down to Campo Valley and then north for about ten kilometers; then we climbed El Pozo Canyon ridge and went down the Naco-zari sandstone highlands, by-passing Fronteras. The big sky was cloudless and we could see into Arizona far to the north. We crossed the chaparral-covered hills to the Rio San Miguel gorges, then into Papagueria—and never once saw another human nor anything that was man made.

When we reached Papago Springs we were trail worn but happy. We were dressed in our blue jeans, cowboy boots, spurs, and modified sombreros. Nadina wore a *vestidura,* but Mother just looked like an Indian; we pretended we were a bunch of ranch workers in for supplies.

We left our animals hobbled at the spring in charge of Eugene and walked into town. There we noticed a few miners. My American friend asked one if there was much gold dust around. The man didn't bother to answer other than to shrug and spit out some brown juice.

I had already given Ticer my poke of gold with the understanding he was to pretend to be foreman of some ranch below the line, and that I was just a vaquero; we figured Miller, the storekeeper, would not recognize me after a year and a change of clothes. Mother and Nadina were making a big to-do out of buying and paid no attention to us, neither did the storekeeper. We loafed around, sampling the hard candy and some cheese, until the women had their purchasing completed. Then Ticer got out the poke of gold.

Sure enough, Miller gulped. "How'd you come by so much dust?"

"The boss gave it t'me t'buy this stuff with," Ticer said slowly, modifying his voice.

"Whereabouts is your ranch located?"

"Too many questions can get a man in trouble," said Ticer, pretending anger, "when its none o' his damn business."

"Uh, sorry, son. We sort of had a gold strike here a while back. Some Papagos came in with pokes of gold. Outsiders found out about it and flocked in but they found nothing. They dug up half the reservation and found nary color. Now they've heard of a strike in the Santa Ritas and they're leaving here. The town'll be dead with them gone."

"Yeah, Pop," said Ticer, softening.

"Those Papagos must have a secret mine," Miller chatted on. "A man called Maricopa Slim got fat old Don Pedro and tied him to a giant sahuaro and beat hell out of him but he would tell nothing. He died from the thorns and the beating. Folks around here thought his tribe would cause trouble, but they ain't yet. There is a band close enough to start trouble and I hear they're not liked by the rest of the tribe. These cowboys of yours, they're greaser-Injuns, ain't they?"

Jim Ticer didn't reply, so Miller rumbled on:

"Well, let's see now—coffee, sugar, salt, flour, choc'late, shears, cloth. Your women like to buy. That one seems to order everything." He indicated my mother. "Is that all right with you?"

"Give 'em what they want," said Jim. "And I want some shells —about ten boxes Remington-30s and ten boxes Colt-45s."

I decided this was a good time to try my English on strangers so I sauntered across the road to the Short Branch Saloon, walked in boldly, and asked for a shot of good whisky.

The barman set a bottle in front of me, but held on to it.

"Say, you ain't a Injun, are you?"

"I am an American," I snapped in English.

"With that mane of hair, you sure look like a Injun," he remarked. "Can't sell likker to Injuns."

I said I hadn't had a haircut for years, and quickly added that my foreman also wanted me to order two ten-gallon kegs of whisky to take back to the ranch. With an order like that thrown at him, the man lost all interest in my nationality. He said he'd have it brought in from the storeroom, and I said the foreman would be in to pay for it. He yelled out the back door and soon two Mexicans came with two heavy kegs. Just then Jim Ticer walked in; I told him about the two kegs and he paid for them, and the barman served us a drink on the house and told us to keep the bottle.

Ticer took the quart, tugged at my sleeve, and we left. He had noticed something I hadn't—others in the saloon were perking up when they saw him pay for the whisky with gold dust. We headed out the door and split up; Ticer went across to the store and I headed back to camp.

Eugene was taking a nap when I got there. I shook him awake and told him in English we could not stay here because some *blancos* had beat Don Pedro to death over yellow iron he didn't have, and we were going to pull out before the whitemen tried to beat us. We lost no time putting the packsaddles on those mules and getting them to the hitch rack at the store. It didn't take us long to get the whisky and supplies loaded and start on our way back out of whiteman's country.

We had barely made the chaparral hills when a shot rang out. My *grullo* mustang stumbled and fell dead with a bullet that probably was intended for me.

I drew my sixgun, took a snapshot at a movement beside the trail above, and a man's body came sprawling down the embankment. Our *shaman* would have called that shot instinct, or maybe I was charmed. I heard a man running and then two quick shots. I saw Ticer with a smoking gun in his hand. We walked cautiously up the trail. There in the distance were two horses tied to a tall mescal stalk.

We examined the dead men and recognized one of them as the tobacco-spitter whom we had asked about gold dust.

"Goddam bushwackers!" Ticer grunted as he took their guns.

And for yellow iron they would have murdered us, I thought, and for yellow iron they are now dead. I would have given them some if they had asked for it. Yet that kind of whiteman would have beaten me to make me tell where I found it.

We took their horses and rode on, leaving the bodies where they had fallen. The coyotes would take care of their final disposition. Alert for more bushwackers, we rode on to Coyote Springs and made cámp. I got out our gift bottle of whisky, while Mother and Nadina got some food together. I told Alchise to stand guard until midnight, Eugene until moonset, Boa Juan to take over until dawn. My intentions were for everybody to get as much rest as possible after a long day, but Ticer got into a friendly argument with Mother about the "King's English" and her version of it, and to save her from utter defeat I remarked that if they'd shut up and go to sleep, I'd stand watch. Mother and Ticer pretended their feelings were hurt. The other men thought I really meant what I said, so they grabbed their blankets and rolled into them.

❦ ❦ ❦

AS I stood watch I could hear the night noises of crickets and beetles, and coyotes were talking to each other in nearby hills. Then there was the cry of a male owl. He wanted to know if it was safe to come into our camp. *Ló-kohí-muhté*—I quickly wakened the camp. Everyone got rifles ready. Then I gave the call that it was all right to come in.

Very soon and without a sound, a tall Apache stood in the waning firelight. A sweeping glance told me he was unarmed, except for a war club looped to his wrist by a thong. A closer look showed it was the white, smoothly polished, thighbone of a man. I felt the old alarm that makes the blood pressure mount, for there stood a stalwart warrior with the stamp of the *Netdahe* all over him.

"I am Ma-Ti-O-Tish," came his guttural voice. "I was a warrior with Beduiat. When he was slain I was badly wounded and a *Nakavdi* held me as his captive. One day someone killed him and the *Rurales* accused me. I fled and was making my way to Pa-Gotzin-Kay when I came upon your camp. I saw this *Innaa* and thought you were prisoners. Later, when I saw otherwise, I called."[3]

3. Ma-Ti-O-Tish, an Aravaipa Apache, and not to be confused with Chief Na-Ti-O-Tish, a Tonto and inveterate *Netadhe* who, along with about sixty followers, was killed by the U.S. Cavalry and Apache Scouts at Big Dry Wash in the summer of 1882. AKG.

Eyeing the thighbone war club, I asked when he had escaped. He said six suns ago and he had slain his last pursuer two suns ago. He said he wanted to come and live with us, and as if reading my thoughts, he added that he took the war club from a big leather shirt soldier. I felt somewhat uneasy around him, but I had the feeling he would be a strong addition to our clan. He was a big battle-scared *Netdahe;* I was only in my seventeenth year, but Chief of a Chiricahua clan in Mexico.

Four days later as we neared the Bavispe *vado* (ford) I sent Boa Juan and Eugene to scout ahead. We plodded on until they came back late in the afternoon and reported that there were many rock-scratchers in the Big Bend flats. I did not want to risk a nighttime encounter with any gold hunters along the river canyon or its tributaries, so we pressed on into the night to Golthlay's one-time base and made camp. This was (and still is) a quiet glen, easily defended from its rimrock. I knew if we had to fight, I would like the protection of those rocks. Out in the open where there is no place to hide, all you can do is to shoot fast and keep riding, but we wouldn't get far that way with a pack train.

It turned into a black, rainy night. We built a crude leanto and made ourselves as comfortable as possible. Ma-Ti-O-Tish was not bothered by the wet weather; he'd probably been unsheltered in worse. The only thing he did was what all Apaches do —he tried to keep his long hair from getting wet. An Apache hates to get caught in the rain because it makes his scalp itch and his long mane very heavy.

To while away the time I told him about our way of life, and when he made up his mind to believe me, he said there must be some *Teneh Chockonen* left who would still fight for freedom. I told him *we* were all who were left free, adding that all others were penned on American reservations.

In the morning we rode on to Pa-Gotzin-Kay and arrived in the late afternoon. Nakai, in charge while I was away, came out to greet us with the rest of the people. Dee-O-Det was there and I gave him the Papago medicine rattle made of tortoiseshell I had picked up at Sasabe. He said he was pleased with it, but his voice took on a rough edge:

"I see you have brought an Aravaipa with you. I married him

to a Mimbreno woman once when we had an inter-tribal ceremony—a long time ago. He is bad of heart."

"You want some firewater?" I changed the subject.

"Enju!" was his quick response.

As the mules were unloaded, the women were in high glee
over the bolts of cloth and the sweet-smelling soap we had
brought. The siblings got more candy, and the ammunition we
divided among the men. Of that we had plenty now for a long
battle, should one come.

Jim Ticer placed one of our two whisky casks on a flat rock,
chocked so it would not roll off. I tapped a half-cupful for Dee-
O-Det, the same for myself, and found a good spot to drink and
relax. I woke up at twilight, very hungry. That night almost
every man was drunk, including Ticer, and only the children
wanted to eat. So I drank my eats, too.

The next morning the cold spring did a good business. The
shaman was there, trying to drink the spring dry. I had a raging
fire to put out myself. Afterward I went over to Mother's fire and
asked for coffee.

"You think that all I have to do is make coffee for you? Why
do you not find a wife?"

"Why should I have a wife when I have such a wonderful and
beautiful mother?"

"Ha! You sound just like your father. You look more like him
as you grow older. You may have all the coffee you want."

I thought to myself as I sipped the coffee, she must be getting
tired of me letting her do all my cooking. Maybe I will look for
a wife. Then I thought of Jedi; she was pert and pretty . . . why
not?

Jedi and her mother Klea were also refugees from American
reservations, by way of Ajo Caliente, to San Carlos, to Mescalero. They had arrived at Pa-Gotzin-Kay by their own efforts
several months after Chee and his mother arrived. They too
were made welcome, but they kept to themselves as Klea was
a cripple and Jedi seemed very shy. She was not yet taken, so
I made up my mind then and there that I was going to court her.
I realized that I must have a go-between and I must choose the
right man for that.

While thinking it over, I strolled over to the garden patch and
picked a few tomatoes. I tossed them into an eddy of the creek

below the spring, letting them float to cool. I had taken up the smoking habit and was rolling a cigaret when Nakai came along.

"Doing, Niño?" he asked blithely.

In the same moment he saw I had tomatoes cooling in the creek, so he rustled up an armful, threw them into the eddy, and then came and sat down beside me.

"Nakai," I said, "I think I will take Jedi for a wife. Will you be my go-between?"

"So, that's what has been bothering you! Does your mother approve of your choice?"

"Answer my question."

"I will see her mother . . ."

"I knew you would. That is why I asked you."

"I just hope your mother does not disapprove," he said thoughtfully. "I think it will cost you plenty for that girl."

"Is she not worth it?"

"No."

We talked the matter over for a while, as we feasted. How good a simple thing like a ripe tomato is, eaten out in the patch! Nakai belched, got up, and left. I stretched out under a tree and fell asleep. I dreamed of the old *shaman* performing the wedding ceremony and I was so happy that I ordered a feast to last a week. The sun went down and I woke up. I walked back to the compound. People were eating. I went to Mother's fire and sat down. She gave me a bowl of stew and some white-flour biscuits.

"I will miss my mother's cooking when I am married," I said.

"Have you found a woman?"

"Yes—Jedi. I think she will make a good wife for me."

"It will be you that marries her," Mother snapped. "She is older than you."

"When I take a wife I hope I do not lose a mother!"

"Nor I a son."

"No chance of that. I have the best mother in the world."

"Again you are like your father," she said, smiling.

Nakai came looking for me; he hurriedly told me he had seen Klea and that her price for Jedi was too high—she wanted two good horses and a bottle of whisky. His attitude riled me, so to show him who was boss I told him to take the horses from my bunch now and tie them at Klea's wikiup. If Jedi accepts them, then take the whisky to Klea.

It is an Apache custom that a maiden has accepted the gift if she feeds and cleans the horses, and that means you may court her. She arranges for you to meet by accident and the courtship starts. It lasts two weeks; then if the man accepts, they get married.

The next morning at daybreak I looked over at Jedi's wikiup and, sure enough, she had already fed and curried my horses. I hurried outside to find Nakai. When I found him, I gave him a bottle of whisky to take to her mother.

I walked down the trail to our spring and waited—but not for long. Jedi popped out from behind a big tree and acted surprised. I told her it was nice to find a beautiful girl in the woods. She giggled and acted coy when I suggested we get some horses and go for a ride on such a nice day. We walked to the corral side by side. I roped out two good horses, saddled them, and brought them to where she was waiting. She mounted the roan, not expecting to be helped. We cantered down the trail a short distance beyond the north rampart, then cut off on a side trail where there was a little clearing with a bubbling spring and ferns growing all around. We dismounted and tied the horses to some bushes. She smoothed a place on the ground and we sat down.

Now that we were alone together I suddenly felt tongue-tied. Jedi had nothing to say either although her eyes were sparkling. My face was burning and my heart pounding. Her heaving breast fascinated me. After a time she shyly remarked that my hair was long as hers and why didn't I cut it? I scoffed that I was not a Mexican. She squirmed a little, giggled, then said she'd braid it. Her quick fingers flew around my head and she wove a braid down over each ear. I told her I couldn't hear, so she made two braids on each side and looped them around my neck. I told her she was choking me; she pointed to my reflection in the pool and we both burst out laughing. After a few more times of braiding it all over again, we became more interested in just cuddling in each other's arms. It had turned into a day I'll never forget.

It was sundown when we returned to the compound, the two happiest people in the world. As far as I was concerned, we were the only two people in the world. I left her at Klea's wikiup, then corraled the horses and walked on clouds back to our wikiup. The cook fires were glowing; Mother was stirring something in the kettle. She looked up and said:

"I thought I would be eating alone this night."

"I am not hungry," I said.

"How did everything go with you?"

"Good. I asked Jedi to be my wife and she accepted."

"Hum. I thought that was the main idea in the first place."

"Mother—how did my father court you?"

"I do not think, by the looks of that woman, that you need any coaching."

Well, I wasn't getting anywhere here, so I went to see the *shaman*. When I got to Dee-O-Det's place and called to him, he came out instead of inviting me in. He quickly informed me there were things he did not want to talk about—until after my courting days.

🌷 🌷 🌷

I WAS up early the next morning and so was Mother. She was making coffee when I saw Jedi ride by toward the north trail. I did not wait for the coffee. I was at the corral, on my horse, and loping down the trail in jig time. As I rode into the bubbling-spring clearing, I saw that Jedi had tied her horse and was spreading a blanket on the ground. She had also brought a picnic basket.

I sat down—and she snuggled beside me. She took a piece of cake and held it to my lips and I nipped her fingers. We laughed and her laugh sounded like tinkling bells. Those tinkling bells, they seemed to enchant me. The cake was like honey. We rolled around like a pair of cub bears playing in the sun—all the while laughing with sheer happiness. Only *Usen* (God) was witness in the endless sky and we knew He would bless us.

Time didn't matter, nothing mattered. All my hates, all my troubles did not exist any more. All that existed was this throbbing, wonderful woman who was mine. I came back to earth when a peal of thunder rolled across the forested hills.

I hugged her closer. I could hear and feel her heart racing. I

Tahza, my father, was the eldest son of Cochise. He died
in the whiteman's citadel of peace, Washington, D.C., on
November 16, 1876

My grandfather, the great Chief Cochise of the C
Apaches. So far as I know no other portrait of
ever made

My father's brother Naiche and his wife as they looked about 1876 when they were on the San Carlos reservation

Golthlay—known to the whiteman as Geronimo—was my mother's brother. The picture above was posed about 1900 after he was interned at Fort Sill, Oklahoma. The lower photo shows my two uncles Golthlay and Naiche on horses with two others: Chappo, left, and Kay-I-Tah

Chappo   Geronimo   Naiche   Kay-i-tah

wanted her more than anything else in the world. How could I wait for two weeks, with only two days of the waiting period gone? A flash of lightning, another peal of thunder—let *Ga-n* (Evil Spirit or Devil) be angry! I would defy him for this woman. Let evil *Ga-n* try to take her from me;[4] I'd protect her from the whole world.

It began to rain, and we covered our heads with cloths from the basket and galloped home in a downpour. When we reached her wikiup she jumped out of her saddle and dashed for shelter. I turned the horses into the corral and got home soaking wet. Mother was not there, so I dried my hair and found some dry clothes. I could hear the rain pattering on the skin roof—why did it have to rain today? I found myself walking the floor, thinking. For something better to do I took all my guns out and examined them. When that was done I sharpened my belt knife.

After a while Mother came in and laid a butcher knife on the table before me. I took it and began to hone it, thinking all the while what life would be like after I was married. I wore off half the edge of that knife before I snapped out of my trance. The rain had stopped. I wanted to go to Jedi's wikiup, but that was against the rules. Neither could she come to mine.

I walked outside. At the other end of the compound some men were whooping up a reverse target game. A ball of husks with a leather cover was thrown into the air and the bowmen shot at it. If the ball was hit, then the thrower would forfeit his bet; if not, he collected all bets. I watched for a while. I borrowed bow and arrow from Chee, and when Kasale threw his ball, I loosed the arrow. It pierced the ball and both tumbled down. Kasale was disgusted. To tease him I reached and yanked the knife out of his belt sheath. With some anger he rushed me. I sidestepped and chopped a stiff hand on the back of his neck. He went skidding on his face. Thinking I had been too rough, I reached down to help him up. The next thing I knew I was on my back and he was on top of me.

"Now I will take my knife," he snapped. "You have forgotten your training—*never trust an enemy*. That is Apache law!"

4. According to mythology when an Apache dies he enters Big Sleep and goes to the Spirit World. There are two rulers in Spirit World. *Ga-n* (Devil) and *Usen* (God). All spirits may return to earth under certain conditions.

❦ ❦ ❦

THAT evening I noticed Mother was cooking a big meal—enough for at least four people. Pretending I wasn't interested, I went over to Nakai's fire and discussed his middleman role during my courting period. Then I returned to our fire. Sure enough, soon Jedi and Klea came by, Jedi carefully assisting her crippled mother. I stood up and invited them to sit and eat with us. We soon got into a lively discussion of the Hako Society (of which I was a member, as were my paternal ancestors) and the Midi Society (of which the Mimbrenos are members).[5]

Jedi's mother said, "I did not know of these things, but neither am I of your race. I am Mexican—Nakai-Ye, as you say. I was hurt in battle. I became the captive wife of Baishan-Chee, son of Baishan, whom my people called *Cuchillo Negro* (Black Knife), who was a warrior of Chief *Mon-achee.*" (Mangas Coloradas)

This was upsetting news to me. I had taken for granted all along that Klea was an Apache. I had noticed Jedi's expression as her mother spoke—hatred seemed to have welled up within her. I reached to give Jedi a pat on the arm, but she drew away. I thought it strange at the moment, but soon forgot it. That she was only half-Apache did fret me a little. Mother must have noticed the change, for she urged us to eat more, but I had suddenly lost my appetite. Jedi soon smiled, then squeezed my hand. I felt better. We got up and strolled to the corral, where I roped two horses and she helped me saddle them. After we passed the guard at the North rampart, she said:

"I think the moon is full . . ."

"Yes, it is called the Apache Moon. The old-time Mexicans called it Apache Moon because it is big, bright, and red. They said there was blood on the moon and that the Apaches put it there."

"It is a nice moon and I love it no matter what anybody calls it," she said, not knowing I had been testing her.

I reached over and patted her shoulder. That was like a spark

5. This stemmed from the Manso culture. AKG.

60

—our horses started prancing and we raced to Lover's Springs as if we were flying through the air. We leaped off, tied our horses, laughing like ten-year-olds, and spread a blanket on the ground. As we were lolling on the blanket, the moon rose higher in all its amber splendor.

"Did you ever hear the story of when *Gotchamo* captured the moon?" I asked.

"No, my darling; tell it to me," she said, laying her head on my arm and snuggling closer.

"Well," I began, "once there lived an Indian chief who was a kind ruler of his people. One night the moon was late in rising because of an eclipse, and a little boy approached the chief all out of breath from running very fast.

" 'Great Chief,' he said with much excitement, 'Gotchamo has captured the moon and is holding her prisoner in his wikiup.'

" 'Now, now, my son. Is this something you have dreamed? Or have you perhaps forgotten that the day of fools is long past?'

" 'Oh, no, Great Chief! I, with my own eyes, have seen the moon bound and struggling to release herself. *Gotchamo* has caused great sadness among all young men and women, as there will be no moon to witness the divine troth of love.' "

"Oh, that is awful," Jedi interjected.

" 'Say no more, my son. Take me to the wikiup of *Gotchamo*. We must release the moon. Even now I see she is late to show her glory to all lovers.' "[6]

"Soon the moon appeared high and with her were *Gotchamo* and his wikiup, and do you know, Jedi, that to this day there is a man in the moon burdened with a bundle of sticks on his back? The sticks are *Gotchamo's* wikiup. He has been burdened with them and is forever searching for his people."[7]

"Oh, Niño, I can see old *Gotchamo* up there now!"

"Yes, I see him, too. He has his wikiup on his back. Let him search. With you here in my arms, I have found what I want out of life."

6. The Apache loved the moon because it ruled the weather and the propagation of the Indians and animals.

7. Alfred Burdette, himself a full-blood Tonto Apache and Lutheran clergyman at San Carlos, told this collaborator that this *Gotchamo* legend goes back ten thousand moons in time. AKG.

Holding each other closely, we went through a phase of exquisite torture and only the spirit of the Maid in the Moon kept us from breaking all Apache chastity laws and all pre-ceremonial laws.

☙ ☙ ☙

DURING the ride back we had agreed not to see each other so often—to keep from breaking any more laws. To make it less hard on myself I joined Ticer, Hi-okee, Nakai, and Eugene at the mine and worked there for over a week. I returned on the next-to-last day of our courtship.

As I rode into the compound, Jedi saw me coming and ran behind her wikiup, pretending to hide. I leaped off, let my horse run free, and ran on in back of the wikiup. She threw her arms around me and kissed me, then twisted away and ran off, calling, "I will see you the day after tomorrow morning."

I was puzzled by her behavior and a bit bothered by it. I went to my mother's wikiup and walked in.

Mother was there with Nadina and they were working on what appeared to be a maiden's wedding dress. Beyond greeting me, they seemed too busy for more talk. I went over to Dee-O-Det's where his understudy told me he was at Chee's for the sacred bestowal ritual for Chee's new baby.

I did not belong there either so I went to bed. I was up early and decided to ride around Lookout Peak to the caves, where my hunters and I had killed the cougar years before. I saddled up and was on the rocky ridge shortly after sunrise. I dismounted, tied the horse to a juniper, and walked over to the rimrock to get a view of the canyon below.

I looked down at the cave along the sandstone ledge where the old lioness had had her lair, and there on the shelf at the cave's portal was my Jedi embracing a Mexican man.

Before my horrified eyes I saw them start the act that I had dreamed of performing after my wedding on the morrow.

Something exploded within me—all the savagery of my ancestors welled up in me. My tortured spirit was screaming to avenge this wrong.

I ran down to where the two were. They heard and saw me

coming and they separated, then the man whirled and grabbed up his rifle. I was unarmed except for my belt knife, but I had momentum. I jumped on him, knocking him flat, grabbed the rifle, and banged the butt against his head. I whirled on Jedi.

"A great wedding present you give me, woman!" I slapped her face until the blood flowed down her cheeks. "Did you have *coito* with this man before I chose you to be my wife?"

"I love him—he is of my race. You are an Apache devil!" So saying, she spat on my face. I drew my knife and flashed it before her face; the tip of her nose flew off.

She writhed and screamed:

"Your people stole my mother and held her in slavery and forced her to mate with your kind! Apache devils! Marry you? I would rather marry a dirty dog!"

Her Mexican man was getting up. I flashed my knife, and as he recoiled, I slashed off both his ears. He screamed, and Jedi whimpered, "no—no."

"Take that *bija-n-ata, gusano!*[8] Take her far away! Do not let me ever see you again or I will kill you and her pups. *Ugashi!*"[9] They left, running.

I needed time to think and cool off, so I got my horse and rode down into Cave Canyon, letting the horse chose his own gait along an old deer trail. It was late afternoon before I was back at the *shaman's* wikiup. Before I could even dismount, he called and said:

"Come in. Now I will talk. I could not have told you what was to happen because you would not have believed it."

Knowing Dee-O-Det as I did, his words came as no surprise.

"It is too bad it had to happen but it was the will of *Ihidnan.*[10] Had you killed her, you still would not have been satisfied. Now, the next time you wish to choose a wife, come to see me first. That is what I am for—to advise you and help you with our people."

Dee-O-Det had a little whisky left in a bottle and he gave it to me. He told me Klea had feared this might happen. Now she might become a troublemaker, and he suggested that the two of us should visit her and resolve the problem. We proceeded

8. Whore, you worm.
9. Go!
10. (The) *Supreme Being* in the Manso dialect.

to Klea's, were invited in, and it soon became apparent she had already made her own decisions.

"I did not know about that man Juanito until too late. I drank the whisky to forget. The horses I will give back. I am leaving Pa-Gotzin-Kay."

That she had made up her mind was breathtaking, but I responded:

"You will need the horses, Klea. It was not your fault that Jedi really loved another man. Then, too, she thought my people had done you wrong."

"When I first became a captive, I was treated cruelly. Baishan saw my plight, did what he could for me, and took me for his wife. I was happy with him and Jedi was our baby. Then he was killed at Corralitos. Now she has done this terrible thing to you. She—they are gone. I will go to Madera where I have a sister."

"You became an Apache when Baishan married you," the *shaman* spoke up. "As an Apache you have rights; as a Mexican you have other rights. It is your choice. I will speak no more about it."

I really felt sorry for this unfortunate woman, but was not sad to see her go. I knew her presence at the rancheria would always bring unhappy things back to my mind. I told her I would arrange an escort to help her cross the canyon.

Chapter 4   1890-1892

Bandits of Basaranca

THE BACKLASH of my misadventure with matrimony littered my mind with bitter thoughts. Dee-O-Det, came to my rescue:

"Go to Sno-Ta-Hae and help dig up yellow iron," he advised. "The Pinda-Lick-O-Ye and the Nakai-Ye say gold is a cure for all evils."

For the past few years we had kept a crew of men mining and guarding our secret mine against the chance that some Basaranca rock-scratchers might stumble on it and seize it. This, I admitted, was an opportune time for me to dig in and help. We needed to increase our hoard of yellow iron, and I needed to work off my smouldering mood. I alternated every other moon, first working at the mine, then roving the nearby hills watching for invaders, but I seldom went down to the rancheria. Mangas-Chee and Nakai—family men—would come and go and by them I sent orders and suggestions to my people.

I began my nineteenth year restless and discontented—as no man should be. Occasionally Mother came up to see me, sometimes accompanied by Dee-O-Det; they always had some advice to offer. The hard work continued and Jim Ticer said the vein of gold seemed to be getting richer instead of pinching out as so many quartzite veins do.

One forenoon young Juh (Asa) came galloping up the trail, his mustang blowing hard. The rampart guard had signalled that Doctor Gutierrez of Basaranca was coming up the canyon trail with an officer of the *tieñ-tjn* (*soldatos*). I called Ticer and the four others out of the shaft and set them to work covering the portal, using old Apache methods of concealment; then Asa and I made a fast ride down to the rancheria. The two Mexicans arrived shortly after I did. Doctor Gutierrez came toward me with outstretched hand. I hesitated, but shook hands with him —why did he bring this stranger to Pa-Gotzin-Kay?[1]

Speaking in rapid-fire Spanish the doctor introduced the stranger as Teniente José Lopez, Fronteras Fusileros; Lopez wore a natty gold-braided uniform and impressed me as the arrogant *godo gachupin* type who habitually looked down the nose at *Indios*. Gutierrez, sensing I did not like any of this, proceeded to explain that they needed *our* help! A dozen Americans and a like number of Mexicans, who had been prospecting along the Bavispe, had taken over Basaranca, killing some helpless citizens. Only recently they had intercepted an incoming *conducta* laden with supplies and had killed all the packers. "The gringos," he said, "were fugitives and the Mexicans were also *profugos*." He had sent for Federal troops, but they could spare only Teniente Lopez.

In the meanwhile Dee-O-Det had joined us and was listening. The doctor, now alcalde of Basaranca, and Lopez both promised me that the Mexican government would be greatly in our debt if we would help to drive the bandits out of Basaranca.

Very unusual, I thought: Mexicans appealing to Apaches to help save a Mexican garrison from Americans. After questioning them, I told them to rest in the shade while I thought it over.

1. Any fair student of history of this period and territory must acknowledge that this attitude of Niño Cochise was not only based on the evolutionary theory of "survival of the fittest," but that he and his (Tahza) clan of Chiricahua Apaches had been pushed as far as they could go. They were trying to build and hold this enclave, as it were, against all intruders and wanted only to be left alone to work out their own destiny.

The Apache based his rights on The People having held this land many centuries before the Spaniards came, took it by force of arms, called themselves Mexicans, and eventually ceded part of it—because they could not hold it—to the United States, their conqueror, by way of the Guadalupe and Gadsden Treaties, all of which immorally preempted The People from their rightful heritage.

When the Jeffords-Cochise-Howard treaty was broken in 1876, Niño's clan had fled deep into this Mother Mountain stronghold to live on what the primitive land provided; they were cunning, daring, courageous, and at times half-savage—but to anticipate and outwit their enemies was a perpetual problem before which they were no longer very sure of themselves. AKG.

Lopez objected, demanding that I decide at once. Some of my men were watching from behind nearby wikiups, I knew, so I waved a hand and five armed braves stepped forth, surrounding us. Lopez quieted down. On the surface the proposition appeared to be our chance to get on the good side of the Basaranca citizens—which might save us the long trading trips to Sasabe—but it could also be a trap.

The *shaman*, speaking in Apache, suggested I call a council meeting. I told him to do so while I went over and told Mother of the situation. She saw no cause for alarm; she believed my instincts would guide me on the right trail, but she came back with me to the meeting ground. I knew she would think of something to entertain Gutierrez and Lopez. By now some of the men had come down from the mine.

I took the chief's position in the council circle and asked for silence. I explained about the situation in Basaranca and said that the two Nakai-Ye wanted us to help them fight. The men began to whoop and holler, but the *shaman* quieted them down. I asked for serious discussion, after which Dee-O-Det called for a vote. The decision was to send an armed group to restore order in Basaranca. I commanded that it be organized at once, and the braves shouted that they were ready to ride.

When I informed Gutierrez and Lopez they appointed me a *Lugarteniente* of the Fusileros! I suggested that they return to Basaranca and make one more effort to get the bandits to leave peacefully—before a tribe of mountain Indians came and killed them. Lopez haughtily demurred, saying he would lead us *Indios* to town now and drive the *ladrones* out or kill them. I promptly informed him that the Mexican had not yet been born who could lead a band of Apache warriors anywhere.

After some spirited discussion it was decided the officials would ride alone down to the shelf of the rimrock overlooking the river town and demand a surrender—and that we would be right behind them, but out of sight.

❧ ❧ ❧

THERE were fourteen in our party, and as we passed the glen north of the rampart, I thought of Jedi. That was where she and

I had ridden. A black rage suddenly seemed to seize me. *"Cat-ra-a ata Nakavdi yù-dastcin!"* (A curse on all Mexican bas-tards,[2]) I muttered to myself, and the *Netdahe* instinct which was part of my heritage grew as we rode down that steep trail to the Bavispe River. Just as we gained the spur above the river a long-range rifle shot banged out. Signalling the column of warriors behind me to stop, I saw Teniente Lopez tumbling out of his saddle. He was dead, shot through the head; some au-thority-hating marksman had scored first!

My men were already spreading out and hiding their horses behind trees and rocks—sons of warriors, they knew what to do even in their first battle. We worked our way on foot down to the river bank, where we saw the miners' sluice troughs and boxes on both sides of the river. No one was working them. Obviously the miners took a siesta during the noonday heat. I told Hi-okee to watch the sluices, and ordered Asa to go with Ticer and see if they could corner the sentry who had shot Lopez.

"We will try some Cochise tactics," I told Gutierrez. "Make a fuss here . . . and a fight there. If you will draw me a map of their strong points in town . . ."

He sketched a map in the sand and pointed to the area where most of the citizens lived. He noted the shacks across the river where the miners lived, then the general store and the main *fonda*, now fortified by the bandits. He pointed to a large boul-der from where he said, "You can see the entire town."

Hi-okee came to report that the miners were coming back to the sluices. I sent him and another man down a channel that had water in it only when the river was flooding and told them to hide behind the big boulder. When I gave a signal they were to yell and fire a few shots to spook the miners. They'd come running to see what was going on, and we would then have them out in the open.

Gutierrez nodded. I gave orders to move out, and we pro-ceeded to our positions. I now noticed a large windrow of dry brush along one end of town; Gutierrez explained it was a brush dam to prevent flash floods from eroding the flats so close to town. I asked him to get me a gallon or two of coal oil—the

2. This is about the strongest language the old-time Apache ever used. There is no profanity, such as the whiteman uses, in the Athapascan language, or in the Manso dialect.

kind used for house lamps. He left, puzzled, but soon returned with a full can.

When the miners began cleaning their sluice boxes I would call to them to surrender, I explained. If they refused, we would set fire to that dry-brush dam. The fire would chase them out, forcing them to retreat across the bare flats to cover. We watched the activity until the sun passed the peak of the canyon rim high overhead, thus casting a premature twilight into the canyon bottom. The miners began cleaning their pans. I cupped my hands and yelled in English, "This is the State Police! You are surrounded. Step out with your hands up and surrender!" Then in Mexican, "*Abajo con sus armas!*"

A man appeared on top of a sluice box and fired his six-gun twice in my direction. My two men beyond the big boulder took that as my signal and started whooping and shooting. The gunman dropped off the sluice box. To my surprise there was no return fire, only a period of silence. Then someone yelled:

"What're yuh waitin' for . . . yuh *culo-gordo* greasers?"

I ordered my bowmen up; several of us peeled off our shirts and ripped them in half, wrapped some arrowheads with the strips, dipped them into the coal oil, and lit them. The bowmen lobbed flaming arrows into the dry-brush dam. Soon flames rose high in the air, a breeze fanning them.

Five of the miners made a concerted rush for the river bank. Our riflemen opened up, and none of the outlaws made it; then three others tried, running like scared coyotes, and met the same fate. A lull followed this stage of the battle. Obviously the miners were changing tactics as we could see men circling back beyond effective rifle range and trying to flank us. Divided into two groups, they rushed our positions at both ends, yelling defiantly. Their rapid gunfire echoed along the canyon walls, bullets whined and ricocheted.

As I saw Jim Ticer go down, his sixgun blazing, I gulped in disbelief—to me Ticer was untouchable. Ma-Ti-O-Tish suddenly twisted half around and pitched to the ground, writhing. The thighbone war club, now blood spattered, still hung by the thong on his wrist. A ricocheting bullet brought me back to my own danger. I saw a huge whiteman charging to gain my cover. He did not quite make it—his gray kepi flew off as my rifle

69

bullet smashed into him. Then I saw young No-Ha-Daya fall and lie still.

By now four outlaws had managed to gain cover between and behind rocks within stone-throwing distance below us. One of them stuck his head above a rock to get a view of our exact position. I heard a shot and Alcalde Gutierrez shouted, "Ha!" He had scored. Eugene was just below me and a little to my right. I saw him aim his carbine and shoot. One of the four jerked up, and Eugene pumped another shot into him.

The two others yelled that they would surrender, and in a moment stood up with their hands held high. Both were Mexicans. One, with no ears, I recognized as Jedi's lover; he had aligned himself with the bandits. I told Eugene and Peridot to seize them—they were the last. Gutierrez and I counted fifteen enemy dead.

Kasale got help and gathered up our dead. I had lost three good men, including our teacher, Jim Ticer. I had the men wrap the three bodies in tarps and take them back to Pa-Gotzin-Kay, along with their personal belongings. Later I gave the thighbone war club to old Dee-O-Det. I made it a point to retrieve Jim Ticer's sixgun. It was a Colt-45 Peacemaker, serial number 88761, patented 1875. I proudly wore that gun off-and-on for a long time.[3]

Alcalde-Doctor Gutierrez congratulated us on our success in destroying the outlaws in Basaranca, adding that the townspeople were preparing a fiesta in our honor and that new shirts and anything else we needed would be provided by the town. We gathered up all the weapons from the bodies, and Gutierrez said the citizens would bury the dead outlaws *mañana*. We rounded up our horses and followed him into town, where we soon got clean and dressed up and were ready for fun.

Strange, these people just a short while ago were in terror of their lives—now they were preparing a gay feast in the plaza. Fair maidens greeted us with seductive smiles and gourds of wine. Wearing a new calico shirt, I strode through the plaza and took my turn in line. When I came abreast of a thinly dressed girl pouring *vino tinto,* she looked at me, then demanded:

3. One day in the early 1920's I gave that gun to my friend and present collaborator, A. Kinney Griffith.

"Were you in the fight?"

"I led it."

"You—you a chief? Da! No beard!"

She turned to Nakai. He informed her that I was Chief, and that he, Nakai, was a capitan! He might have informed her that I was a pure-blood Indian and therefore could not grow a beard.

I had my hour later when Alcalde Gutierrez introduced me to the crowd as Chief Niño who had directed the victorious battle. Soon those señoritas vied with one another for a turn to dance with me. I'd have none of them. To show my contempt, I asked the older women to dance—and I am sure the *damas* enjoyed it as much as I did.

I finally saw Eugene, and asked, "What did you do with the two prisoners?"

"Prisoners! What prisoners?" he asked, feigning surprise.

"The two you were in charge of, *'stúpido!'*"

"Oh, those, well—ah—some people wanted to talk to them. They seemed like family people. They gave me this." He held up a gold watch and chain and chattered on:

"It was dark in that *cárcel*. I turned to the light to see the time. Well, the door was open . . . and when I turned back those two were running out the door . . . and there was some shooting before they got to the river . . . so, no prisoners."

The fiesta lasted until nearly daybreak. None of us was in shape to travel, so we slept in the barn with our horses. I think mostly everybody in Basaranca slept till noon that day. As we finally made ready to ride, Gutierrez and another man came, each carrying a goatskin of wine. We loaded them, and as we bade the doctor and the townspeople farewell, they assured us we were welcome to come to Basaranca to visit or trade whenever we felt like it.

As we rode out past the cemetery we saw they had erected a headboard over the mass grave of the miners. It read:

HERE LIE THE REMAINS OF THE BANDITS OF
BASARANCA BROUGHT TO JUSTICE BY ALCALDE
PABLO GUTIERREZ WITH THE HELP OF
FRIENDLY INDIANS FROM PA-GOTZIN-KAY.

❧ ❧ ❧

WE arrived at the rancheria that evening and held our burial ceremony, which everyone attended. The *shaman* chanted and beseeched *Ihidnan* to be kind to those now gone to Big Sleep. Later, as was the custom, I told of the battle, adding that we had right on our side, which had given us the advantage all the way. Every warrior then told his version; finally came Eugene's turn. He stood up, and when all eyes were on him, said:

"I do not wish to talk about it." That was all.

Dee-O-Det went through the closing rites, the council broke up, and we men drank the two goatskins of Basaranca wine. It was sour but potent. I staggered to our wikiup and to my cougar-skin on the floor. In my sleep I again fought the battle of Basaranca. In the dream I saw Jedi was the leader, but somehow she escaped.

I awoke in a bad humor. I was soon at the spring, drinking to put out the internal fire. Other men came, drank, and left. Dee-O-Det came but he just filled a jug and left. I sat there thinking: Why does wine make you feel so good? It tastes better than whisky. Yet after one has so much he goes to sleep, and when he wakes up—why does he feel so terrible? As I was pondering this my mother appeared as though from nowhere with a gourd of liquid.

"Here, my son. Drink this. It will make you feel better."

I raised the gourd to my lips; it smelled suspiciously like mescal mixed with pine pitch. I took a swallow and it tasted good. I drank it all and handed the vessel back to her. The Apache seldom says "thank you"; it is an unspoken thought, signified by a glance skyward.

"It is the same as I fixed for your father after victory dances. On the way up I also gave Nakai some of the medicine."

The stuff was already taking hold and I was feeling better, so I looked up Nakai. He was out in back of his wikiup, running a deerskin over the breaking board. He handed me a pelt; it was as soft as any I had ever felt. We went inside his wikiup. Nakai was married to one of old Juh's orphaned daughters, a good Chiricahua, and she was busy making a pair of *kabuns*, while crooning some tune. Hanging from a rack was one of the most beautiful buckskin *jaquetas* I ever saw. There was a swastika charm of gold worked on the left breast; a Cibolero Cross of silver on the right side was inlaid with turquoise, jet, coral, and mother-of-pearl. On the sleeves each bit of fringe was tipped with a silver bead or an oblong turquoise spangle. My admiration of it must have showed, for Nakai said:

"For one like that I will take three tanned skins, some silver, gold, and turquoise—and some more of your mother's medicine!" His wife whispered something to him, then he turned back to me. "Do-Sa-Le says she will make you a jacket better than this if you will just replace the deerskins—well tanned."

"Say no more, it will be done," I replied. "I will replace *all* the stuff. How much in trade is one of these jackets worth, would you say?"

"Oh, about three good horses."

"I can see all my warriors will be wearing these fancy *cueras* —and walking. Foot men are no good in the mountains. Say, Nakai, I will make a bargain with you: I will appoint you war chief."

"Oh? Why?"

"Well, if you own all the horses, what will my men ride?"

From there I walked over to Eugene's place. Lying on a tarpaulin in front of his bachelor wikiup were fifteen sixguns with belts and holsters and four carbines. He was checking the weapons captured at Basaranca. I helped him a while; then we stored them in the communal kiva, later to be issued to men who needed a weapon. We each decided we needed one now; he chose a shiny nickel-plated Smith & Wesson and I chose a Colt Frontier Model made in 1881. I shot it a few times and decided it was a good gun.

❧ ❧ ❧

MY current problem was the half-dozen or so braves of my own age, any one of whom might get the urge to take advantage of me because we had grown up together. Nakai was a good man and I thought he deserved anything I could throw his way. Although he was devious and ambitious, he never tried to go over my head. But this little Eugene needed watching; he was smart and would go a long way in life. Mangas-Chee and Al-chise also kept an eye out for the main chance. All of them needed to be slowed down or they would have everything worth owning around the rancheria. I went over to see Dee-O-Det. He bade me enter. When I was seated he remarked that I seemed to have grave doubts on my mind.

I told him that some young men were trying to gain tribal wealth, which was natural enough, but I did not think it should be done at the expense of others. Was I within my rights as clan chieftain to prevent it? He promptly informed me that any spoils of war belonged to all, and that there was an old tribal law made by the Hako Society to that effect. As a Hako it was up to me to enforce the law, and it would take a ten-member council of the Hako to change it. Shrewdly, he then added that most of those young men I had in mind had greedy, pushy wives. That was the main reason why they were seeking wealth, but that I need not worry too much as only the Hako council could control or confiscate, and then only with the ap-proval of the chief and the *shaman*. Old Dee-O-Det had hit on a point I might never have thought of . . . .

Bluntly, within a few minutes, I had learned more about people and Apache law than I had known in my lifetime. I must have murmured out loud that I had better remember it, too, or I'd soon find myself sucking the hind tit around here. Dee-O-Det snorted, "See me more often and you will learn more."

❧ ❧ ❧

SEVERAL weeks passed and we had settled down into normal routine when Nakai came in from Sno-Ta-Hae with ten deer-bladder bags bulging with gold dust and nuggets. He informed me our gold stock could be much better handled if it were melted into bars. He had seen a blast furnace in Basaranca, and since it was no longer in use there, why shouldn't we buy it?

That was good thinking. I had been pondering a trading trip to Basaranca now that we need not make the long trip to Sasabe. The river town did not have the wide variety of Ameri-can goods that Sasabe had, but it had other things to make up for it. When I told Mother about it she promptly came up with a long list of needed stuff—she could not write but she had a fine memory—including those big cast-iron pots that could make enough stew to feed the whole clan at one sitting. I had thought of buying some beef cattle of the new shorthorn breed the Mexicans were developing to replace the native longhorn.

The following forenoon I saddled Hammerhead and rode up to the mine. Nakai and two others had a huge pile of ore at the shaft entrance, and they were throwing plain rock off to one side where it tumbled down the slope. They ignored me, kept on working, and I just sat there and watched. Every now and then Nakai would make some loud remarks about how much better they could do this with a blast furnace. This was all for my benefit so I let them work and sweat. Finally tiring of the game, Nakai came over and extolled the new vein of red gold, saying if it was not just a pocket that would peter out, we'd soon be rich. So a blast furnace would save time in smelting the ore he had before something happened. He was pushing again, and I prodded him with questions until he got irritated. When I had the answers I thought I needed, I told him to put Chee in charge and we would go after the furnace in the morning.

Back at the rancheria I found a stranger in camp. My mother seemed to know him. We were used to having tribespeople dropping in unexpectedly. A score or more had drifted in since Golthlay had surrendered five years before; some stayed, some went on. Even the Apache Kid and the fearsome Mickey Free paid us a visit now and then. We did what we could for them. This one, however, I instinctively disliked: here was another *Netdahe!* He was a well-built warrior of about twice my age and his movements reminded me of a cougar. Mother, eyeing me, said:

"Niño, this is Apla-Chi-Kit. He has lived on the San Carlos. He got into trouble and had to leave; he wants to live with us."

"Until the man hunter (Mickey Free) shows up," I said to myself. As chieftain, it was up to me to make a decision, but I shirked it. I walked over to the *shaman's*.

"Ha! You have a strange one and you do not trust him," Dee-O-Det greeted me.

"Who is he?"

"He is a bad one with a knife. Taglito once told me he worked

75

with the army—before we left our beloved homelands. I myself think he is faithless and treacherous."

When I returned, Apla-Chi-Kit was at the table with mother. He was eating like a wolf. Mother seemed happy, so I went away. I was busy the remainder of the day, getting ready for the trip to Basaranca, went to bed late, and was asleep by the time the noises of the rancheria subsided.

❦ ❦ ❦

NAKAI woke me in the morning and said the fires were hot. Mother made corncakes and had wild honey to go with them. We were on our way to Basaranca before the sun was an hour high. There were nearly thirty men and women in the caravan, for this was to be in the nature of a social visit as well as a business trip. I had ordered the men to leave their rifles, or carbines, at home, but every other man could carry a belt gun or belt knife of his choice. We were at peace with the Basaran-cans, I pointed out, and arriving fully armed was not exactly trusting. I inspected the column now and then, as was my cus-tom, and at one turn in the trail I saw that Apla-Chi-Kit not only had a belt gun and a knife, but was packing a carbine in his saddle boot. Since he was riding in the rear with Mother and Dee-O-Det, I said nothing, but I was uneasy.

We made it down Juh's Pass to the river bend without mis-hap, then around and up the flats to the spur along the base rock. Here I ordered camp made in the side channel, while Nakai and I rode into town to apprise Doctor Gutierrez that we had arrived. We dismounted and tied our mounts to the hitch-ing rail in front of his small hospital. I knocked on the door and a pretty nurse opened it, inviting us in.

Gutierrez looked up from his desk as we entered. He shouted a greeting and told us to make ourselves at home. The nurse brought three glasses with a bottle of cool wine, and while we sipped it, I told the alcalde-doctor that Nakai wanted to buy the blast furnace that was no longer in use. Gutierrez chuckled and said Nakai could have it just for the taking. I then mentioned we had half the tribe with us and that my mother had a long list of supplies she wanted to buy. The doctor nodded happily.

76

It seemed Mother was on his list of favorite people. He beamed and said he would have the people make a *baile grande y fiesta* for tonight. I figured now was the time to get my little idea settled before any partying, so I told him I had in mind buying about twenty head of cattle, prime cows and bulls of that new shorthorn breed.

"We will gladly sell them to you, Niño, and at a good price," he responded. "We have more cattle right now than we have men willing to herd them, and our stores are well stocked. The *conducta* has just left; we took all the stuff they had and paid for everything in gold. There is more gold along the Bavispe than I had thought, it seems. Our men are doing well, for once, but I am worried."

"I thought everything would be calm and peaceful after our recent battle . . ."

"Mexico has many desperados." Gutierrez shook his head. "News of gold gets around, and we do not have the armed protection we should have. The military is at odds, and most towns do not have authority to employ and arm a police force. We have over three hundred men, women, and children here. Of that number there might be sixty men able to fight."

"If it is arms you need, it seems you should be able to buy them."

"It is not that simple. You see the Diaz government has fear of being overthrown and has banned the possession of arms. True, the gringo gun-smugglers will sell to us—but there are always spies around to report any violations to Diaz, and the guilty parties will be shot."

"Well, then, I will quietly return the rifles and all but three of the pistols we took as spoils when we fought the bandits of Basaranca."

"If you will give me those, Niño, I can organize a police force that will let our citizens breathe easier."

After we settled those matters I rode over to the main *abacería*, where our men were loading the six pack mules with provisions the women were buying. Apla-Chi-Kit was with my mother; Alchise was with his mother, Nadina; Mangas-Chee was with his mother, Neo-Dina; Dee-O-Det was fussing around as a *shaman* should. With the loading over, we all returned to our river-bend camp, unloaded, unsaddled, and secured our camp so that a few people could guard it.

When the women were dressed in their new Mexican finery they started for town in a group. Apla-Chi-Kit, Mangas-Chee, Ealae, Nea-Ot-Toden, and Alchise went with them. Dee-O-Det, Hi-okee, Klan-O-Tay, and Eugene went with me. Nakai had somehow disappeared. As we drew near town, the strains of "La Paloma" came floating through the air. It was fiesta time, sure enough, and many couples were dancing in the plaza. There was a big *ramada* over the center of the plaza and lanterns hung from the rafters. Musicians were grouped everywhere, strumming their guitars.

Some of my men chose the first girls they came to and swung them onto the floor; but I looked for the pretty *muchacha* who had scoffed at me for being so young. I saw her dancing with Apla-Chi-Kit. She saw me and broke away from him, running toward me and calling, "Oh, there is my Niño—my big chief!" She held out her hands. "Dance with me, my Niño!"

A rough hand thrust her aside and there stood Apla-Chi-Kit, still wearing his gun and knife, his face ugly with rage.

"Ho! You a chief . . . you steal my woman! I will kill you and I will be chief!"

He drew his knife but unbuckled his gun belt and flung it into the crowd. A circle began forming around us. The spirit had changed from gaiety to anger in the space of a few breaths.

"We will fight with knives, like true Apache men," the *Netdahe* snarled. "Ha! But you tremble with fear—you have no stomach for Apache steel!"

"Why do you vow to kill me?"

"You are not fit to be chief of people who trust you! You have betrayed us to the enemy. You ordered us to leave our guns. Then you sold them to the *Nakavdi!*"[4]

"You are a liar!"

He lunged and stabbed at me, and I leaped aside and jerked my knife from its sheath. Just as I brought it clear, he stabbed again and his point slashed the inside of my right arm from elbow to wrist and ripped into my hand. As the blood spurted, my knife clattered to the floor from a useless hand. I had not yet struck a blow, yet I was half-disabled.

4. I have often wondered how he got that notion.

I dropped to one knee and retrieved the knife with my left hand. I whirled as I straightened up, but he stabbed me in the neck. I could feel a quiver in my legs as I leaped aside. Even so I knew I had the advantage of being younger, quicker, lighter on my feet than he. We circled each other, looking for an opening to deliver a fatal thrust.

I slashed him across the chest. He stabbed at my stomach. My feet slipped in my own blood. I pretended loss of balance, and he rushed in for the kill. I leaned to the right; he moved to intercept, and I thrust in from the left. I brought my knife over in an upward thrust with all the strength I could muster. The point of my weapon disappeared under his chin and penetrated to what must have been the top of his skull. I twisted the blade and thrust again.

His knees buckled; his body quivered in spasms and wrenched the knife from my slippery hand as he hit the floor.

I tried to pull the knife from his throat. I had to put a foot on his neck to dislodge the weapon. The people closed in and kicked and spat on the body to show their contempt. One man stooped and hacked off the head.

I felt sick and wanted to vomit. My knees shook, and two men grabbed me as I started to fall; one of them was Doctor Gutierrez for I heard his voice ordering me carried to the hospital. I remember feeling him work on my cuts. When he got through with me I must have looked like an Aztecan mummy.

I heard the doctor tell someone to carry me to a bed. I started to get up, but the nurse took hold of me. I saw that my mother was holding me also; Kasale, Eugene, and Hi-okee were standing by, and Dee-O-Det was chanting a medicine song.

I tasted and smelled chloroform and was sick but I felt a soft bed under me. A pill was pressed into my mouth and I had some water. I have heard it said that an Indian is stoic and never shows pain. Well, I don't know if we *show* it, but I know we *feel* it. There was fire in my stomach, wrist, hand, arm, and jaw. My chest pounded with every beat of my heart and this night it had come close to stopping its beating forever. I was on fire all over, but the pain was going away. Now I was getting cold and everything seemed to recede.

Sometime later—as in the world of dreams—I heard Dee-O-

Det tell someone that Apla-Chi-Kit was no good. He had worked for the White-Eyes and had helped the soldiers slay Apaches for gold. (I could not open my eyes as he kept sprinkling *ho-denten* on my face as he talked.) He also mentioned Mickey Free and said, "That Feared One came last night and was vexed because Niño killed Apla-Chi-Kit and someone else made away with his head."[5]

Mother aroused me in the morning. The doctor was with her. I felt dizzy. I had fever and cold sweats. Doctor Gutierrez took a quick look and said:

"Niño, I have to open that arm wound and scrape the bone. During the night you struggled, and your bandages tore loose —infection has set in."

He gave me a pill and told me it was Veronal for pain. Huh! He laid my arm open and wet it with antiseptic and left it open. He worked on my jaw and my stomach. Then he gave me another pill; those pills did not seem to relieve the pain much, but they made me feel sleepy.

Once nurses brought soft food, and I tried to eat. My jaw was so sore I could not chew, but I could swallow. Mother, constantly at my bedside, mashed the stuff and gave me some wine. I could drink that. I lay there thinking: I won the fight, but what did I win? The right to live in pain? I almost wished I had not won. I knew Apla-Chi-Kit was not suffering. I knew he died instantly.

"Mother," I said, "will you ask Dee-O-Det for some *shaman's* soup and *shaman's* tonic, and mix them with eggs, milk, honey, and whisky? And, Mother, put much whisky in it."

"The *shaman* and I will make you some strong medicine."

Most of the townspeople came to ask how I was and if there was anything they could do.

I lay there and throbbed, swinging back and forth from hot to cold, and I cursed Apla-Chi-Kit's ancestors for giving life to a mad dog—a *Netdahe* dog—who had craved to take my life and my position in our tribe.

I lay on my back for two months, wasting away. The doctor said I went down to ninety pounds. Finally my spirits returned

5. There was a notation in the *Scouts Journal* at Old San Carlos that Mickey Free had been ordered by Al Sieber to track down Apla-Chi-Kit but there was no notation of the final discharge of the order. AKG.

and I began to get some strength back. One morning the doctor said:

"You are getting better, Niño. You can walk around some now, and when you get a little stronger, you may return to Pa-Gotzin-Kay."

Chapter 5   1892-1894

Tesorabi

THE ANNOUNCEMENT that I could return home made me feel better. It seemed to me I had been in the hospital a lifetime.

When mother, Dee-O-Det, and I entered Pa-Gotzin-Kay the people were out to greet us. They were chanting as we rode in:

> *She brings Ciyé back,*
> *She who gave him life and gave him to us.*
> *She brings him back.*
> *He whom he gave shelter and food,*
> *Tried to take his life.*
> *Now that one is gone.*
> *No longer will he sell Apache life;*
> *For he is gone.*
> *Never more to breathe, he is gone.*
>   Enju! Enju!
> *She brings him back,*
> *She who gave him life and gave him to us.*
> *He is our chief, he will always be!*
>   Enju!

It was good to be back in the red hills of home. Here the weather was cool and pleasant. Mother insisted that I take it easy, as did Dee-O-Det, so I loafed around for a week or two.

Nakai, Eugene, Chee, and others were busy at the mine. Occasionally I caught a glimpse of Nakai coming or going, and one morning I called for him to wait for me. We sat on a rock and I told him to bring me up to date.

He began by telling how he, Eugene, Chee, and Kasale had bought four more mules and packed the blast furnace and crucible up from Basaranca in two trips, how they had reassembled it and got it going with good results. It had turned into another dry summer and the deer were scattered and hard to hunt, so our herd of cattle had dwindled to sixty: twenty-six cows—only two tame enough to milk—three bulls, and thirty-one calves and yearlings. It took a lot of meat to feed our clan, which now numbered fifty.

Nakai invited Mother, Dee-O-Det, and me to his wikiup for supper that night, and afterwards he presented me with the fancy thigh-length buckskin jacket his wife had made for me. Dee-O-Det took this occasion, over a cup of Do-Sa-Le's homemade mescal, to relate how the council members had reacted to the report he had made for me of my fight with Apla-Chi-Kit.

The *shaman* then gave me the benefit of his memories of Apla-Chi-Kit in the past. He revealed that Apla-Chi-Kit had been a born *te-iltcohe* (troublemaker) who, as a child, was the clan thief and as a youth could almost out-perform the *Netdahe* in violence. And when things went wrong—as they often do for a man of his mentality—he escaped tribal justice and joined up with the whiteman at Fort Apache. From then on he was a renegade who worked with both groups—whichever paid him the most at the time, or gave him the most pleasure.

Now I understood Apla-Chi-Kit's attitude. He thought I was afraid to fight, that it would be easy to take over and run my clan and seize our hoard of yellow iron—or he might have sought a reward for turning us in as renegades. My mind was now at rest. No longer would his hate-distorted face bother me in my sleep.

The next morning at dawn I felt good, and wanted to do something constructive. The thought came to me that I owed Nakai three deerskins. I found my bow and arrows and walked down to the garden patch. Sure enough, a moss-horned buck and two does were feeding on our corn. Who said the deer were scattered? Nakai, the politician! I fitted an arrow to the bowstring, drew the string back, aimed, and let go. The buck dropped, kicking. Before the startled does could collect their wits, I had two more arrows on their way. I bled the deer, then walked back up the trail. When I got to the compound I was tired. A half-grown boy, Young-To-Clany, was chopping wood for the central fire. I told him I had three deer down in the garden and had bled them, and asked him to pack them up to the kiva for me. He replied he would even skin them if I would give him a hindquarter of one of them. I agreed. I knew Dee-O-Det had made him a *shaman's* understudy—and I also saw a trick; he would show the boy how the old-time Apache cooked deer, and get a choice quarter for himself at the same time.

I lay down for a while and began to wonder if that was what Dee-O-Det was up to. Was he going to make a batch of *shaman's* soup? Well, I would find out tonight.

I dozed off and it was twilight when I woke up. The *shaman* should be cooking the meat by now. I went over to his fire. There he was, and he was roasting a whole haunch on a spit. I hunkered down and watched. He was chattering away, telling me how good the old-time meat was—how different it tasted from our new way of cooking it—and he would prove it.

When it was done, he gave me some. It *was* different. In addition to being over-salted, that old rascal had literally studded it with green chili peppers. He had used an awl to make holes every thumb-width all over that haunch and inserted a small green chili, making the meat's taste so hot that it burned like fire. It was so different that I could not swallow it. I did not want to offend him, so I mumbled some excuse and left. I went back to Mother's fire; she had a pot of pintos and cornbread ready.

"I just had some of that old-fashioned venison, cooked by Dee-O-Det," I declared, grasping the water jug.

She began to laugh. "Ho! Hot, huh?"

"So that is supposed to be old-fashioned."

"The *shaman* thinks so because when the Chihuicahui-Chockonen first met the Spanish, they were given some chili peppers. I think Dee-O-Det lived in those days."

"Well, he's gray enough and wrinkled enough," I admitted.

After eating Mother's cooking, I went back to Dee-O-Det's. I was curious and wanted to ask questions. He was chewing on the deer shank when I arrived.

"Who are the Chockonen?" I asked.

"Teneh Chockonen: people of the Chihuicahui Mountains."

"Then we are Chockonen?" I pressed.

84

"We are of the Teneh Chockonen!"

"And they liked that hot meat?"

"No. It was the Mimbreno, Tudairvia, whom the Nakai-Ye called 'Delgadito The Slender,' who showed me how to cook meat this way."

"I am glad I am not a Mimbreno."

"You did not like my meat?"

"No. It would make me drink water all night."

"Whisky makes you drink water—you like *it!*"

"Your meat does not make me feel the way whisky does."

"You are not old-fashioned like me," he snapped.

I could see I was getting nowhere, so I bade him pleasant dreams and went home. Mother asked if I had found out what I wanted.

"Who ever finds out anything from that old coot?"

"He is wise, do not forget that. He knows things that are not known to other men."

🌱 🌱 🌱

IN THE morning I made a bargain with the *shaman's* understudy to tan the three deerskins, then I rode up to the mine. The men had ore piled everywhere; the blast furnace was fuming and the crucible bubbling. I dismounted, tied my horse, and walked to the mine entrance. Eugene was sitting on a pile of rocks and sorting them like ears of corn. He must have read my mind for he said:

"I am sorting the soft ones from the hard ones."

"I have never heard of soft rocks!"

Nakai came out of the stope pushing a wheelbarrow of ore and dumped it at Eugene's feet.

"What's he doing?" I asked, indicating Eugene.

"I told you what I was doing!" Eugene said angrily.

"Yes, but let me hear it from Nakai."

"It is called high-grading," Nakai explained. "The ore that is very good . . . we crush in that." He pointed to a hand crusher. "That which is not so good, we crush in that." He pointed to a mule-driven arraster (rock crusher). "Then we smelt it in that." He pointed to the blast furnace. "At 1945.5°, gold melts and runs into these refractory molds—and is twenty-four karat, pure gold. Teacher Ticer taught us all about it."

I knew it was complicated, but to keep from appearing too stupid at some later time, I had to find out now. I told Nakai to show me how much gold he had stored. He led the way down into a stope and there, covered with a sheet of canvas, was a pile of gold bars about a foot high and two feet long. He explained that they weighed the bars and tried to make them sixty ounces each, but that they varied from fifty to seventy ounces, depending on the smelt. After some more discussion, I rode back down to the rancheria.[1]

In a few weeks, after the fall harvest, we made another trip to Sasabe. Mother had insisted on Sasabe, but this long trip galled me and set me to thinking: Sasabe was more that 600 kilometers round trip over rough trails and took about two weeks of constant riding from dawn to dusk, depending on how long daylight lasted, the weather, how experienced the packers, how heavy the loads, and luck—and all for a stock of the whiteman's luxuries! We could afford them, but were they worth the effort? Couldn't we do well enough at Basaranca, or even Magdalena, or go back to our old way of living off nature? My mother and my *shaman* outvoted me.

🌿🌿🌿

THE Season of Little Leaves, 1893, arrived—late. After two dry years this spring was a little too cool and wet, but we got the garden and fields planted. The rains increased and the year turned out to be the never-to-be-forgotten "Time of the Floods." Old-timers in the region talked about the floods as long as they lived—certainly I never forgot them. The Sierra Madre—Continental Divide—is by nature a backstop for storm clouds coming from either east or west, and this year from early spring until late autumn the mountains were the backstop for a continuous

1. Our forefathers believed that *oro* (gold, yellow iron) must be a magical force—or why did the Spaniard destroy great nations for it? Jim Ticer gave my generation the answer: "Gold is *everything*," he said. "Get it any way you can. With enough of it you can rule the world." He had coached Nakai, Chee, and Eugene how to mine and smelt it—me, he taught how to manage it.

mass of rain clouds. The many canyons, draining out of the mountains into the desert arroyos, were constantly at flood stage, whereas in normal years most would be dry at least nine months out of the year. On the upland Pa-Gotzin-Kay shelf we were in no danger of being flooded, being surrounded by numerous deep canyons through which the relentless waters swept, but we could not cross the torrents for our periodic trips for supplies for a year. So we were forced to return to our former primitive way of life.

In spite of the incessant rains, we were happy. Some men worked in the gold mine, others split logs and built bigger and better wikiups and kivas. Nakai and I taught school. Some siblings tended the livestock, others roamed the hills for wild meat. We even went back to eating rabbits. What crops were not rained out grew twice as fast and big as normal, and crews were kept busy fighting back weeds that seemed to grow a foot each summer night. The women were industrious, as was normal, making and repairing clothes, weaving baskets—busy with family chores from dawn until they went to bed with their men at night. We all missed the whiteman's luxuries to which we had become accustomed, but we made the most of what we had. Even Mother had gone back to combing her hair with the *nité* stone, as she had lost her comb and was too proud to borrow one.

❦ ❦ ❦

SPRING, 1894, arrived with normal weather, and we had just finished planting when a trail guard sent word that a stranger was approaching. It turned out to be a Doctor Gutierrez, and we congratulated each other on having survived the year of the floods.[2]

He had been concerned about us, he said—not having seen or heard from us for so long—and his other worry was that Sonora and Chihuahua were again being overrun with *yangui* bandits

2. The researcher can find records of the "Time of the Floods" in the Sonora Archivos, Hermosillo, when the State's economy dropped to near zero due to the fact that people could not travel, yet hundreds had died of drowning on the lowland Sonora desert! AKG.

and local bastards. Mexico was too poor to furnish Federal troops to protect the back lands and the *paisanos* did not have arms to defend themselves. Would we Apaches again come to their aid should Basaranca be attacked? I said we would and asked if Basaranca would come to the aid of the Apaches if Pa-Gotzin-Kay were invaded? Gutierrez had a bottle of American whisky in his saddlebags and while we drank it we pledged our all to each other; then decided the two of us alone could wipe out all the outlaws in Mexico.

When the bottle was dry it occurred to me I'd better let the people in on this decision. I knew old Dee-O-Det had been watching us and he called a council meeting. When the members were seated at the fire I introduced Gutierrez just as I would introduce a stranger. This Apache custom was designed to put everyone at ease, showing malice toward none, for in council everyone was presumed equal. Then I explained the fears of the alcalde of Basaranca that outlaws might again invade the river towns, adding that they might even come to our almost inaccessible hills and accidentally find us. Fast-thinking Chee remarked that would be "our chance to gain more guns in the form of spoils, so let them come—the Pinda-Lick-O-Ye must be good for something![3]

The council members got their heads together and words flew. Again the *shaman,* as spokesman, announced the council had decided that the matter rested in the hands of the High Chief. The meeting broke up and I took the *shaman* and the doctor to our wikiup, where Mother poured three cups of mescal. Dee-O-Det raised his cup and saluted the alcalde, and after that stroke of diplomacy he tossed off his drink as if it were water. Then he nodded and left.

"He is a remarkable man," Doctor Gutierrez sighed. "I wish I knew how he does it."

It was late and I felt weary, and Gutierrez looked weary. I took him over to Ticer's former wikiup where he could spread his bedroll, and then I headed for my cougarskin in Mother's wikiup.

Mother was serving us cakes and coffee for breakfast when Eugene, Hi-okee, and Klan-o-tay came by. Eugene said they

3. Indians were not allowed to buy, or own, guns.

would ride to Basaranca with the doctor as they had to get a grate, or cone, for the blast furnace. I nodded, and they left to get horses. Gutierrez was still eating, and as long as he kept eating those cakes, Mother kept putting more before him. She won. He stood up and said:

"Your breakfast cakes are delicious, Señora Tahza."

"How did you know that name?" Mother demanded.

"I came across an old magazine called *Leslie's* from somewhere in the United States but it was published in Spanish. It was about your husband Tahza, who went to Washington with an Indian agent called Clum, and it told that your husband died of pneumonia, and that the young chieftain left a wife, Nod-Ah-Sti (Niome), and an infant son, Niño, who had fled to Mexico."[4]

Mother turned and walked away. Although Gutierrez seemed sincere, I had a sudden feeling that there was something wrong here in the High Sierra.

After Gutierrez and Eugene left, Mother and I had a long talk with Dee-O-Det. The old *shaman's* conclusion was that the doctor was just being friendly and had no ulterior motives. The morning wore on and I got to thinking about those bands of outlaws. Being bandits, they would also rustle cattle. I realized then that I hadn't looked in on our herds lately. I roped my rangy hammerhead bronco, hackamored and saddled him, and mounted quickly. I snubbed the hackamore around the horn so he couldn't lower his head as he got set to buck. He was ornery that way, when not ridden often, but was a good horse for a long ride.

As I mentioned earlier, Pa-Gotzin-Kay was located on a mountain shelf about a kilometer wide and five kilometers long. Our rancheria compound was in the center for convenience sake; our fields were on either side, and the open range was beyond. To see the cattle I had to ride one way, then double back to get to the other herds. I kept old Hammerhead hoofing right along. I found our cattle in small bunches, often in hard-to-find places, but they seemed fat and contented. I counted sixty-nine head.

With that off my mind I hit the trail up to the mine. Hammer-

4. Article based on a letter written by John Clum dated July 8, 1876.

head didn't like that, as he wanted to return to the home corral. I quirted him out of that notion, and we arrived at the mine in late afternoon. There was no one there, but I looked around. Everything seemed *ya-laǹ,* but even so somebody was going to get a tongue lashing for leaving the mine unguarded. The crude blast-furnace apparatus was standing alone like a weird pile of rust. It's leather bellows had been patched many times, and it's innards were in disrepair, waiting for the grate Eugene had gone after.

When I got back to the compound, Eugene had just ridden in from Basaranca. He said:

"The alcalde sends word that a band of *blancos* and *gusanos* are moving to set up a stronghold at Tesorabi. The alcalde and his men will advance from Basaranca and try to engage the *tsít-à-gi* (outlaws) before they fortify themselves."

Tesorabi—close by our regular trail. If anyone occupied that old walled pueblo it would be the closest threat ever to Pa-Gotzin-Kay. I forgot all about giving the tongue lashing to Eugene. I went to see the *shaman.* He was waiting for me as usual.

"Victory will be yours," he said before I could open my mouth. "And here is your charm, but you will not need it." Old Dee-O-Det and his prescient mind! "No man can take your life —only *Usen!*"

Our party of twenty warriors was on the trail in short order. We arrived near the fork of the Juh's Canyon trail well before sundown. I had sent two scouts ahead to see if the old barrio was occupied, and they returned saying there was no one in sight. I then put Chee in charge and told him to hold this position until he heard from me—unless the *guerrillos* entered the town.

I pushed old Hammerhead into his trail-covering lope and made the remaining distance of about eight kilometers in record time. Basaranca was as active as a beehive in springtime. A group of about thirty militiamen was lined up in haphazard formation in the plaza, the alcalde and a sergeant standing by. Beyond them was an ominous-looking rig with a long black tube within a shield on an axle between two big cartwheels. Pablo Gutierrez, proud in his dual role of doctor and alcalde of the town, said that this was their cannon and that Sergeant Tomas had made it out of parts of old blast furnaces. Tomas

Bill Greene took this photograph about 1901 at Pa-Gotzin-Kay and it is the only one I have of the rancheria. The man at the left is Dee-O-Det but I am not certain who the women and the child are

OPPOSITE: Mickey Free, the Apache Indian scout who worked with the U.S. Army for many years in Arizona and Mexico

ABOVE: General Crook (No. 10) at the parley at Cañon de los Embudos in 1886. Naiche is No. 2, Geronimo is 4, and Mickey Free is 7. The others are: 1. Faison, 3. Roberts, 5. Kay-I-Tah, 6. Chatto, 8. Maus, and 9. Bourke

BELOW: At Fort Bowie in 1885 some civilian scouts and packers with General Crook (No. 4.) and: 1. Tom Jeffords (Taglito), 2. Horn, 3. Bourke, 5. Newsman, 6. Mickey Free, 7. Wratten, 8. Houston and 9. Sieber

Signal Peak, overlooking Dragoon Springs and Dragoon Canyon, entrance to Cochise's stronghold. It was fenced in 1950 to keep out vandals

BELOW: Cochise Head towers above the rugged surrounding country in the Chiricahua Mountains where Cochise located his main stronghold

had once worked for an arms company in Mexico City, and he added that my Nakai and Eugene had helped him in their spare time. Well, well!

Although Gutierrez was very proud of his weapon, I refrained from expressing my opinion as to its value in these mountains for Indian-type warfare. I brought up the subject of prompt action and tactics for the coming battle (that did not include cannon) and was surprised when both the sergeant and the alcalde agreed to my plans.

As I rejoined my men, the moon rose. It was full and amber red. The Apache Moon. I had been told how in 1880 Golthlay had sacked this old walled pueblo on a night like this. It was the time of year when the daylight was long, nights short and cool and clear. We took turns catnapping and standing guard all night.

At daybreak, hearing distant rifle fire, I saddled up, rode to a high point, and saw our outriders had ambushed a bunch of bandits. And I noted the Basaranca men advancing slowly up the canyon trail. We were grouped in fours. I rode with Nakai, Kasale, and Eugene at my side to the outskirts of our line. I gave the sound of a screech owl, followed by the yapping of a lone coyote. Chee came to me. I told him thirty Mexican militia were in position in the dry wash at the bottom. He reported fifteen of the *guerrillos* were lurking behind the old walls, but they were held down by his men posted on the cliffs.

I joined the Mexicans and had them advance to the spur of the cliff overlooking the town. My braves were firing intermittently. The invaders must have had plenty of ammunition as they kept up a heavy return fire. At first Chee had said he thought there were about fifteen of them. Now it was apparent there were at least twice that number of the enemy and none of them seemed to be watching for an attack on their rear. Soon heavy rifle fire came from a spur on the cliff. The main group of my braves was attacking from the right flank, as planned. The invaders stampeded and ran for their horses. I waved Gutierrez the signal, and he ordered the charge. We had the enemy surrounded and out in the open. They began to drop under our combined force. Riderless horses added to their confusion and panic. Five men surrendered to the Mexicans— avoiding us Apaches.

Eugene, Kasale, Hi-okee, and Boa Juan began gathering up pistols and rifles. The *sergeanto* counted the dead, while I went to see what my losses were. I had only one wounded—Klan-o-tay, who had accidentally shot his little toe off.

The Mexican militia had no losses. The *guerrillos* lost by count twenty who would pass for Americans, one who was definitely a Pima Indian, one Zambo, and thirteen of Mexican origin—a grand total of thirty-five.

Our losses: one wounded Indian and a lot of ammunition!

I rounded up my braves and we rode into Basaranca, following the militia. When we arrived the news of the victory was given to the people, and a big celebration was planned for the next week—but starting now. There would be a dance that night. I told Chee to remain there and help Gutierrez with the preparations. Then I had Eugene and Boa Juan pack our share of the spoils—an assortment of rifles and revolvers—and the three of us returned to the rancheria.

Dee-O-Det greeted me, knowing I came with a victory and primed to celebrate. He had the people assemble, and I told them of the week-long celebration in Basaranca. All those able to ride could go; those too feeble to ride would be held in the saddle if they wanted to go. It seemed that everyone wanted to go. All pitched in to help. With a lot of yelling and laughing and confusion and a few minor hurts, we finally saddled thirty-seven horses. Eleven people remained at the rancheria.

I had all the oldsters ride in the saddle, with the younger people mounted behind to steady and keep them from falling, though few needed assistance.

The *shaman* rode with me, and as we passed the outskirts of Tesorabi, the vultures were already circling high in the big sky.

"The Mexicans say that town died of fear," I remarked. "Golthlay raided it fourteen years ago and they never came back."

"Yes, I know, but was it in favor in the eyes of *Usen?*"

"I do not know. You, the *shaman,* should know."

"I could have told him. Golthlay never asked."

"Did he not ever ask you for advice?"

"He was not of the Hako or the Midi—he did not believe."

"So now, I hear, he is farming somewhere in Okla-homa. Geronimo a farmer! I do not know where that is, do you?"

"I do not need to know."

As we rode into Basaranca, we were met by cheering people. We were quartered on the hill overlooking the main part of town, where three young men helped with feeding and caring for our horses in a large corral with a water trough. The barn was stocked with fresh hay. We cleaned up, and everyone picked a place to sleep later. We were told that anyone who wished to eat was to go to the side plaza where food and tables and wine barrels were set up.

We started to walk into town along the main *avenida,* passing a huge *álamo* tree from one limb of which dangled three men and from another limb two more.

"What's this?" I asked Chee.

"Those are the five *blancos* who surrendered to the Mexicans. The alcalde declared the town under martial law. They were given a trial, found guilty, and were promptly hung. Good, huh?"

We came to the large plaza where there were better things to see.

"Oh, there is my Great Chief!" shouted the *muchacha* who had danced with another Apache on another night.

"The last time you said that, I almost got killed," I retorted.

"Oh, but you are not dead," she laughed. "You will dance with me tonight?"

I put an arm around her slim waist. "Let us go behind these bushes and talk about it . . ."

"Aa-ieh! You men, you are all alike!" She laughed again as she ran off.

❦ ❦ ❦

TWO officers in parade-dress uniform approached me. One was Alcalde Gutierrez, who saluted and said:

"Chief Niño, may I present my commanding officer, Colonel Mendoza de Vega."

"This is a privilege," said the colonel, waving a salute. "I have been hearing about you, Chief. General Torres and I arrived with our troops from Hermosillo but an hour ago. Were we a little sooner, we would have ridden to victory with you."

"It would have been an honor," I said.

Gutierrez then asked us to join him in a *saludo* to the victory. We entered the *Oro y Plata Cantina,* where a smiling bartender served us brandy and we drank to the future of Basaranca and her Indian allies. Then we drank to each other's health and to the health of everyone we could think of until we ran out of healthy people; then we left and went our separate ways.

I ran into the *shaman;* he was at the wine barrel. Nearby, the dance music was in full swing. He started to sing: "Hai-hai-hai! Eeeyiioo! Hiiieeeooo!"

He went into a wild whirl that I recognized as a medicine dance. People gathered and applauded him. He took another swig of wine. This time he really gave them their money's worth—it was a combination medicine dance-rain dance-war dance.

The crowd roared and the old man did an encore; then sprang to the top of a long table near the wall, undid a "possibles bag" at his belt, and began handing out good-luck charms.

Dee-O-Det knew how to attract people. Several hours later he collapsed from too much wine, and three of his admirers half-carried, half-dragged him to the barn, although they were about as bad off as he was.

I danced into the wee hours of the morning and I think I danced each time with a different woman. Then when my eyes no longer told me what they saw and my legs began to take me where I did not want to go, I retired to the barn. I stumbled into the *shaman's* bed and there on his left were three young Mexican soldiers. Nearly out, I lay down on the *shaman's* right and did go out.

Late morning found five sick people—three soldiers, one *shaman,* and one Indian chief. Dee-O-Det looked around and saw the soldiers and then noticed me.

"Tudish!" croaked the *shaman* as he departed for the horse trough. Once there he entrenched himself, flat on his belly with half his head submerged, and seemed to be breathing water.

I saw the alcalde coming and he too looked as if he had been doing a war dance.

"Where were you last night?" he grunted. "I looked everywhere! I couldn't find hide nor hair of you."

94

"We were dancing!" croaked the *shaman*.

"I even had your mother looking for you. Our guest of honor was General Luis Torres and he wanted to meet you."

"Oh," I said.

"I have waited all my life to see this general," Gutierrez continued. "He may be the next *presidente* of Mexico."

The alcalde led us over to the military plaza. Nakai, Eugene, and Sergeant Tomas were getting the cannon ready for some tests. These tests were to be in keeping with the victory celebration.

Two years previously this young inventor, Tomas, had discovered by the trial-and-error method that cannon could be made of cast iron, as well as of brass. His first model was constructed with a three-inch water pipe (called black pipe in those days), and was mounted on an axle between two wagon wheels. The cannon fired two rounds before the barrel burst and a bystander was killed.

Tomas made a heavier barrel. The shot that was about to be fired would be the third from the thing, which was now mounted on a heavier carriage reinforced with strap iron. Everything was in readiness. The townspeople were gathered around but they kept at a safe distance. Tomas lit a torch and applied it to the fuse. The fuse sputtered—then BAA-ROOM!

A huge cloud of red-and-blue smoke enveloped the cannon and the crew; then odd-shaped pieces began falling out of the air. When the smoke blew away the only thing intact was the trail spade. At the same time, across the river on a barren slope, there was a huge dust cloud that arose from the explosion of the ball, for the projectile also had a fuse that was lit by the original explosion. The crowd cheered.

Tomas, scratching his head, stood there; Gutierrez walked away, shaking his head. With that we separated. I sought out Mother and we walked down the *avenida* until we neared a restaurant where the smell of baking tamales was overpowering.

"Mother, would you like to eat some tamales in that *fonda?*" I asked, pointing to the restaurant.

She nodded, I opened the screen door, and we walked in. A

waitress came for our order. She was a girl who had danced with me the night before. She nodded at my mother and turning to me asked:

"How many legs has this cow?"

I ignored her question and ordered six tamales and a bottle of red wine. She brought the wine first. I opened the bottle and poured Mother a glassful. She sipped, then exclaimed, "This good!"

The waitress returned with the tamales, two plates, and the necessary silverware. I put three tamales on Mother's plate.

"Since when does my son wait on me? I have been waiting on you ever since you were born!"

"Just do not eat with your fingers here."

The meal over, we went out on the *avenida* and she told me how well she liked that restaurant.

"I do not have to serve, they serve *me!"* In the next breath she asked, "Will there be another dance tonight?"

"Yes, I think there will be a dance every night."

"I have watched the maidens dance and they do things with their feet that are strange. That is not the way of our dances."

"No, but to them *our* dances are strange. And some of them dance like cows with five legs."

Dee-O-Det was standing on the next corner. He was enjoying life here in Basaranca. He was a friendly fellow and spoke to all who passed. Then I saw the parish padre greet him. Each turned to size the other up as they passed, like two strange dogs.

The padre then headed my way. As he came abreast, he spoke:

"Good afternoon. Will all you folks be at the Way-of-the-Cross service this evening?"

"We have brought our *shaman* with us," I answered. "That was he you just passed."

"I invite you to come and worship God in our church."

"We do not know Him—we know only *Usen.* We pray only to *Ihidnan.* To someone we do not know, how can we pray?"

At that point the conversation foundered. We walked away. Mother asked me what he was talking about, and I told her I didn't know and didn't think he did either. No Apache *shaman* would ask strange people to worship.

"These are peculiar people; so are the Americans. They want us to forsake our way of life and adopt theirs, or they get mad."

"Yes, son, wars can start because of things like that."

"My mother, I have a feeling that he is a false padre. He wanted all of us Apaches to come to his church tonight. He would have us all there in a peaceful mood, off our guard, and he could have us all massacred by the State troops under that new general. I think it best to move our people out before tonight."

Mother was so surprised at my words that for once she was speechless. I called for Nakai. He came running and I told him to get Eugene and the men, and to tell all our people quietly that we would move out before sundown.

"Niño! Eugene and Tomas and I want to build a new cannon!"

"You can stay, but send Eugene to me."

"I will go get him, Chief."

Eugene and the *shaman* came almost together.

"Eugene," I said, "these people are not of our blood and they have different ways, they have different beliefs. Their padre talked to me just now; he wants us to come to his church. If he asks someone else of our people, violence might break out. Now what I want you to do is to tell our people quietly that we are moving out, and to get ready to move."

"How is it you are giving me these orders when Nakai is really the chief under you?"

"He is not of our blood. These are his people. He may not understand. Besides, he said he wanted to stay and help build a new cannon."

"I would also like to stay and help them," he replied.

I nodded and Eugene left. Dee-O-Det, Mother and I walked to the alcalde's house and found Gutierrez had just departed for Hermosillo with General Torres and Colonel de Vega and would not be back for a week. I did not like that, either!

Soon everyone was busy saddling the horses and strapping gear to the saddles. It was about midafternoon when we rode out of Basaranca. The Bavispe was running higher so we cut around to the main ford. Enroute neither the *shaman* nor I had much to say. My thoughts were busy with a question: Why is it those people think everything they do is right—and that all others should go along with them?

We paused to rest at Juh's old rancheria, and looking down the steep trail toward the ford of the Bavispe Barranca, I wondered what General Crook must have thought when he first rode into this hideout.

It was about two kilometers from the bottom of the canyon up this trail, which was so steep and narrow that a horse could not turn around. On many switchbacks and overhangs the outside stirrup swung over a breathtaking gorge. In most places one side rose to a sheer cliff-face, the other was thousands of feet straight down. If fighting had broken out while Crook was on the trail . . .

"A yard wide and a mile deep with Apaches lurking on both sides," it is said Scout Tom Horn had remarked. "Once you have started, you are committed—come hell or high water."

I lapsed into deeper reverie, recalling when as a lad I was out with a deer-hunting party. We looked down on one of Crook's columns—led by Captain Henry W. Lawton—struggling down this same trail.[5] Dee-O-Det broke into my reverie.

"You have minor troubles?"

"To tell the truth," I said, "I think perhaps that padre does not understand us. How could he know of *Usen?* Even I do not know Him. I have never seen Him, have you?"

"Nobody has ever seen Him. He is the Great Mystery. *Ihidnan* —Supreme Being. He lives up there in the endless sky, the Spirit World. So, being a mystery, how could anybody know Him?" The *shaman* continued with a note of wonder in his voice, "I think maybe this God of whom the padre speaks is also a Great Mystery, and he knows no more about Him than I do about *Usen,* except that He is a mystery. I heard once from an old man that back in the days when the padres first came they told Great Chief Tulac that the Indian was this God's children the same as the White-Eyes. Tulac answered him by saying, 'The White-Eyes must be His favorite, because the Indian is always hungry and cold since the White-Eyes came.' "

5. I happened to have with me a captured Mexican bugle that had been given to me by my Uncle Golthlay (Geronimo). Mischievously, I blew my version of "Boots and Saddles" loud and clear. Even today I still chuckle at the confusion that caused on this narrow wilderness trail. Then I blew "Charge!" When the echoes died away I blew "Recall." I have been told the incident was never mentioned in Lawton's official report to Crook. But a news item in some magazine or other caused wry chuckles in the War Department.

"I think the Great Chief was right," I agreed. "But if the whiteman's God is so good, why are they not with Him instead of here?"

When I got only silence for an answer, I motioned our column to move out. We made it into Pa-Gotzin-Kay shortly before nightfall. All of the fires except Mother's and the central fire had to be rebuilt. With the fires going, we roasted four turkeys we had shot along the canyon rim. We had brought no groceries from Basaranca, so we had to make out with what we had at hand.

I slept well that night, and daybreak found me up and dressed. I fed the fire, put the coffee water to boil, and waited for Mother to get up. She was up just as the water boiled. She put the coffee in and set the pot back to steep.

During breakfast I told her I was going to change the storage place of our yellow iron and that I would put the council in charge of it. I had some fears, I explained, and even if they were groundless, the change would do no harm. Mother agreed, and I went over to the *shaman's* wikiup; he was about to take his morning walk so I walked with him. I told him of my plan to have three carefully chosen council members move our gold bars from the mine to a secret storage place, and he approved.

That evening he called the council together and they voted on the seven men most qualified to handle the project. They were Mangas-Chee, Nakai, Kasale, Neo-Ot-Toden, Nah-Shis-Tor, Hi-okee, and Eugene. Dee-O-Det and I stepped to one side; I told him I trusted Nakai but he was a Mexican and he got along too well with them. Dee-O-Det said Chee had a wife who talked too much. Kasale and Eugene were rejected because they had not attended the meeting. The *shaman* then called the council back to order.

"Will the three men I call step forward and make themselves known to the chief?"

This, of course was a formality, as I knew every person in the rancheria. The three were Neo-Ot-Toden, Nah-Shis-Tor, and Hi-okee. They were the three youngest men on the council. As they were assembled, I knew these husky young braves would take no time at all in stowing the gold as planned.

Dee-O-Det and I escorted them to a cave in back of his wikiup at the foot of the cliff. The cave, which at one time must have been inhabited by Yamparikas, was a place known to only a few of us because the *shaman* had sealed it soon after the clan arrived. The entrance was now overgrown with weeds and brush. We reopened the cavern and the five of us crawled in and looked around. We decided to move the gold bars in after moonset.

We all knew the power of the yellow iron and its effects on the minds of men, and how it might affect us sometime in the future. This wealth belonged to all of us Chiricahua Mansos and so by hiding it, where no stranger would ever find it, it would be safe should we be forced to move without it. An invader could take Sno-Ta-Hae and could work it but our hiding place would be far enough away that we could slip in and remove our gold bars at any time.

I was concerned not only about the local Mexicans but also the American outlaws, who seemed to come and go almost unchallenged. Then that Basaranca padre had me worried. The Mexicans obeyed their padre better than they obeyed their alcalde. I believed that padre was *à nèt-j* (a spy) sent by General Torres, who might one day be the *presidente* of Mexico, the doctor had said.

Some Mexicans are good: the doctor was a good man, and he ran a good little town on the whole. He had explained much of their government to me. Yet he said those in power have fear of being thrown out of power. Dee-O-Det admitted he did not understand those things either, but he emphatically did not trust a Mexican, unless he first proved himself. He said to me, "I do not like that padre."

We went our ways, having agreed to meet later when the rancheria was quiet and *Gotchamo* gone from the sky.

I walked the shadowy trail to the garden, found my favorite rock, and sat down to think. I could hear the creek bubbling and an occasional swish as a bat swooped through the night air after an insect. The moon was nearing the horizon. I studied it, amber and serene, but Apache legends broke back into my mind.

The races—why were they so different? Why did the *españoles* come to the Mayan shores and drive us Indians north? Did their God tell them to come and take our homelands away from us? If so, I certainly wanted nothing to do with Him!

Why did the White-Eyes come west, drive us Indians out, and take away from my father the land on which I was born? Why did the whitemen take away our Chihuicahua homelands and, as they said, *give* us reservations? How could they give us something that already belonged to us?

Would the Mexicans now try to take Pa-Gotzin-Kay from us?

I had dour thoughts that night in September, 1894. Even tribal lore, handed down from father to son, did not help much. All I could see was foreigners—pushing at us Apaches since 1540. We had protested at first. We got nowhere; then we fought. The *conquistadores* had superior weapons and kept on pushing. They saw our pastoral hills abounding with wildlife—the great and small animals of forest and desert. These, to our way of thought, were our animals. Yet the invaders took what they wanted. They did not ask for it—they took it.

They brought animals that were strange to us. We found *them* good eating, so we took them. It was either that or starve! Did they not take ours? Then they called us thieves and, if caught, we were hanged or shot. Another reason to fight back and try to drive them from our homelands.

Then the *conquistadores* found the yellow iron and the white iron on our land. They made crosses of it and held them up before us—was this their Deity? They became so greedy that we could not even claim the air we breathed as our own.

I sat on that rock in the garden and I swore that some day I would have the answers to those questions. Today, as I write, I am in possession of the answers. I do not dare to write them—not because of fear of retaliation, but for fear of embarrassing some descendants of those foreigners.

A fox barked not ten feet from me, bringing me back to reality and out of a nightmare of thought. The moon was nearly down. I stood up and stretched and walked over to the *shaman's* fire. He and Hi-okee had some coffee on but it wasn't what I'd call good. Soon Neo-Ot-Toden and Nah-Shis-Tor arrived, and the four of us headed up to the mine. Dee-O-Det remained to prepare the cave. It took us three trips to carry down the gold hoard and store it in the cave. The *shaman* was sitting on top of it; it was well guarded.

Chapter 6   1894

Taglito!

MOTHER and I inspected the food stock in the communal kiva and found we were low on just about everything. Only corn was plentiful; this year's crop had been good. Tomorrow, we decided, we would head for Bisbee in Arizona. Jim Ticer had told me about Bisbee. He said it was bigger and better than Sasabe. Mickey Free, on one of his brief stopovers at our rancheria, mentioned it as lying just north of Naco Springs. Judging from all I had heard, I figured it would be several days shorter than the ride to Sasabe. The only thing wrong was that Bisbee was an American town, but I was determined to try it. Autumn was a good time for traveling.

Alchise, Boa Juan, and I checked the saddles, *aparejos, armas, modulas,* tarps, straps, ropes, then the horses' and mules' shoes. We would take ten pack animals since there was so much we wanted. Besides Mother and Nadina, I would take ten men, and leave all the others to guard the rancheria. This should make a force strong enough to handle any bandits that might take a notion to ambush us for our yellow iron or any *soldatos* who might question us enroute.

That night at the council, I explained that we needed to replenish our supplies, told about our new destination, and got council approval for the trip. We were slow getting started the next day but we made the Bavispe Bend *vado,* crossed the canyon, and camped, having traveled almost forty kilometers.

The second day our trail was slightly westward and north. Afternoon of the fourth day found us at Naco Springs. We had by-passed Campo and Pozo on our right, the Fronteras Presidio far on our left, then the Mina Oro sand traps. At no time had there been a fence, or marker, let alone a gate. In fact we could have ridden for days in any direction from Pa-Gotzin-Kay and not seen a fence. The first people we saw were a clan of Pima Indians camped at Naco. They seemed surly and down on their luck. Mother and I confronted their head man, Joaquin. He eyed us beligerently. It was easy to see he had larceny on his mind. I waved a signal and five of my braves stood up from the underbrush in a grove of giant sahuaro and displayed their ready rifles.

"Ugh! Apotches!" Joaquin grunted. "We go now."

"What was he up to?" asked Boa Juan after the Pimas left.

"Robbery. He wanted the skins we are going to trade."

"What skins?"

"The ones we left home." And I added, "Or maybe the ones we are wearing."

"Ugh! Red niggers!"[1]

We camped at the springs, and in the morning headed north. We had not gone far when we were stopped by the border patrol, an eight-man squadron. An American sergeant questioned us. I told him we were Pimas from Rancho de San Jose, headed for Bisbee to buy our annual supplies. He nodded dubiously as his men looked us over. Luckily all our rifles were hidden under the leather *armas* that covered our saddles and packsaddles. He waved us on. We rode for about four kilometers and camped at another spring, which we later found was called Mule Gulch.[2]

Knowing the *blancos* did not like to see Indians riding around in their towns, I told Mother and Nadina, who looked neat and happy in the fluffy dresses they had put on that morning, to walk into town and have a look around. They were gone so long I began to get worried. I walked in to see what was happening. Asa and Alchise followed in case I was being followed. I arrived at the biggest store, the Phelps-Dodge Mercantile, and there was Mother at a counter, buying like mad, so I joined her.

1. A colloquialism in the Southwest since Old Bill Williams, mountain man, started it in 1830.

2. *Brewery Gulch: Frontier Days of Old Arizona,* by Joe Chisholm, Naylor Co., San Antonio, 1949. AKG.

❦ ❦ ❦

A TALL well-built man with a short red beard and rusty hair
that hung to his shoulders walked in. He stopped inside the
door and his gaze fastened on my mother for a minute or so,
then he strode to the counter and said:

"Niome!"

He picked up my mother and swung her around as though
she were a child and kissed her—and she kissed him right back.

"Taglito!" she exclaimed. "I never thought to see you again!"

"Niome—Nod-Ah-Sti! It is glorious to see you!" He was speaking in flawless Apache.

"Taglito, it is glorious you come back to us!"

Like a pair of long-lost Apache sweethearts those two
couldn't take their eyes off each other. Here was an occasion
that made Mother forget about buying, and she and Taglito
walked out of the store, hand-in-hand. Nadina and I followed.
Outside they paused and came back to this world, and Mother
said:

"Taglito, here is my Ci-yé."

I put forth my hand. "So you are Tom Jeffords."

"Neen-yo! You are the spittin' image of your father." He
smiled, grabbing my hand and sizing me up with sharp brown
eyes. "You are as tall as he, but not as heavy."

We walked back to camp, and when Tom saw our men, he
was astonished; he said it was like walking into a warriors'
camp in the old days. They gathered around and I introduced
them individually, then added, "He is called Taglito by his
friends."

"E-Chi-ca-say! Taglito!" (Greetings, Redbeard, our brother!)

"I knew your fathers," Tom responded. "All were good warriors under Niño's grandfather, then his father."

When I told him we were living in Pa-Gotzin-Kay in the
Sierra Madre, he told me we were running a big risk by coming
here. The Territorial law said no Chiricahui could live in
Arizona, so if anybody asked we must say we were Pimas and
friends of Tom Jeffords. Everybody seemed to be talking, but
Mother got in a few words again, telling some men to fetch

wood and water so she could make coffee. Tom chuckled and asked me if women ordered men around in our tribe now, and I whispered, "Only Mother does—she is the Queen Bee." He nodded and understood.

"I have heard so much about you, Taglito, from her," I said. "It is as though you have always been with us. She told me about whitemen taking our Chiricahua land and giving us new land. Taglito, how can you give me something that is already mine?"

"Well," he chuckled, "I can only try to explain. If you accept it without question, I will think you're touched by White Painted Woman. 'Beware of Greeks bearing gifts,' is an old truism, Niño—you might get a Trojan Horse."

I did not exactly understand, but that started me off. I, myself, now recognized the intelligence that had attracted this man to my grandfather, Chief Cochise, some twenty-five years before.[3] We had our heads together, me firing questions and Taglito giving answers. Mother brought coffee but Taglito kept on talking. He cleared up my mind on several things that had been bothering me.

Mother and I pressed him to ride with us to Pa-Gotzin-Kay and he agreed. He said he had been prospecting, but was not doing well, so maybe this would change his luck. I told him we had good luck; we found yellow iron, and I handed him my buckskin pouch of dust and nuggets.

"Boy, howdy!" he exclaimed. "That's *rose* gold!"

Mother took him by the arm and started walking back toward town. I could see what was on her mind, so I told Kasale to break camp and bring the pack mules into town. Nadina and I started walking. I gave Tom my poke and asked him to buy two five-gallon kegs of whisky. I would stay with the women. It was late afternoon by the time he returned with the whisky, and we were already loading the mules. We moved out with the twilight.

Taglito led us down a dry-wash trail in case that Pima clan was waiting for us on the main trail. We followed it for a time, then cut around the manzanita ridge to avoid the border patrol and Naco Springs. Tom knew of a marshy strip of land along

3. *Arizona Characters,* by Frank C. Lockwood, Times-Mirror Co., Los Angeles, 1928. AKG.

the east base of the ridge with water and tules all around. Deer came from the hills to drink; javelina and wild burros came in from the arboreal desert. We made camp back from the water hole to avoid disturbing the wildlife. We unloaded our horses and mules, watered them, and hobbled them in the grassy swales. Kasale posted a routine guard. We built no fires for they could have been seen from a wide area; besides, it was not yet cold in the lowlands. We ate a cold supper, then everyone found a place to bed down. When I woke up the sun was shining in my eyes. Mother and Nadina were making breakfast.

"Rise an' shine, Taglito!" I yelled, speaking English for the first time in his presence. We had been conversing in Apache, as English was a strain for me; also Taglito had a broader vocabulary than many Apaches.

"That sounded like army slang t'me. Who taught you?"

"An American who came to live with us," I answered. "He taught all of us. He was called James Ticer."

Right away Tom wanted to know more about Ticer and I gave him my impressions of the man from the time we found him up to the time he was killed in the battle at Basaranca. Tom seemed to think we had been mighty lucky in more ways than one. He called to Mother and said:

"Niome, Niño tells me you speak English."

"Yes, Taglito. I spik Unglis pretty some good."

"You do fine, Niome," Tom replied—in Apache.

"Taglito, do you not spik Unglis like me?"

Somehow he avoided giving an answer. I helped him out by quickly describing our battles at Basaranca and Tesorabi, and why they had occurred. I mentioned that we were on friendly terms with the alcalde-doctor, but that I did not trust his townspeople nor their padre. Tom nodded.

Mother noticed his coffee cup was about empty so she refilled it. He gave the upward glance of an Apache "thank you" and mentioned how lucky we were to be sitting on a gold mine at Pa-Gotzin-Kay. He pointed out that without it we would be living like primitive Indians or, as in the old days, by raiding and would have the Mexicans hounding us. Also, if we raided in Arizona, the Military would be very embarrassed, as their final reports stated there had been only one or two old Apaches who did not surrender with Geronimo and Naiche.

Taglito!

We had a hearty laugh over that. Then I hopefully explained that with our gold we might one day be allowed to come back to Arizona, buy some good land, and live on it as farmers. He scoffed and said we'd need enough gold to buy half the politicians in America to do that, and hire a battalion of lawyers to boot.

❦ ❦ ❦

IN THE morning we took an old trail south across the Cananea hills, angled alongside of Black Mountain, then skirted a stretch of lava, letting our animals pick their own pace. The following forenoon we wound around a pine-capped mesa with a broad valley beyond. Later that day we neared the Sierra Medio and the Continental Divide—as Tom called it—loomed in the distant haze. By afternoon the ground got rougher, full of potholes, large and small, and we angled up a nearly dry arroyo toward mountains on our right. There was a stretch of mesquite and madrona and a spring of cool water, and we made camp. The remains of our previous campfire could be seen, with no sign of anyone having been there since. At Tom's suggestion the next morning, we veered a little to our left and soon we were crossing the rolling hills of a vast range. Clusters of cattle were here and there, some so close we could see the Z brand on their shoulders, others so far away they looked like bugs. Tom, who had been riding back in the column with Mother, loped up beside me.

"That's John Slaughter's San Berdoo Springs Rancho. Did himself proud buying it. Too bad half of it is in Mexico. We'll have to drop in on him while I'm down this way."

We reached the lower campsite—one of a half dozen used by the Apache war parties of old—unpacked, and hobbled the animals in the scrub-oak grove beyond. I heard a shot and went to investigate. Taglito had killed a deer and was already bleeding the animal.

We carried the buck to camp and had plenty of help cleaning it. I never knew whether it was the close association with this frontier scout out of the past, or if they were just plain hungry, but some of this generation's warriors suddenly reverted to the primitive; they gleefully grabbed the deer's intestines, stripped out the contents, and began eating the still-warm organs until they were sated. Continuing their orgy they began whipping left-over strings of gut around until all were a dirty mess. I couldn't do anything with them; Mother did not try, but Taglito brought them back to the present by throwing several of them into the water hole.

Next morning we were slow getting started. We picked up the Rio Agua Prieta course, which was almost dry, and followed to its junction with the down-Bavispe Barranca. By midday we had crossed the canyon and were up in the highlands. We camped in a cedar park within a semicircular escarpment that we Apaches call *Cos-codee,* meaning "No Escape." It is known in Southwest history as "Chi-hua-hua's Hideout."

Tom Jeffords, who had ridden many a wilderness trail, slowly shook his head and said, "Looks like our trail's plum disappeared!"

"This is where Golthlay first started to talk surrender with General Crook," I said.

"You mean to tell me 'Rosebud George' Crook put his troops over these trails after old Geronimo?"

"With the help of some Apache scouts he made it. See that rocky point over there? That is where we came in. We go around this point—and there is the trail home."

"Is there any other way out?"

"Yes, but the military did not know of it. Up on that cedar ledge there is Cos-codee Pass, just wide enough so you can lead a horse through. This is as close as the soldiers ever got to Pa-Gotzin-Kay," I explained. "The Apache scouts kept our secret and once in a while some came to visit us; then we'd all have a good laugh."[4]

We made a rest camp, got a fire going, and put on a pot of coffee laced with a pint of whisky Tom happened to have in his saddlebag. Everyone sat around listening to him tell stories of the old days. Finally Mother asked, "Taglito, what happened to you after you resigned from the reservation?"

"Oh, I just loafed around Tucson for a while. You see, before I became Agent I had to be bonded. Well, it took the government

4. *Mickey Free, Manhunter,* by A. Kinney Griffith, Caxton, pp. 97, 118, 120, 129, 159, 175, 176, 200. AKG.

a long time to refund the bond. Then I went to Tombstone and did some prospecting and found a fairly good vein. I sold it and drifted over around Owl Head Butte in the Tortillitas. After some months I found it—silver. I made enough to set up a ranch on the south side and I live there now."

"What happened to that evil *Mister* Clum?" Mother asked.[5]

"Well, Clum resigned when he couldn't keep all the promises he made to the Indians on the San Carlos. He went to Tucson and started a newspaper. He sold it and went to Tombstone, where he started another paper—*The Epitaph.*"

"What did they do with all our people who surrendered?" young Chi-hua-hua asked, probably thinking of his father.

"At first they were sent to Fort Pickens in Florida. The climate was bad for them, so the army took those who survived to Fort Sill in Oklahoma, where they are now farming. Your father went to Big Sleep there."

Lolling around, we had all become so relaxed that some heads began to nod. There is nothing as restful as a midday nap on the trail, and nothing so startling as a wolf howl from the nearby rocks. Boa Juan, on guard and the only one awake, shot at it, and missed. Several of us bounced to our feet. Laughing, we named the place Sleeping Rock. Soon Alchise called that the pack train was ready. Taglito and I mounted and rode to the head of the column. The afternoon wore on and only the creak of packsaddle leather and an occasional click of a hoof against a loose stone were heard above the breeze in the scattered pines along the silent hills.

❦ ❦ ❦

WE plodded into the rancheria after sundown and The People were out to greet us. The *shaman* saw Taglito and his old eyes lit up.

"Taglito! Is it you or your spirit?"

"Dee-O-Det! I thought you had gone to the Spirit World."

"I am not ready to go to Big Sleep for long time." The *shaman* held up both hands, fingers spread out, twice. "I still have so

---

5. The emphasis on the *Mister* was Mother's way of expressing contempt.

many teeth. I feel young again. The *zagosti* [6] leaves are growing again after last year's rains, and I treat all the Old Ones with them."

"You have the secret of longevity," Tom smiled. "You are a good medicine man. I remember once when you wanted to give *golinka* (skunk) oil to my blood brother when he had a toothache. It smelled so bad he would not let you come near . . ."

"And I remember once I almost got you married."

"Yeah, and once I beat you shooting the bow, remember?"

"Yes, and to get even I stole your clothes when you were in swimming."

Two other Old Ones approached. One walked with a stick and his hair was as silvery as Dee-O-Det's. Once he had been one of Cochise's bravest warriors. He hugged Tom Jeffords and tears came to his eyes as he said:

"Taglito, I have wished many times that I might see you once more before I go to Big Sleep."

"You must not go to Big Sleep now that I am here, O-Tee-Boa," said Taglito. He turned to the other. "Oh, ho! Here is Fle-Cha-Ka-Eda-Ty-gee! You were one of the braves who helped me learn the Apache tongue and coached me in Chockonen customs."[7]

Now there were tears in Taglito's eyes as memories of the glorious past crowded in. And so it went until Tom Jeffords was greeted by all who remembered him, was introduced to those who had heard of him. When the greetings were finally over he followed us to Mother's wikiup.

Tom asked about the New Order Law we had in effect in Pa-Gotzin-Kay, and Dee-O-Det explained how it worked. Mother and I added a few points: the Old Ones were no longer abandoned; instead the old men now helped in the fields,

6. I had, on several occasions, seen Dee-O-Det grab a handful of certain brownish leaves and eat them with obvious relish. Once, when he was not around, I tried a mouthful but soon spat them out as they were bitter. I also knew the women sometimes used them to spice a stew. Many, many years later I found out that *zagosti* leaves were a blood conditioner, and that present-day chemists make a medicine from them called *Coumadin*.

7. For fascinating research on this trip to Pa-Gotzin-Kay and other travels of Tom Jeffords, see the magnificent Dr. Joseph A. Munk Library of Arizoniana in the Southwest Museum, Highland Park, Los Angeles. Also Arizona Pioneers Historical Society, Tucson. AKG.

tanned skins, and made arrows, and the old women made clothes and cooked for the young people who did the strenuous work around the rancheria. Our New Order called for community cooperation—everybody worked and everybody shared equally in our results.

Tom could see that our system was sound and he seemed to give the credit to my mother. He said some of the so-called civilized peoples ought to try Niome's way. She had done what the American government was still trying to do; had, in fact, tried on the San Carlos and failed. And why? Too many dishonest White-Eyes! Remembering her recent past when Golthlay bought whisky with captured gold and then got drunk and cruel, she said we now managed our gold so that everybody benefited thereby. She suggested Dee-O-Det and I show Taglito our gold.

I called Hi-okee, as he was one of the custodians, and we took Taglito to the secret cave. The sight that met his eyes caused him to exclaim, "Holy Toledo! You have more gold here than I have ever seen before!"

"Here, have a chunk," I said, handing him a bar. "If you want more, you will have to work for it. Tomorrow, I will show you where that came from."

Back at the wikiup, Mother set out four cups and served us from a wicker-covered jug, then placed the jug beside us.

"Your New Order has indeed changed the Apache," said the amazed Jeffords. "I never dreamed I'd see it. You're living in clover. Women with a voice in the affairs of men, and whisky served from a wicker-covered jug!"

"We are going to have stew with much beef, onions, and potatoes, and with *zagosti*," Mother smiled. "And for after we will have the peaches in the can."

Later I reported to the council about the trip to Bisbee and how Mother and I had been found by Taglito. The council cheered and called, *"E-Chi-ca-say! E-Chi-ca-say!"*

Dee-O-Det called for a vote to celebrate with whisky, and the motion was carried with alacrity!

Taglito stood up and asked to be heard. This procedure was not new to him; he had been heard in Cochise's councils and his voice was weighed in the decisions of those councils. When everyone was quiet, he spoke: *"Ish-lá n y-ag-itná*

Is-d-áh!" (Drink now . . . talk tomorrow!)

By midnight there was not a sober man in the rancheria. Many fell over where they sat. Morning found the spring doing a rushing business, as it always did after these celebrations. The *shaman* had his choice spot as usual, and I was busy doing my part in trying to dry up the spring. Tom crawled under a nearby tree and went to sleep. I did likewise.

This way of Apache life went on for several more days. Eat a little; drink a lot. Sober up; then get drunk again. In between times Dee-O-Det and I took Tom on tours of the south and north portions of the shelf. He was amazed at our progress in "starting from scratch in a primitive land, and growing into a tribe of fifty-five people" (his count), and we talked our heads off.

"There is one thing I have always wanted to know, Taglito," I said one evening. "Where does the difference lie between us and the whiteman? I know it is not our color. What is it?"

"Niño, you have asked me a question I do not believe I can answer."

"Then, if you cannot see the difference, there is no difference . . . or is it because you do not want to?"

"The difference is that when an Indian is asked a stupid question and a truthful answer would make him look stupid, he says, "I do not want to talk about that."[8]

"In that case I have been asking too many questions—and getting that same answer; even you give me that same answer. Who am I supposed to ask . . . myself?"

"Well, it is sort of like making love to a beautiful woman— it is a time when a man must act for himself."

"But I must act for my people! Taglito, you and I know that the whiteman craves gold. He will cheat and steal and kill for it. If we gave you all our gold bars, could you buy the Dragoon Mountains for us? Then we could go there and live in peace. We would raise cattle and farm and hunt."

"Niño, as I have explained to you earlier the Territory of Arizona is afraid of the Chiricahui and will not let any live in the Territory. You can blame Geronimo, and the newspapers, for that. All Apaches must live on reservations that the government has provided. Besides, the government owns the Dragoon

8. Means: *No comment!*

Mountains and land and will not sell. So forget it. You are much better off here than you would be in Arizona." Then he added, "Let well enough alone."

Old Dee-O-Det had been silently sitting by, listening. Now he stood up, said, *"Hi-dicho,"* [9] and headed back to his wikiup.

After a period of thoughtful silence Tom got up, stretched, and said:

"I'm going to hit the blanket. Wake me up tomorrow noon."

I followed him into the old Ticer wikiup which I now shared with him. Somewhere in the darkness outside a baby was crying. Taglita said softly:

"You are right about getting land, Niño. *Usen* has quit making land, but he keeps right on making people."

9. "It is finished," or "the end."

Chapter 7   1894-1895

Yaqui-yori

I T WAS the Season of Red Leaves, October of 1894. We had spent a restless night; the horses had been kicking up a fuss, the mules and burros had brayed off and on all night. Possibly a grizzly or a cougar had been prowling nearby. To avoid the added noise of barking, we kept no dogs at the rancheria.

After breakfast Tom Jeffords and I saddled our horses, loaded two pack mules, and were off. It was less than two kilometers to Sno-Ta-Hae as the eagle flies; but after crossing a small canyon and dodging rocks and bushes, we had to cover about three kilometers to the mine at the base of a box canyon. A born prospector and miner, Taglito eyed the area for quite a spell. We removed the rocks, brush, and trees placed by our men to conceal the diggings whenever they were away.

We lit candles and crawled down the shaft to the main stope, and Tom soon found where to look. He dropped to his knees and his experienced fingers began probing the vein between two strata of rock. He took a hand pick and began tapping and prying. I stood by and watched. Soon he exclaimed:

"Boy! This is rich! Whitemen call this jewelry rock."

"Indians call it yellow iron," I laughed. "But now Sno-Ta-Hae has a whiteman's name: Jewelry Rock."

He continued tapping and prying. I caught the fever and joined him in the effort. It was hard, dry work and we lost track of time. Finally I climbed back outside and noticed it was near sundown. I unstrapped a water bag and returned to the shaft. Tom was fingering dust and nuggets into a deer-bladder poke.

It was dusk when we climbed outside. We unpacked and un-saddled our four animals, watered them, and staked them out to graze. We made camp and talked about gold mines until long after we had supper and were bedded down. Taglito figured we had dug out twelve ounces which at $20.00 an ounce made $240.00 in whiteman's money.

In the morning we discussed other known mines in the vast Sierra Madre: the most mysterious was Scalphunter's Ledge,[1] variously described as a gold-filled ledge, a cave of gold, a hole with gold bars buried in it. I had heard our old *shaman* men-tion it; I thought I knew about where it was. To get to it we would need to cross the canyon at Hauchaneria, then ride south for five suns.

We packed up and rode. Since the trails were unfamiliar, we often relied on instinct and the sensory organs of our horses. The mountains abounded with elk, deer, and other wild ani-mals, which meant trails that always led to water. We mean-dered through what Taglito called "unbelievedly rough country" for days. We skirted the rim of *Barranca de Cobre* (Canyon of Copper) to where it widened out into an amber-red plateau. Superimposed in the eerie formation loomed a solitary monolith of harsh red stone like an island reaching to the sun; this weirdly shaped red ledge was our goal. It had taken us six days, and in all that time we had not seen another human being.

Taglito was satisfied that this was Scalphunter's Ledge and we began searching. We gave it up after four days. We found no sign of a gold ledge or a gold cave, no old or new mine. Nor did we find any sign of a gold cache, although Apache legends say a Spanish pack train loaded with bullion was buried there.

Picking up an old Indian trail, we recrossed the Bavispe and

1. The Mexicans claim it is a red monument to the thousands of their people slain by Indians. The Indians say it is a monument to the redmen slain by the Mexicans. Dee-O-Det claims a band of Apaches led by Chief Ca-Co-Chama had attacked a mule train laden with gold bullion from Tayopa. Under the cover of a dark moon a group of scalphunters led by Mustang Gray ambushed the Apaches and killed and scalped them. The legends say that during the bloody battles all the water bags became ruptured. Also all the horses and mules escaped. The scalphunters were trapped. Now the ghosts of those Evil Ones hover over the grim monolith and cry for water in dark-moon nights.

headed back north. We spent several days exploring the fabulous Tayopa ruins, a day at Las Chipas, another at El Tigre; then we cut east back across the Bavispe to Rio Escondido. We rested there two days before riding on to Hachinero and Beduiat's former base camp.

One evening while enroute we each shot a blue grouse and prepared them for supper. This reminded Taglito of another day, and the smell of roasting grouse took him back to the evening when Tesal-Bestinay, my grandmother, had roasted one for the High Chief, my grandfather. "Cochise had been ailing and was becoming thin and gaunt.." Taglito spoke almost in a whisper. "He needed food, but to eat was like putting knives inside him.

"He was in constant pain and the medicine men and the reservation white doctor were unable to stop his internal bleeding. Tahza, your father, was there with his mother, Tesal-Bestinay, and Naiche was there with his mother, Nali-Kay-deya, and your mother was there, along with Dee-O-Det, Nochalo, Poin-sen-ay, Skin-yea, and others. I was about to make a fast ride to Fort Bowie to bring an army doctor when Cochise forbade it saying that time was too short. He pointed overhead and said when the next sun was there he would go to Big Sleep.

"The Chief went on to say he would meet me up there in the endless sky where all brothers meet again in the Spirit World. He began telling his sons and subchiefs things a man with responsibilities must tell when he knows his time has come. No one interrupted. To know a man like Chief Cochise is to know a great man. It is a privilege that comes only once in a lifetime, and he is waiting up there for me to join him.

"True to his prediction, *Chies-Co-Chise* died that day of June 7, 1874. We helped the women dress him in his finest raiment. We buried him in that bottomless cave by Signal Rock, along with his best horse and his favorite dog. As previously agreed, the women went down into the oak grove and painted their faces black and did their keening, and we let it be known that the Great Chief was buried there beneath the black oaks at the entrance to the stronghold."

Taglito came to the end of the story I had heard before from my mother and it was essentially the same except for some of the people named.[2] Taglito rolled a cigarette and nodded with finality. I stretched out on my blankets, deep in troubled thought. Tesal-Bestinay was my father's mother; Nali-Kaydeya was the mother of Naiche. Why had not my mother told me these things? Why hadn't the *shaman* told me? Maybe it was another case of Indian philosophy: *Had you been there you would have known; you were not, so you do not need to know.*

It got cold during the night. In the morning I told Taglito we had been meandering one whole moon and that I was getting homesick for Pa-Gotzin-Kay. We packed and headed back, intending to hole up for the winter.

We worked north through the Sierra Medio foothills and approached the long-deserted hacienda of the *Godo* San Rafael de la Zanza family. The main house had been nearly destroyed by fire. It was sometimes called Burnt Ranch. The legend was, as I remember, that lightning had struck it during a summer storm many years before; others said it had been raided so many times by Apache and Navajo war parities between 1790 and 1820 that the *Godos* had abandoned it. Another story was that Golthlay had burned it when last he raided it. Cochise, I had heard, seldom raided there because the Rafael family raised good horses and he took only a few now and then when he needed them, and never molested the people.

The next morning was my turn to round up our animals and saddle up while Tom made breakfast. Home was just two easy days away. A chattering bluejay followed me to the old corral and perched on a top rail. It screeched so much that I threw a rock at it. A small whirlwind blew up dust and the jay flew to another tree, keeping up the insistent screeching. Another jay joined the first and lent its voice to the din. I watched them for a spell, then walked over to investigate, feeling that something in addition to myself had caused the jays' ire.

Beside a small pool I found a man lying face down, his back covered with dried blood. I knelt down and saw he was breathing. I turned his head; he was a whiteman of about middle age. He groaned a little and seemed to be regaining consciousness. I unbuckled his gun belt; there were six spent shells in the gun

2. *The Apache Indians*, 129–30, by Frank C. Lockwood, Macmillan Co., New York, 1938. AKG.

and the belt was empty. I cut the bloody shirt from his body and found a bullet wound ranging from the right rear shoulder blade and emerging under the armpit.

I called to Tom Jeffords and he came on the run. He took a quick look and said, "I know him! He's Buck Green—has a ranch bordering Slaughter's on the San Berdoo."[3]

We pulled off our bandanas and wrapped them around the wound. We had a half-empty bottle of whisky in one pack, and I ran and got it. When we gave him whisky the man came to, started to struggle and mumble, and I made out the words: "Damn bushwackin' Injuns . . ."

I spoke in English and told him not to move, and he seemed to understand. Then he mumbled that he had been looking for strays when the Mansos Apaches jumped him. This was a shock to me as I knew my men had not done this and we were the only Mansos in existence. Tom gave him another swallow of whisky and followed it with several swallows of water.

"Say!" the man squinted up at me. "You're a Injun—but not one of them! Those who jumped me were Yaquee!"

Yaqui! Yaqui had invaded Apache hunting grounds! That thought sent a sudden shiver through me, jarring me out of a complacency that I now realized had been growing within me —and in my people at Pa-Gotzin-Kay, too, for that matter. My Apache fighter instinct boiled up.

Taglito noticed it and tried to calm me down by making off-hand introductions all around. I then realized that we had to get this man patched up and get him home. Tom said Buck Green was virtually a neighbor of ours; I recalled having seen cattle with his R/V brand grazing within thirty kilometers of Pa-Gotzin-Kay, but we had never been near his ranch house.

Taglito mentioned an old medicine man remedy—wild honey! He suggested I scout around and find a hive. Meanwhile, he would make a litter of poles and blankets and strap it on our red jenny. As it turned out I was lucky. We all were. I soon found a prime beehive in a nearby tree stump and got stung only a few times. I plastered Green's wound, front and back, with thick globs of honey—a natural healer and a bleeding inhibitor. Obviously he had lost a lot of blood, but he seemed to be perking

3. See notes on San Bernardino Springs Rancho in the Munk Library of Arizonia, 1908, Southwest Museum, Highland Park, Los Angeles. AKG.

up. Tom had rigged up the litter; we packed Green on it as comfortably as possible and were on the trail.

We rode at a fast walk, no faster than a smooth trot on level areas, and stopped about every hour for a rest. At every stop we checked our patient and the litter and at one point Buck Green got to talking:

"So, you're Niño Cochise... heard 'bout you ... what you doin' down here in this country?"

I told him Tom Jeffords and I were just drifting through, prospecting. Green went on slowly: he had missed some steers and was blaming those hold-out Apaches as he knew a bunch were still somewhere up in the mountains. He had seen two 'Pache boy deer hunters and asked them if they'd seen any strays and they said no, but he always figured an Injun was a liar anyway. So he kept lookin' and found Injun tracks on top of cow tracks leadin' over to Fraud Canyon. He realized now they were Yaqui *calzados* (cowboys), and they had ambushed him; but how he got over by Burnt Ranch was a damn mystery.

I asked if he had shot any of them, and he said he sure tried, but he got hit from behind and the next thing he remembered was waking up where Tom and I found him. Tom reasoned the Yaqui knew he wasn't dead so they carried Buck up there. They figured Apaches would find him, and knowing he would think he was still in Fraud Canyon, he'd accuse the Apaches of stealing his cattle, and we would kill him for what they had started.

I felt like pointing out a few facts about Apaches he may not have known, but I just said I did not like having a bunch of *Yaqui-Yori*[4] cast the lance at me.

At our next stop Tom fished some jerky and leftover hardtack from our packs, and while we were chewing on them, Green said maybe General Torres was getting the Yaqui riled up against the whitemen—sort of playing both ends against the middle.

Our sick man grew sleepy but did not seem overly weak, so we rode on and made good time until nearly sundown. Then we made camp for a while in order to water and graze our animals. I knew Green would last as long as that honey plaster stayed fresh, but when it turned rancid he'd be in trouble.

4. The Yaqui takes the *Yori* oath to kill all outsiders.

There was no moon but the sky was dotted with diamonds as we pushed on. It was well nigh midnight when we rode into the Rancho Verde gate. Green's wife, two children, three cowboys, and four dogs greeted us with noise. We got him inside and into bed. Someone got supper for us, and the cowboys took care of our horses and mules.

It was decided that Taglito would remain at Green's and I would ride to Basaranca and get Doctor Gutierrez. Walt Duman, Green's foreman, and I made a hard ride up the foothills and crossed the Bavispe into Basaranca by daybreak. We routed the doctor out of bed, and I explained what the emergency was. I relaxed a little when he and Duman were riding the Rancho Verde trail.

Then I pushed on to Pa-Gotzin-Kay. Old Hammerhead seemed to know what was expected of him; also he knew this was the way home. I thought to myself as we loped along: General Torres, whom Buck Green talked about, must be the man Gutierrez almost introduced me to in Basaranca a few moons back. The doctor thinks Torres will be the next *presidente* of Mexico. Again I had my doubts about the good doctor, though I would wait and see . . .

Torres might be afraid of me for some reason or other. Colonel de Vega might have set the general to thinking I posed a threat to his rise in power. Somehow, he had perhaps got the Mexicans' traditional enemy—the Yaqui—on his side and was using them to rile up the American cattlemen. These in turn would think hold-out Apaches were the rustlers and would attempt to wipe us out, thus saving the general and his gaggle of *gusanos* the trouble. It was the crazy kind of plot to expect; and if a band of Yaquis could make it through without been seen, there could be more.

I had shirked, unthinkingly, my tribal responsibilities for a month. Maybe the Yaqui were in Pa-Gotzin-Kay now!

Today, historians call us Apaches "marvelous horsemen, capable of astounding feats of endurance,"[5] and by their standards they are right. But did they ever consider our half-wild horses? Old Hammerhead was running with head straight out, ears back, and nostrils flaring, loping with the rhythm of a

5. *The Mustangs*, by J. Frank Dobie, Little, Brown & Co., Boston, 1952. AKG.

machine and without any direction from me. He would run that way until he dropped dead. He had that inborn reserve to carry on, but by the time we arrived in the rancheria, he was blood-and-foam streaked, had thrown all four shoes, and his hoofs were bleeding.

I had Boa Juan take care of him, and later we turned him out to stud, never to be ridden again.

※ ※ ※

I LOOKED around; things appeared normal. I found the *shaman* supervising a group of women making candles; nearby two old men were grinding tule seeds into powder for him. I talked with him a little and told him to wake me when the sun was overhead. Then I went to our wikiup; Mother was not there.

I stretched out on my cougarskin and was soon asleep. The next thing I knew old Dee-O-Det was shaking me and helping me to my feet. We went to the council ring; Mother and only seven men were there. I told them of Buck Green and how the Yaquis had ambushed him as he was tracking his stolen cattle in *Cañon de los Embudos*. Green's riders had told me the Yaqui were now camped near Chi-hua-hua's former rancheria.

The men realized that if a band of Yaqui raiders could get that close to us without being stopped, they might come closer. When I told them I wanted to capture a live Yaqui for questioning, they agreed wildly.

I told Mangas-Chee to get fifteen men ready for war, and soon the war drums began to beat. I ordered the drummers to be silent. Some lurking Yaqui spy might hear the drums, and I wanted a prisoner so I could learn what was behind this Yaqui invasion.

When Chee yelled that they were ready, I mounted a bay gelding and looked around; ranged behind Chee were Alchise, Ny-Oden, Boa Juan, Kasale, Hi-okee, Kersus, Klan-O-Tay, Nah-Shis-Tor, young Chi-hua-hua, young Juh, Peridot, Neo-Ot-Toden, To-Clany, and Achinera, all familiar faces of Basaranca and Tesorabi war trails—Apaches all!

Suddenly I felt better. We pushed our horses hard through the north rampart and down the trail. We had all worked up a sweat before we sighted the ledges overlooking Chi-hua-hua's old hideout. We circled the north rimrock, dismounted, and crept close to the top, out of view from the canyon's bottom. I pointed. Chee knew what I wanted, and he and two braves felt for their weapons, especially their belt knives, as they disappeared down the lateral trail.

❦ ❦ ❦

IN about an hour they were back with a very battered Yaqui. *"Yori,"* I said, "you have not long to live, if you do not talk straight. I want to know why the whiteman was taken to Burnt Ranch. I want to know who has betrayed the Yaqui into such a dishonorable deed." Drawing my knife, I continued, "Talk straight, only once—*itna-iltc-'he!"* (Tell me no lies.)

He gushed a stream of mestizo Spanish. "Luis Torres he say he make Yaqui grand man when he be *presidente* if Yaqui help fight, he say all *blancos* and Mansos mus' be kill."

"For that, Yaqui, you can go with your life. You tell your *nant-án* to move his people out of this canyon now because, by dark, Apache will kill all Yaqui that are here." I aimed a kick at his departing breechclouth. *"Ugashi!"* (Go.)

We crept closer to the edge and watched and waited. Twilight gradually cast weird shadows in the canyon. There were about ten Yaqui down there, with campfires burning. They were roasting a yearling beef.

"Yaqui!" I called out. "I told you to go!"

A turbaned warrior stood up and scanned the rimrock ledges. It was obvious he could not see us, nor be sure of our location from the sound of my voice. Defiantly he made the universal gesture of insult to any Indian.

I gave the signal. The turbaned man and two others fell under our first volley of carbine fire. The others scattered like rabbits, and were shot and killed as such. When the shooting ceased for lack of targets we rushed down to seek out and kill any who might be hiding. We counted twelve bodies—one of them was Cuchillo Alto, a *Yori* chieftain of some renown. There were no women with them. We picked up all of the weapons we found worth taking and started home.

I did not think we would have any more Yaqui trouble. Nevertheless, I stationed guards night and day at additional points along the trails to Pa-Gotzin-Kay. We were back about midnight; I rode over to Mother's wikiup and dismounted. To her questions I replied with quick facts about Taglito and Buck Green, about our Yaqui fight and the Nakai-Ye general's orders.

The next morning, old Dee-O-Det confronted me as I staggered from the wikiup. I asked:

"Where are Nakai and Eugene?"

"You will ask your good friend, the doctor," he sniffed. "He is sleeping in Ticer's wikiup; he rode in after you last night."

Surprised, I went to the old wikiup and called Doctor Gutierrez. He sat up and mumbled. "I came to tell you the rancher will be all right. Your honey plaster saved him."

"Where are Nakai and Eugene?"

"Those young men are going places. They left for Hermosillo with General Torres. He has commissioned them both captains!"

"Ha! That was very generous of the general! One of those men was my subchief, the other a war chief. I have not discharged them from my service. They have deserted!"

"They have a bright future, Niño; the general has promised them much, when he is the *presidente.*"

"And what has he promised you, doctor?"

"When he starts his march on Mexico City, I will do what I can to help his noble cause," Gutierrez replied patriotically. "We now have soldiers stationed at Basaranca . . . I am in command. The general spoke of you, too. He has sympathy for the *Indios.* At my request, he will make you as any other Mexican citizen, with the same good standing."

"Yes, Alcalde, I know the general spoke of me. He spoke to Cuchillo Alto of me and now Cuchillo and his men lie dead in the canyon, though the general spoke to them of my death."

I turned and left the wikiup.

"The Nakai-Ye are unpredictable people," the *shaman* said as I met him. "Shall I call the victory dance?"

I led him away to inform him of the treachery of General Torres, and of Nakai and Eugene. He was promising great things, even to the Yaqui, for when he became the *presidente* of Mexico. Now that his plot had failed, what would he try next?

❦ ❦ ❦

SEVERAL days later the canella hills lay under a blanket of white, and the endless sky was hidden by lowering clouds from which more snow was falling. Tom Jeffords rode into the rancheria and came to our fire. A boy led his horse and our two mules to the corral.

"Buck Green is doin' all right. I stopped at John Slaughter's on the way here . . . told Slaughter about you . . ." Then abruptly he shot out, "Niño, what in the hell was that fight at Chi-hua-hua's all about?"

So I had to explain all over again about the Yaqui being tricked into invading us by General Torres, about Nakai and Eugene joining his *charro* army, and about Doctor Gutierrez. I added that I was sure the padre was a spy and the chief troublemaker.

Taglito silently thought all that over as he eyed Mother and Nadina who were cooking over the same fire.

"Niño! Taglito!" Mother called. "Food is ready; eat now, talk later."

Tom was hungry, as a man always is after a long ride. Later, while puffing his cigaret, he told me that when Buck was able to get around again he wanted to introduce me to all the American ranchers in the Sierra Madre. All were losing stock either to the revolutionists, the Yaqui, or to professional rustlers.

I agreed and mentioned the four or five steers wearing the R/V brand near the Yaqui camp. I said we left them there, figuring the Yaqui would have left them there, too, as evidence pointing to us, which would give the white ranchers and *soldatos* a good excuse to ride in and cut us down.

"Well, these hybrid people often do crazy things," Tom said. "Mexico has been plagued with generals and stupid dictators as far back as I can remember—always men in the field trying to cook up a revolution and grab glory. Now I'll give you a little advice, Niño: Buck Green has a good idea. He said all the ranchers in these parts should get together. He wants you in, too; in union there is strength, as the saying goes."

Dee-O-Det joined us, holding a quart bottle of whisky firmly grasped by the neck. He handed the bottle to Tom, who pulled the cork, took a good swallow, and handed it to me. I did justice to its contents, then passed it back to the *shaman*.

"Niño, do you know Tennono Kelzel?"[6] Taglito asked.

"I have heard of him."

"Buck said he lives on the east side of the mountains. He also has a stronghold on the Arros River on the Chihuahua side. He knows you, because he told of the fight you had in Basaranca a couple years back—remember?"

"I remember I killed an Apache in Basaranca and some worm came and cut the Apache's head off and put it in a bag . . ."

"Well, that was Tennono Kelzel, a *Yaqui-Yori!* He had a friend who wanted *that* head, though I don't know why. Anyway, this Kelzel hates Torres and all Mexicans, but he is friendly with the Americans.

"Now comes the good news, which is why Buck is so keen on getting organized," Tom continued. "Kelzel, High Chief of all the Yaqui clans, rode in to Buck's yesterday, along with other chiefs and a medicine man. Kelzel took his stand with us. He denounced Cuchillo Alto; he cussed Torres. He will help fight all the spicks any time, any place. That knocks General Torres on the head. Your troubles are over—at least for now."

"That's the best news I have heard since Golthlay kicked a skunk! Dee-O-Det, start the victory dance."

"Aw, hell!" Tom groaned. "Here I was figuring on a good night's sleep."

Two moons rolled by and Buck Green, now recovered, rode into Pa-Gotzin-Kay with his wife, Anna, and their two half-grown sons. Their visit was an unexpected surprise to us, but Taglito pointed out it was the proper thing to do—to thank us personally for saving Buck's life.[7]

6. The name was revered by the Yaqui as was the name Cochise by the Apache; it was also loathed by the Mexicans as much as was the name Geronimo.

7. It was then that I learned what the whiteman meant when he said "thank you." Like *a-co-'d,* it is an expression of gratitude, but Taglito also pointed out that the expression covered "a multitude of sins" and that I should beware— but not in the case of Buck Green.

After these amenities were over, I told them that we were preparing to go on our annual midwinter bear hunt and would they care to come along? They said they would be happy to go bear hunting with their newly found Apache friends. The hunt was a success: when it was over we had exterminated a lot of predators, including wolves and cougars, and the Greens had a load of fine hides to take home and place on their ranch-house floor; we also had enough bear grease around the rancheria to oil all the guns and pomade all the women's hair for years.

Chapter 8 1895-1896

Pinda-Lick-O-Ye

CHAWN-CHISSY (Ghost Face or Winter) walked softly that year and April found us Apaches fat and sassy. Nothing untoward had happened. When the first west winds blew, I put Klan-O-Tay in charge of preparing the fields and garden, Hiokee I put in charge of mining operations, since Nakai and Eugene had gone over to the Nakai-Ye. Mangas-Chee was my subchief and as such was overseer of the rancheria in general.

That evening before the council, I spoke of Buck Green's winter visit with us, the rumors, our fears of a Yaqui invasion, and of the Mexican glory-hunters as the cause of our troubles. To secure our position, I proposed a trip to Green's ranch with Taglito, Mother, and Nadina. Chee would be Chief while I was away, but I'd take Kasale along to camp at Green's and be the vedette to relay messages between Chee and me.

If there were no further threats to our peace, we would ride with Taglito to Owl Head and stop by our old tribal Dragoon Stronghold. Leaving in the morning we would be gone about one moon. The council members put their heads together, and soon the *shaman* nodded and said; "The council has approved your decision."

I discussed regular tribal matters with Chee: planting the fields, caring for the livestock, and keeping the trails guarded. Hi-okee packed the six pokes of gold I would take along, since Taglito had suggested he could cash them in at Tombstone.

I was excited about this trip, about seeing the land where I was born, twenty-two years before. I wanted to see the white-iron mines that has caused the trouble that sent us into exile.

We left early, and as we arrived at Green's ranch, the slanting rays of the setting sun cast a glow like foxfire through the tops of the tall tamarack trees that made a park of the four-acre yard and shaded the rambling log-and-stone, two-level ranch house. A huge barn, smaller buildings, and corrals were set back beyond the grove. Palo verde, pyracantha, and other evergreens lived up to the owner's name for a perfect setting: Rancho Verde (Green Ranch).

Buck rushed out to greet us. "Howdy! Howdy! You made it."

"What th' hell did you expect?" Taglito chortled. "We know the trails and we're not the kind who ride into an ambush."

"All right! All right!" Buck grinned. "I know you can out-Injun the 'Paches! I could've too if I'd lived umpteen years with 'em like you have, you old maverick."

As we dismounted, Taglito kept on at Buck. "You going to pour us a drink or do we have to drink what little we brought?"

"You bring any money t'pay for it?" Buck fired back.

"Sure—depends on what the price is. D'you run this outfit like the old Butterfield Stage stations, where the drinks were poor and the prices dear?"

Before Buck could retort, Anna Green called from the veranda, "Hi—Niome and Nadina! Come on in. Let those men have their fun. Buck made some home-brew for them."

On the veranda where a bar was set up, we had a choice of whiskies, wines, and brandy. Tom chose Old Granddad; I picked Old Overholt, because it had an appealing picture on the label; and Buck, not to be outdone, took Old Crow. We soon demanded refills. Then, after dinner, we settled down to smokes, brandy, and talk.

Kasale was all set for his vedette duty; Mother and Nadina would remain at the ranch until Buck, Tom, and I returned from visiting the American ranches along the east slope of the Sierra Madre.

Sunrise the next morning found us well along the south trail. I had chosen a prime grullo stallion for this trip, and Taglito was riding his rangy claybank mare. He maintained that mares were better than studs for long rides as they had no outside interests unless in heat. Buck, on a roan mustang mare, apparently thought the same way. My grullo stallion was intrigued by this strange mare and continually tried to sniff at her. We Apaches looked at it this way, a horse was a horse so long as it could cover the trail; when it could not, quite likely it would be meat, either for us or the wolves. My stud's desires irritated me and I jerked him away until, after an hour out, he caught me off my guard and got his sniff. Buck's mare promptly kicked the sniff out of him. He was a good horse after that.

Four hours of hard riding brought us to a big ranch house built of pine logs; you could still see the stumps where the trees once stood. There was a large shed filled with hay, corrals in every direction, a barn, a squealing windmill, and a leaky tank. We stopped to water our horses, and we drank from the tank's pipe. Tying our horses to a long hitch rack, Buck hollered, "Anybody home?" A tall blond woman came to the door. She recognized Buck and invited us in. She said Ammon would be back soon and for us to make ourselves to home; then she turned and went out the back door. I started to roll a cigaret, but Buck said, "Don't smoke in here." Before I could ask why not, the front door swung open and a big whiteman came in.

"Howdy, Jim!" said Buck, surprised. "Meet Captain Tom Jeffords, and this is Chief Niño Cochise. This, men, is Ammon Tenny's closest neighbor—Big Jim Grey."

"Howdy, gents," smiled Grey. Then he looked at me and said, "I knew there were Apaches up in th' mountains. But I never heard of any raids, so I've been wonderin'. How many in your tribe?"

"All that did not get railroaded," I answered, not caring for any more conversation until I could size him up.

He turned to Tom Jeffords and asked if the stories of lost gold mines had brought him to the Mother Mountains. Tom said he was just visiting with me and he doubted there was any gold in those hills.

"There must be," Grey insisted, "or else somebody found Tayopa. These Yaquis coming in sure bring a lot of it when they need rifles and shells."

The tall woman came back in with a pitcher of sweet cider, served it, and left again. Grey pointed out of the window at a cloud of dust far down the road. A short time later the "they" proved to be Ammon Tenny and five Yaquis. One turned out to be Chief Tennono Kelsel—a *Yori* if I ever saw one.

We were introduced all around and were on our second cider when a lone rider cantered up to the house. He was admitted and casually introduced as Mr. Chase.[1] I guessed he was in on the powwow.

Tenny invited us into the parlor "to talk things over." The Yaqui chief asked Grey if the load of guns had arrived yet. Grey replied that they were in his warehouse in El Paso and he'd fetch them across the border soon. Kelzel grunted and handed Grey a full leather poke. He opened it and poured some of the contents on the palm of his hand, and I saw some nuggets as big as a pinto bean. He seemed satisfied.

Kelzel looked at me and asked in Yaqui if I was there to buy guns. Although the Yaqui tongue is similar to the Apache, I had to hesitate to consider his meaning. In Apache I said I was going to Arizona with my white friend. He scowled and wanted to know which one, and I motioned toward red-bearded Taglito.

"I do not trust whitemen," Kelzel said, "but I do need guns."

"I trust my friend, but I do not trust others," I continued in Apache.

Kelzel switched to Spanish, speaking slowly, and was easy to understand.[2] "They want gold. They want to come to my land to search for gold. They say there is much gold in these hills. So I want guns to guard it."

"Have you heard the talk about the Mexican general?" I asked, changing the subject.

"Ugh! He speaks with a forked tongue. Torres told me that he wanted the Mansos driven out of Mexico, and if the Yaqui would do this, he would make us big. Now Torres has been discharged from the army by President Diaz. Carranzo of Chihuahua is the big man. I know that Cuchillo Alto was told to kill you, but he was not smart enough. I told him so. I also watched you kill Apla-Chi-Kit in Basaranca. After you finished him, I came in and cut off his head."

I asked, "Did the general give you a good price for it?"

The Yaqui thought for a while, looked around, then muttered:

1. Later I was told that Cairo Chase represented a New York magazine publisher, and was a friend of General Crook.
2. Jim Ticer once told me that some Indians spoke "mission-trained Spanish," and they pronounced each word distinctly and every syllable as if it too were a word.

"He said 'I am indebted to you.' "

I knew Tom was listening to all this. The other Yaquis were blank-faced, but the white ranchers were beginning to fidget. I asked Kelzel what he wanted of me. He replied he wanted me to help fight all Mexicans who wave the red flag. He was to ask the whitemen to unite with the Yaqui; would I also? I asked Taglito in Apache what he thought of it. He said it looked like somebody was riding backwards on his horse, for he had never known the Indian to ask the whiteman for help. Tom had answered me in Apache, much to Kelzel's surprise, and Kelzel growled:

"There is only one *blanco* who can speak Apache like that! You must be the man who was Blood Brother of Cochise!"

The three of us came to an understanding, and Taglito made our decision known to Green, Chase, Grey, and Tenny. Everybody shook hands all around, and Chase asked Tom if he was the man who was the first Indian Agent of the Chiricahui.

When Taglito admitted that he was, Chase continued; "I was visiting at the Warm Springs Agency back in '77, when your successor, John Clum, captured Geronimo, Victorio, Nanay, and Loco . . ."

"This man Clum did a lot of bragging about how he 'captured' them, I recall."

"Well, 'took charge of them,' " Chase amended. "Did you ever hear the whole story?"

"More than what Clum printed in his paper. The truth is none of those Apaches were ever *captured.*"

"Well," said Chase, "I was there and had a front-row seat. Those Indians were loafing around the Agency and keeping out of trouble, as far as I know, when Clum came with orders, his orders, to remove them to the San Carlos. He sent word to Geronimo to come to the blacksmith shop to talk to him. Geronimo, not thinking anything was wrong, stepped into the dimly lighted shop and before his eyes became used to the half-dark he was seized, irons put on his legs, and a gag in his mouth. Clum tricked each chief that way and hauled them all off to Hell's Forty Acres. Clum wanted glory, and he didn't care how he got it."

"Yes—and sometimes he made the same mistake twice."

While the two were talking, I was studying Kelzel. I remembered seeing that Yaqui face in Basaranca. I had thought him to be a Mexican, he was dressed like one, then. Eugene had told me the man who had cut off the head had first kicked and spat on Apla-Chi-Kit after I had killed him. Now, with Kelzel standing there, I asked him why he wanted the head of Apla-Chi-Kit.

"There was a *blanco* who wanted the head of a famous bandit called *Muerte* (Death)," replied Kelzel. "He paid me to take it, and not being able to find the bandit, I took the Apache's. It was easier and I did not think you would care."

I told the *Yaqui-Yori* in no uncertain terms that I thought he was a big liar! I put my hand on my knife, but Kelzel just scowled and turned away. Everyone seemed to run out of words after that.

Tom, Buck, and I shook hands all around again, said good-by, and then hit the trail back to Rancho Verde. With that long ride on an empty belly ahead of us, we made camp about five kilometers down the Morelos Canyon and ate some jerky Buck had in his saddlebag. In the morning it was raining, but we made it to Buck's ranch that noon. We found Kasale had taken up residence in Buck's barn and was showing Buck's boys how he braided his long hair—that was all he had on his mind.

❦ ❦ ❦

AFTER a hearty breakfast next day, Mother, Nadina, Tom, and I headed north. Because of rain we made an early camp by the lower San Bernardino Springs. In the morning we rode the remaining ten kilometers to the fabulous old ranch house, where Tom made us acquainted with John and Viola Slaughter.[3] Our route was westward below the border. We crossed it a day later at Naco Springs and made camp in Mule Gulch, later called Brewery Gulch. I asked Taglito about what made the water green. He said:

"Copper. Coronado found it and called it the Copper Queen. Copper is man's oldest metal."

While we lolled around, he went into town. He returned in the afternoon with news. "The Territorial Legislature, in win-

3. *The Southwest of John Horton Slaughter (1841-1922)*, by Allen A. Erwin, Arthur H. Clark Co., Glendale, California, 1965. AKG.

ter session, has relaxed some old laws. Chiricahua Apaches, if any are still around, may now travel through the territory on visits, providing they are under the guidance of responsible white people."

That was good news. Taglito also brought some staples, as we were low on provisions. The next day we arrived near Tombstone at about noon. He decided to skirt the town and take a direct trail to the Dragoon Mountains. We made dry camp in High Lonesome Pass and the next day rode through the noisy town called Gleeson. As we were passing through Tom remarked that this place was one of the white-iron (silver) discoveries that had wrecked the J-C-H peace treaty. We continued in silence for about ten miles, and then the broad and long Sulphur Springs Valley stretched before us.

"We are getting close now," whispered Mother.

Taglito pointed east across the big valley to a high range of mountains, dark under a blanket of pines. "That's the Chiricahua Range, Cochise Head and Cochise Peak. The east, or Main stronghold, was there. The west, or Dragoon Stronghold, where you were born, Niño, is to our left a few more miles."

We made it into a parklike oak grove that narrowed as we proceeded, and we were in the Dragoon Stronghold. The land of my forefathers! It was such a glorious place I felt like getting down on my knees and giving praise to *Usen*. Mother sat under an old oak and cried. Finally Tom and I unpacked and unsaddled our animals, watered them, then hobbled them to graze under the trees. We had covered fifty miles that day.

"Tomorrow you can look around to your heart's content . . . relive old memories," Tom said softly, and put an arm around Mother. "Don't be sad, Niome."

"I am sad, Taglito," she said in a weak little voice. "The warm west winds blow but Tahza will not be here to meet me as in the old days."

We rolled our blankets out and soon were asleep. The singing of birds awakened us. Taglito had a fire going, and we breakfasted on bacon, hotcakes, and coffee. After a while he smiled wryly and suggested we "make yourselves to home" for a few days. He wanted to visit around a little, see Jim Brophy of the Chiricahua Cattle Company ranch, and then see Colonel Henry Hooker at the Sierra Bonito Rancho and maybe make a deal for a few head of those new white-face Herefords the colonel had imported. He left, riding east where, no doubt, he had some "visiting around" to do, but mainly he knew we three Apaches wanted to be alone.

Nadina remained in camp, and Mother led me up an abandoned trail to a plateau, or shelf, near the top. Spread before us was what was left of a once-proud rancheria, now silent and weatherworn under the everlasting sun.

"Here our wikiup was where you were born." She looked up at a tremendous tower rising to the sun, like a bulwark of the shelf. "This is Signal Peak." We climbed around its west base and there were several crevasses, one of which seemed bottomless. She pointed again. "Here the Great Chief is buried." It was the most peaceful place in the world.

She took me a half-mile or so along a winding old trail through small glens, where once wikiups stood below the west face of the mountain rim to Council Rock; then on a long walk to Treaty Rock, where Taglito (Captain Thomas Jeffords), Chief Cochise, and General Oliver Howard had made peace and signed the treaty.[4]

Nearby, in this world of solitude and boulders, was another rampart called Eagle Rock that looked as though *Ihidnan* had placed the boulders to make a breastworks that no evil spirit could breach. There were short canyons, and sheer cliffs rose to heights of possibly a thousand feet on three sides with Signal Peak towering on guard over all. There was but one way to get in, and if guarded, ten warriors could hold off 10,000 invaders. So, this was the place. No wonder I had often longed to see it. Now I did not want to leave it.

"I can not bear to stay very long," Mother sighed. "It seems strange here without The People. I remember too much that hurts me . . ."

I sighed too. "I think I know how it is with you, Mother. With The People gone, it is but a ghost of the past—a place of the Spirit World."

After another period of looking and listening, she said, "It seems that I can hear voices . . . like echoes of the past . . . they seem to be pleading for something. Do you hear them, my son?"

---

4. Many people today think they are the same rock but they are a mile apart.

Then after a pause, "I know now. They are the spirits of the past. That is what keeps the White-eyes out . . . they cannot face their misdeeds."

🌱🌱🌱

FOR the next two days we just lolled around camp; Mother and Nadina made a few short excursions, while I spent my time dreaming. However, I tacked up the loose shoes of the horses and mules and made some minor repairs to the packsaddles.

The following day Taglito returned, and we sat around the campfire and talked late into the night. Taglito and Mother drifted into another reminiscent mood and I listened to their words, but with thoughts of my own.

The whitemen called this land Cochise County. They must have thought something of my grandfather to have named his land, given by treaty—although they had preempted it—after him. Then why take it away from us at all, I thought—unless it was for silver. Yes, that is what it was—silver, white iron. They thought it was no good for the Indian. That must have been it, the silver. Well, I had *gold* in Pa-Gotzin-Kay! They could keep the white iron—I liked yellow iron.

Taglito seemed to have been reading my mind, for he said:

"It's about time we got rid of those six pokes of your gold. We'll head for Tombstone tomorrow and turn it in for paper money—easier and safer to pack along. And we've got to get you used to the whitemen. Remember one thing, though. You're supposed to be a Mexican. There's a lot of them around these parts, and you *sabe* their lingo—so you'll get by. Tell them, those who ask, that your name is Ramon Rodriguez and you are from Tucson. And if some galoot calls you a greaser, don't get your Apache up! Just call him a gringo and let it go at that."

"My name is Ramon Rodriguez and I'm from Tucson," I repeated.

"Good, and you speak English. We will hold all our conversations in English. Now, don't forget."

"I won't. Have you noticed I'm using don't, ain't, won't, it's, and yeah, just like you and Buck?

135

❧ ❧ ❧

THE next morning Taglito and I were off to Tombstone. As we rode down the western slope of the Dragoons and continued west, he pointed to where my people sometimes camped in the winters; the summer rancheria was in the distant Chiricahua Mountains.

Soon the craggy west walls of the stronghold were behind, and the vast San Pedro Valley lay ahead. We passed Soldiers' Hole, where some off-duty cavalrymen had dug for silver, and later a pile of stones marking the spot where Poin-sen-ay killed three whisky traders back in 1876.

We were now down in low-lying land, broken with dry ravines and small hills. A herd of javelina popped out around us and scooted into the clumps of prickly pear that grew along the ravines. There were a few cattle tracks through the patches of sagebrush and cactus. We could see the red courthouse and the outlines of Schieffelin Hall in Tombstone. We came across a road and followed it to what Taglito called "the abandoned Consolidated Mine." There were large structures with elevated endless-chain dips to carry silver ore to the smelter, there to be made into ingots.

We rode in and soon tied our horses to the hitch rack in front of the Tombstone Bank. The Wells, Fargo office was located upstairs on the theory that it would be harder to rob. We dug out the six pokes of gold from our saddlebags and climbed the stairs.

A two-gun guard glowered at us, but when he recognized Tom, he waved us in with a smile. A dour-faced man took our names and descriptions, then weighed the gold—twelve ounces to the pound, Tom told me. He came up with "21 lbs., 8 oz., and 4 dwt." At $20.00 an ounce it amounted to $5,200.00 plus.

Sour-face counted out fifty new $100.00 Federal Bank notes and gave them to Tom, plus $200.00 in $5.00 gold coins; he scowled even deeper as he tried to figure the four pennyweights, so Tom let him get away with it. Tom then packed the notes into a money belt he wore under his shirt, remarking that I wore nothing under my jumper but my skin. The gold coins he divided equally with me for "eatin' money."

Outside he led the way to the post office to see if there was a "a talkin' paper" from either Buck Green or Kasale. Postmaster Emil Sydon said, "No mail, Tom," so we walked back to our horses, rode around to Dunbar's Stables on Third and Fremont, and left our mounts to be taken care of. We walked back to the Oriental Saloon and pushed through the swinging doors and up to the bar. The saloon was not crowded—just two men at the far end of the bar, and four others at a card table.

"Whisky an' two glasses," Tom ordered.

The bartender slid a bottle and two glasses toward us. "Where yuh fellers from?" he asked.

"Over Tucson way . . . and through the Dragoons," I answered and glanced sideways at Tom for his reaction.

"Yeah, we're doin' a little prospectin' hereabouts," Tom supplied, laying a gold piece on the bar. "Here's to yuh!"

"Say, how come you wear your hair long like an Injun?" the barman asked me.

"Oh, we been out in the hills quite a spell," Tom said quickly. "I got mine trimmed a while back, but Ramon is too tight to spend two bits; said he could get an extra drink on that."

"Ya know," said the barman, still eyeing me, "that guy, if he had on a blanket an' a headband, he'd look like an Apache!"

Over my Apache shoulder-long hair I was wearing a sloppy Mexican sombrero, and I had on a pair of American denim pants, a dirty blue jumper, and Texas boots. I laughed. "Well, I've got Mexican blood in me and there might have been an Apache behind the woodpile."

The bartender went into a fit of laughter. "Here, let me buy you guys a drink." He poured our glasses full. Turning to me, he asked, "What did you say your name was?"

"I didn't say, but it's Ramon Rodriguez."

"Yeah, well, that's a greaser name all right."

To change the subject, I guess, Taglito asked about some old-timers in the area from the first silver strike to the present, and the barman gave him a rundown on all of them and others. When he got to his version of the Earp-Clanton shooting match, Tom cut him off short.

"Yeah, well, folks get all mixed up now and then. Now I'll buy a drink . . . have one, bartender?"

"Yeah, I need a snort after all that palaver." He looked at me: "Ramon, my name is George Fowler. Introduce me to your pal."

Tom stuck his hand out, saying, "Sorry, I didn't think to mention it. My name is Tom Jeffords."

"Oh, for Christ's sake!" Fowler's eyes popped wide. "So you're Tom Jeffords. And I told *you* all that!"

We left, checked into the Grand Hotel, got cleaned up, then had dinner at Cashman's. After a few drinks in some other bars, we went to our room early. It was my first night in a hotel.

❦ ❦ ❦

"NEEN-YO," Tom said, still speaking English as we jogged along the next morning, "I reckon that by now you can see the best way to get along with the whiteman is to speak well of everything or else not say anything."

I got to thinking: old Taglito was right again. I could not go around with a chip on my shoulder and not expect to have someone knock it off, and maybe part of my head with it. As long as I kept my mouth shut, I was accepted—my visit to Tombstone had proved that. I made up my mind then and there I was going to join them. It was a proven fact that I couldn't whip them. I didn't think I could forget the past any more than the whiteman could; but what's the use of trying to ride a dead horse?

I told Tom what I'd decided to do. I had a goal and I was going to make it—but I would *not* cut my hair! He snorted and said he wasn't worried about me any more. I would manage to get along with the Pinda-Lick-O-Ye, and he gave me one of his rare smiles. I have remembered that smile and those words all through my life.

Back in our camp in the Dragoons that night I told my mother how I tried to copy Taglito; that it was not what he said or how he said it but what he didn't say that counted. Mother seemed pleased. One by one we began all to bed down. I kicked a few stones aside, spread my blanket, stretched out on it, and wrapped it around me—just like any other Indian.

❧ ❧ ❧

WE got an early start the next day and headed north, avoiding
the occasional farming settlements. We stopped only to water
our animals and have a drink ourselves. It was a long day. The
next day we by-passed Benson, a cowboy town, and by dusk we
reached an ancient Indian campsite along the nearly dry Rio
Santa Cruz. While our women made camp, I took care of our
four horses and two mules. Taglito shot four rabbits in the
brush, and with what we had packed along, we had a good
supper.

The next day we by-passed Mission San Xavier and Sentinel
Peak and clumped over a wooden bridge at Congress Street in
Tucson about noon. Our first stop was the post office and finding
no "talkin' paper" from Buck Green or Kasale, we assumed
everything was normal at Pa-Gotzin-Kay.

We hitched our animals at a long rack in front of the Shoo Fly
Restaurant. Taglito led the way in, with Mother and Nadina all
wide-eyed, and stopped at a table covered with a red checker-
board cloth. There was little said between Tom and me as our
women were saying it all in what they thought was good English while staring around the large dining room.

A man in a white coat came and said, "Well, howdy, Mr.
Jeffords!" And Tom called him "Rusty." After we were seated,
Tom ordered four rib steaks rare, with all the trimmings. Rusty
said he'd bring us four good ones even if he had to go butcher
a steer. He soon returned, smiling, with a big bowl of soup, from
which Tom ladled out four small bowlfuls.

Nadina and Mother kept on talking and laughing as they ate
the soup. After a while Rusty brought the steaks on a large
platter. He gave us a dish of a new kind of potatoes called
"French fries," a bottle of brown stuff, and one of red. He asked
if we wanted anything to drink besides coffee, and Mother understood enough to quickly say "lemon-dade." We each forked
a steak. I don't know who got the best one, but I have never since
seen a stack of such good steaks. I was doing all right with mine
until Rusty came with a pitcher, clinking with ice. Tom
reached for it to fill our glasses. Mother reached at the same

time: Tom fumbled, and Nadina playfully slapped his hand. That upset the pitcher and the lemonade spilled over everything and everybody.

Tom muttered a dirty word. The other diners, whom so far we had not even noticed, began to laugh. Rusty at first was inclined to laugh it off, too, but someone in back yelled "Ge-ron-i-mo!" A woman screamed, and a man growled "Aw, shut up!"

By then it dawned on Rusty that Taglito's three companions were Apaches. He said two nasty words and Tom told him to shut up and get us another table. He took us to a table next to an open window, and we settled down to finish the rib steaks, French fries, biscuits, and canned peaches. People had quieted down, and we were sipping our coffee when Nadina suddenly grabbed mother's bare steak bone and her own and tossed them out the window to several dogs she'd noticed. Soon there was quite a commotion outside, which Mother stopped by leaning over the sill and yelling rapid-fire imprecations in Apache.

An uproar of both screams and laughter bubbled up in the dining room, but soon quieted down again. Rusty, looking sheepish, brought us more coffee and a big pie fresh from the oven.

"Appa-pie!" Mother exclaimed. "Like at Buck's!"

Tom cut the pie into quarters and dished up the four pieces —sure enough it was apple pie.

Rusty came back to ask if there was anything else we wanted. Tom shook his head. Rusty said the bill was "a buck-ninety." Tom gave him a five-dollar gold piece and a sly wink.[5]

Outside, I noticed familiar swinging doors and I headed that way, but Tom grabbed my arm and we untied our animals and rode down to the next corner to Ochoa's store. There Tom told our women to wait with the horses. He and I went in and bought sugar, flour, beans, lemons, potatoes, bacon, syrup, coffee, salt, and some canned stuff. I also bought a Barlow pocketknife.

We camped at Steam Pump Ranch that evening, and the following day we made it to Taglito's ranch at Owl Head in the Tortillita Mountains. The green ranch house was surrounded by young giant sahuaros and a white picket fence which needed repairs. The yard was clogged with weeds, grown dur-

5. Tucson *Arizona Daily Star*, May 9, 1896. AKG.

ing Tom's long absence. There was a well in the back yard with a hand pump which, when primed, gushed clear water.

While he opened the house and showed the women around, I unloaded the mules and unsaddled the horses. The barn had eight stalls in it, but the granary and haymow were empty. So I turned the animals loose in a fenced pasture out back.

We had just finished carrying the supplies into the house when I noticed two horsemen approaching. I called to Tom and he came out on the porch to see if he could identify them. I saw they were whitemen and one had a rifle in his saddle boot. Our saddles were still on the porch so I yanked the carbines out and handed one to Tom. Soon he handed it right back.

"That's Billy Fourr . . . and John Rockfellow!" he said. "Wonder what they want?"

They rode up and dismounted and there was some good-natured banter. Then Taglito introduced me as Ramon Rodriguez. He introduced Mother and Nadina as my mother and aunt. Billy Fourr, a bowlegged old rancher with a spread on the northern slope of the Dragoon Range, had been an army scout and packer. He had a message for Tom: some Eastern people wanted to buy his mine here at Owl Head. John Rockfellow was a schoolteacher who dabbled in mining; he wanted Tom to make an appraisal of his latest silver strike. When they began talking about the days when Cochise and Geronimo kept the country in an uproar, Taglito told them my true name—and that kept us talking far into the night.

TAGLITO was, as usual, the first one up in the morning. He had coffee boiling, bacon frying, and was stirring hotcake batter when I got up. He had a long griddle that held eight cakes at a time. I let out such a wild Apache war whoop that the two guests on the porch bounced out of their blankets. Those hotcakes were good and the sowbelly was terrific. Mother told Taglito that he was a better cook than she, and vowed that if she stayed around him very long, she'd get as fat as Nadina. That really did it. Have you ever heard two Apache women give each other back-handed compliments? We four men had an uproarious treat that lasted nearly all morning.

After the visitors left, Tom and I rode east about a mile to-ward a solitary butte—its outline resembled an owl's head—in the desert and climbed a road rutted by recent seasonal rains. On the side of this butte, about halfway up, the road came to an end on the tailings from a shaft that yawned black like the open mouth of some prehistoric monster. We staked our horses out to forage in back of a shed. The shed had both front and back doors propped shut with large rocks. Adjoining it were a smoke-blackened, brick-oven smelter with a bellows for draft and two ricks of mesquite wood cut in short lengths for fuel. This was the blast furnace used to melt the ore in order to separate the silver from the rock. Taglito said it was the old Mexican *fuego* process.

Inside the shaft we lit lamps. A battered wheelbarrow stood in the drift; several shovels, a beat-up single jack and a pick with broken handle leaned against the face. The wheelbarrow was half-filled with ore, and I picked up a chunk. It was heavy, indicating that it was loaded with white iron. About waist-high I could see a lode that was about a half-inch thick. It looked like pure silver to me and ran the length of the stope. Tom admitted the vein was a full eight inches wide, but that it might pinch out. When I remarked that it also might get wider farther back he said I was the first Pollyanna Apache he ever knew, but that he did want to expose the vein more so those Eastern people could see that they were not buying a pig in a poke. He showed me how and where to dig; we worked until late and didn't get home until after dark.

Mother and Nadina had jerky stew waiting for us; after eating we rolled cigarets and settled down. There was always plenty of Indian talk at a time like this, and we discoursed on the back-shooting of Mangas Coloradas in 1863, the slaughter by whitemen of Chief Eskiminzin's tribe of Aravaipi near the old Haunted Corral in 1871, and the death of Chief Cochise in 1874. Mother and Nadina twice brought up the name of Mister Clum, but Taglito switched them to thoughts of our people languishing in Florida, the others scattered on reservations, and how good our life was in comparison.

When Tom and I had put in three hard days in the stope he seemed satisfied—at least he said so. That evening we were too weary to talk about the past, and we certainly did not worry about the future. Tom and I were so tired we hardly noticed that the women had cleaned the house, changed the furniture around, fixed the stovepipe, cleared up the yard, burned the trash, and even repaired and whitewashed the fence.

꒳꒳꒳

NEXT morning the four of us were riding south; unencumbered with pack mules, we made good time through the giant sahuaro forests of Tanque Verde, thus by-passing Tucson. That night we camped in a manzanita grove a few miles beyond Benson. In the morning we had to ride several miles out of our way to find a gate through the barbed-wire fence the Southern-Pacific had strung along both sides of their miserable tracks. By midafternoon we entered the mouth of Mescal Canyon and Billy Fourr's range. His ranch was just south of the present-day freeway that streaks through Texas Canyon.

Traveling at a leisurely pace the next day, we made it to Tombstone by afternoon and set up camp in the old cavalry bivouac grounds. Tom and I then rode to the public-school building, which backs up to Boothill Cemetery and fronts on infamous Allen Street. Inside, Tom opened the first closed door we came to. John Rockfellow greeted us. We talked awhile, then decided this was as good a time as any for Tom to make the appraisal of Rockfellow's silver mine.

We rode southeast to Slate Pass and turned south along a granite reef. Along its base was the prospect hole. We dismounted. Compared to Tom's diggings, this looked like a gopher hole. The hole appeared about twenty feet deep and ran almost level. I held the horses while Tom and Rockfellow went in. I had rolled and smoked a cigaret before they came out, each of them toting an armload of ore. Taglito studied the rock and found a good streak of white iron in the slate. He mumbled something about pumice. The silver vein might get bigger, heavier farther in—or it might not. It was a gamble. Anyway, there was no sign of running into water.

They discussed the prospect for a spell, then Rockfellow invited us to his house for supper. He explained that his wife, Flora, was from the East and had read a lot about Chief Cochise and his famous blood brother, Taglito. And now that the legendary Taglito and the noble chieftain's grandson were so close by, it would be a shame to disappoint her . . .

Well, we headed back to town with him. By the time we arrived at the Rockfellow house, however, I was boiling mad. We had told him several times that my mother and aunt were waiting in camp for us at the edge of town, but he gave no invitation to bring them in to join us.[6] When we arrived his young son, Philip, and a tail-wagging collie ran to meet us. We entered the house and Rockfellow introduced us to a very attractive woman.

"Flora, I want you to meet a friend of mine. This is Tom Jeffords, the blood brother of Chief Cochise, and this is Cochise's grandson, Niño!"

"Oh, my, Mr. Jeffords! I never thought I would meet anyone as famous as you!" Then turning to me she asked, "Do you speak English?"

I was about to acknowledge the introduction in English when Rockfellow winked at me and said to his wife, "Flora, you will have to address him through Mr. Jeffords."

"Well, tell him I said welcome to our home," she smiled.

I turned to Tom and said in Apache, "This is going to be embarrassing to somebody."

He answered, also in Apache, "Yes, but it was his idea. Take off your hat!"

As usual I was wearing my tribal headband, so when I took my hat off, my hair tumbled over my shoulders. I was wearing an off-white wool cowboy shirt, a silver-spangled belt with sheath-knife, jeans, and boots and spurs. Flora Rockfellow took a ladylike glance at my appearance and her eyes came to rest on my hair. She said to Tom:

6. Taglito later told me Rockfellow had heard about our Shoo Fly Restaurant episode, and feared a sequel. Having his eye set on a higher goal, he had to watch his step; right after our visit at his house he moved to Tucson to accept a professor-of-mathematics position at the Territorial University.NC.

See *Log of an Arizona Trail Blazer,* Copyright 1933, by J. A. Rockfellow, published by Arizona Silhouettes, Tucson, 1955. Although this is an excellent piece of early Cochise County history, it contains no mention of the Jeffords-Apache women incident. AKG.

"So this is the great Cochise's grandson. He does not look at all impressive to me."

I was still irked over that slight to my mother and aunt, and not caring to carry this farce any farther, I spoke in plain English:

"I'm sorry, ma'am. Had I known beforehand what your husband was up to, I would have tried to appear more impressive."

That poor woman lost her composure for a moment. Then she said, "I think we have both been victimized. May I get you gentlemen something to drink before supper?" Without waiting for a reply, she bustled out of the room.

"You spoiled my joke," Rockfellow said. "Flora didn't think Indians could speak our tongue."

"Serves you right," Tom grunted.

Silence fell in the front room until Mrs. Rockfellow returned with a decanter of whisky and some glasses.

She asked me a lot of questions at dinner that night: What I thought about the way the whites acted, what they were doing for the Indians at the present time, and so on. I told her I did not know much because I lived in the Sierra Madre of Mexico with my tribe and had not surrendered.

She then wanted to know if I had come here to surrender. When I told her I was just visiting with my friend, Tom Jeffords, she looked baffled. I explained that when Golthlay, my uncle, surrendered back in 1886 there was no more raiding in the United States or Mexico, so we Apaches became ranchers and farmers and miners. We came to trusted whitemen like Tom Jeffords for advice. She ignored all that but asked me to repeat the name of my uncle.

"Geronimo!" I almost shouted. "In Apache we call him Golthlay. He was my mother's brother, and Naiche was my father's brother.

"I must ask your forgiveness for saying you were not impressive. You are more than that—you are fascinating. Where did you learn to speak English so well?"

"There was a schoolteacher who became one of my clan because of personal circumstances and he taught the whole clan to speak English. Some to read and write. Had he lived, he would have taught us arithmetic too."

"What happened to him?"

"He was killed in a battle at Basaranca."

"I knew it! Apaches always fight."

I explained to her about the American outlaws who were terrorizing border towns and how the alcalde of Basaranca had asked us to help drive them out, but that in doing so, I had lost two of my best warriors and our teacher. When we were about to leave, she said, "You are the most fascinating man I have ever met, Mr. Cochise."

"You had better call him Chief or he might scalp you," her husband told her with a smile.

"I think Mr. Cochise is more of a gentleman than you are, John Alexander Rockfellow," she said with a defiant note in her voice.

I thought she was right, but said, "Mr. Rockfellow, I am wondering if you can help me get a few school textbooks—English grammar, penmanship, arithmetic, and such—used books will do."

"Of course!" he responded. "Right here in my library. Give me a few minutes and I'll have enough to fill your saddlebag."

We said our farewells, headed for Allen Street, and went into a saloon for one quick drink. Our friend, the gabby bartender, George Fowler, greeted me with:

"Howdy! You ain't got that hair cut yet?"

"If I had, I wouldn't have money for a drink," I answered. "But Tom shaved the other day; he does that once a year."

Fowler laughed and set out a bottle and two glasses. Just then, Scott White, the sheriff, walked in and stopped beside us.

"Tom Jeffords! Man, am I glad to see you! Saves me a long ride. I got a message for you."

"Yeah? What is it?"

"It's a crazy telegram—came this afternoon. I left it at the office, but here's how it reads: 'Buck Green says that Kasale asks how many legs has a cow.' "

"Ha!" I exclaimed. "I understand it."

"What does it mean?" Taglito asked in Apache.

I fired right back in Apache, "Once in Basaranca I was drunk and got into trouble with a woman when I told her she danced like a cow with five legs. Kasale helped me out. Later we joked about it. Before we left Buck's, Kasale and I agreed that if any trouble came up, we'd use that expression as a call for help."

146

We downed our drinks, said *"Ya-lan"* (good-by) to the sheriff and the bartender, and headed for the swinging doors. As we went out Fowler yelled, "Hey! You said you was a greaser—that sounded like Apache t'me!"

Mother and Nadina were furious when we arrived in camp, but they soon forgot their anger when we told them about Kasale's message. The three of us prepared to return to Pa-Gotzin-Kay; Tom would return to Owl Head. Our horses needed re-shoeing, what with the hard ride ahead, so we stabled them at Dunbar's and left word with the night man to have them shod the first thing in the morning. When we bedded down for the night my mind was in a turmoil, but level-headed Taglito finally got me calmed down.

Chapter 9   1896

Red-flaggers

THOSE two women of mine were not as good a trail crew as Taglito and I were, but what they lacked in efficiency they made up for in determination. Following a day of constant riding we were in Mexico, having slipped past the border patrol after dark. We had covered about sixty miles, and the Rancho Verde was only another day's ride ahead. The next afternoon Kasale spotted us while still a mile away and rode out to meet us.

"*Shis-Inday!*" he called. "*Shis-Coza-Idia!*" (Hail to the Chief! Hail to the Queen Bee!)

It was good to hear an Apache greeting again. Kasale told us some of the things that had happened in our absence while we rode in to the ranch house.

As soon as we dismounted, Mother and Nadina stretched out flat on the ground and closed their eyes. The trip had been hard on them, especially on Nadina. It was like the old days when the clans were often on the move, sometimes riding a hundred miles in a day and a night. Our ride from Tombstone had had some of the same urgency—although no one was pursuing us —for we did not know what lay ahead.

Buck Green was glad to see us, and his boys led our horses to the barn. I explained that Tom Jeffords had to stay at Owl Head to show the Easterners his mine. Anna Green and her servant came and took Mother and Nadina into the house. I yanked off my grimy shirt, shoved my face into the run-off of the horse trough, and gave my head and shoulders a good dousing. Buck tossed me a burlap bag and I dried off, feeling better. He led the way to the porch and nodded to the big swing. He went inside but was back soon with a clean shirt and a bottle of Old Overholt. He proceeded with the news.

In our absence, Kasale had been busy scouting and keeping in touch with our rancheria, while Buck and his men had been out, especially the past week, rounding up cattle and working them down close to home. The six other ranchers had been losing beef and had caught several red-flaggers who were rustling them. The ranchers had sent a protest to President Diaz, but had not received an answer as yet. The self-made General Luis Torres had picked up a following and was a thorn in the Americans' side; also he was dreaming of taking Diaz' place on the presidential throne.

I recalled things Taglito and Buck had told me about Torres: he had about as much chance as a snowball in July against Diaz. Old Diaz was heap smart, had an organization, and had been top man for a long time. He was elected in 1876, missed out in 1880, but went back into office in 1884 and had been in ever since. People were always trying to throw him out, but none succeeded. Always the revolution, always the red flag, always the promises—that was Mexico in the 1890's. But recently the reinstated Governor General Joaquin Terrazas of Chihuahua had again lined up with Torres, and between them they had about 1,000 *revolucionarios*.

Buck and I had both heard Chief Kelzel curse those generals. Also Kelzel would not have joined the American ranchers to protect their cattle, except that he had lost cattle to Torres and Terrazas and was afraid he'd also lose his head. Torres had sent Colonel de Vega to confiscate cattle for so-called back taxes; then Torres and Terrazas added the cattle to their own herds on their own haciendas. The ranchers, especially the Americans, had the most to lose, as Diaz had talked them into buying Mexican real estate in the first place.[1] That was the reason for the meeting Buck, Tom and I had with Chief Kelzel, Ammon Tenny, and James Grey a month before.

Four years earlier, when peace was restored with the Yaqui tribes, Diaz allocated 6,000 plots of land to them. It was part of

1. Part of the U.S.-Mexican Agrarian Act of 1888, brought about by the Mormon efforts to colonize in the States of Chihuahua and Sonora. AKG.

the land that had been granted to them by the King of Spain. Within two years the Yaqui were again at war with the Torres-Terrazas faction and other generals in Durango and Sinaloa. The generals had double-crossed them, but managed to convince Diaz that the Yaqui were to blame. So Diaz offered any soldier who would kill a Yaqui fifty pesos for the ears of the victim. The Yaqui took the *Yori* oath and went a bit farther—they took the whole head of the Mexicans. Then Generals Izabel, Corral, Belandres, Zapata, and one with the lustrous name of Luna Luz (moonlight) pitched in with Terrazas and Torres. Hundreds of Yaqui and other Indians were rounded up, killed or taken prisoner and sold into slavery for seventy pesos each.

Cajeme, the Yaqui High Chieftain at that time, appealed to Torres. Torres had him thrown from the governor's palace and put in an adobe-walled place. (All walls were made of adobe brick. They were also used as a backstop for bullets from the firing squad.) Kelzel, who succeeded Cajeme, went *Yori* mad, and the Yaqui fought like the killers they are until beaten by Mexican regular troops under Ramon Corral and Luna Luz. The *soldatos* sacked all the Yaqui barrios in the bottom land, and raped and beat the women—many of them to death. I had all that on good authority. It was easy to see why Kelzel would have nothing to do with any Mexican leaders. The Yaquis had been treated as badly as we Apaches were by the Americans, except for the raping by the Mexicans. The White-Eyes did not try that on us.

❧ ❧ ❧

AFTER a good night's sleep Buck loaned us fresh horses, for ours were used up and needed a rest. We took the short cut up Juh's Canyon and went on to Dry Canyon, by-passing Basaranca and Chi-hua-hua's old stronghold. Near Bubbling Springs we were challenged by a young vedette who was so glad to see us that he stumbled and his rifle went off, the crack banging across the canella hills.

A band of braves galloped up, with Chee at their head, and escorted us the rest of the way. Everything had been going well during my absence, Chee explained enroute, except that Dee-

O-Det, the *shaman,* had been a stickler for proper law. Now that I was back to take over, the troubles were mine. All of our people were out to greet us as we rode in, and Dee-O-Det rushed to embrace me, saying:

"You have saved me from going mad! I have sad news for you. Our friend, Doctor Gutierrez, has been executed in Basaranca. The charges were treason!"

"That Torres!" I exclaimed. "I knew the doctor was wrong trusting him! What happened to Eugene and Nakai?"

"They are making cannon and gunpowder," Chee replied, "under orders from Torres. Basaranca is now an arms factory."

"Have you talked with them?"

"I talked with Eugene. He is married now and seems to be worried. He is not the Eugene we used to know."

Saddened, I looked away. Eugene and Nakai had accepted commissions in Torres' militia, and had thus made their beds. Doctor Gutierrez, it seemed, had refused to go along with Torres' rotten schemes, so Torres had him shot. Had he only listened to me, he would yet be alive.

I made up my mind that I would attempt to see Eugene. I wanted to avenge the murder of my good friend, the doctor of Basaranca. I turned to my old confidant, the *shaman,* questioning him further about the death of Gutierrez, but all he knew was what some new people—who had come to live at Pa-Got-zin-Kay—had told him. I followed the shaman and Chee, and just beyond the edge of our compound, I saw alien wikiups—certainly not Apache.

"Buenos días, Señor Jefe! Adentro!" A tall Opata stepped out of one wikiup and greeted us.

We walked in as invited, and the *shaman* asked him to tell me of the doctor's death. He told how General Torres talked out of the side of his mouth, but to the doctor's ears it was truth and he heeded. He was a fine man; he had helped the Opata much. Then one day Gutierrez was told to be a tax collector; to go to the Opata and demand the tax. This tax was their small herds of cattle. The doctor argued, but the general was short-tempered and sent soldiers to collect the tax. They took the men prisoner and sold them as slaves; they raped and murdered the women and children. When the doctor found out, he had words with the general, who then ordered the *soldatos* to execute him.

The tall Opata launched into a tirade of his own troubles. They were all that was left of the Sonoran Opata people. Their chief was shot in the back after he had surrendered to the *soldatos.* Twelve Opata were able to slip away into the mountains, but they were starving. When Chee caught them butchering one of our calves they knew they were finished. Instead Chief Chee had been very good to them and brought them in and these three families would like to stay. He was called Sanchez—Emiliano Sanchez. As the oldest he had been chosen to speak for the people.

"Emiliano, you will be Chief of these, your people," I said. "I am Niño of the Apache. Dee-O-Det, as you know, is the chief of our council—you will answer to him. Chee is my subchief. Come to me tomorrow and I will give you weapons."

"We are indebted to you, Chief Niño."

Dee-O-Det, Chee, and I returned to our compound. We parted after I told Chee he and I would ride to Basaranca in the morning. I was determined to have a talk with Eugene and Nakai. I could see Nakai throwing in with the Mexicans. But Eugene? No, even if he was married into the race! However, as Chee had said, Eugene, a full-blooded Apache, was not the Eugene of old.

❦ ❦ ❦

THE following morning Chee saddled two horses while I made us some hotcakes and coffee. Mother was not yet up. We ate, then after a quick ride down the north trail to the river bank, we went as close to town as was possible without being seen. Chee had already informed me soldiers would stop us at the gate and question us. And since we were Apaches that would be enough to get us adobe-walled by them. We tied our horses and worked our way along the brushy bank to the large boulder overlooking the unused sluice boxes of the erstwhile miners. Chee pointed out Eugene's place—a square *casita* with a red brick chimney.

Now we had to wait and see. I was still somewhat weary after my hard riding of the past few days, so we sat in a tree's shade and relaxed. Late in the afternoon I awakened, looked around, then nudged Chee. We talked in whispers, and at dusk worked closer to town, keeping well hidden. Soon a light came on in the *casita*. I gave the cry of the male owl three times and waited. Then I saw a form on the roof of the *casita*. I gave the call again. A female's plaintive call answered. It was Eugene. I gave the lonesome call. This time as he answered, Eugene leaped off the roof. I crept closer to the house.

"Ho, my brother," I greeted Eugene. "You are having troubles?"

"Well, you were gone so long and I did not know what to do."

"About what?" I asked impatiently.

"About the killing of the doctor. I was told that if I did not obey orders they would get Nakai to lead a battery of cannon to Pa-Gotzin-Kay and kill all of us."

"Do you think Nakai would lead them to us?"

"Not willingly . . . but he is not a true Apache."

Eugene revealed that he was head man of the gunpowder makers and they already had enough sacked to blow Basaranca sky-high. When I suggested we do just that, he informed me that we wouldn't have a chance—he was the only Indian in Basaranca and any other would be shot the instant he was seen.

We discussed the problem further, and I understood why Eugene was acting in so un-Apache a way. He had been trapped. I had my answer, so I started back to Chee and the horses. Basaranca was unsafe for me. Had I walked through that gate, I would now be a dead Indian. Torres did not like the way I had handled those Yaqui he had tricked into invading us. Now, I realized, he was building up his forces while playing the waiting game. Hermosillo City was too hot for him to manufacture weapons in; likewise Chihuahua City for Terrazas, because of the railroad and nearby large towns that Diaz visited often. Terrazas and Torres were both rattlesnakes playing the same game, bucking President Diaz as well as robbing the Indians and the American settlers.

We got back to the rancheria around midnight, but I was up at daybreak. Over breakfast Mother and I discussed the unpredictable Mexicans; then I sought out Dee-O-Det and told him to call a special meeting of the council.

I informed them that our brother Eugene was working well for us in the Nakai-Ye town. He was in a position to see to it that changes in the world around us did not affect our life here in

153

Pa-Gotzin-Kay. In Mexico there was one Strong Man, their *Nant-án,* who worked for all the people, but he had constantly to fight off peasants who were trying to overthrow him and take his place.

It was these *siblings 'O'-ndi mba sitz 'n' Na lti-i-gi-na,* (little coyotes that pop up out of holes like gophers) we must guard against for they try to steal the ranchers' cattle, as they stole from the Opata and the Yaqui in the bottom lands. They would try to steal our cattle, take our gold mine, our mountain fortress.

But we would protect ourselves. When crossing flat lands, if we saw soldiers, we would take to the mountains. If they pursued us, we would fight on our grounds. We would help the American ranchers in both Sonora and Chihuahua, and they would help us. Fully united, we and they would fight in the valleys, the hills, the canyons, and in the mountains. Together we would meet the Mexicans head on and destroy them. This was the treaty our brother Taglito and I had made with the ranchers.

The *shaman* conferred with the members, then gave me the approval sign. Glancing skyward, I left. The *shaman* followed me to Mother's fire and sat on a log. Chee and Kasale soon joined us. As I talked about the trail guards, there came the rhythmic beat of a horse running up the shelf trail. Chee leaped up and ran to meet him. Asa, the outrider trail guard, talked to Chee for a moment, then turned and loped back down the trail. Chee came back and said:

"Buck Green comes."

In a short time he rode in and dismounted. After the greetings to our assembled men, the dust-covered rancher told us that other ranchers, along with Kelzel and some warriors, were waiting at Chi-hua-hua's old hideout for permission to come in. Kelzel had refused to ride right in because "Chiricahua trail guards shoot and then ask 'What do you want?' A dead man could not answer."

I did not like all these strangers riding into Pa-Gotzin-Kay. But since Buck seemed to know what he was doing, I had to go along with it. He had been riding since before daybreak, so Mother brought him a cup of coffee and some food. I told Hi-okee to take one man, go to the old hideout, tell Kelzel and the others waiting there that Niño Cochise was ready to meet them, and to escort them up through the rampart.

Emiliano came over and I introduced him to Buck. He eyed Buck carefully, then told him—with me as interpreter—that he had never met a *blanco* before. He began telling Buck what Torres had done to the Opata on the Yaqui River flats. Before long Buck, Emiliano, and I got hot just talking about the outrages of Mexicans with their evil laws that enriched the *ricos* and suppresssed the *Indios*.

The *shaman* suddenly began making sign talk to me; when I nodded, he got up and left. Shortly he returned—with two bottles. That old rascal! In my absence he had somehow acquired some whisky, but it was good stuff to have at a time like this.

Other men began to line up as the bottles passed from hand to mouth. Emiliano soon was feeling good, and Buck began to brighten up. To get a chance to talk with him alone, I suggested we take a walk up to Lookout Peak. We hadn't gone ten steps before Emiliano was right on our heels. I told him it was a hard climb but he just smiled. I had a man up there with a telescope that Tom Jeffords had given me. I told Buck we could see how far the ranchers had come and would know when to expect them.

From this point with our twenty-power refracting telescope mounted on a tripod we had a close-up of hundreds of square miles of wilderness.[2] We could scan the canyons of the Yaqui, Arros, Escondido, Azul, Moctezuma, Naco-zari, San Bernardino, De Los Embudos, Ocho Rios—except some of the bottoms —as well as much of the Bavispe Barranca; Basaranca was hidden from view.

Klan-O-Tay, the lookout on duty, informed me that Hi-okee and Boa Juan had just disappeared under the trees below Beduiat's Bluff, where a canyon branched off to the Bavispe. I adjusted the four-inch lens of the telescope to fit my eyes and took a look. I could see the sunlight reflect off the water hole where a horseman paused to let his mount drink.

Buck took a look and grunted; "You sure can see all over hell from here, can't you?"

2. These were twenty- and forty-power telescopes made by Bausch & Lomb for the Army Signal Corps; along with binocular Field Glasses they became Quartermaster surplus after the Apache campaigns of the 1880's. AKG.

I took another look. By now there were by count twenty-five riders strung out along the trail. At the pace they were coming I figured it would take them another hour to get to our rancheria. I squatted down and rolled a cigaret. Emiliano was surprised when I struck the match with my thumbnail. These were the whiteman's sulphur matches, and he got his nose too close in his curiosity and went into a fit of coughing.

I quickly took him about twenty-five steps down the slope to the guards' wikiup and found an xusage (a skin bag) half-full of water. Between the whisky and the sulphur Emiliano was going through agony. He stretched out and closed his eyes. Buck soon came and, eyeing Emiliano, snorted, "He wasn't feelin' any pain till you stuck that match under his nose."

When Buck and I arrived back in camp, the noon meal was served. The old *shaman* came strolling over to our table.

"Hum-m-m. Good-looking meat and potatoes—the coffee smells good too," he hinted. He was seated at the table before Mother could even get him a plate. Much as I like the crusty old coot, he sometimes got under my skin. I was about to say something about it when Mother called:

"Ciyé . . ." (Son)

From where we sat I could see the trail up to Lookout Mountain. Emiliano was coming down, slipping and sliding. I called and invited him to eat with us, but he ignored me and kept on going in the direction of his camp.

🌱 🌱 🌱

A LITTLE later Kersus, a guard, came on the gallop to tell me a man was nearing the south rampart. He looked like a Tarahumari, was on foot, and carried a white flag. Strangers coming here was getting to be a habit, but I told Kersus to bring the man in. As Kersus loped off down the trail, Buck sat down under a tree and pulled his hat over his eyes. I felt drowsy too, but before I could doze off, another guard came with the man carrying the white flag.

I looked the stranger over; he was middle-aged, thin, dirty, naked from the belt up, and appeared nervous or scared. His body was a color between gold and copper. A typical Indian, but not as dark as sunburnt Apaches. I waited for him to speak.

"I am called Jemez, Benito Jemez," he said in a mixture of Mexican and Tarahumari. "I am *cacique* of the Tarahumari, once a great nation; now we number but three hundred and have been driven from our lands in Temosachic. When we were finally beaten, I fled with my people to the mountains, with no weapons. There were two thousand *soldatos* in the field against us. The man I succeed was given *ley fuga*[3] when he surrendered last year. He was called Imochic. Now I have come to you. We are starving."

"Where are you located now?" I asked.

"We are three mountains to the east on the Chihuahua side. We seek a place where we may heal our wounds. No one is safe from tax-hungry *Nakavdi*—no, not even *colonizadors* (Mormon settlers) whom they made to hate us with their lies. They told the Americans that Tarahumari stole their cattle, so they shoot us on sight."

"No more will they shoot you on sight," I replied. "You are on the whiteman's side now—I will see to that."

"No comprendo . . ."

"We Apache will give you food and a weapon; then you may return to your people. Do you have horses?"

"None, Chief Niño. We ate them."

At a signal from me Dee-O-Det went to the communal kiva and brought a rifle and a handful of shells. Mother gave Chief Jemez a shank of roasted venison and he ate like the starving man he was. As with most Indians of Northern Mexico he was poor, hungry, downtrodden, scared. I told him to bring his people, that we had a place for them, and that I would then explain why they were on the side of the American ranchers. A horse with a homemade hide saddle was brought for him. He mounted. I warned him not to eat that horse—I wanted him returned. And I added in emphatic Manso Apache, *"Ata-B'n-ata-yeyn huf'tan!"* (I wish you fruitful work!)

He nodded and loped down the trail. I thought to myself: Hummm.—300 more people. How am I going to provide for

3. "Ley fuga"—Mexican dialect for "law of flight." The military authorities were good sports—in some ways. They gave some prisoners as much as 50 paces head start before the execution.

them? I can feed them for a while, but not for long, or we'll all go hungry . . .

🌿 🌿 🌿

MOTHER was busy with preparations to feed Buck's coming ranchers, and I told Chee to have two beeves butchered for the day after tomorrow to feed the 300 Tarahumari, and two more for the following day. Later I told Chee to earmark about twenty sacks of corn, potatoes, and pinto beans, and ration some coffee and chili peppers.

I got to thinking how when we Apaches came to these mountains we ate rabbits and moles and nuts for a long time. We were afraid to leave the mountains, and down through the years they had been good to us. I had grown to love these mountains and I vowed never to leave them again. One day I would become part of them—forever. Wars are fought to see who owns the land, but in the end *it* possesses man. Who dares say he owns it—is he not buried beneath it?

Those thoughts made my brain weary. I sat down to smoke and think. Buck woke up and began to talk. After a time a guard came and reported that the ranchers were passing Bubbling Springs. I lookd down the long circle of family fires. Our rough plank tables were being set with plates and cups. Two large pits of coals were roasting sides of beef. Other fires had pots of boiling beans with chili, whose aroma could be smelled from afar in this mountain air. Indian corncakes were baking on hot rocks; potatoes, onions, and carrots had been put into the stewing pots. This was indeed to be a feast.

In my family wikiup I changed my everyday clothes for regalia more fitting to receive visitors. Dee-O-Det had changed his shaggy *shaman* outfit for a fancy medicine-man habit, and Mother looked regal in her moleskin outfit.

With Kasale in the van, leading our three horses, the guests filed into the compound and dismounted. Some of our men and boys took the visitors' horses to a small glade where they could have water and graze. When the greetings were over we gathered around the tables. Mother, Nadina, Buck Green, Ammon Tenny, Jim Grey, John Brewer, Nephi Parks, Jess Fisher, Al

Bower, Benito Escalante, and Dee-O-Det sat at my table. Several heavily armed cowboys, Chief Kelzel and his five Yaqui, and Emiliano Sanchez and his oldest son occupied adjoining tables.

Nothing much was said about anything except the food, but when all had gorged themselves, Dee-O-Det invited the men to take places in the council circle. The ranchers moved to a semi-circle around the council fire, and the chieftains gathered on the other side with their followers behind them according to their rank. As host and Chief, I took my place in the center—and felt small. I got hold of myself and addressed the council:

"Members of the council, we meet tonight with the ranchers of the Sierra Madre who are being robbed by the heads of state. They are being threatened, if their taxes are not paid, that their property will be confiscated. All of you know that the Yaqui, the Opata, and the Tarahumari, who were unable to pay their levy, were driven from their homes by the red-flaggers. Many of these people lost their lives. I think all of you members of the council have heard of the pitiable ordeal of Tarahumari Chief Jemez.

"The purpose of this meeting is to consider these poor people, along with those here tonight who are about to be dispossessed. I ask that you hear these people and decide that we help them repulse their enemies, as though they were our enemies. I have spoken."

The *shaman* conferred with the council members and then announced that we would hear from the ranchers.

"I am one of the ranchers from the Chihuahua side," said a middle-aged man as he stood up. "My name is John Brewer. The President of Mexico, Porfirio Diaz, encouraged Americans to invest and colonize in Mexico. I and my fellow ranchers have done this. We have created employment for the Indian vaqueros, who serve us well. Now Governor General Joaquin Terrazas, of Chihuahua, has, without authority of the president, raised our taxes to support an army to overthrow the president. Governor General Luis Torres, of Sonora, has joined forces with Terrazas. Porfirio Diaz has troubles of his own in other states and informs us he can give us no Federal aid . . .

"It is my opinion that we must protect ourselves, but to do this successfully I must ask your help. I request that the well-known Apache fighting prowess come to our aid. In return for this we ranchers will see to it that all who help get repaid. We will furnish weapons and we will furnish food. We will furnish seed to those who are farmers; those who raise cattle we will give a good start. That is about all I have to say."

Buck Green, spokesman for the Sonora-side ranchers, got up and seconded Brewer.

Dee-O-Det polled the council members, and then announced we would stand with the Americans against the red-flaggers. I stood up and spoke of the problem of the Tarahumari. They would arrive in two days and would need help (which I had promised), and they in turn would help us. I stressed the fact that they had about 100 men who would be warriors with a vengeance if they were supplied with weapons.

Big Jim Grey said, "I have 500 rifles that I ordered for Kelzel. He could spare 100."

I turned to Kelzel. "I will buy 100 of them from you."

"Will you pay on delivery?" he asked, spacing his words and syllables, as was his custom when he spoke in Spanish.

"I will pay in gold. What is your price?"

"I will take 1200 reales for them. There are 200 rounds of shells and a blanket that go with each gun." He added that I could pick them up any time at Grey's ranch. I told Dee-O-Det to fetch a sixty-ounce bar of gold. He disappeared for a time. When he returned with the bar of gold and gave it to Kelzel, he said slyly; "I hope they are not muzzle-loaders."

Someone translated that and Big Jim almost blew up. "They are the new Winchester Model 94, 30/30 carbines! Pick them up any time you're ready!"

I announced that tomorrow would be a day of rest. The following day the Tarahumari would arrive and there would be a feast, after which I would pick up my guns. Dee-O-Det dismissed the council. Being the *shaman* that he was, he managed to dig up one more bottle of whisky and a large *jarro* of mescal, and the men all gathered around.

❦ ❦ ❦

THE sound of wood being chopped awakened me before sunup. I went out to Mother's fire. There was plenty of still-warm beef left over. After our guests had breakfast, I had Chee take a mixed group of ranchers and Yaqui, and Kasale take an English-speaking group on a tour of our rancheria. My idea was to keep anyone from wandering around and accidentally discovering Sno-Ta-Hae. The day wore on with everybody busy, leaving little for Dee-O-Det and me to do as overseers, except keep Buck Green interested as he followed us around. Sunset came and a purple mist settled over the mountains— the *shaman's* sign of clear days ahead. After supper Dee-O-Det called another council meeting and the talk came mostly from the ranchers—all of whom had the future uppermost in mind.

The next morning shortly after sunrise Hi-okee galloped down from Lookout Peak and reported the Tarahumari were winding up Juh's Trail, all on foot except one. I figured they must have traveled most of the night and that they would arrive before midday. There was an air of expectancy in the rancheria.

As they came, I could see that the smell of food quickened the footsteps of the weary. There was the sound of human breath hoarsely drawn and the scuffle of feet. It was a haphazard movement that became a relentless march as it neared the compound, then a rout as the slowest tried to keep up with the fleetest. Chief Jemez came straight to me, dismounted, and silently handed me the reins of the horse.

For a time there was a weird babble of voices that soon lowered to the noise of hungry people eating.

After the eating orgy was over, with even the bones gnawed, I called for attention and got it.

"My friends," I spoke loudly, addressing the ranchers, "This is Chief Benito Jemez and his Tarahumari. They are our allies and I will supply them with guns. They need much more, as they were forced to flee with no more than the rags on their backs. They need horses, cattle, blankets, seed to plant, harness, axes, hoes, rakes—anything to help them get back on their feet."

Buck Green was the first to hold up a hand. He stated he would pledge thirty horses, all broken to ride. John Brewer pledged a like number, and Ammon Tenny followed suit. Jim Grey, a little cautious, said he would supply thirty within a week; then Jess Fisher of the San Bernardino ranch pledged thirty. Nephi Parks said he would send up a dozen milk cows; Al Bower pledged grain; Escalante pledged a herd of goats.

One hundred and fifty horses! Emboldened by this response I asked for farm tools, blankets, cooking utensils, sugar and salt, and got positive promises from the ranchers. Buck stated that he was for me—whole hog. Brewer became quite vocal on a different angle: "I am with Niño all the way, and I figure if he and his Indians protect us, then he is entitled to our help. And if he wishes to buy special items, I will see that he gets them. Won't we, Mr. Grey?" he added rather sarcastically.

"Whatever you say, Mr. Brewer."

Buck whispered in my ear, "He damn well better agree with Brewer. It's mostly Brewer's money that runs his whole she-bang." Then aloud, Buck said, "Grey, since you're the sutler below the San Berdoo, we will buy from you what we need. Have you paid your taxes?"

This brought laughs from everybody but Grey. Kelzel eased over to me and whispered in Yaqui, "He is the man who paid me to bring him Apla-Chi-Kit's head."

"What!" So that was the kind of man Big Jim Grey was! He paid bounty-hunters to do his work. The thought gave me cold chills.

"He is a very hard man," Kelzel added, "but he pays well."

"Then why do you not earn it honorably?"

"I will next time."

"If he ever picks my head, I'll take yours!" Then I added, "I will be in for the rifles tomorrow."

I walked away. I did not like the way Kelzel talked. The ranchers were getting saddled and ready to ride out. I felt a hand on my shoulder and turned—it was Chief Jemez. The expression on his face told me much. I glanced skyward, but my mind was still on Grey and his head-hunting consort, the *Yaqui-Yori*.

I led Jemez to a cleared area beyond the compound and told him to have his people settle down there for the night. He called out an order and his people came, moving promptly. They were not only tired and ready to rest, they were obedient. He held up a hand for silence and introduced me as the High Chief of the valiant Apache to whom he had sworn allegiance.

He pointed out what I had done for them this day, and then asked if any still believed the tales of Apache atrocities told to them by the *Nakavdi* officials? He asked further:

"Are the tales you heard of the Mansos true? How about the food now in our bellies that have been empty so long? Does it look true when the Mansos and the *blancos* give us weapons, blankets, horses—make us feel like men again? Do you believe the Mexicans' lies about the Apaches?"

The response was a resounding *"No!"*

My people were mingling with them and helping as much as they could, handing out pieces of clothing and balms for over-eating, and the *shaman* was sprinkling *hodenten* and chanting a song.

I went back to Ticer's old wikiup to be alone. My thoughts centered on Kelzel. Was he really a friend—or a cunning enemy? Was he a friend to anyone who would pay him to be? Or was he friend only to the man Grey? Perhaps I had made an enemy of him. Did I now have two deadly enemies?

I was pulling off my *kabuns* when I had my most troubling thought. Here I had 300 Tarahumari, twelve Opatas, five Yaqui, not to mention my own tribespeople. I had nearly 400 people on my hands and most were unarmed. Until I got those guns from Grey, we were virtually helpless. The winds of treachery had been blowing, and if Torres and his red-flaggers were told how vulnerable we were, they might get the notion to surround us and wipe out all of us, his enemies, in one swoop. Pa-Gotzin-Kay would run red with blood.

I pulled my moccasins back on. Only action would soothe my troubled mind. The rancheria was quiet as I stepped outside on silent feet. I first sought out Jemez and told him to get ten of his best men quietly and meet me. I passed up the five Yaqui left as a token of good will by Kelzel, for I did not care to put myself in a position of having to depend on them. When the ten Tarahumari were assembled I issued them weapons from the kiva and sent them out in pairs to watch the hill trails for the rest of the night. I put Jemez in charge. These extra scouts, added to my own vedettes, would see anything strange that moved within many kilometers. I went back to bed and got a few hours sleep.

❦ ❦ ❦

I WAS up before dawn and roused Mangas-Chee and Boa Juan and had them assemble all our men of warrior age who were not on guard duty. Then I instructed young Chi-hua-hua and young Juh to have Chief Jemez gather his tribe and move them to the grassy flats just west of Bubbling Springs. This was one of those remote mountain meadows sheltered by a rocky ridge and an impassable spur of the towering Sierre Madre. In case of trouble the refugees would be within reach of Pa-Gotzin-Kay, yet safe.

The other men and I took fifteen pack animals and left without breakfast. We rode hard cross-canyon and arrived at Grey's ranch by high-noon sun. This was one of the hardest rides for both man and beast that I had ever made, but under the circumstances it was necessary.[4]

Chief Kelzel was there and knew we had come for the guns and blankets. Jim Grey came out of a big shed and waved to us. When we were shown which piles were ours, I had the men wrap each rifle with a blanket and keep track of the count. When they were finished, there were only eighty—we were short twenty rifles. Kelzel, standing nearby, must have read my mind.

"I counted one hundred," he said in Spanish. Then he snapped in his native tongue, "That's what you bargained for and that's what you get!"

"Kelzel, I will give you time while I smoke a cigaret to produce those rifles." I eyed his belted bowie knife and put a hand on my own. "Maybe you are thinking of taking my head for Grey. Better start, *Yori*, your time is smoking out."

He walked toward the shed door and passed Grey coming out. Grey came over. "I didn't think he'd do that, Niño," he said in a low voice. "Don't let that ornery Yaqui get you riled."

4. In later years historian J. Frank Dobie wrote that the Apache could get more out of a horse than any other race of men. We proved him right, I think.

I told him I was fond of my head. When he demanded to know what this talk of heads was all about, I told him he ought to know—he had sent Kelzel after Apla-Chi-Kit's head.

"Was that horse thief a friend of yours?"

"He was no friend of mine or any other human being—he was a *Netdahe!*"

"Well now! I'm glad to hear that. Then we are friends?"

"We have to be. We face a common enemy."

The twenty guns were brought out, promptly loaded on the pack mules, and we left in a hurry. We would get the ammunition for these when we came back for the horses. We made it to Rancho Verde, where the Greens served us a belated breakfast, dinner, and supper all in one. We decided to take only fifteen horses from Buck and let the Tarahumari pick up the rest. These were all we could handle over the steep trails getting back to the rancheria. Winding up the escarpment on Juh's Canyon trail in the moonlight, we found our loads were too bulky to get by some of the narrow switchbacks. We had to unload and hand-carry some of the guns, for a skittish mustang or mule might become overbalanced and plunge over the side. Both animal and cargo were valuable to us.

It was dawn when we made the rancheria. We had pushed our horses and mules over more than 100 kilometers of rough mountain trails between dawn and dawn and all of the animals made it. Dee-O-Det was up and I asked him to call in all the old rifles our men were using and issue them new ones. The old but serviceable rifles went to the Tarahumari with shells for each.

❦ ❦ ❦

THE following day ten of us Apaches, accompanied by fifteen mounted Tarahumari, picked up sixty horses at the Tenny and Brewer ranches. Brewer showed me some farm tools he said we could have. Among them was a heavy plow. He showed us how to disassemble it so it could be loaded on a packsaddle. He also pointed out a homemade harrow, but I declined it in favor of rakes and hoes for Jemez' people. I helped the men load up, then told Chee to take the Tarahumari and head home with the cumbersome supplies. I would follow later with the Apache crew, driving the herd of horses.

First I rode over alone to Campo Santo Naco-zari-Oste to see Pablo Mendoza, a well-known saddle maker. The old *sillero* informed me he was very unhappy with the last deal the Sonora governor gave him. Being Mexican himself, I thought he should have known Torres would pull a fast one. He showed me a stock of about 100 low-grade saddles, equipped with scabbards, pouches, and saddle blankets. When I asked him what he wanted for the bunch, he threw up his hands. If I would take them all, he'd be so happy he'd let me have them by paying only for his time: 200 pesos in gold. He admitted that some were good, some not. Thinking my silence a bad omen, he threw up his hands again and told me to take my choice at two pesos each. I began a more careful examination, and he became impatient. He shouted he would put them all in excellent shape —and throw in the bridles!

I nodded acceptance and dug two $100.00 American gold-back bills out of my shirt pocket and handed them to him. His face went blank. I explained the advantage of paper over coins—at two pesos gold per dollar I was paying him double his original asking price. While he was mulling over the unfamiliar currency, I told him I would be back soon with sixty horses for sixty of the best saddles. He was to work over the other forty to be picked up later.

When I got to Brewer's it was too late to go back to Pablo's. We pitched camp near the full corrals, which were being guarded by my braves. One of Brewer's Mexican wives brought us fried chicken. We ate eggs and white bread for breakfast, and it was midmorning before we had roped and hackamored sixty mustangs, most still half-wild, and were on the trail to Campo.

Old Pablo greeted us with a smile of pride. He had sixty good saddles piled up. We proceeded to cinch them on the horses. Many were so unruly that it took us all morning, but we finally made a dust-raising start out of there and headed for the hills.

We herded the horses into the Tarahumari encampment and then the real confusion began. It was sundown before all those mustangs were brought to bridle, and with a man in each saddle. Although they were not the world's best horsemen, those Tarahumari were like white kids with new hobby horses; what they lacked in experience they made up for in energetic delight.

While this was going on, I detailed to Jemez how to send a band of men to Parks' ranch and slowly drive back the twelve milk cows, another group to Escalante's to get the herd of goats, and a third group to get the sacks of grain at Bower's farm.

Dee-O-Det was at Mother's table, as was his habit lately. He started to vex me with comments about taking two days for a trip that normally would take three. I explained that I had to get all the weapons and horses before the Nakai-Ye tried to invade us, as well as our winter's provisions before bad weather came. We must make at least two trips to Bisbee, I told him, because we now had so many more mouths to feed. He realized all this, I think, and was secretly proud of my endeavors but had a perverse way of showing it—something like eating the chicken, then serving me with a bowl of feathers.

So I asked him if there was a law against a man eating a bird and leaving the feathers for his friend. When he said there was, I asked him if there was one that allowed the High Chief to skin an arrogant *shaman,* as I needed a *shaman's* skin on the wall of my wikiup. The old coot cackled and left with a full cup of Mother's hoarded coffee.

Noticing Chee teasing a nearby maiden, I beckoned to him and he came running. I told him we would have to make a quick trip to Bisbee, that he himself would not be going but he was to organize a trail crew to handle a column of about twelve pack mules. I would prepare the list of supplies to be bought and give them paper money to pay for it. I wanted to go, but I was more needed here to bring in the rest of the horses and stuff from the ranches.

That night I dreamed a lot. I envisioned the *shaman* had me trussed and hung upside down from Ticer's tree. He was sharpening his ceremonial knife and telling me he was going to skin me: did I want the cut to start up the back or down the front? I woke up at that point. I had drunk the evening before from the *shaman's* bottle and I began to wonder if the old coot had put a magic potion in that stuff to make me dream that way.

Leaving Chee in charge at the rancheria, I took Kasale and ten other riders and headed east. It was an average day's ride to Grey's ranch in the wooded hills on the Chihuahua side, but again we made it in half the time. Grey came to the front door and greeted us. He said he had the rest of the ammunition packed and a bunch of broomtails in the corral yonder. When he mentioned that he was "Jim" to his friends, I dismounted and shook hands with him.

We picked up ten cases of shells and tied one on each side behind the cantle on five saddles. Grey had several wranglers help us cut out my choice of thirty broomtails from the corral. Those broncos were as wild as the north wind. Obviously some riders were going to have fun breaking them to the saddle. The Tarahumari would have that pleasure. Instead of crossing the canyon, we drove to the Bavispe flats and crossed below Basaranca. This was the long way home, but an easier trail on which to control the broncos; also this trail went by the Tarahumari camp in the mountain meadow. We left the broncos there.

The next day I took the same group of braves and we rode to Rancho Verde where Buck Green pointed out the remaining fifteen horses he had corralled for us. He rode with us to the great San Bernardino ranch of John Slaughter where we tarried only long enough to pick up the thirty horses promised us by Jess Fisher, the foreman.

These thirty horses were good ones: half-feral, half-domestic snip-nosed Barbarie referred to as "Barbs" and prized by all good cowboys. We herded them back to Rancho Verde, camped there for the night, and the following afternoon we were back in our rancheria.

Now, with two herds of horses, saddles, a stock of new carbines and ammunition, our combined tribes were a fairly well-equipped force, determined to defend our homelands, come what may.

🌷 🌷 🌷

THE days had passed swiftly since our visit with Tom Jeffords. Our people were starting with the harvest; the weather was clear, warm by day and chilly by night. It was the autumnal equinox, 1896.

The trail crew rode in from a seven-day round trip to Bisbee. Hi-okee, the leader, reported everything was as ordered, but while crossing the Naco-zari hills they had once taken refuge in a rock canyon while a group of fifty heavily armed red-shirts rode past. With eight-to-one odds against them, they had employed Apache concealment strategy instead of battle tactics and had come through without firing a shot.

That evening Chee was late in coming to the council fire. He reported seeing through the telescope a column of soldiers moving up the Bavispe Bend and heading eastward toward Chihuahua.

In the morning I called Kasale; he came right over. I told him to turn over the new supplies to the Tarahumari and let their chief make the distribution. He nodded and walked away. When I yelled after him, he whirled and came back. I told him just to get the stuff ready, I'd ride over and fetch the Tarahumari. He nodded and, this time, ran. Old Reliable, always willing. Before I had finished my coffee, a boy came with my saddled horse.

The Tarahumari camp was a beehive of activity; many brush huts with thatched roofs were already up and more were being built. Beyond them was a pen half-full of goats, a cattle corral with a partial roof, several brush-and-rock corrals teeming with horses, and in back was a yard with riders on bucking horses!

Chief Jemez rode out to greet me. After praising him for his people's accomplishments, I told him of the supplies ready to be picked up. He said he would send men to get them. He invited me to have *cerveza* with him. They had no tables as yet, so we sat on the ground and sipped the green beer that a pregnant young woman served us.

"My wife," he explained. "I did not notice if you have a wife. Do you have one?"

"We have more young men than young women," I replied and changed the subject. "I am thinking of sending several of my warriors to your camp to advise you on Apache offensive and defensive strategy. We must coordinate our forces in case of an emergency."

"I had not thought about that. I have been thinking only of food and shelter for my people."

"There are many nuts to be gathered up there." I pointed east to the pine and piñon forest. "There are groves of mescal and mesquite loaded with beans there." I pointed to the rolling hills to the west. "For meat you will find many deer, and bighorns and turkeys come down to these meadows for the winter. Your men should not have much trouble finding meat for your people. But no shooting, unless there is trouble. The sound of gunfire travels far in the mountains—although the *soldatos* are seldom seen in the winter. Use bows and arrows, and traps."

🌱 🌱 🌱

I WAS not home more than a half hour when the Tarahumari came with Jemez leading. Behind him rode ten young women and about thirty men brought up the rear. They headed for the stack of supplies, but Jemez dismounted and walked up to me.

"I have brought a present—you may give these women to your young men."

I gave the women another glance and called, "Dee-O-Det, come here!" Finally he showed up. "Dee-O-Det," I said, "here are some fine maidens. They are to be given to our unmarried young men. How long has it been since you have married a couple?"

Completely ignoring me, he began to chant in Apache, "This is good! This is good! Now we will be strong. Ten strong maidens and ten strong young men I will marry this night!"

"Hold your horses!" I interrupted. "It seems to me you are in one big hurry to get these girls married off!"

"The quicker the better, my chief!"

"Now you listen to me, you old coot, and you listen well. These maidens will get the privilege of choosing their own mates, and they will have the regular ceremony, you hear?"

But that old *shaman* never heard a word I said. Mother arrived and took charge of the girls. The first thing she did was to feed them, then she took them to the garden spring and made them take baths. She found a large wikiup for them and they were allowed outside only as a group. Word of their arrival had spread and already our young men were gathering nearby.

But Apache lovemaking was a complicated ritual. For instance, since the maidens were given to me, the young men had to offer me a price for them. That's what I thought until Mother set me straight on the Law of The People. Since I myself had no wife it was Mother that had to be reckoned with. In other words, she was the "Mother" of all those maidens. Had I been married, my wife would have been the mother of them, since they were a present to me.

I realized that old Dee-O-Det was going to override the custom. But I made up my mind that every girl was going to have the proper wedding ceremony. When I accosted the *shaman* about this, he informed me I had changed our ways of living on the grounds that the old ways did not fit the world of today. I pointed out that my changes were for a better life, not to change from *Usen* to the whiteman's God. I would never change *Usen's* wedding ceremony.

"Then it shall not be changed," he said reluctantly, "but how will you get them to marry?"

"*Usen* will see to that. Our young men will do the rest."

"Will you take one for yourself? An unmarried chieftain is never heard of . . ."

"I do not want to talk about that," I said flatly.

He had an inscrutable smile on his face as he walked away. Mother called me into our wikiup.

"My son, this is Maria—Maria Jemez."

Chapter 10 1896

Golden Bird

THERE COMES a time in every man's life when The
Woman comes along. That woman can undermine a man's
mental stability as quick as a wink—and make him like it. This
was that time in my life. When mother introduced Maria
Jemez, as I recall it, my mind did flip-flops.

She was, indeed, a dainty bit of femininity. Slim and lithe as
a fawn, the top of her head came just to my shoulder. Her glossy
black hair encircled an oval face of unbelievable golden hue.
Her black eyes sparkled like stars. I gulped and ducked out of
the door. There was much giggling going on as I left.

I went over to the *shaman's* wikiup. I told him he was right;
an unmarried chief is never heard of, and that I would be heard
from. He gave me an appraising look and dug up a jug of
whisky. That old coot and I had the biggest drunk I ever had;
I do not mean *one* of the biggest, I mean *the* biggest. There has
never been another to match it. When it was over three days
later and my mother got through telling me my conduct and
that of the *shaman* was beneath our dignity and that we had
spoiled the wedding plans, I did not feel so good. Neither did my
partner of the three days' revelry.

When I was able to ride, I took four men and four pack mules
and headed for Rancho Verde. Buck Green, standing on his
front porch, waved us in. A big veranda with two benches and
a swing ran the length of the tamarack-shaded ranch house
and we all sat down. I began by telling Buck about the need for

a signal system[1] between the ranchers and us up on the mountain, for if a shooting war started, we needed to know what was what. He knew my telescope on Lookout Peak scanned a wide expanse of territory and could even center in on this porch in his snug little valley were it not for the tall trees.

We discussed what to do about Grey's, Brewer's, and Tenny's locations, hidden behind distant mountains. He came up with the idea of using an army-type heliograph to send signals from various high points to be relayed to those ranchers. And if he had a telescope like mine, we could aim them at each other at stated intervals. We could also use the semaphore system. We got into details and decided that since I had the most men, and the kind best adapted, I could send about ten braves each to Brewer and Tenny for liaison work. Grey already had his Yaqui. Our Indians would act as couriers as well as scouts and/or warriors in a group strong enough to hold a regiment of red-flaggers until a stronger force could come.

We needed an organization strong enough to repel any force Torres or Terrazas could send against us at any time. Buck said that Colonel William C. Greene—his uncle and silent partner—had recently protested to President Diaz, who replied that he was unable to give us armed support at this time and that we must defend ourselves. Diaz also pointed out that he had little control over the taxes to be paid. That was up to the governors.

We talked over a code system of signals that would be acceptable to our compatriots. A former U. S. Cavalryman, Buck described the Signal Corps system of heliostat flashes by day and lantern swings by night. He said he would get a heliograph outfit from Grey and mount it on the roof of his barn. Our next problem was how to educate our Indians—especially the Tarahumari, who could not read or write in any language. Tireless runners, they believed in having an objective pointed out to them and running in that direction with the message. Buck agreed to get in touch with the other ranchers, explain our

1. For centuries the Indians had maintained vedette points and signal peaks in the Sierra Madre and other mountains from the Rio Grande to the Rio Colorado—even before the conquistadores invaded Apacheria in 1540. The points were at various distances up to about twenty kilometers apart and were manned at all times; fast runners were used, then riders on fast horses; smoke signals were sent up by day and pitch torches were waved by night. Our code system was a forerunner of the wigwag system used by the Army Signal Corps.

plans, get their cooperation, and then call another meeting. His wife, Anna, called us in for a quick dinner and we all sat at the long table: Mexican Mixtecas, Apache warriors, a white family. It never occurred to any of us that we were setting an example of interracial solidarity; we were friends with a common cause and that was that.

From there my men and I took the little-used road that wound through the canyons to Campo and Fronteras. It was dark when we arrived at Pablo's. The *sillero* had the last few saddles done, but not all of the bandoliers and shell pouches I had ordered on my previous trip. He promised to work all night if we would wait. We made camp beside the nearby water hole and after an uncomfortable night, and with only tortillas for breakfast, we finally loaded up and headed home.

It was late afternoon when we arrived at the rancheria. I was warmly greeted by Mother and Maria, but I pretended I was still a little put out and returned their greetings with a grunt. Maria reached out to take the reins of my horse. This was obviously some of Mother's skullduggery, but I said nothing and gave her the reins. She led the horse toward the corral, and I went over to Chee's wikiup but found he wasn't home. I went back to our fire.

Mother had arranged a table nearby for the five maidens still unmarried. But tonight she placed Maria at our table on my left. Now, I thought, this mother of mine is getting me bound and bundled. Well, so be it! When the food was served, out of the clear sky I asked:

"Do you like me, Maria?"

"Niño!" Mother exclaimed. "That is no way to do. You must not ask such questions where others can hear."

I repeated, "Maria, do you like me?"

She nodded, eyes downcast.

"Enju," (I have spoken) I said, using the tone which meant that was all.

"Ciyè!" (Son) said Mother.

"Ci'cima." (Yes, Mother)

"You have embarrassed Maria."

"She does not mind, do you, Maria"?

The golden tint of her face was flushed like rose gold as she shook her head. My mother beamed.

When I was through eating I stood up. I didn't know what I had done to that poor girl, but her eyes were like black diamonds as I walked away. It occurred to me that my idioms in her Tarahumari tongue were as strange to her as my Apache was, but I didn't care. I left and went to old Dee-O-Det's wikiup, intending to inquire into a point of the wedding-ceremonial law. The *shaman* wasn't home, or else he saw me coming, for he did not answer my call. When I returned to the table, Chief Jemez and Chief Emiliano were there, drinking coffee.

As I took my place beside Maria, she leaned closer to me; Mother pulled her by the arm and got her to move away. This bit of by-play made her father beam, but flustered my mother. I pulled Maria right back and whispered that we would take a walk. There were rules that maidens could not be alone with their chosen until they had their rights bestowed upon them by the *shaman,* but I said we would change that. She looked at my mother askance, but I used a little more gentle persuasion and we walked off with my arm around her waist—and right into the *shaman!*

The *shaman* gave me an enigmatic look and turned away. When he was out of sight, I took the trembling girl into my arms and pressed a long kiss on her lips. I could feel her body go limp. I led her back to our table.

🌿🌿🌿

THE council was called. I took the center and told of the events of the past few days and of future plans. I explained Apache battle tactics to the Tarahumari and the Opatas; my intention was to change these primitive Indians into hunters instead of being the hunted.

In the morning my head was full of Maria. I got back to normal as survival problems crowded into my mind. I saddled my favorite mount, a big sorrel stud, and rode out to see how our cattle were doing. I met Maria on the trail. Not too surprised, I asked: "Where are you going, Maria?"

"Just riding—I am . . ."

"Do Tarahumari girls, when they are to marry, meet their chosen just by accident?"

"It is not so to be, oh—but we always manage."

"Enju." I laughed. "How did you know where I was going?"

"We of the Tarahumari are trackers good. Tell me, my Niño, does *enju* mean what?"

"When *atá*[2] says *enju,* it means I am glad, satisfied, it is good, it is enough, I have spoken—depends on the inflection," I replied, chuckling over the way she got her words mixed up.

"Glad that I came, oh, are you? Glad I came I am. Ride with you may I?" she warbled in rapid order. "Going where, are you go?"

I pointed south toward Mummy Mountain, and made a circular motion, meaning to ride around it. She questioned the wisdom of riding in circles, but I pointed out to her that if she wanted to be the wife of an Apache chieftain, she must obey his wishes without question. I did not explain to her that my purpose was to size up two old animal trails that led to Mummy's top—up-and-down trails to the summit where I wanted to set up a signal station. We circled around to the far side, talking and laughing—changing only once or twice to the serious things of life. At the summit we dismounted, sat down, and viewed the mountain world.

It was sundown when we arrived back at the rancheria. Mother, intently eyeing us, wanted to know where we had been. I told her we'd met by accident while I was inspecting our livestock and grazing conditions. I again took Maria by the hand and led her to the *shaman's* wikiup. The way I saw it, five days had passed since our betrothal. Time was drawing near; when I mentioned that, she giggled and squeezed my hand. At the *shaman's* I called, "Dee-O-Det, are you home?"

"No! But come in. I am just preparing to start the old puberty ceremoney—and you wish me to instruct Maria?"

"You and your foresight!" I said under my breath.

I turned to leave and Maria started to follow, but he detained her, saying:

"I will acquaint you with our puberty and nuptial rituals.

2. The word *atá* is a puzzler to non-Indians and frequently to the Apaches themselves. It might stem from P. Tomas Manso himself. (Manso was the only Spanish Missionary who had any good influence on the Apaches, circa 1626–1656.) It means various things: I, me, you, he, him, she, her and sometimes they or them, depending on how it is used, the nuance or the emphasis.

After today you cannot look upon Niño until the moon has had his fourth look, and then you may only touch him to indicate he is to be your husband. Then you must go into the abode of White Painted Maiden and there answer questions of all who ask, except your chosen. He will not be allowed to see you until the fifth day, and then, my child, you will be wed and you will go with him to the sacred wikiup and you will stay there with him for a quarter moon. After that you and he will come back and live with The People forever. That is Apache law."

He led the mystified girl to the seclusion of the big wikiup reserved for the maidens.

Back at our fire, Mother said I must eat at Chee's fire until the wedding, as she would be busy preparing costumes for the bride to wear. She whispered that ours would be a Chockonen high ritual such as few here in Pa-Gotzin-Kay had ever seen, except the Ancient Ones. She recalled with pride when she had had that sacred ceremony and the great Nochalo was the *sha-man*. The High Chief, my grandfather, gave them their first present—the baskets that we ate cold meat from—and those she would give my bride as our wedding gift.

That revelation did something to me. Tears almost began in the corners of my eyes. I hugged my mother, and knew at that moment she was the best friend I would ever have. When she disappeared into the maiden's sanctuary, it seemed that she was going forever, and a great loneliness came over me.

I went to Chee's wikiup. Chee was sewing, modifying his bandolier. I watched for a while, then asked how he was coming with the lookout stations. He said he and Kasale had run tests that worked fine, both day and night. They flashed and got return flashes from Buck Green's ranch.

With the big event four days and nights away, I decided that in the morning I'd take a ride all by myself. I needed something different to do. I needed to refresh my memory on some old vedette locations and I'd try to scout a new trail to the Chihuahua side, a trail that might come in handy one of these days.

In the morning I had breakfast at Chee's. Ealae fed us beans with chili, coffee, and ashcakes made of mesquite flour and beef-tallow shortening—a standard diet in those days. I told Chee I intended to take a ride and asked him to come along.

Young Emiliano was cleaning out our horse stalls when we

arrived, and I motioned toward the sorrel. He eagerly bridled the stud, and as I cinched my saddle on his back, it was apparent the Opata lad was popping with curiosity. So I told him Chee and I were going to try to find another trail along the east face of Huachinero Mountain. He quickly informed me he knew of such a trail—an old bighorn trail—that he would be happy to show me. I told him to get a horse out of the corral and bring a rifle.

He was soon mounted, armed with one of our old Remingtons in the saddle boot, with bulging saddlebags, and with a bandolier of shells over his shoulder. I asked him how old he was and he said he was twenty summers, he thought. So, he was only two years younger than I, yet I had taken him to be about fourteen. He was small and his thin face seemed to be that young —another example of the Mexican Indian's starvation existence. I had another idea. I told him I would make him a war chief under his father with six men: two of his Opata, two Tarahumari, and two Apache. He bounced in his saddle as if he were sitting on cholla burrs, and gleefully said he knew how to lead men and fight—like the bushmaster!

I told him I wanted him to fight like an Apache, and to lead the way now. The three of us rode—mostly in silence—until the sun was nearly overhead. We entered a deep gorge—one of those narrow clefts into which the sun shines only at high noon —where the trail was so narrow one's stirrups touched both sides. No horse could have turned around here, but it was a great short cut for anyone riding east or west. I called a halt when we emerged on a promontory. Before us lay a picture of barren brown-and-craggy terrain, of hills and hollows of bare lava buttes on the volcanic side of the Sierra Madre—nothing like our green Pa-Gotzin-Kay.

I asked young Emiliano about water, and he said there was water only where the *ocho rios* join—even then somtimes one has to dig for it. When I asked why "eight rivers" he said they were rivers only when it rained. He pointed northeast and told of a Yaqui village about three small canyons over, a barrio of Kelzel's. He mentioned a small spring in Naranja Canyon about halfway there. I asked if Kelzel was his friend, and he said he knew of him but did not trust him. On further thought he mentioned having as a friend a *Yaqui-Yori* named Doroteo

Arango[3], who was Kelzel's nephew and a small chief. But since the *Rurales* were hunting him he must be a good friend.

We voted for that "small spring in Naranja Canyon" and found it in a brush-clogged grove of hoary orange trees and what remained of some weather-beaten adobe walls. Some long-dead Spaniards had obviously lived there and had planted the Valencia orange trees around their hacienda. We drank, then watered our horses. The sun had passed its zenith and we were hungry. Chee and I had forgotten to bring food, but Emiliano came to the rescue with turkey jerky and mesquite cakes. It was a hot afternoon as we sat on the wall by the spring and ate. The salty meat increased our thirst but there was plenty of good water.

We climbed back up the bighorn trail, then circled south along the up-Bavispe rimrock, from which, had we had field glasses, we could have spied on one of Kelzel's rancherias along the Yaqui Bend. This had turned into another one of those 100-kilometer rides, and it was nearly midnight when we reined in at the home corral. At the compound I saw that there was nothing cooking over Chee's fire, but there was activity at the big wikiup of the maidens. Obviously one or more would be getting married in the morning. Chee's wife sleepily put out some food, and after eating, I spent the night in Ticer's old wikiup.

❧ ❧ ❧

THREE more days dragged by, then came the big night: the time of the choosing. That evening the White Swan Dance started and everything was in order. Dancers with white plume fans were performing, gyrating around the *shaman* and his specially built altar while he sprinkled *hodenten* on them to ensure fertility. They moved to a dry tree that symbolized barrenness. A very old woman and a young woman were standing nearby, both wrapped in the same blanket. The *shaman* began to chant. The young woman held forth an ear of corn and waved it over the heads of the dancing maidens. The old

3. The Yaqui name of the man later called in America Francisco Pancho Villa.

woman attempted to wave a twig of the dry tree, and the young woman fought her and dislodged the twig from her grasp. The young woman again waved the corn.

I felt a hand on my arm. I turned and saw Maria, who turned and walked away. I started to follow but Nadina pulled me back.

The maidens were taken by my mother to the abode of White Painted Maiden, their part of the ceremony had come to a close. That night I dreamed that my Maria was really White Painted Maiden . . . and as her husband I was made Chief of the Spirit World. I had hardly begun my reign when I was awakened by someone hammering on a piece of iron. I dressed and went to Chee's; Ealae had breakfast ready. I sat down with the problem of last night's dream. After eating a little I headed for the *sha-man's*. He pretended to be busy at his altar but I demanded an audience.

"Now, what troubles you, young man?" he asked in his most dignified manner. "If you had a dream—forget it!" he snapped. "Most young men about to get married do . . ."

"Dee-O-Det, I have come to my *shaman* for advice. Instead he ridicules me."

"I have asked what the trouble was."

"The dream—the dream I had—I think it was symbolic. I dreamed that my Maria really was White Painted Maiden and she made me Chief of the Spirit World. Then just as I was beginning to rule, I was awakened by someone hammering."

"Humm. Humm. That was a good omen. It means that you will never be slain in earthly battles. You may live forever. Some go to Big Sleep and sleep forever, while others go and come back to live again and again . . . when they become used to the Spirit World they live forever. Humm, yes. You are a chosen one—you will never have fear . . ."

I left him, my head more in a whirl than ever. To pass the time I went to the barn and helped Boa Juan, Neo-O-Toden, and Nah-Shis-Tor shoe some new mustangs—and twice nearly got my head kicked off.

At dawn of the fifth day I was awakened by Nadina. She placed an armful of clothes by my bed and motioned to me to hurry. And hurry I did. I made a swift examination of the clothes, holding my breath. Here was the finest costume of

Indian regalia I had ever seen. I did not stop to wonder where those two women of mine had acquired the ceremonial costume; I just proceeded to put it on.

There was a headpiece of woven wool in three colors, artistically encrusted with agate and turquoise; it fitted snugly and held my hair in a roll over my shoulders. The jacket was knee-length, trimmed with beaver fur; the *kabuns* were knee-high, turned up at the toes, the most comfortable I had ever worn. The entire outfit was made of bleached elkskin and embroidered with thousands of tiny shells and beads. While getting dressed I heard the people singing, led in the rituals by the *shaman* as he kept time with his sacred spirit rattles. There seemed to be so many voices with an un-Apache accent that I guessed the whole Tarahumari tribe was on hand for the wedding ceremony. The songs ceased suddenly and became a chant:

> *White Painted Maiden,*
> *Her day for the ceremony of long life . . .*

Hurriedly I stepped outside. Then I saw Maria! She had just emerged from the big wikiup and begun the slow, measured steps of an actress making her dramatic entrance upon the stage—this was *her* day indeed!

The crowd continued to chant:

> *White Painted Maiden*
> *Lift your eyes to the sun.*
> *White Painted Maiden*
> *Bright in the sun.*

Maria's face was radiant in its golden hue; her head was bare, her glossy black hair combed and brushed out over her shoulders; and she was clad in a cloak of spotted jaguar-kitten fur. The gold armband of the Apache diety was around her left arm, and on her breast was the symbol of the rising sun—a hammered plaque of gold the size of her hand. It hung by a strand of gold cord studded with agate. It rested on a shield, painted on her silk bodice in the four colors that represented the earth, water, sky, and sun—*terte, quesa, mie,* and *holos.* Her breasts were firm, rising and falling under the multicolored shield. Her full dress—made of hundreds of white moleskins—spread out far behind her, and she advanced with the majestic mien of a princess accepting the acclaim of her people.

Drums were beating and the people were both cheering and singing. I felt a tug at my arm; it was Nadina. When I hesitated as if still in a dream, she repeated the tug. She walked part of the way with me and I managed the rest to where the *shaman* was bending over his altar; he pointed to where I was to stand.

Maria's father and mother joined her and brought her to a place beside me; stalwart To-Clany took a position along the other side; the people crowded closer. The drums upped their tempo for a time, then softened to a low rhythm, but the people kept up their chanting. The adulation to White Painted Maiden went on, adding more stanzas. Dee-O-Det, chanting to himself, picked up his silver ceremonial knife and held it high.

Suddenly the rancheria became quiet. While the *shaman* continued to hold his pose, my knees began to ache. I felt Maria sway a little, and I wondered if it were proper to lend her a steadying hand.

Finally the *shaman* stooped, picked up and then raised a long pine-needle-tipped wand in his right hand, and moved it in a stately arc above our bowed heads. A breeze, fragrant with conifer scent, stirred around us; *hodenten* dusted down on us. Maria began to tremble and, custom or not, I took her arm.

The *shaman* knelt before the altar facing us, reached across, and motioned for our hands. He gently grasped Maria's right hand. With his knife he swiftly made an incision in her wrist. He quickly grabbed my left hand and made an incision in my wrist. Her mother held Maria's hand, a *shaman's* assistant grasped mine, and Dee-O-Det quickly bound our bleeding wrists together. I could feel the throb of our excited pulses as our blood mixed. The crowd began to sing:

> *Now for you there is no weather;*
> *For one is shelter to the other.*
> *Now for you there is no fear;*
> *For one is protection to the other.*[4]

4. Songs for wedding ceremonials are joyous praise offered for the everlasting sun, the endless sky, the fragrant air, the majestic mountains, the great rivers, the might of warriors, the chastity of women, the glories of White Painted Maiden. And above all to *Usen* who gives us all these things for which we thank Him—but we never beseech Him.

As they pressed forward singing, sometimes the same verse, sometimes new ones, always in the same rhythm, Dee-O-Det again sprinkled *hodenten* on our heads. His voice boomed:

"There are two bodies, but now there is one blood in both and they are one and the same person." He pulled the binding from around our wrists. *"Enju!"*

We were surrounded, yelled at, pummeled, gifts were thrown at us. The great ceremonial cape hindered Maria, so I lifted it off her, shrugged out of my beaver-trimmed jacket, and tossed them both to my mother.

Maria pulled on my hand; we broke clear and began to run, soon gaining on the following crowd. She led me to some cedar trees along the cliff-base where two boys were holding two matching white horses, saddled with the finest gear.

The horses carried the R/V brand; I had not noticed Buck Green around that morning, but good old Buck had furnished those white horses. We mounted and rode south through the rampart, then over a ridge crowned with autumn-gold trees. Beyond, in a small level glen between jutting boulders but almost hidden by a clump of ancient piñon trees, snuggled an inviting wikiup. Its open door faced east in the direction of the Mother Mountains.

We dismounted and tethered the white horses to the nearest tree. Arm-in-arm, Maria and I entered the wikiup. The interior seemed like another world, although it was furnished with the best of Indian handicrafts. There was food and drink if we wanted it—even my cougarskin was there. The air was rich with the aroma of autumn conifers and tiny bells tinkled as I closed the door. Maria came closer into my arms. We were really and truly in a world of our own.

🌷 🌷 🌷

MORNING came and a golden glow seemed to fill our honeymoon castle. I stepped outside. The world reflected the incredible blue of the endless sky and the sun beamed down in all its glory. The canella mountains and red canyons were spread clear and calm in the transparent air.

As Maria came and took my arm, the sun enhanced the gold

of her skin, and from that moment on I called her my Golden Bird.

She began to tease me into making a fire; her voice warbled like a sage wren singing its morning song. It was traditional that the bride should prepare the first meal for her husband. She gave me the fireboard and drill and I twirled it. A wisp of smoke soon came from the fireboard and she blew on the sparks. A small blaze started and I eased the kindling off the board onto twigs piled below.

Whatever it was she prepared for our first breakfast I don't remember, but she insisted the *shaman* had instructed her to take me to the spring for our first drink. When we got to the spring I had to brush the ferns away so I could dip up an olla full of the cool water. Arm-in-arm, we started back to the wikiup, playfully jostling each other, spilling water on ourselves.

The day raced by. When the moon came up, we boosted each other to our feet. If old *Gotchamo* in that moon was watching us, he must have thought we were the craziest two people on the face of the earth. Back in the wedding wikiup, we ate some cakes and then bedded down on the cougarskin.

More days passed, making love, having fun, laughing; we laughed at everything, including the world and ourselves. A woman is naturally helpless when in a laughing mood—at least an Indian woman is—and on a honeymoon what woman needs to be anything but helpless with her husband around?

We ate when the pangs of hunger overtook us. The Apache honeymoon lasted ten days when observed traditionally, but the days passed uncounted as neither of us thought to keep track. The one event that might have been irritating under ordinary circumstances occurred about the sixth day. There were two quail left in the frying pan from our previous meal and we were very hungry. I made a fire, and Golden Bird filled the coffeepot and put it on to boil. Then she removed the quail, poured water in the pan, and as it heated she swabbed a rag on a stick around in the pan a couple of times. She wiped the pan dry, put the quail back in, set the pan on the fire, and knelt close to watch that it did not burn. I knelt beside her to move the coffeepot to a better position and the little imp bit my ear.

I bit right back. Before we were through playing, the pan was wreathed with blue smoke and the quail were burned black. We wound up going to bed without supper, but you are only young once.

Early in the morning, I awoke hungry. My Golden Bird was still in dreamland. I dressed quietly, took the bow and arrows, and went to the spring. Just before I got there, I heard turkeys clucking and saw several about twenty steps away. I fitted an arrow, loosed it, and it sped true, impaling a fat young gobbler. I had him dressed out when Maria came to the spring. That day passed all too quickly.

The following morning the two white horses were back, saddled and tied to the nearest tree—the *shaman* was keeping tabs on us. It was his way of telling us it was time to pack up and come back—the honeymoon was over.

My thought switched to reality and almost gave me a headache. Maria, too, looked sad. We followed an old deer trail and soon were on Lookout Mountain. I helped my bride to the ground and we walked to the telescope. Hi-okee popped out of concealment beyond a nearby rock and greeted us.

He told me Buck Green had sent a signal message that Torres had notified him that if he did not pay his taxes in thirty days, the state would foreclose on his property. The other ranchers did not get the same warning and Buck thought this was some trick. Nevertheless Chee had taken Kasale, Jemez, and Emiliano and they had gone down to Rancho Verde for a conference.

Maria and I mounted. We walked our horses down the steep rocky slope until we hit the flat area. Then we slapped heels to the white Barbs and fairly flew into the rancheria.

Chapter 11   1896-1897

Mountain Battery

DEE-O-DET was out to greet us and, as usual, he fired answers before I could ask questions. In my absence he had received several urgent messages from Buck Green, saying that conditions were worsening between the ranchers and the generals, and the Mexicans were accusing the Americans of inciting Indians to ride again the trails of war. It was another case of spies crying spy, but after centuries of mistrust between us what could we expect? Buck had called an emergency meeting and Dee-O-Det had sent Mangas-Chee with ten warriors to represent us, telling Chief Jemez to take thirty Tarahumari men and ride along in a display of solidarity.

I knew Chee would do the right thing, but I finally got a question or two asked. Judging from the answers, I decided this was just another case of an old war cloud with a different shape. When I mentioned that, the *shaman* looked away, his wrinkled features inscrutable.

Maria began tugging at my sleeve and pointing—behind Mother's wikiup stood a good-sized cabin made of split logs of pine and cedar. I followed her lead as she ran to the handsome one-room building. The cabin had three windows made of the oiled skins of fawns pulled so thin one could almost see through them. There were cougarskins and bearskins on the floor; serapes and blankets hung along two walls; and a bed was built in the far corner. There was a stone fireplace in the side wall, a moveable table, and a bench pegged to the wall. My rifles and sixguns hung on a wooden peg that projected from the wall above the bed, and there was a coal-oil lamp and a lantern.

Mother came in and, warbling with delight, Maria led us around for a closer inspection; my reaction was that for once I'd have a warm cabin, like Buck's. Mother, pleased with Maria's reaction, finally said she had food ready for us. We went over and Dee-O-Det was at her table, already eating. Eyeing Maria and me he remarked it was a cruel fate that brought us ten maidens to build up our people, only to let war come and destroy us. I told him to stop worrying and eat, and he said all the white ranchers were agreed not to pay the tax that Terrazas and Torres demanded, so what could I expect? Irked, I told him this still did not mean war. The generals would settle for a reasonable tax when they saw the cattlemen meant business. He sighed with relief, took a bigger bite than ever and, chomping away, said something about the optimism of youth.

🌱🌱🌱

LATER I walked down the path to the garden and sat on my favorite rock to think. Twilight was settling in the canyons when near-silent footsteps aroused me. It was Chee—back from the emergency meeting.

Chee was his usual smooth self as he reported how things looked bad at first, when the ranchers saw a dust cloud and estimated at least 500 men were riding toward Rancho Verde. It turned out there were only sixteen *soldatos,* dragging dead limbs of trees to make believe they were a large force. When they arrived and saw Buck Green was ready for them, they hoisted the white flag.

Their leader was *El Carneicero* (The Butcher) Batista, now *Capitán-general* of Police in Basaranca. He said Governor General Torres had instructed him to collect such taxes as the ranchers thought due, and that next year there would be a set tax which the governor believed would meet the ranchers' approval. Buck gave him 500 pesos gold, got a receipt, and they left. Buck now thought that as long as we Apaches were on his side, Torres would not start a ruckus around here.

That sounded simple enough; but judging from what little I knew about Torres, I didn't think he was the kind of Mexican who would back down so easily. I gave Chee a nod and we headed for the council fire. The *shaman* had already called the men together. He opened the proceedings, and Chee held up both hands for silence.

"Our High Chief had important things to do, so the authority fell upon me to help prevent a war," he said, with a perverse sense of humor. "To Buck Green goes all the glory—he did the negotiating. My warriors and I stood by to win or die. We won; there will be no war—at least not until next spring."

Someone asked in a loud voice:

"Did our High Chief attend to those 'important things' he had to do?"

"Yes. He seems to have had a wearing time."

This bit of innuendo brought laughter from the men.

"You had a report to make, Chief?" Chee grinned.

Before I could respond, someone uttered an impolite remark and this in turn brought laughter—also reprimands when the men got home. After that meeting, every man in the clan got the cold shoulder, I heard later. My mother nagged poor Dee-O-Det just for laughing. Ny-Oden, one of my youngest fast-talking, slow-acting warriors was the big one who asked at the council if I had done my important thing. He had missed out on getting himself a Tarahumari maiden—he claimed he was sparking over at Chief Kelzel's with a "wacky Yaqui," as he called their women, because they shout "wacky" when they cheer their men in handball games. He got derided by his own family, his mother and grandmother nagging him for being too slow to get himself a wife. Now he and Boa Juan were the only two young men not married.

Chee, unabashed, and Ealae came over later to see the inside of our cabin; he had helped to build it while we were honeymooning. After a quick look around, he remarked he was going to build a new one with three rooms—one for his four children —Ealae added they would put in an iron stove, so she would not have to cook outside when it rained.

"That good!" my Golden Bird exclaimed. "No more hair wet —wet foots!"

I resolved then and there to buy a stove on our next trip to Bisbee, one that could be taken apart for easy packing. And to let everybody in general know who was boss in this new wikiup

I told Chee to get packers and twelve good pack mules ready for a trip to Bisbee.

In the morning when I awoke there was no Golden Bird by my side. She was busy at the fireplace. She chirped that food was ready, gave me a kiss, and helped me with my tight riding boots. After breakfast I saddled our white Barbs, and Maria and I rode first to Chief Emiliano's camp. I caught sight of young Emiliano and called to him; I told him that we were going to Bisbee and I wanted him to help get mules, horses, and trail gear ready. He almost fell over his own feet, he was so eager to do his full share.

Next Maria and I loped over to her father's rancheria. It was, as expected, a camp bustling with active people. After the usual amenities with her mother and father, I told him what I wanted. He called an order and soon four good men were ready to help. Back at our rancheria we laid out trail equipment, making certain everything was in good shape. I was very glad for this help as most of my best men were still with the ranchers, helping them with their fall roundups, even though the red-flagger scare had passed. Through it all Maria was at my side or at my heels, helping, laughing, or humming a cheerful tune.

❧ ❧ ❧

THE following day we were out bright and early. Emiliano helped to saddle the white Barbs and the little pinto Mother liked to ride. Jemez and his four men joined us, and I noticed that the *shaman* had no trouble mounting his single-footer bay gelding. Dee-O-Det was a remarkable man—one of our legendary characters. Thin and leathery like all old Indian men, he was nearly 100 years of age. According to his own calculations, his only child had her puberty rites "the night the stars fell."[1] Now, in November, 1896, his thinning white mane hung over his shoulders, but his narrow-lidded eyes were still keen and sparkling.

There is something about riding long distances that is not

1. A comet in 1835. AKG.

conducive to talk. Even Dee-O-Det rode mostly in silence, but late in the afternoon he made a pithy remark about young men who would take an old man off on a long ride and fail to remind him to bring his favorite saddle pad.

Evening shadows were settling in the Piñon Springs meadow, although the sun was still shining on the surrounding peaks, when I ordered camp made for the night. Deciding to go hunting, I took my twelve-guage Ithaca double-barreled scatter gun and headed for the nearby pyracantha brush. Maria tagged along. Maybe she brought me good luck—I got eighteen cotton-tail rabbits with ten shots. The women cleaned and broiled them. The *shaman* was still in a silent mood, but he ate one whole rabbit and two corncakes, washing them down with water. We could bring no coffee on this trip; we were out of it at the rancheria.

Everyone, tired, started making their beds; Maria made ours far back from the fire, the *shaman* made his near the fire. He remarked he was not tired but might as well bed down as there was nothing else to do; I sided in with him, saying I felt I could have ridden 100 kilometers this day. Mother said we spoke with a crooked tongue and should go to bed.

In the morning, while the other men got the animals saddled and packed, Dee-O-Det, Jemez, and I watched and talked. We discussed hectares of land; number of weeks in a growing season in the midlands vs. the lowlands; how much corn and bean seed should be planted next spring to feed 400 people.

As we rode out, old Dee-O-Det began to sing. When a *shaman* sings it is *something* to hear, but this time it wasn't so bad.

> *When you plant in the spring,*
> *You hope in the summer it will bring,*
> *A good harvest in the fall,*
> *A good life if there is enough for all.*

🌱 🌱 🌱

LATE on the third afternoon we neared Naco Springs near Bisbee. Alchise, who was our outrider, came loping back and reported two whitemen were camped at our usual spot. I signalled the column to close up and we rode in, halting in a loose semicircle facing the two cowboys at the water hole. We stared silently at them and they glowered back, but not for long. The odds of fourteen trail-hardened, mounted Indians with twelve big pack mules had an overwhelming effect—especially when the mules began to push on to the water. Muttering about a bunch of "goddam greaser Injun," the cowboys packed up and rode out, heading west toward the Chivatera hills.

Everyone had comments and laughs over the incident as we unsaddled our animals and watered them. We made camp but decided it was too late to go into town to do the buying, so for supper we made do with what little we had left in our packs. Then Chief Jemez and I thought we would walk in and look around. Young Emiliano overheard us and begged to come along. He had never been in Bisbee nor had Jemez, so it was up to me to guide them. I asked the other men to remain in camp, then we three went into town. Emiliano, wide-eyed over the many strange sights, soon became a nuisance so we left him to watch a cockfight while we went into the Copper Queen Saloon. The bartender greeted me and asked, "In for supplies?"

The smell of the saloon excited my taste buds and I promptly forgot my good intentions to stay sober. The barman must have noticed this for he slid a bottle and two glasses to us, saying, "I've got plenty Monongahela in outsize barrels. I got small ten-galloners and the large twenties."

"I'll be in to load up tomorrow. Tonight I'm celebrating."

"Your friend, the tall guy with the red whiskers—ah—Tom Jeffords, how come he didn't come in?"

"Oh, he's busy these days, but he'll be in . . ."

I paid him and we took the bottle and went outside; we sat on a sidewalk bench and soon Jemez and I were feeling fine. When the bottle was empty I went in and bought another, and then took a notion to go back to my Golden Bird. Crossing the field back to camp I tripped and fell, almost breaking the bottle. Jemez helped me up, though he wasn't in any better shape himself.

We had two irate women on our hands when we got to camp —not for getting drunk but for staying away so long. Maria had had all kinds of forebodings. She thought those cowboys might catch me off guard and kill me. I was able to talk her out of her anger, but not Mother. Dee-O-Det meanwhile got the bottle; he jerked the cork out with his teeth, tipped the bottle skywards, took a deep breath, and tipped it again. I grabbed it away from him. Mother snatched it away from me, saying, "You have had enough."

"I will have one more," I said and wrenched the bottle from her grasp.

"Hako!"[2] she snapped.

"I too am a *Hako*," said Jemez, "and will have one more."

"And I," said the *shaman*.

"Hakos!" my mother snapped. When the bottle was returned to her it was empty. "Hakos!" she repeated contemptuously and threw away the empty bottle.

Jemez and I lay down and passed out on the spot. I woke with the sunlight hurting my eyes and my stomach full of butterflies. I made my way to the spring where I found Jemez.

"Is that water any good?" I mumbled.

"That is a dumb question," he gurgled.

When we got back to the fire there was no one around, but then I found the forgotten young Emiliano lying flat on his back and snoring softly. I toed him awake and he said some man gave him red wine, but he was able to come back to camp. He, too, needed water. My hangover began wearing off a little, and we talked about this and that until I saw Maria coming across the field, running as only she could run. Boa Juan and Ny-Oden were following her, walking, so I knew there was nothing amiss. I went out to meet her, and the sunlight accented her happy face, although it was no longer the golden natural color I loved so much; she had ridden too many sun-drenched trails with me.

"Your mother the mules wants you to load," she said rapidly.

Jemez called loudly for his men and they ran over. We all pitched in and soon led the mules in to the hitch rail in front of the Phelps-Dodge general store. Mother and Alchise were waiting. She had a mountain of merchandise stacked on the porch, including a Pottstown kitchen stove. At Goldwater's nearby Nadina had bought a pile of wool yarn; it looked as if she had bought out half that store. We finally got everything

2. An insult. The Hakos are a society of people who always take but never give.

packed on eleven mules and I sent Jemez back to camp with them, telling him to get our gear together and I would be there as soon as I took care of one more purchase.

I led the biggest mule across to the rear of the Copper Queen. The saloon-keeper rolled out four ten-gallon kegs of whisky and helped me pack them in pairs, end to end, in heavy tarps. We hefted them up on the *aparejo* and double-diamond-hitched them high on each side of center. For once the best "workhorse" of our mule herd groaned. Figuring at five pounds a gallon for the whisky and fifty pounds for the kegs and another forty for the *aparejo,* that ornery mule had a load of nearly 300 pounds. But he was a prime brute and he could take it. I paid the man and led the mule back to camp, where everything was ready—even my white stallion was saddled.

We made Balsa Chipa that night; this was at a fork in our return trail. The other fork curved through the range of the Cananea Cattle Country, part of "Uncle" Bill Greene's domain. It was easy to make fifty to sixty kilometers between dawn and dusk here, even with a loaded pack train. No fences, just a sea of browning grama grass with blue skies above. Three days later we arrived at Pa-Gotzin-Kay shortly after dark.

Along with our whole tribe, Chief Emiliano was there to greet us. I gave the Opata one keg of whisky. I had already turned one keg over to Jemez of the Tarahumari and the other two went into our new cabin for safekeeping, for the time being. The Apache does not steal from the Apache, but that does not mean he will not take a drink. I made my report to the council, then went to bed dog-tired—as did everyone else of the trail crew.

When I got up the next morning I thought I might live another day. After breakfast I saddled my ridge-running roan and headed for Lookout Peak. Hi-okee was on the job manning the telescope. I asked about Chee and learned he was in the guards' wikiup, playing cards with the off-duty men. Hi-okee told me nothing worth mentioning had come up for over a week, but he didn't mind keeping watch—it was either that or gamble, and his Tarahumari wife did not want him to gamble. He said she was a squaw-ballplayer[3] and lost more often than not.

While he was talking, I took several quick squints through

3. Shortly after this incident she was hit on the head by a volley ball during a game and it killed her.

the telescope. I thought to myself that if I had just one more such station on the Chihuahua side, we could command a good view of the vast eastern slopes of the Mother Mountains. Kelzel's main Yaqui rancheria was on the Chihuahua side; but so far he had been evasive about setting up a lookout station there. Anyway, I would put it up to Buck Green, the cattlemen's association having recently elected him their general. He in turn would propose it to Jim Grey, who controlled Chief Kelzel.

Back at the rancheria I felt content: winter lay ahead and the Mexicans had made no new moves; they were not likely to before next spring, so I had plenty of time to plan strategy. But, just in case, I sent Chee and a crew to Magdalena to pick up rumors or facts on any troop movements in the lowlands. Besides, he needed a change, and as he was the tribal mechanic, he wanted to buy a few "extras" such as axes, saws, nails, and other metal items. We had a good harvest that fall and my people would not go hungry. It had been a busy year; now there was time enough to take it easy.

🌱🌱🌱

SPRING of 1897 came, and life on the rancheria perked up with the change of seasons. My thought turned back to the red-flaggers—they would become active with warm weather at hand. Therefore I ordered our garden enlarged, our corn and potato acreage doubled, and got the plowing started. Chee, Jemez, and I coordinated each phase with the Tarahumari so we had plenty of help at both rancherias. The weather was right and the planters started only a day behind the harrowers. Everyone, old and young, had been put to jobs they were best suited for. Dee-O-Det dusted the land with his sacred *hodenten;* Mother made gallons of lemonade for the thirsty and kept everybody busy. Fearing a break in the weather one forenoon, I needled the *shaman* into trying for a miracle to hold back the cold front just half a day so we could finish planting the finicky pintos. To my surprise he accepted my idea and disappeared. When next I saw him he had a crew of six men, each straining under what I thought was an empty whisky keg. He asked me to line up the people in six rows, as he had what was needed to make everybody happy. Not in the least suspicious, I had them line up and each was given a cupful of what looked like and tasted like lemonade—but with a difference. That old fox had filled the whisky-impregnated wooden kegs with lemonade *and* had added a quart of the real stuff to each keg! The field workers went back to their jobs with renewed vigor and finished the bean planting after dark that evening, just before the weather broke. His drink had done it—and that "magic" concoction was known as *"Shaman's* delight" as long as Pa-Gotzin-Kay existed.

❦ ❦ ❦

WE now had everything planted except the potato patch and a few days more would make no difference there. That night I dreamed I had established smoke-signal fires across the vast mountain chain and was receiving word of red-flagger movements from the Chihuahua side.

Next day Maria and I rode north on our white Barbs, pausing for a brief visit at her father's rancheria, then going on through Chi-hua-hua's old rancheria and down to the flats where the sidewash would hide us from curious eyes in Basaranca. We watched for unusual activity for a little while, but it was raining hard so we left. We arrived at Rancho Verde after dark, and Buck Green came in response to my knock.

"Well, howdy! Glad t'see you. Just in time for supper."

He took Maria by the hand and they disappeared into the kitchen; I soon heard women's laughter, along with the clatter of dishes, and used the occasion to grab a quick drink from Buck's bar.

At supper I went into detail about my new signal-system plan. Buck almost stopped eating when I said it would be handled as in the old days when Victorio and Naiche were giving the American cavalry a lot of exercise. He recalled that those two had been great hell-raisers. We would place vedettes at intervals on peaks with signal fires going all day. To signal, green brush balled up in a blanket or a hide, would be put on the hot coals. The man on the next peak would see the smoke and relay it to the next, and so on.

Buck figured that was the best we could do until we got more telescopes and some heliographs, *if* we ever got them! The way things were it took two or three days to ride around from the Chihuahua sides, depending on which trails the courier rode. With signals it would be possible for me to get the message within an hour—and then four or five hours of hard riding would bring me to Rancho Verde.

We were in agreement all the way, even to forming an Indian guerrilla army to fight for our rights. Although Buck had a statement from General Torres that he would get a fair *censo de contribuyentes,* he said he did not trust his bond any farther than he could "sling a bull by the horns uphill."

I mentioned that as Maria and I had passed by Basaranca we had seen that inside the town walls was a big new building, some kind of factory, perhaps, by its looks and the stink of black smoke pouring from two smokestacks. That confirmed Eugene's word last year that Torres was increasing gunpowder production in Basaranca; they made cannon there, too, but cannon are useless without powder. We got to supposing what would happen to that town if we could get into their powder storeroom. It would "raise hell worse than Geronimo" if that powder plant should blow up at about the same time they were ready to make a hostile move in our direction.

Later, over a brandy, I mentioned that Eugene was still stuck there, but I would get in touch with him. The only thing was— that walled town scared me. Buck thought he might get Grey to snoop around a little, as he was trading in Basaranca.

The way I saw it, Eugene was an Apache by birth and heart, even though he was now married to a Mexican woman and they had a baby. I was confident he'd never betray us at Pa-Gotzin-Kay. Buck suggested that some of my fears were groundless. No cannon could be hauled out of Bavispe Canyon close enough to shell our rancheria. I explained to him how guns are taken apart and toted on pack mules.

"Yeah—the old army mountain-battery stunt!" he grunted. "Niño, make every effort to get Eugene to come back to our side!"

I told him I would do my best on the way home. Then I suggested we take a quick ride over to Grey's tonight. Grey had his brand on Chief Kelzel and was our best hope for Kelzel's coming in on our signal plan. Buck agreed reluctantly; I knew he had a bellyful of that border-jumpin' Jim Grey and his head-hunter Yaqui friend. So did I, but I saw no other way to gain our objective. We told our wives where we were going—but not when we'd be back.

❦ ❦ ❦

BUCK loaned me a dark bay for the ride and chose a black for himself—a warrior never rides a white horse at night if he has a choice. At the Grey ranch we dismounted by the hitch rails in the lantern-lit area in front of the warehouse. Big Jim Grey, with a ready rifle, leaned out of a window of his nearby house and called: *"Qué pasa?"* When he recognized us he withdrew the rifle and jovially invited us in. He set a pot of coffee to boil in the kitchen, and before it was cool enough to drink Buck had outlined our new signal plan.

"Muy bien," Grey said. "Kelzel's stronghold is on a mesa that overlooks a heap of Chihuahua. I'm about the only whiteman ever to visit his bailiwick by invitation, and I saw he has a clear view of a helluva lot of country. He wants no *blancos* messin' around. He's got four or five outposts, too—about like yours, Niño. I'm for your plan, men, but the hitch is to get that ornery Yaqui to work with us.

"I finally picked up two U.S. Army surplus forty-power telescopes and four pairs of marine field glasses at Fort Bliss.[4] I really got lucky when an old pal quartermaster shipped me two heliograph outfits. They're the kind that made General Miles famous.[5] I can get more. Got the whole works stashed away at El Paso. I can train Kelzel's men to use 'em, with a little help from you, Buck—*bueno?"*

Buck nodded and said we had three peaks to locate them on; he named peaks I knew had been used by the Apaches in the old days, so I bought the two Grey had and ordered two more.

4. Curious about these frontier types of optical equipment, I checked with Willard LeBlond Greene, Patent Attorney, of Scottsdale, Arizona, who is a Bausch & Lomb expert. He said the 1880-90 model B & L telescopes of twenty to forty power with 4″ refractor lenses are good for up to thirty-five miles on a clear day, and six to seven power field glasses up to twenty miles. AKG.

5. These were Mauce heliostats with 8″ mirrors; their effectiveness was limited only by prevailing sunlight and shadow conditions. AKG.

We discussed details until the coffeepot was empty, and then we left. This visit with Grey had raised him a notch or two in my estimation. When our horses settled down after the first brisk run down the home trail, I proceeded to talk Buck into coming with me when I saw Eugene; he agreed. We arrived at Rancho Verde as the early-bird roosters were crowing. Rather than awaken anybody in the house, we flopped down on a convenient pile of hay to sleep. One of the ranch hands doing morning chores found us there, so we staggered into the house. While our women fed us, we explained what we were up to. Then we left, riding fresh horses.

🌱 🌱 🌱

IT WAS noon by the time we arrived close to Basaranca. Buck and I proceeded to scout on foot, leaving Maria to watch the horses. When we got above the red *casita,* I made the call of the female white-winged dove, figuring Eugene would be home for the noon siesta. Soon came the male dove's answer and a man leaped Indianlike over the wall.

"Niño! I have not seen you all winter," said Eugene. "What have you been doing?"

"Doing Apache work!" I snapped. Then I said in English, "You remember Buck, don't you?"

Eugene nodded. "I am watching my chance, then I am going to quit this stupid army. They are always late in paying. They say they cannot collect any taxes . . . and that they are going to make the army collect the taxes from the cattle ranchers . . . Torres now has ten cannon here."

"Ha! And he has cannon powder that must be stored here in some building—which one?" I insisted. "When you quit, I will blow it up. With no powder, what good are Torres' cannons?"

Eugene pointed out the gunpowder storage building and said, "You leave that to me—just give me the signal. I will fix it so one burning arrow will set it off. Then I am going to New Mexico and live on the Mescalero reservation. I'd be ashamed to come back to Pa-Gotzin-Kay and I am sick and tired of these *gusanos.*"

"All I can say," Buck remarked, "is your *gusano* general is a goddam liar. I happen to know that I and *all* the other cattlemen paid our taxes last year. If there is anything you want, let me know."

Eugene nodded. "I might need a couple of horses, Buck . . ."

Back at our horses, Buck mounted, waved good-by, and loped off in the direction of Rancho Verde; Maria and I headed our Barbs up Juh's Trail to Pa-Gotzin-Kay.

Chapter 12 1897

Mexican Standoff

THERE had been no trail guards on duty as we rode up from the canyon, not even at the north rampart, and this sudden laxity in our guard system gave me some concern. We found the entire clan gathered between Ticer's tree and the big kiva. Even a few Opata and Tarahumari were there, all looking solemn and stunned. There was not a smile of welcome in the crowd!

"*Qha'n tayl-t-alu-ká?*" (What is going on around here?) I demanded.

Mother, her eyes wet with tears, said, "Dee-O-Det is gone. We fear he has gone to Big Sleep. We are preparing to paint our faces black."

I was speechless. Mother related that he had been seen starting on his morning walk but had not returned. She sent search parties but, finding no trace of him, they feared he had fallen into a canyon, or a big cat had eaten him, or old age had overtaken him.

I leaped from my horse. In my anxiety, I failed to look before I leaped and I bumped a small child, knocking it down. The child began to cry and all the women cried and wailed in sheer sympathy. Not so my Golden Bird; she had remained mounted and I heard her voice through the din:

"*Ol-lo!* Look!" She was pointing. "There the *shaman* is!"

Even her horse was looking, his ears pointing to the edge of the clearing where a dense copse of cedars hid part of the entrance trail.

I started out to intercept that old coot and give him a harsh piece of my mind. But I drew up short, holding out my arms to stop everybody. We all stood and stared in awe.

There Dee-O-Det came, walking with a slow, measured stride, trudging toward the compound—*and he was leading a huge old graybeard deer by the nose!*

Talk about a *shaman's* magic! The camp became as quiet as a cave. Even the child stopped crying. I don't think anyone even breathed as we watched his silent approach across the clearing, his eyes downcast—a pathetic old figure, leading a docile old buck. As I remember it, I wondered if I was seeing things. This certainly was something unnatural!

When the *shaman* reached his wikiup he paused, his head moving slowly as if in deep thought. Then he released the buck's nose and it just stood there, motionless.

Dee-O-Det stooped, picked up a *mano* from one of his big *metates* and, raising the stone up high, smashed it down on the buck's forehead. The buck dropped.

Dee-O-Det let out a weird triumphant yell. I ran over to him as fast as I could.

"I do not want to talk about it!" he snapped in his high-pitched voice before I could say anything. He stared down at the huge, gray buck, then looked back up at me and cackled, "I will call the council for tonight. I will have much to say then."

The attitude of the people suddenly changed from gloom and despair to relief and happiness. Life went on as usual for the rest of the day, but with an unusual amount of speculation, laughter, singing, and chatter. When Dee-O-Det called the council, that evening, everyone attended, even the youngsters. Actor that he was, knowing he was the cynosure of all eyes, he dramatized his report:

"Old man as I am, when I got up this dawn to take my customary walk to commune with *Ihidnan* (Supreme Being) and observe the glory He bestowed upon us here in Pa-Gotzin-Kay, I determined to take a longer walk. I imagined myself a young man again, not a warrior but a man at peace with the world. I walked far. I walked down to the fern glen which we call Bubbling Springs. When I arrived the sun was warm and I was tired. I sat down to rest and admire our canella hills and fertile glens. I must have fallen asleep. When I awakened the world was peaceful and quiet, only a bird chirped. I looked around.

"There, not more than twenty paces from me, a large doe was drinking from the pool. Behind her, with equal calm, stood an old buck, the biggest these old eyes of mine had ever beheld. Here was one of *Usen's* great manifestations. It was meant for me and me alone. Had I gone to Big Sleep—and was this the Spirit World?

"Here, something told me, was *Usen's* gift to me—the past-prime buck I needed to make my annual potion of *shaman's* soup. Silently, carefully, I stood up and drew my knife. Something compelled me to walk toward the apparition. I then saw the buck had the doe's tail in his mouth. With one stroke I cut her tail off, right between her and the buck. The doe took one long leap across the pool and hit the other side, running . . .

"The buck did not move a muscle—this astounded me. Why his weird action, or lack of action? It brought on thoughts of *Usen* coming from the Spirit World to put a curse on me for my rash act of harming the friendly deer. My mind was crowded with thoughts of dire things about to descend upon me from out of the endless sky.

"Blood was dripping from the buck's mouth, so I blew *ho-denten* on his head. Then I saw that his eye on my side was white, like a white stone in his head. I saw his chest move in and out with normal breathing, and reality came back to me with a rush. This buck was deaf and stone-blind from old age. I also knew the way he got around was to hold the doe's tail in his mouth and thereby let her lead him.

"I made no further effort at being quiet. I grasped the bleeding tail-end between my thumb and forefinger and pulled gently. Sure enough, the blind buck, thinking the doe was still there and ready to go, responded to my pull. Keeping a firm hold on that stump, I turned and he turned; I walked slowly back toward our rancheria—you all saw me coming.

"At my medicine ring it was an easy matter to pick up a *mano* and hit him on the head, killing him. To-Clany[1] helped me put

1. In 1931 "Young" To-Clany, repatriate from Pa-Gotzin-Kay by way of Carlisle Indian School, was the last of the old-time Apache *shamans*—a rank not recognized since about 1919—at San Carlos Reservation. He gave this narrator his recollection of Dee-O-Det's blind deer episode and it was essentially the same as that of Niño Cochise. AKG.

him in the boiling pot—hide, hoofs and horns. Nothing is wasted, and I will have good *shaman's* soup tomorrow. *Enju!"*

He had spoken. Though I knew a little about *shamans,* and a lot about this crafty old one in particular, I couldn't think of anything to say. I had long ago realized that one could expect almost anything from old Dee-O-Det!

The people cheered and began talking among themselves. When the council broke up, Maria, Mother, and I headed back to our cook fires. I sat there and drank coffee for a long time—long after the women had gone to bed.

🌷🌷🌷

MOTHER asked me next morning if I had seen Eugene. I told her of my talk with him at Basaranca; of his fear of the Nakai-Ye, and his desire to go to New Mexico because he was too ashamed to live with us again. To set her mind at ease I said the Nakai-Ye made him that way after he married one of their women. I was thinking of placing him and his family at Ammon Tenny's ranch, out of harm's way, yet close by.

Just then Chee came by with some planting problems as if nothing else mattered. And he was probably right. Did I think the weather and the moon were right now for the potatoes? I told him to ask the *shaman,* but he insisted I come down to the field with him. I spent most of the day there. Everything had been planted except the seed potatoes we had packed in by mule train from Brewer's farm. Then I went to the corrals to check over our horses. Many had been ridden so hard lately that the feet of some needed attention.

The next day and the following one everyone was out in the fields planting potatoes. By sundown everyone complained of aching backs. Only Chee, the wise one, who had been seeing that the potatoes were cut properly and supplied to the planters, had not been bending for long intervals. When I commented about that, he told me to remember my sense of humor and my oft-professed deep love for the land.

Dee-O-Det shuffled up behind us. He had been doing his part in planting by singing and sprinkling a mixture of *hodenten* and pulverized cattle dung over the newly planted rows to assure a bountiful crop. The planting would be finished in one more day, he remarked, but to ensure a fruitful season he did not have enough *hodenten.*

"Well, now! You *cannot* be out of *hodenten!* We must replenish your stock," I answered, glad for any excuse that would take me away from the back-breaking labor. "Yes, Dee-O-Det, we will go to the tule springs in the morning. I never fight with history—but with the future, yes!"

San Bernardino Springs was a long way to go just for tule to make *hodenten,* but I would kill two birds with one stone: I had to see Tenny about placing Eugene. That evening I told Maria and Mother that Dee-O-Det was out of *hodenten* and that we would take him to the springs tomorrow to gather tules if they'd like to come along. Maria was delighted, but Mother showed no enthusiasm until I told her we'd cross the line to John Slaughter's ranch—Taglito's friend—to buy food at his store, and she need not pack much along for the trip.

When morning came, I found more sore muscles than I was aware that I possessed. Poor Maria! She opened her eyes, turned over and groaned. I shook her fully awake; we got up and crept over to Mother's fire. She had made coffee and was frying eggs and baking ashcakes[2]. The smell of coffee made me forget all about my soreness. The *shaman* appeared as if from nowhere and Mother motioned him to the table.

"Seems like everybody who worked in the fields yesterday is hungry and sore," I remarked. "Are you sore, Dee-O-Det?"

"No, I am not sore. I am used to working hard."

"Yeah—I noticed how hard you worked scattering your *hodenten* around the field and singing."

"I feel young again. I had my *shaman's* soup."

"How long does it take to learn to be a *shaman?*"

"Are you thinking of becoming a *shaman?*"

"Well . . . I like hard work."

2. Ashcakes were made of either ground mesquite beans, or pine nuts, stored from the previous gathering. Shortening was bear grease, tallow, or any other available animal fat; honey, when available was mixed in with the dough. They got their name from being patted flat and baked over preheated stones. We, at Pa-Gotzin-Kay, ate them only during in-between seasons or whenever we were short on store-bought supplies.

"You must know many things to become a *shaman*—and you must learn the songs."

"Where did you learn to sing?"

"When you two stop talking and get the horses ready," Mother snapped, "Maria and I will pack what we need."

"Niño will get the horses while I sharpen my sacred knife for cutting the tules," said the *shaman*. "The knife has to be just so, you know."

"Yes, I will get the horses," I agreed, "while Dee-O-Det gets his sacred self ready."

"I am not sacred, but this is sacred work . . ."

"If you two do not stop fighting with words like *Los Goddammies*," stormed my mother, "we will never get started on this sacred trip!"

☙ ☙ ☙

I SADDLED the two white Barbs, a gentle black for Dee-O-Det, and the pinto for my mother. When I brought them, mother chased me back for a pack animal to carry the food down and the tules back. I saddled a mule. I held the pinto while Mother mounted; though it was not necessary, it pleased her—an Apache warrior's daughter. Maria swung into her saddle and the old *shaman* mounted.

San Bernardino Springs, flowing out of the surrounding brush- and grass-covered hills, were the headwaters of the San Bernardino River which flowed south to the Bavispe. The area had been a major camping point on the Apache and Navajo war trails for centuries. When the Ignacio Perez family established a hacienda nearby in 1882, the Indians left it unharmed for a time—they knew the *Godo*-Mexicans raised good horses and cattle, which would be far easier to take than to raise themselves.

When the Mexican Governor General issued the scalp-hunting *pronunciamiento* in 1842, the Apaches sacked the hacienda in retaliation. My grandfather, Chief Cochise, and his Chiricahui and Chief Mangas Colorados, with his Mimbrenos, teamed up for the raid.

After the Gadsden Purchase was ratified in 1854, a new international boundary line ran through the abandoned ranch, putting about two-thirds of it in Mexico. The ruined hacienda buildings were in the northern third, now Arizona. The main springs, causing a large *ciénaga* (marsh), were about eight kilometers to the south—in Mexico. By 1884, when John H. Slaughter bought the ranch from the descendants of Ignacio Perez, the once-proud land grant of 73,240 acres had reverted to wilderness.

❦ ❦ ❦

WHEN we arrived at the springs to gather tules, I had little thought for ancient history. It was the present—1897—that counted. We picked a campsite and unloaded the mule. The heaviest part of the equipment necessary for making *hodenten* was the two large *manos* and *metates* that the *shaman* used for a preliminary grinding of the green tule seeds; after sun-drying at the rancheria, this would be ground into powder with small *metates*.

Dee-O-Det, Mother, and Maria set up camp and I took care of our animals. Then I set out to gather firewood in the brushy area about 400 yards away. I had gathered nearly all I could handle when I noticed that a group of about five men had camped at this secluded spot. On closer examination I saw signs that indicated Apaches—the way the fireplace was built and the look of the places where they had bedded down.

The spoor was fresh, not a day old at most. I wondered who they were and what they were doing. None of my men had any reason to be this far north at this time. When I got back to camp, I told the others about it and we all went to the campsite.

"They are Apaches!" Mother said. "Maybe Chiricahui!"

We made a thorough search of the area. The *shaman* remarked that maybe they were some dissatisfied people from the San Carlos; I pointed out that there were no Chiricahui at San Carlos but they could be from the Mescalero. If they were Chiricahui, we should have met them on the trail or when we came by Chi-hua-hua's old hideout.

"They left in a hurry," Mother said through tight lips. She held up a few links torn from a gold watch chain. *"Has-kay-bay-nez-ntayl* (Brave-and-Wild-and-will-Come-to-a-Mysterious-End) *wore this when he came to Pa-Gotzin-Kay once!"*

I said, "The Apache Kid!"

Mother nodded, troubled. She wanted nothing to do with the *Netdahe.* They were troublemakers. We talked it over, and then I rode to Slaughter's to ask if he knew of any Apaches other than us in the area.

I tied my Barb to a post of the fence that enclosed a big yard and had just stepped into the yard when Slaughter opened the front door of the main house. His foreman, Jess Fisher, was with him and they called greetings. We went into the front room and Slaughter asked about Tom Jeffords. I said Tom was home on his ranch, and also that Mother, my wife, and our *shaman* were camped down on the south part of his ranch gathering tules. We were talking about Buck Green and Jim Grey and our progress in setting up the heliograph system when there was a clatter of approaching horses and the creak of saddle leather. Slaughter went to the front window.

"Hey, what's this—the whole U.S. Border Patrol?" He chuckled. "They after you?"

I joined him and saw about thirty cavalrymen riding in and forming a circle in his front yard, guided by the infamous Mickey Free.[3]

Slaughter talked with the officer in charge and soon both came back to the porch.

"Five *bronco* Apaches broke out of the reservation," Slaughter explained. "Lieutenant Averill, here, wants me to guide them to the lower ranch were Geronimo used to camp."

"Mickey Free knows very well where that is," I remarked, but the lieutenant ignored my comment.

Slaughter turned to me. "Averill says those *broncos* have committed at least twelve murders and burned ranches, and their tracks lead here. Say, Niño, you're camped on the southwest part of the ranch—notice any sign?"

3. See *Mickey Free, Manhunter,* by A. Kinney Griffith, Caxton Printers Ltd., Caldwell, Idaho, 1969. Also Griffith in *Old West,* 2 vols. Summer 1968, Western Publications, Austin, Texas.

"Yes. I came here to ask if you had seen them, but we got talking about other things."

"Well, I'll get a horse and then you can show us where to pick up the trail."

"Say, young fellow," the lieutenant condescended to address me direct, "you want to be our guide?"

"No."

"Oh, I thought you were working for Mr. Slaughter."

"No," interjected Slaughter. "He has a place in the Sierra Madre."

"Are you a Mexican?" asked the lieutenant.

Again Slaughter interrupted. "He is an American."

"That's what I thought by the way he speaks."

I was breathing easier by this time. I did not want to get mixed up with the U.S. Cavalry, or Mickey Free, or any runaway Apaches—least of all with the Apache Kid. Slaughter and Fisher hurried to the barn where a Mexican stableboy saddled two horses. I mounted my horse and reined away from the cavalry column. Young and eager, the lieutenant was snapping orders to his men as they mounted. Let them go, I thought to myself; I wasn't holding them up. Besides, that fair-haired White-Eyes didn't need me; he had Mickey Free, the best guide and scout in the Southwest. When Slaughter and Fisher joined up, the cavalry moved out, Free riding a short distance ahead, scanning the ground, in the manner of the instinctive man hunter he was.

Slaughter trotted his mount up beside me and said in a low voice, "Do me a favor, Niño. Show me where those *broncos* were camped." For him to ask me was an entirely different matter. I nodded. "Sure, John; glad to."

We passed the place where I had left Maria, Mother, and Dee-O-Det. There was no sign of them; undoubtedly they had heard our approach and were well hidden. We rode on and I showed Slaughter where the *broncos* had camped. It was getting dark and hard to make out anything else, so the patrol decided to move back across the border and camp. I took my leave so as to get back to where my people were camped.

"Thanks for your help, young fellow," the lieutenant called. "My name is Averill . . . what's yours?"

"Niño."

"What is your last name?"

Again Slaughter came to my rescue, saying, "Adams," and I repeated "Adams" and rode off into the darkness.

I rode to where our camp had been and soon heard a distant nighthawk scream. That nighthawk was Dee-O-Det. I followed the call and found they had moved camp to the far side of a wooded hill and had no campfire. The only light was the stars. As I rode in, they all began talking at once, trying to tell me that a large body of soldiers had passed by, but they did not know whether they were Mexican or not. I explained that I had been with them and that they were Americans, below the border.

I was hoping the *shaman* would let it go at that, but he demanded to know what such a large force of Americans was doing south of the border and why I was riding with them. Maria's manner was that of a woman who has confidence in her man, and Mother was quiet, so I told them I had guided the soldiers to the camp of the Wild Ones. Then Mother rebuked me for riding against people of our own blood. I defended myself, saying these *Netdahe,* even though of our own people made it hard for us who wanted to live in peace. They had murdered some white people, and if they came to us to hide, they would give us a bad name. What if Mickey Free and the soldiers tracked them all the way to Pa-Gotzin-Kay?

The *shaman* scoffed that it was just the soldiers' say-so—the bad-eye half-breed scout would not lead them to us. By now Mother was in deep thought, for she knew as well as anybody that even Golthlay had never trusted Mickey Free.

Maria, whose knowledge of the *Netdahe* was only from hearsay, laid a trusting hand on my arm. I took her in my arms and hugged her. She had shown me that a wife can make burdens lighter for a husband—a lesson I have never forgotten. I was so relieved that I ate a second supper that night.[4]

---

4. I never saw Lieutenant Averill again. I did hear rumors that the *broncos* had scattered into the mountains on both sides of the border. Though I saw John Slaughter many times after that, the subject was never brought up. Historians have found evidence, however, that ranchers shot two of the fugitives, two were hunted down and killed by the relentless Mickey Free, and only one escaped—the Apache Kid.

❦ ❦ ❦

IN the morning I looked around, saw what had been done the day before, and decided that Maria and Mother alone could easily gather enough tules to keep Dee-O-Det busy. They could spare me for a few days and I wanted to go to Tenny's ranch and make a place for Eugene. Mainly I wanted to be riding—I was restless, impatient. I talked it over with them and they agreed.

I went by way of Rancho Verde, arriving there about noon. Buck was beyond the house, digging some holes. He dropped the shovel when he saw me. He wanted to know how come I was alone, and I told him I'd left Maria, Mother, and Dee-O-Det at the springs to go on gathering tules and was on my way to Tenny's and Grey's.

Buck explained that he was building a schoolhouse, as time would allow. His wife, Anna, would be the teacher, but she might have a problem with the children in this widely scattered region. The American Ranchers Association—as they now called themselves—had figured that since the Indians gave them protection, they should live right on the ranches that they protected. The Association would furnish them houses, schools, and commissary, and put them on the payroll. That school idea sounded good to me, and Buck's idea of having the families stay right on the ranch would make protection available at all times.

Anna fed us in the kitchen, and Buck said he would ride with me to Tenny's; I was hoping he'd think of that—riding the trails in those days was risky business for a lone rider, what with *bronco* Apaches and red-flaggers around.

As we headed up the valley I noticed his fields had been planted; the season here was actually two weeks earlier than ours up on the shelf. I could see potatoes, beans, corn, oats, and a field of clover. With normal rainfall he'd have a good crop. But he had something on his mind. I thought he looked worried, so I prodded him and he let loose:

"It's the same old crap. The goddam laws here in Mexico. There's no honest legal protection for landowners, Indian *or* white. The Federal Government tells us to apply to the State Government for protection, but *that's* what we want to be protected *against!* We have, you know, protested to both Torres and Terrazas that the taxes are exorbitant, and that under present conditions we cannot operate. We were told by the governors to protest to the Federal Government. We did, and were referred back to the State Government—always the Mexican standoff.

"We held a meeting last month and decided to protest to the American Consul. We did this and were told we were creating an 'incident.' The same old runaround. So now there is nothing to do but take the bull by the horns. And that, Niño, is where you come in. Technically, you and your people are Americans. If worst comes to worst, I think the Ranchers Association can get the American Government to recognize your clan as Americans. The Association feels this will bring in the protection of the American Government in case the Mexicans try to confiscate our property—which they sold to us under false pretenses."

I remained silent. I had to mull over what he had said, but with all that off his mind he was in good spirits for the rest of the trip. When we arrived at the Tenny ranch there were at least twenty horses tied to the long hitch rack. Some of the horses were bedecked with handmade Indian *armas,* several wore gaudy, hand-tooled caballero saddles, while others wore sweat-stained vaquero saddles; all had rifles in the scabbards.

We strode up onto the porch. The front door was open so we walked in. The room was crowded with men. My roving eyes took in Jim Grey, John Brewer, Benito Escalante, Chief Kelzel, Francisco Villa (Doroteo Arango), and some others— I did not know.

"About time you two got here," Ammon Tenny called from the center of things.

"I didn't know you'd set a time. We just came on a hunch!"

"I sent you a message the other day," said Tenny.

"Who did you send?" Buck shot back.

"Pablo—that saddle maker from Campo rode by and said he was going to deliver a saddle you'd ordered. John Slaughter's not represented either."

"There's something haywire somewhere," Buck grunted.

"I've not seen Pablo for a month. Maybe there's a red-flag spy operating in these parts—and bushwacked old Pablo . . ."

"Terrazas and Torres both have spies out, so we'll hire a few of our own," replied Tenny, speaking loud and fast. "We'll give Niño the details of what we're fixing to do, and the progress being made on the new signal system. We want full agreement all around so there'll be no slip-ups. We've got to work fast. Things are shaky. The revolt against Diaz is growing, and we're slap-dab in the middle." He paused for breath and looked at me.

"Niño, you people were born in America just like us. What we want you to do is furnish us with two Apache men for each group we will set up for the sole purpose of defending American interests. This is in line with your original plan." He grinned and continued, "Cholos can't read Mansos so we'll be using our heliostat system. Jim Grey will give you the lowdown.

"Chief Kelzel will work with us, his Yaqui are naturally Mexican Nationals, so if the Yaqui are captained by Americans, the Mexican government can't charge us with fomenting revolution."

I got the feeling there was a big *if* in this somewhere, but Tenny went on and I listened.

"The Yaquis feel the same as we do. They don't want to have happen to them what happened to old Emiliano—his Opata tribe was wiped off the earth and his people, any who were left, were sold into slavery. Now," thundered Tenny, "we can prevent that from happening again if we all stick together. What is your answer?"

There was unanimous agreement and the meeting settled down to informal discussion among groups. Soon plans were made to organize and be ready to meet trouble head-on when it started. The ranchers wanted to weed out the Mexican Cholos since no one could be sure which side they were on. They seemed pleased when I pledged Apaches to captain teams of Yaqui and Tarahumari tribesmen. I was pleased also by the confidence accorded me and my men. Tenny abruptly adjourned the meeting and I realized this was no time to bring up my problem about Eugene—I would just send him over as a team captain.

212

That was it. We were dismissed and virtually told to get moving. Had that meeting been held at either Pa-Gotzin-Kay or the Rancho Verde, everyone would have been served a big drink and a good meal. There were low mutterings as the men mounted and rode out—some in pairs, some in groups.

Buck and I rode at a moderate pace. Our horses were still tired, and now we were too. It was getting dark and there was no moon. Since we had not been fed—not even given coffee— we decided to camp and make do with what we could scrape out of our saddlebags. Over a final cigaret, Buck, who had been somewhat morose, suddenly let go a blast at Moroni Mormons running scared and yelling for help every time Terrazas or Torres sneezed. But, when it was up to Brewer, Bower, Parks, and Tenny to pitch in with more than guff to help a gentile, those Mormons came up with an alibi that could lead you to believe they hoped the gentile would fall flat so they could move in and take over his land. That was a new angle—maybe the big *if.* I certainly would not have thought of it, so I shoved it to the back of my mind to recall in the future.

We got an early start in the morning, separated at the *vado* of the San Bernardino below the springs, and Buck headed off to Rancho Verde while I loped on to our camp near the tule swamps. Mother greeted me and Dee-O-Det began telling me how much *hodenten* material they had gathered. I nodded, but not seeing Maria I asked about her. The *shaman* told me she was hunting rabbits so they could have roast rabbit tonight, as they were afraid to go into Slaughter's and buy food because the Wild Ones might still be nearby. I looked at the sun; it was afternoon. For some reason I had an uneasy feeling.

I galloped out, skirted a swampy tule area by cutting through a goatnut swale, and soon met my Golden Bird, who was lugging eight rabbits. And I was worried about her!

"Oh, back is my husban'!" she trilled. She dropped the rabbits and made a dash at me, almost knocking me flat as I dismounted. "Many rabbits I have—carry them I could not."

"I think I will make you our new hunting chief," I laughed.

"Hunting Chief of tribe I am." She waved her primitive rabbit-hunting stick.

We cleaned the rabbits and put the meat in the spring to cool.

That night those rabbits with boiled tule roots tasted as good as a charcoal-broiled T-bone steak tastes to me today.

❦ ❦ ❦

SEVERAL months passed; we tended our fields and watched the crops grow and nothing outstanding happened. But at about noon one day a trail guard brought word that there were five armed men entering the old Chi-hua-hua rancheria and headed up-trail to Pa-Gotzin-Kay. They turned out to be Buck Green, Ammon Tenny, Jim Grey, Tennono Kelzel, and an Apache who looked familiar.

After the greetings, Tenny got down to business. The ranchers had come for help in their annual roundup. I knew it was getting close to roundup time. Mother, always thoughtful, called our visitors to the table before we could get anything decided. She and Maria had started a big beef stew, with chili pintos and fresh tomatoes, the minute they heard people were coming.

"You people sure eat good here," observed Grey and leaned back with a sigh. Beats the slop my squaw puts out."

"Either feast or famine—that's us," I said, and turned to Tenny. "How many men do you want?"

"Oh, about a dozen riders: the ones you want to be captains in case of trouble."

Tenny had donated thirty horses last year but now wanted them back—with riders on them! However, aside from the roundup, this was the time of year when the *revolucionarios* were most active, and Tenny went on to tell of fighting going on around Corralitos, Dublan, and Casas Grande. Being the closest settler to that area, he feared the trouble would backlash on him. Buck, Grey, and Kelzel had little to say.

As I listened, I knew I would lend him the horses and riders, but I kept looking at the Indian with the familiar face. Then it dawned on me: it was Kay-Pesh! When Crook's soldiers first came to Chi-hua-hua's rancheria to talk surrender with Golthlay, Kay-Pesh and I, boys of about eight, did not want to be captured so we ran to hide in a nearby cave. In we went—but it was already occupied by a family of skunks, who resented our intrusion and showed their dislike for us in no uncertain fluid terms.

Fearful of capture, we never uttered a sound, although the stench was almost more than we could stand. But there was nothing we could do, being temporarily blinded and so nauseated that death would have been preferable. I was thinking of all this when I stepped around the table to him:

"Kay-Pesh!" I said, and he nodded questioningly. "You still stink like *golinka!*" I chortled. Although we had been speaking in English, I let the Apache word for skunk slip in. "Where have you been all these years?"

After a spell of laughing, I learned that they had been put on the San Carlos Reservation but soon were transferred to White Tail (Mescalero), and thus escaped being sent to Florida. When his mother died he left to come to Pa-Gotzin-Kay, but met some Yaqui and stayed with them. He was now a *capataz* (foreman) over Indians and Mexicans for Mr. Tenny. The Mexican vaqueros did not amount to much. They would not keep their families close to the ranch house but camped far back in the trees. They stole beef to feed them and also gave so much to their friends and relatives to take home that now Tenny had hired Yaquis to ride herd on thieving Mexicans as well as on the livestock. I told him I had a good Apache warrior named Eugene—whom he might remember—with a personal problem. I asked if he could use him back in the hills, where the Mexicans would not see him. He nodded and said a good Chiricahua was always welcome with him.

Then I mentioned that several months previously five Apaches had escaped from San Carlos and were seen at San Bernardino Springs, and I wondered if he had heard if they had been caught. His firm reply that he had never even heard of them allayed my doubts. It had been my way of testing to see if he had been one of them.

Chee, Hi-okee, and others joined us and we got to talking cattlemen's business, red-flaggers, and our need for more practice on the helio stations. Buck related that after he and I had parted at the San Berdoo *vado* he had found what was left of Old Pablo, the saddle maker—his decomposed body showed signs of having been shot in the back. There had been no sign of his horse or his mule—nor of the silver saddle he was to deliver to Buck. This time Buck blamed a Mexican spy.

The conversation dragged on and finally it was agreed we had attended to everything. When they had all left and were out of sight, I began to wonder what all this would lead to.

Later that evening I had the *shaman* call the council and I made a report on the decisions made at the meeting with the ranchers. I appointed the absentee Eugene war chief for ten braves: two Apaches and eight Tarahumari, to be chosen and sent to Tenny's within a few days. After the council broke up, Dee-O-Det remarked that our way of life at Pa-Gotzin-Kay was due for a change that would be good for some; for others, he could not foresee—perhaps good also. I knew when the old man spoke in a way that did not seem to make sense, he was downright serious. I thought it best not to question him. But his words kept haunting me, and it was much later that his meaning revealed itself.

That night I lay on a sleepless bed. My thoughts seemed like a ghost whispering that there were times in the Great Scheme of Things when we had no control and certain things that men did lasted only for a time and passed with their passing, never to return. Later, other people looked back and perhaps thought they would not make the mistakes of their ancestors. Were those thoughts in the minds of others when the plan for the way of life in Pa-Gotzin-Kay was born? Could it disappear, too, never to return?

The next thing I knew I was being awakened by a gentle shaking. I opened my eyes and there stood my Golden Bird—she was real, she would be with me forever. I took her in my arms but, laughing happily, she broke away and ran to the table, shouting that she was hungry and could not wait for me. As we ate I told her we'd ride over to her father's rancheria and borrow some of his men to help with the cattle roundups. I saddled up and we rode, galloping all the way like two kids without a thought except the pursuit of happiness.

Jemez was pleased to see us and invited us to have *cerveza* with him. Maria declined and ran off to visit her mother. I did not like this green beer, but customs are customs. And, as custom permitted, I told him I wanted eight of his men to help the ranchers with their roundups and that I needed an equal number to help me move some cattle from the north pasture to the south; I also remarked that we both should lay in a supply of dried beef, along with more venison, for if bad trouble started and we must fight, we must also eat.

"Trouble will come," he said, "but not soon. The Mexican people are not very hungry this summer. Only when hungry are they desperate, and then the men who are leaders must also be in the right temper. Only then will real trouble come. Young Emiliano has asked me for a hundred warriors if trouble starts. I told him maybe thirty."

I knew Emiliano was ambitious but, unless he was going to start a revolution of his own, he did not need any men. When I questioned Jemez on that point he shrugged and said he had not given it any thought, but Emiliano had the earmarks of a leader. I agreed that when wars come there are always young leaders who rise to the occasion and Emiliano might be one of them.

"That is true," Jemez agreed. "It takes young blood to face the uncertainity of defeat or victory. But Mexico has thousands of men under arms. For myself, I am too old to fight against such odds. But, I will fight to protect the lives of my people here. To fight for a cause that never ends—no! War never again!"

This old Tarahumari *cacique* (chief) spoke from experience. And I knew what my forefathers had faced in the past.

Chapter 13   1897-1898

Soldier-chief

I T WAS the Season of Golden Leaves and we were out in the fields shocking corn when Tom Jeffords unexpectedly rode in. After hearty greetings, he announced that he had a friend visiting at John Slaughter's ranch he wanted me to meet—an officer in the U.S. Cavalry who was looking for volunteers. America might go to war with Spain and needed the support of all American citizens—especially Indians and cowboys who were good horsemen and good fighters. I promptly reminded Taglito that we were mere Indians to the Americans—if they gave us any thought at all—and we had nothing to do with any war they were starting. When he began to object I told him I'd do anything for him personally. But America—no!

I then explained that we might have a war on our hands right here in Pa-Gotzin-Kay any day now, and I needed all my men to protect our own property. Would his American friend come and help us if we needed him?

Tom knew I had been married but when Mother and Maria joined us, it was the first time he met my wife. He hugged and kissed Maria and Mother. My mother had overheard just enough to catch our mention of war and wanted to know more.

"Who is America going to war with?" she asked.

"Spain."

"Spain? Are they Spain Indians?"

"No, Niome, they are, well, a big nation like America . . ."

"Oh, they are White-Eyes?"

Taglito nodded uncomfortably.

Today I live in Arizona where this photograph was made last year

When I was acting in Hollywood in 1925 I had this photograph taken

Teddy Roosevelt in Dakota territory, looking much the same as when I first met him

At the Miller Brothers 101 Ranch in Oklahoma, Golthlay
(Geronimo) posed in a silk hat in a 1906 Pierce Arrow
car with other Indians

"So now the whiteman fights himself! *Taeh!* I thought it would come to that! Hot dam!"

"Nod-Ah-Sti, you do not understand."

"Taglito always call me Nod-Ah-Sti when he is angry!" Mother fired back. "*Niome* understand. *Niome* know that we here in Pa-Gotzin-Kay have had peace many seasons, with plenty to eat. And *Niome* can remember that when our braves were on war trails, old people, children, and women were starving. *Niome* understand that war will take those we love away from us and we may be put on reservation. *No,* Taglito! Even you can *not* talk war here!"

I thought I had better come to my old friend's aid.

"My mother," I began, "Taglito does not want us to go to war —it is a soldier-chief who is looking for young men to go to war with him. I will not spare one man to help *Los Goddammies* make war. I will fight only to defend my people, or what is dear to you and the people of Pa-Gotzin-Kay."

"Oh, then you do not want us to go to war, Taglito?"

"I only wanted Niño to talk with this soldier-chief, who one day might be the Great White Father."

"My husband, Tahza, tried to talk to one who was the Great White Father. He died trying."

"But he did not know him before," Tom put in. "It makes a difference, Niome."

"I see no difference. The Great White Father sits on his Great White Throne and makes war . . ."

Maria, who had trouble following our exchanges in both Apache and English, nevertheless made the clinching remark. "We fight Spain . . . they fight us . . . right here . . . we then fight . . . I am Tarahumari . . . Apache now!"

Dee-O-Det, swinging his medicine bag, also joined us. He greeted Taglito and said he showed no signs of the seasons that had been added since last he'd seen him, and that this visit must bring good news for some and bad for others. But then only a *shaman* could understand those things. Glad for the interruption, Tom raised an eyebrow, grinned, and knowing the Indian's mysterious ways, gave him the Apache handshake.

The *shaman* nodded to the old scout and motioned for us to follow him. He led the way to his large, new split-plank cabin that Chee had shown us how to build. He felt around by his bed and came up with a half-full whisky bottle. He passed it around and, after the first drink had been gulped, cleared his throat.

Launching into a dissertation about the values of a *shaman* to a tribe, he touched lightly on our present tribal welfare, but cast gloom when he said good things cannot last forever. Sometimes bad things last longer; sometimes what was thought to be bad, turns into good; but he emphasized that good and bad times change, though few could see when—until the time came. And I knew from past experience that he was right. Taglito knew it as well as I did, but Dee-O-Det, being *the shaman,* had to remind us of it.[1] He maintained that Pa-Gotzin-Kay was good, but he forecast that it must die to make way for a better place. Those of us who loved Pa-Gotzin-Kay would also die and become a part of her in the Spirit World, where we would be long-lived. Those who deserted her would mourn the comfort of her love to keep them warm in Big Sleep. It is the will of *Usen*: it shall be so.

Dee-O-Det had served with the great Cochise, Beduiat, Juh, Naiche, Golthlay, and now was serving me. He knew the power and the ways of *Usen*. He said the time he dreaded was near at hand, that I must do my best, and Taglito must help. I knew the old *shaman's* prescient mind was in full swing, but I could ask no questions, nor could I chide him for his feelings. I loved this old man like a father.

I had him call the council for that night. There I spoke of what Taglito wanted me to do. When the inevitable question of this soldier-chief arose, I turned to Tom and asked him to explain.

Taglito said the soldier-chief was called Teddy Roosevelt. He said he was his true friend, and that most people thought that one day he would be our Great White Father. And he believed it would be a good thing for the Apache chief to know him.

Dee-O-Det exercised his rights and remarked that things are strange: whiteman fights whiteman; Mexican fights Mexican; Indian fights Indian. Has war taken the place of *Usen?* It was fitting that the Apache chieftain talk with this white chief—he

1. In the old-time Apache tribes, a *shaman* was counselor, diplomat, prophet, secret confessor, and all-around prime minister, as well as religious instructor and educator; the same personage was also a medicine man, doctor, and even a witch doctor—the Apaches being superstitious people.

might find what makes people fight their own kind. When the council so voted, I asked that five armed men and Dee-O-Det accompany me on the mission. Granted. That left twenty braves to man the lookout stations in case of an emergency. My wife and my mother were to go along and, of course, Taglito.

☙ ☙ ☙

GETTING an early morning start, we rode hard and by noon our horses were drinking from Lower San Bernardino Springs. Looking toward the rolling back-up hill, I saw five people riding at a lope in our direction. I recognized John and Viola Slaughter, followed by three soldiers. Taglito waved his hat to them and we waited.

The three soldiers were a sergeant, a lieutenant, and a lieutenant-colonel. They swept up to the water hole, and as the men dismounted, the colonel displayed an ease that showed he was at home in the saddle. Maria, Mother, and Viola Slaughter brought their horses closer together and began chatting. My men remained mounted, but Dee-O-Det, Slaughter, and I dismounted during the introductions. I sized up the colonel: Here was a man who would naturally attract attention in any setting. Although not tall, he shadowed Slaughter when he stood beside him. Slaughter was slim, five feet six; the colonel about five feet eight and husky. Prestige, power, and self-confidence seemed to emanate from these two men.

Colonel Roosevelt was very pleased that we Apaches spoke English—accented and garbled though it was.

"So you are the grandson of the late Chief Cochise?"

"Yes, I am."

"Do you do much fighting with the Mexicans?"

"We do not bother them and they do not bother us," I replied, tongue in cheek.

"How do you live if you don't raid them once in a while?"

"We are cattlemen and farmers now, sir."

He nodded as if he had known what my answers would be. "Tom Jeffords has told me about you and your people, Niño, and I am impressed. I like talking with you," he went on, smiling and impressing me. "Mr. Slaughter has been good enough to show me his ranch. I did not know that most of it lay in Mexico, as I am looking for American volunteers."

I had been so interested in watching this man that I did not notice that we were now almost alone. Off to one side, two of my men were making a fire for the women, while others were caring for the fifteen horses. Slaughter, Taglito, and Dee-O-Det had their heads together. The man who was to become the twenty-sixth president of the United States then asked how many people I now had. I told him 300 Tarahumari, sixty Apaches, and what few Opatas were left after the Mexican soldiers overran them. I then added that America had millions of men. Why, therefore, did he seek volunteers in Mexico?

He took polite objection to that, pointing out that Tom Jeffords had told him—and history showed—that we were American Apaches, and he wondered if we had ever thought of returning to the United States? He said "Uncle Sam" (Taglito later explained this term to me.) had established reservations for all Indians and that they had a good life on these reservations. I almost bit my tongue to keep from telling him that Tom Jeffords could vouch for quite the opposite. I just said that many Apaches had escaped from those reservations because, with or without walls, they were prisons and an Apache loves his freedom.

I saw that I had not made my point so I continued, "Many escaped Apaches have told me that 'piece of land set aside for the displaced Indians'—a whiteman definition—is a living hell. Besides, until recently there was a law in Arizona Territory that said no Chiricahua Apache could live there in his native land—not even on a reservation. In other parts of your country, if I am found, I run the risk of being an Apache off the reservation without a pass or a dog tag. Whitemen are suspicious—they will think I am a Wild One, or *bronco,* because I let my hair grow long. I have been back in Arizona several times, but only in the presence of a trusted whiteman like Tom Jeffords am I safe. Otherwise they may either shoot me, or arrest me and send me to Florida, to Fort Apache, or to Fort Sill, where they have imprisoned others of The People.

"Here I am free. I now have a herd of more than 100 cattle. I have 100 horses and mules. I have crops planted that will feed 600 people for a year."

The colonel was itching to interrupt so I paused.

"They don't just arrest people because they are Indian," he said. "They arrest people who commit crimes. You have not committed any crimes here or in America. If you came to America and were self-supporting, you would be treated just as any other citizen."

We continued our exchange until Mother called us to the campfire for something to eat. We had brought along *maletas* (bags) stuffed with dried beef, vegetables, and serving utensils, but knives, forks, and spoons had been overlooked. Everyone got a tin plate and cup and lined up by the fire. Viola Slaughter and Mother were dishing up, and Maria handed the colonel and me a cup of coffee each and a plate of food.

Colonel Roosevelt thanked her and remarked that I had a very pretty and vivacious wife, and how many children did we have? I answered we had none yet, but expected to have sons and daughters.

He said he had six children, two daughters and four sons.[2] He looked around, and was nonplussed for just a moment when he saw others eating with their fingers. He shrugged and said:

"Well, we have a choice: either be fastidious and go hungry, or enjoy it."

I found a log to sit on; the colonel, licking his fingers, came and sat beside me. He remarked that this life was bully—like that on his old ranch in Dakota. We were silent for a while, eating and thinking. When his plate was clean, the colonel asked, "Where did you learn to speak English? You speak it very well."

I told him the story of Jim Ticer, adding that Ticer's influence on us would always be present in our way of life. We talked about wars, past and present, and of the threat of war with Spain in Cuba. I asked him the reason for this war, and he replied it was to free the people of Cuba. I told him I did not understand why there should be a war to free the people of Cuba, when the Americans had fought a war with us Apaches to take our freedom away from us in our homelands.

A strange expression clouded the colonel's face, and staring intently at me, he patiently began to explain the reason lay in

2. Ethel, Alice, Archibald, Kermit, Theodore Jr., and Quentin. AKG.

who the Great White Father in Washington was at the time it all happened. Just then Slaughter, Taglito, and Dee-O-Det joined us, Slaughter saying that they had a long way yet to go and it was getting late. I muttered under my breath. I might have had the explanation of the eternal ways of man within my grasp, but man had intervened.

Off to one side, the women had packed up, and the men had the horses bunched. The soldier-chief turned back to me as we stood up. "I have the feeling that some old-time Apache tactics might come in handy. Are you sure you cannot spare me a few men?"

When I shook my head, he sighed. "Well, thanks anyway. If you ever come back to America to live, ask John Slaughter or Tom Jeffords to get in touch with me and we will have another visit. Possibly I can do something for you."

He swung into the saddle, wheeled his horse around and rode close to me, saying:

"Maybe you're not missing much, Niño."

"May you be victorious in the war, Colonel Roosevelt."

The whole party was mounted when one of my young men, riding bareback, suddenly farted. Whether it was the sudden explosion or vibration, I will never know, but his skittish mustang leaped northward and came down southward, bucking furiously. All of the other horses simultaneously began bucking in sympathy, and the next few minutes were consumed with a medley of shouts, creaking saddle leather, the noise of plunging horses' hoofs. The red dust that was kicked up created an amber glow in the afternoon sun.

The action ceased as suddenly as it had begun. When quiet came, none of the riders had been unseated. The gallant soldier-chief waved his hat and galloped off, still laughing. His voice came drifting back:

"You *geronimos*[3] put on a good show . . ."

I watched him disappear over the hill with the Slaughter family. Had I not been in the position I was, I would gladly have ridden with him; he was that kind of man. Whether you were Indian or white, as long as you belonged to the human race you

3. When Theodore Roosevelt was inaugurated as President on March 4, 1905, Geronimo rode in his inaugural parade. AKG.

immediately saw him as a leader and respected him.[4]

Taglito had elected to remain with us for a couple weeks, and we got to talking. Night fell before we realized it. We made camp, talked some more, and finally bedded down. The next morning we headed for Rancho Verde—two hours' ride away. After a very enjoyable visit there with Buck and Anna, we started back to Pa-Gotzin-Kay.

We forded the Bavispe and headed up into the mouth of Juh's Pass to where the trail forked to the short cut known as "a yard wide and a mile deep." The other fork led to an easier climb but a much longer trail. Before taking either trail it was customary for riders to stop here, let their mounts blow, relax a little, tighten cinches, and look around.

Young Alchise, my ever-active *segundo,* walked over to Benito's Bluff, a point from which he could scan the up-trails and the world of canyons. He hurried back to report seeing eight horsemen, two tied to their saddles—either dead or captives.

Our people stayed back while Taglito and I went with Alchise for a look. Through my field glasses I could clearly see the riders—six red-shirts and two Yaqui prisoners. They disappeared, then reappeared behind rock ledges or trees, going away from us and up to the Chuipac balsa flats. A sweep with the glasses revealed ten or twelve more riders who looked like Yaquis coming out of a blind canyon. At any rate they were enemies of the captors, because there was rifle fire. Though we could not see all that was going on, we could sense who was winning.

The Mexican red-shirts were losing. At this distance we could only be observers. After a time I told Alchise to take the rest of our party on to the rancheria. Taglito and I would come home later. I knew Maria and Mother would object, but I was sure this was the right thing to do. As soon as they were out of sight, Tom and I headed back down to the ford, cut across, and picked up the warriors' trail. The Yaqui were now our allies, but we did not hurry. Yaqui and Nakai-Ye—they had crawled out from under

4. The next time I heard of Colonel Roosevelt, he and his Rough Riders had charged up San Juan Hill in Cuba to win an important victory. That news aroused my savage Apache heritage, and I had a twinge of regret that I hadn't gone with him when he offered me the chance.

rocks together. I was quite sure of the outcome of the battle.

When we got to the battle scene only the losers remained—and their heads were gone. The bodies were in diverse spots, where they had taken cover. Tom remarked that "whoever had gone into the head-huntin' trade sure knew his business." I recalled that Kelzel, the *Yaqui-Yori* chief who spoke Apache and true Spanish, was a thorough man.

We rode on and picked up the Yaqui's trail, heading east across the balsa flats. It led toward Ammon Tenny's, Jim Grey's, or Kelzel's nearest rancheria. As we neared the Tenny ranch in the twilight, I saw Buck Green and Kasale ride into the yard ahead of us.

"I thought you were headed home," Buck called.

"We were until we saw some Yaqui murder six red-shirt *soldatos* who were slavers—by the evidence."

"How do y'know they were slavers?" Buck asked, looking around.

"They wore uniforms of the State of Chihuahua and this happened in Sonora. The line is back there."

As usual the long hitch rack was crowded with saddled horses. We dismounted and pushed horses aside so we could tie our mounts. Buck suddenly shouted, "Lookee here! This is the fancy silver saddle I ordered, on this black. By God it is. And that's old Pablo's black gelding." He scrutinized the dozen or so other horses. "Tenny flashed me a message right after you left this morning, askin' me to come over. Humm, there's a skunk in the bushes here somewhere . . .

Tenny saw us riding in and waved from his front door. "Howdy, gents. Eugene said you'd show up soon. Did you see old Pablo's horse and your saddle, Buck?"

"Yeah—what's going on around here?"

We went on in to the big front room; Jim Grey was there, but Chief Kelzel had everyone's attention. I heard him say that now they knew the new system the slavers used, they would destroy all who set foot in Yaqueria.

The two Yaqui who had been rescued gave their first-hand account of the event: they had been scouting and had come to a spring. They were thirsty, so they leaned their rifles against a tree to get down on their bellies to drink, thinking it was safe. Suddenly they were overpowered, knocked senseless, and tied to the backs of horses like carcasses of meat. When they finished their tale, I complimented Kelzel on a neat job of cutting back there.

"I would like to take the credit," he replied, speaking in his usual slow, modulated voice (which impressed many people but always annoyed me), "but the captives, when they were freed, could not be restrained."

"Kelzel, I agree with you that the slavers got what they deserved. What I do not like is the way they stink up my land. It takes a *gusano* a long time to rot and blow away. The wolves and buzzards won't eat them—their bodies are too tainted with *pulque* and red peppers."

He shrugged, his face blank as usual. He usually knew what was going on, for though his people did not live in one stronghold, they were scattered in clans not too far apart. His outriders had reported red-shirt activity, and Alberto and his brother Saenz, who lived with their families in Canyon Diablito, were told to take their turn watching the western cattle range. When they did not return, Kelzel took men to follow their tracks. He elaborated about how the trackers had found the scouts' horses tied to a tree near a water hole. They began looking around and soon found the rifles leaning against a tree, then signs of a fight and the tracks of many shod horses. They read the signs and knew they could head off the slavers at Chuipac Canyon, if not sooner. Kelzel and his men came up behind the slavers and there was a fight—but not much of a fight. Kelzel added with pride that not one of his men had been wounded. He admitted that they had crossed a part of Apache land, but not as an act of war; just as we could cross theirs since we were allies and worked for the same boss.

I could see why this *Yaqui-Yori* was considered the best manhunter in all Mexico. He overlooked nothing. In reality, I found out later, he was a cattle detective employed by Tenny as well as by Grey. Somehow I was glad he was on my side. I would have hated to have him trail me. I think highly of my head. I asked him if he always cut off the head of his quarry. I had the Apla-Chi-Kit killing in mind, an episode I will never forget.

"I once hunted criminals for the government—and others,"[5]

5. It had been a custom, and may still be, for the *Rurales* to coerce certain criminals into tracking down an escaped outlaw. In his earlier days Kelzel had

he replied. "Sometimes I need to study my quarry a long time before I engage him, then I only bring in his head. In these mountains it is too difficult to bring in a body. I hunt only those who are wanted dead or alive. It is too much trouble to bring in a live one, and by bringing in the head, there is no argument when I claim the reward."

"Those six you left on the Sonora side will not pay you any reward."

"Oh, yes they will. I am now Federal District Administrator —Terrazas notwithstanding—and as such I am informed of their operational methods. I will collect phantom pay[6] on them. Besides, their heads will grace the entrance to my stronghold, and my people will know there is a power of justice and reprisal for those who sell human beings into slavery."

He turned away. Somehow, I couldn't help admiring the man and his devious, grim brand of justice. I approached Taglito, who was off to one side talking with Kasale, Kay-Pesh, and Eugene. I joined in. While we were talking, Kelzel and a helper walked past with two gunny sacks that were stained red at the bottom. A shiver ran through me as they passed. It has been said the Apache is the most cruel when dealing with his enemies, but I say they are amateurs compared with *Yaqui-Yori*.

Outside we were mounted and ready to leave when Kelzel showed up again. This time he was leading the late Pablo's black gelding and on its back was still cinched the silver saddle.

been convicted of a heinous crime, but instead of being imprisoned he was given the option of hunting down another criminal the authorities were unable to capture. Kelzel made such a success of it that he was blackmailed into other man hunts and he always brought in the head of his quarry.

6. Phantom pay accrues when a top-ranking officer or a *caudillo* keeps the name of a soldier killed in action on the pay roster and pockets the pay himself. This was also a practice of the Mexican Government's authorized bounty-hunters, who had been known to collect as many as three times at different district offices where a reward had been posted for a certain criminal. Tennono Kelzel, Catholic-mission educated, a legend in 'his time (1840–1916) and with considerable oblique mention in the Chihuahua State Archives, became anathema to all Mexican Christians, but was idolized by his tribespeople, the pagan Yaqui. Such divergent characters as Pancho Villa and the Madero Brothers turned on him, yet had found occasion to employ his peculiar talents to hunt down outlaws or even an opponent whose only crime was in being on the other side of the political fence. After accomplishing his dark deed Kelzel was liable to blackmail; to pay it, he was sometimes forced into assassinating another "enemy."

Kelzel quietly handed the reins to Buck, nodded, and walked away. That gesture made that *Yaqui-Yori* a few friends for life.

❦ ❦ ❦

TOM and I stayed at Buck's that night and were on the trail shortly after sunup, arriving at Pa-Gotzin-Kay that noon. Chee was first to greet us.

"I just got word that Buck is coming with news about Kelzel. He should be here before dark."

"But we just left him!" I said.

"Good signal system we have, huh?" Chee retorted.

Buck Green rode in at dusk, and said briskly:

"Thought I'd better not tell you this over the system. Kelzel just got a letter signed by President Porfirio Diaz and the Administrator of Agriculture, saying that those parts of his lands in Sonora that had been confiscated were hereby restored to him in perpetuity and that he, Kelzel, would not be responsible to Torres for taxes. Also he would be furnished with an irrigation system that could be paid off on a crop-value basis. He's all fired up and will make preparations to move his people as soon as possible. How d'you like that!"

I replied that if Kelzel accepted all that at face value, he was not as smart as I had thought. Buck added that Kelzel thought Diaz had had a complete change of heart and would back the Yaqui against Torres and Terrazas. Jim Grey also thought it a good deal and had agreed to stock Kelzel with cattle.

"And you?" I asked.

"I think the same as you do, Niño. It's a goddam trap. I believe in Kelzel, but I don't trust the spicks. They can change their laws faster than a lawyer can say 'I object!' The odds are that Kelzel and his people will put up a new barrio and get the land in shape for farming, then Torres will tax him anyway, and if he doesn't pay he'll be choused to hell an' gone."

"And," Tom spoke up, "there'll be one mad head-hunter. Anyway tomorrow I'm going back to Owl Head."

We joined the *shaman*, Mother, and Maria at the supper table in our cabin. Over coffee, Buck got us into a fit of laughter as he told how he had stopped off at Basaranca on the way up and had looked in on Nakai, who was now a major in the Sonoran army. Nakai told him that Terrazas had sent in an order for two tons of black powder. They had loaded it on a big wagon to haul it over the old *carreto* road to Chihuahua City. The driver was an inveterate cigaret smoker and the wagon had not got very far when *"bluie"*—it went up in a cloud of smoke, taking driver, swamper, and mules with it.

🌱 🌱 🌱

NOW our crops were in, except for the potatoes. We were late digging them, but not too late. The whole clan was out working, and it seemed we had dug up a mountain of spuds and carried them in baskets, bags, and blankets up the hill to dump them in a cave near the gold cave.

When that was over I sent a pack train to Bisbee for our winter supplies, and when it returned, I organized a hunting party of Apaches and Tarahumari. We had forty men to do the hunting and an equal number of women to dress our kills and keep camp. The sky became overcast the morning we started out and by noon it began snowing. By nightfall the snow was knee-deep, but by morning it had quit snowing and the weather turned cold. This drove the bears into hibernation and the deer down into the canyon flats. In three days we had fifty-four deer, five bighorn sheep, and nine cougars hanging, and it took us three more days to pack the meat back to the rancheria.

It snowed more and more till the vast Sierra Madre range was covered in white, and the mountains remained snowed in, making it our worst winter in Pa-Gotzin-Kay. When spring came we were like a people returning to life after hibernation.

🌱 🌱 🌱

ON the morning of the first day of spring, 1898, I rode up to Lookout Peak. The vedettes were all at the station; they had built better wikiups for shelter and for places to cook, as well as for storing food and supplies. Chee was in charge, and we were talking when my eye caught a flash from Beduiat's Butte;

Chee acknowledged it and then read off the message:

"Ask Niño to ride with me to Chihuahua City . . . will await your reply . . . Buck."

I told Chee to ask why, and he did some flashing with the heliograph apparatus. The returning flashes said:

"Bring ten men . . . I must pay taxes . . . and see Kelzel."

I asked Chee to tell Buck I'd be there tonight: then I was off down the trail to the rancheria. I called for young Chi-hua-hua and told him to get Hi-okee and Boa Juan and seven other stalwart braves, fully armed, because we were heading for Chihuahua City and maybe some trouble.

I saddled a prime mustang stallion, and my men rode similar tough, mountain-bred horses. Buck Green met us as we dismounted by his hitch rack that evening, and next morning we hit the trail south. Good old Kasale, now like Buck's right hand, rode with us. We hit the old Spanish *carreto* road and stuck to it most of the day. The next day we crossed the up-Bavispe at Huachinera and headed south. By noon of the fourth day we hit the Arros flats and came to a new adobe village of some fifty *casitas.* I knew Kelzel had about 200 families in his main tribe and counting five people per family as an average he still had more building to do, but the barrio was well laid out along wide *avenidas* with a large plaza in the center.

Across the plaza in front of the biggest building was a block-letter sign, ALCALDE. Another sign attested that the new village's name was BOREGA CITY.

As we dismounted and tied our horses to rails provided for those who came on official business, who stepped out of the front door but Chief Kelzel, hair slicked in two long braids, and decked out in a velveteen suit like a *godo.* He looked the part of a top *haiga!*[7]

He welcomed us to Borega and sonorously said he had been expecting us. He explained how they had worked day and night all winter to get this much done. At this low altitude the winters were mild, and they had put in winter crops. His cattle had increased, his people were clearing more land for summer grain—but the whole area lay wide open to raiders from all sides!

7. Meaning either very rich, very powerful, or very crooked. AKG.

His office building was also his home. It was constructed of raw adobe, at which the Yaqui excel. Living quarters were in back with a spacious living room with whitewashed walls. Huge, hand-hewn logs formed ceiling beams and from each hung a shaded kerosene lamp. The chairs were handmade, hewn out of timber and padded with sheep pelts tanned to a surprising softness. A handmade, long table was placed in the middle of the room, and on it a woman was setting a wet, wicker-covered jug, indicating that it had been cooling in the spring, and some glasses of the old-fashioned mouth-blown type made by Guadalajara artisans. I had the feeling that either Chief Kelzel had a gold mine or he was collecting a heap of phantom pay.

Above the gurgling of wine being poured, Kelzel's voice sounded:

"This is the finest wine that can be obtained—there is none better anywhere."

In these surroundings, dressed as he was and with his *haiga haciendado* manner, one would never believe this was the dreaded *Yaqui-Yori* head-hunter of Mexico.

As Buck and I raised our glasses to him, his woman brought in a white cotton tablecloth and we held our glasses till she got the cloth spread. A girl of about sixteen appeared and began setting the table.

"My second youngest," said our host. "I have three—living. You should begin to have a family, Niño. I hear Chief Jemez is becoming impatient."

"Give me time, give me time."

"Women who ride much seldom have babies," he replied jovially. "It took me two years to get the first one started—after that it was easy."

"Mine never had any trouble at all," laughed Buck. "And they just keep showing up."

I chuckled at that, knowing Buck had only two children.

Then came Kelzel's wife with a great platter of steaks, followed by platters of fried onions, potatoes, and cornbread. Out back I could hear Yaqui maiden voices giggling and the deeper voices of young Apache men; Kelzel had assured me that my men were dining equally well with his family. While we ate we discussed the maintenance of the signal system up north that he'd left only partially manned, and the disposition of tribal warriors in case of a war this summer. Kelzel then showed us the President Diaz letter restoring his lands to him; it was just as reported, so after discussing it, we left.

When Buck and I rounded up our men after the conference, we saw it was nearly sundown and the men were restless. We decided to spend the night several miles upstream on the banks of the Arros River. While we sat around the fire Buck told me the reason why he had to go to Chihuahua City to pay taxes, even though his property was in Sonora. It seemed that Colonel Bill Greene—one of the few true American friends of President Diaz—had arranged with the Federal Government for all the American ranchers' to pay taxes at Chihuahua City as it was now Northwestern District headquarters. The ranchers now called themselves "The Consolidated Cattle Company of Chihuahua and Sonora," and I was a full member. A branch office was at Buck's ranch, the main office at Colonel Greene's in Cananea. Jim Grey was to have a branch office for his Chihuahua holdings since some of his land joined Kelzel's and Kelzel was winter-feeding Grey's cattle. It was becoming more and more clear that Kelzel knew what he was doing—but did the others?

Dawn saw us on the trail, winding easterly through a range of forested hills. A stagecoach drawn by four small black mules met us and we paused to let it pass; then came a mining region where lines of creaking ore-laden ox-carts clogged a yellow, dusty road. We soon left the road to make better time alongside of it. We reached Madera that evening, where we camped and traded off two horses that had split their hoofs. We recrossed the winding Arros for the last time at Temosachic, a sun-baked but prosperous mining town, and camped and ate supper in the local *fonda*. On deeper into Chihuahua the region seemed more "settled"—there were many ranches back in the grass and brush.

❦ ❦ ❦

WHEN we arrived in Chihuahua the townspeople eyed us suspiciously, and we surveyed them with equal suspicion. This was a big town with too many people. We probably were a rough-looking bunch. As we reined up in front of the governor's palace, Buck felt for his money belt under his shirt, making sure it was still there. He said it was best if he went in alone and for us to keep our eyes peeled outside. He had been inside long enough for me to feel uneasiness when suddenly he appeared, waving several sheets of white paper and with a smile of success on his bewhiskered face. He shouted, "This calls for a drink."

I told the men to stay by the horses and keep watch on our rifles in the saddle scabbards. Buck and I sauntered over to the cantina and found only six people in it. In one corner was a band platform on which a dancing girl was clicking castenets and trying to get attention. At the bar we ordered whisky and the barman set forth a bottle of Old Crow. Buck said we'd take the whole bottle, and asked if they served food. When assured that they did, he ordered a potful of chili con carne with fourteen serving plates. We had a drink of the whisky, and then asked for a couple of gallon jugs of tequila. When the barman obliged, canny Buck made a great to-do of searching for money in his pockets but finally came up with an American double-eagle.

"Dios! Veinte pesos oro americano!" the barman exclaimed, and began to scratch around in drawers looking for change. When he went into a back room, still looking, we picked up our purchases and walked out for, as Buck said, he could keep any change for a tip. The bunch of us made camp in a secluded spot about five kilometers out of town and ate and drank till we were tired, sluggish, sleepy.

The next morning at daybreak luck temporarily ran out on us. Rudely awakened, we found our camp surrounded by six heavily armed men in the gaudy leather shirts of *Rurales*. Young Chi-hua-hua, an explosive type when rudely awakened, shot one of the *Rurales* in the back before anyone else was attuned for action. The Mexicans whirled in confusion but we Apaches, seeking our way out of the ambush, shot and stabbed until there was only one man left. We let him run until young Chi-hua-hua fired the last shot—a long-range one—and that was that. As we examined the bodies, we recognized one—the man who had fled. He was the barman who had had trouble making change at the cantina.

234

On our return trip, we sent Kasale along with the men to make camp at Borega while Buck and I again visited Kelzel. He greeted us royally and we bargained with him for fourteen fresh horses to replace our tired ones. By the time we were on our second jug, Kelzel owned fourteen used-up mustangs, and I was the owner of fourteen prime horses that wore undecipherable brands, but showed fine Barb and Andalusian blood.

Three days later we were back in Pa-Gotzin-Kay. Mother, Dee-O-Det, and others crowded around me with enthusiastic welcomes. Maria threw herself at me. "My husban'!" she exclaimed. And getting her Apache and Tarahumari rhetoric mixed up, "Am so glad for you me to see!"

Chapter 14 1898-1899

Back-stabbers

AFTER weeks of constant riding I decided to do some walking for a change. I headed for the cliff-face and crawled up to a small spur, below which was the red shelf on which our rancheria lay spread, verdant under the spring sun.

I was proud of my part of the world—my land. Regardless of the old *shaman's* prediction that Pa-Gotzin-Kay would die, I felt secure in my belief that it would live forever in these remote mountains. Only a few enemies knew of its existence, and I knew that they were aware they could not muster an assault force strong enough to invade us. Then, too, friendly tribes within a radius of up to 100 miles would ride to our aid at our first sign of need, while the American ranchers in the region were our proven friends and were in constant touch. What other troubles did I have?

I worked my way around to the bighorn ledge and climbed to the summit—a short but seldom-used route to Sno-Ta-Hae. At this point I sat down to regain my breath and I got to musing over the tales spun around great treasures of Apache gold and Yaqui silver here in the Sierra Madre. Within my view were El Tigre, Las Chipas, and Tayopa, the most fabulous of all Aztec-Spanish mines, and other ledges of yellow iron and white iron. Minerals abound in the Mother Mountains: gold, silver, turquoise. I crossed to the regular trail that wound around the spur from our rancheria to the mine. The place had the atmosphere of having been abandoned. The spring rains had washed away all signs of recent human endeavor; weeds were crowding the tailing dump; the old blast furnace was rusty and leaning as if tired of it all. According to legends much gold had been taken out of Sno-Ta-Hae by the invaders and shipped to Spain. Certainly it had been worked before we discovered it and took out nuggets and rose flake that we melted into bars, as well as loose gold to turn into paper money and use for living expenses.

"My husban'!" Maria's trilling voice broke into my thoughts. "Looking everywhere I have been for you. Doing what here at the mine? For more gold are you to dig? Oo-whee! All day have been gone you and have eat nothing. Let us home and eat go. Starved I am; for you I have waited."

"All right, Golden Bird," I replied and kissed her tenderly. "I will race you down the trail."

She was off like a jackrabbit, and I was right behind her. She got to the spur where the main trail led to camp a dozen strides ahead of me. Ah, those Tarahumari runners! That young woman could outrun a deer. She hit the main trail, still gaining on me, and dashed on down to the rancheria.

❦ ❦ ❦

A FEW weeks of garden and field work passed and then a message from Buck asked me to come down when it was convenient. Convenient! No time like now, I figured, for I never cared for farming.

I told Mangas-Chee to choose a man and saddle five good horses. I told Mother and Maria that we would ride down to Buck Green's ranch, and maybe over to Tenny's. Chee chose Boa Juan, now best all-around man in the clan. Although popular and attractive to women, he had somehow missed getting a wife when Chief Jemez had brought in the ten maidens from his Tarahumari tribe. Lately he was showing signs of wildness, and I agreed with Chee that a little time away from the rancheria would be good for him. I sent a runner up to Lookout Peak to tell Hi-okee to flash a message to Buck that we were coming.

We were soon mounted and riding. I led the column, Maria was directly behind me, then came Mother, Chee, and Boa Juan. Shortly after dropping off the first rimrock near Chihuahua's old hideout, I noticed about twenty head of cattle grazing in a small glen. I wondered what cattle were doing there this time of the year and tried to make out their brands.

Two shots in close succession banged out from the rocks and brush around the glen. My white Barb's front legs doubled up and he went down, throwing me face-down in the trail. I yelled to the others to dismount and take cover behind the rocks. At the same time my horse was struggling to get back on his feet. I felt a numbness in my left knee.

There were more shots and I glimpsed Chee levering a spent shell out of his rifle. I couldn't see Boa Juan but I saw Maria and Mother scrambling to safety. Their horses acted confused, jumping a little after each shot. My horse was still trying to get up as I crawled over and jerked the carbine out of the saddle scabbard. I had yet felt no great pain in my leg—it was just numb. A bullet kicked up dirt near me, but I was already diving for cover. I saw gunsmoke rising from the brush beyond the glen.

Another shot sounded and again I saw gunsmoke. I heard Chee fire, then another shot from my side of the trail. Both Maria and Mother had rifles, but I didn't know if they'd used them. Boa Juan appeared out of nowhere and dived into the cover beside me. Speaking in a low voice, I pointed out a way around the ambushers to get them from the flank. He disappeared, and I motioned to Chee to advance on the other flank. He took off, skimming through the brush like a cougar stalking prey. I fired two shots into the most likely spot in the scrub-oak patch, spacing them far enough apart to keep whoever was hiding riled up.

From our vantage point the rest of the terrain was clear enough to sight anyone trying to escape. As two riderless horses appeared on Boa's side of the brush, two shots banged out and the horses dropped. I regretted that, but on the other hand those gunmen would now have to walk.

I looked back to where my white Barb was lying and could see his sides heaving. He was suffering, and making fading efforts to get up. Gradually his heaving sides stopped. Our other four horses, their hackamores dragging, had moved back, working away from the noise. I looked toward Maria. She hung her head but in a moment leaped up and ran like a doe to my side. She threw her arms around me and wept silently.

Then came a nerve-tingling scream that I recognized as the old Apache victory cry. Boa Juan leaped out of a clump of bushes, waving his blood-stained *cuchillo* in one hand, two rifles in the other.

Mother rushed over, took one look at me, and yanked out my belt knife. She slit the jeans along my left leg, exposing a bleeding wound just above the kneecap. Maria took cloth and began to fashion a tourniquet, while Mother went into the woods nearby. She soon returned with what she called *Yerba santos Mer.*[1] She and Maria chewed the stuff into pulp and made a poultice mixed with some *hodenten* the *shaman* always made us carry in our personal fetish bags. Those two wonderful women soon had the wound plastered and tightly bound.

Chee and Boa Juan were working toward us, each dragging the body of a man. I took a close look but did not recognize either. "Two less border freebooters," I said.

"We are riding back to Pa-Gotzin-Kay," said Mother firmly.

Boa Juan went to catch our horses. I told Chee to cover the bodies with brush and to help Boa Juan pull my white Barb off the trail.

Riding double with Maria, I arrived back in the rancheria, where Mother started to clean the wound and Maria ran to fetch the *shaman.* She came back on the run but old Dee-O-Det came calmly into the cabin. He had his medicine bag with him.

"Oh, so," he said, eyeing my leg. "Trouble on the trail, eh?"

He then went into a dance and some sort of chant that I had never heard before. I got my first good look at the wound. It looked awful but such things always seem worse than they really are, especially to the wounded one. The *shaman* dabbed it with vile-smelling skunk oil, all the while singing his weary song. He danced around me several times and sprinkled me with some sort of concoction, then stopped as suddenly as he had begun.

"I must have some hair of his horse's mane and some of the tail hair—and some of its blood."

"What for?" I growled, somewhat exasperated.

"Do not ask! Do as I say!" he snapped in his shrill voice. "I may yet make medicine that will drive away the evil spirit."

1. A scented herb the ancient Indians used to coagulate blood from wounds. It was also used by the Mexicans.

I nodded to Boa Juan and he was off like a shot. I must have dozed off, for the next thing I clearly realized was that Boa Juan was there with a thick tuft of white mane in one hand, a hank of tail in the other, and with generous chunks of the animal to provide the blood required. The *shaman* removed the bandage while Mother and Maria stood by. He applied a new poultice of hair, blood, and some other evil-smelling stuff, then rebandaged the leg, all the while chanting some weird tune. It did not bother me much during the night and I slept fairly well, but in the morning when I tried to get up I could not bear any weight on the leg. It was stiff from the bandage and would not bend.

Maria served me breakfast in bed, and a little later the *shaman* changed the bandage. I could now bend the knee a little. The *shaman* was still making his medicine. Every hour or two he wanted something. Whatever it was, it worked, for I had no more pain. Finally he asked for the outlaws' rifles. Luckily Boa Juan had brought them with the hair and meat from my horse, saving another trip down the trail. Dee-O-Det got more stuff from my mother and my wife—always it took just a little more of this or that to make his medicine work.

My people trooped in and out, singly and in groups, full of desire to help, and Chee and Boa Juan were there constantly. Chief Jemez came in to see how I was doing; he had his Tarahumari medicine man in tow but Dee-O-Det would not let him touch me.

Jemez' smooth brown face looked pleasant and calm, but when the usual amenities were over his face tightened. He got right down to what was really on his mind.

"Chief Niño, I hate to bother you at a time like this but something must be done. One of your young men has gone too far with some of my young women. He has been seen in my camp on many occasions. He was one of our favorite Apache visitors. But now five of my young maidens are sorry. All five of them are pregnant—and not one is wed!"

"Five!" I exclaimed. "How do you know they are pregnant?"

"Oh, they are—and it is Boa Juan's doings!"

Jemez and I discussed the problem until I became convinced. I offered various forms of restitution, but he would accept none, saying I had already done much for him and his people, but that the unpleasant situation must be solved.

He left without offering any solution himself.

As I mentioned earlier, Boa Juan was the tribal ladies' man. He was always teasing and flirting with our young women. As I have also said, Apache chastity laws are strict and any man or woman who oversteps them is severely punished. So far, in our hideout existence, Boa Juan was the man who had come closest to breaking that law. Apparently, when he had tired of not getting anywhere with our young Apache women, he had turned his attentions elsewhere. After more serious thought, I called him into the cabin for a serious talk. The outcome of it was that I gave him all the currency left in my money belt— about four hundred dollars—and some orders:

"You remember that red house with the red light in front of it at the end of the main street in Sasabe? Take this money and a good horse and go there. Pay in advance for a month's residence and all other accomodations provided. When your month is up, go elsewhere—but do not come back here."

I never saw that stalwart Apache brave again.

🌱 🌱 🌱

CHEE came to sit beside me, rolling a cigaret for me and one for himself. He recounted some instances in which border-hoppers made the old main trails risky unless we rode in a strong group. All northern Sonorans and Chihuahua citizens knew this and fought back, usually with small success. The gunmen would raid on one side; then run over the line when pursued.

He showed me a letter—taken from one of the bodies—addressed to a Mexican in Tucson from a Mexican in Chihuahua, a man working on Tenny's ranch. I though that possibly there was a rustling—and—smuggling organization in cahoots with some *gusano espio* who worked for Tenny. There was one thing sure—the death of the two Mexican ambushers had broken a link in the chain. Undoubtedly Tenny, a staunch and true man, knew nothing about it. I resolved to see him, and also Kay-Pesh and Eugene. Chee said it was the same old story with a new twist from the times when Golthlay raided Mexican *conductas*.

When I thought of what Golthlay did to the Mexicans—and

what the Mexicans did to him—I became confused. No doubt it was revenge, for the Old Ones said that when the Mexicans killed his wife, Alope, and their children at Janos, in 1858, Golthlay went *Netdahe*.[2] Chee believed it all went back to when the first Spaniards came; all the others had followed their lead. Then the whitemen came and took what they wanted. This in turn caused the Indian wars. He said a man could go crazy trying to figure out who was to blame.

Maria came in with a bowl of soup, thus ending our appraisal of the past. She offered some to Chee. He declined, saying his wife, Ealae, expected him; also he had promised to teach his nine-year-old son how an owl makes its cry.

Mother came in and asked in her best English, "How do your leg feel?"

"Not too bad," I answered, also in English.

"What are you two saying?" Maria asked in Tarahumari.

"Why don't you learn to talk better English?" I asked in Apache.

"Oh, some day I learn, I think, if my husban' learn me will." Maria laughed.

Dear little Golden Bird—how I loved her!

�),🌷🌷

THAT evening, to no one's surprise, Buck Green rode into the compound, leading a white horse. He tied the animals to the rail and sauntered over to the cook fire.

"Niome, will you trade me some chuck for this white horse so that you may present your son with it to replace the loss of the other?"

"I trade, Buck. Eat with Niño in cabin."

I was lying there looking out of the door at the new white stallion. What a beauty! Buck came in and said he was the younger brother of the Barb I'd lost, also a brother to Maria's mare. I started to thank him, but choked up.

"Well, Niño, you looked heap good on a white horse. All the ranchers are concerned about you. Chee told me about it over

2. See *The Indian Wars of the West*, by Paul I. Wellman, Doubleday & Company, New York, 1954, pp. 421–3.

the signal system. Kasale asked how many legs has a cow? I asked if a doctor was needed, but he didn't know. The other ranchers seem to think it was bandits, mainly interested in loot. Sonsabitches! We drive off cattle thieves at least once a week."

Maria had gone out to inspect the new horse, and Mother brought Buck a plate heaping with food. I told Buck about the letter found on the dead gunman—and about its implications. He wasn't much surprised. Right about then the *shaman* walked in.

"Howdy, Dee-O-Det!" Buck greeted him. "How you been?"

"I have been making much medicine."

Buck grinned. "Well, you have a prime case."

The *shaman* went out and began to sing and dance and toss *hodenten* on the horse. The young stud, not used to such goings on, kicked at the old man.

I yelled, "Dee-O-Det, stop kicking that horse!"

The old *shaman* threw another pinch of stuff on the horse and went into another dance, uttering mournful sounds. Then he came back to the table and sat down, all out of breath.

"Now," he said, "that stallion will never die from a bullet."

Then he gave Buck and me the treatment. We laughed and I said, "Give Maria what you gave us. I do not want her to die from a bullet either."

"I do not have the power to save her from bullets. I am studying on that now, maybe I will be able to—maybe. Let us not talk about it."

As Mother set a platter of food in front of him, he whispered to her, "Niño thinks I was kicking his horse. I do not understand, for it was the horse who was kicking me. Will you tell him for me?"

Buck and I both heard the remark. We burst into laughter.

"Why do you laugh?" asked the *shaman*.

"Buck just told me a funny coyote story," I answered.

"Oh, do you know the Coyote stories?" he asked Buck.

"Only the one I just told Niño. I'll tell it again for you. Old Coyote met a man. Coyote said to himself, 'Man is supposed to be smarter than us, let me find out.' Coyote took out his eyes, began to roll them on the ground, and said to the man, 'I bet you can't do that.' The man looked at Coyote and said 'I will bet you can't do this,' and he bit Coyote on the leg. Coyote got mad and was going to bite the man. The man said, 'Hold on, Coyote, if you want to win that bet, you've got to bite yourself. I am a man and I bit a coyote.'

" 'Coyote got smart and asked, 'What did we bet?'

" 'The man said, 'Whoever wins this bet is the smartest.' This made Coyote mad, and he said, 'I can do it,' so he took a big bite out of himself. *'Owoo!'* yelled Coyote, 'I can bite even harder than you can. '

" 'Coyote,' said the man, 'you are getting smarter and smarter.'

"That night when Coyote was lying in his den licking his wounds he said to himself, 'That man's bite didn't hurt much, but my bite *really* hurts! Man is tricky.' "

"I have heard funnier tales than that," said the *shaman,* and left.

"Do you think the old boy caught on?" asked Green.

"Sure he did. At first he believed I thought he was kicking my horse. It put him in a ridiculous position to try to explain. And you coming up with this Coyote story made it worse."

Mother suggested that Buck take Ticer's wikiup for the night. She helped to put me to bed, and Maria made sure I was comfortable before she stretched out beside me and snuggled close. She pulled the blanket over her head and pretended to snore.

In the morning I limped outside where Maria and Mother were making breakfast. Buck sat on the log by the table, sipping coffee. His big bay gelding, Maria's white mare, and my new white stud were hitched to the rail, saddled and ready to ride. My new mount was a beauty, and I think he knew it. I limped over to get acquainted with him. My best saddle—the one Naiche gave me when I was twelve—was properly cinched on, and the horsehair hackamore was a beauty. I took the reins, led him over to the log, grasped the horn, and swung into the saddle. The Barb pranced a little as I headed him down the trail toward Jemez' camp with Maria and Buck following.

The minute we passed the rampart, I let the Barb run. His stride was magnificent—like riding in a rocking chair—and what a single-footer! Down the ridge, Jemez' guards were on duty but let us go unchallenged as we rode into the meadow. The fields were all plowed, some planted. We rode directly to the central wikiup. Maria's ailing mother came out, not asking us in. She said; "He—is not here."

"Where is he?" I asked.

"Jemez left for Chihuahua to see if the government order came through to resettle us on his land." She waved an arm back and forth overhead, meaning many days might pass before he came back.

"Did he get a letter from the governor?" Buck asked.

"Yes, and it says that Kelzel got one, too, and that he was told that Governor Terrazas had authorization to reinstate the Tarahumari, and he has gone to see about it."

"That makes me think the Diaz Government is either trying to forestall a revolution," I said to Buck, "or double-cross us. Giving Kelzel's land back might neutralize him; and Jemez— it might alienate him from us."

"Niño, that is good thinking, and I am thinking right along with you. It's the same old double-crossing, back-stabbing Mexican standoff!"

We took our leave and returned to the rancheria. As we dismounted, Buck held on to his reins.

"I'll call a meeting of the ranchers as soon as I'm home," he said. "I'll get Colonel Bill Greene to attend—he's a friend of Diaz—and knows how to handle the big boys. I'll let you know the time and place."

"I hope Jemez gets back in the meanwhile," I said, "and reports on his trip, so we'll know what's what. And the first chance we get we must have a council with Jim Grey; he has a good business handling guns and ammunition. So far, he has just sold to people friendly to our cause, I think. However, Torres and Terrazas will eventually try to grab Kelzel's holdings. He is getting rich and they can't stand it. And Kelzel is not the man to stand for a back-stabbing. I think that old *Yori* can be trusted, but it's a good idea with so much at stake for us to cover our trail."

"How d'you figure he can be trusted?"

"I liked the way he acted when we saw him in Borega. You remember, Kelzel's offer came from President Porfirio Diaz through Terrazas, proving that it was a Presidential Proclamation. He showed us the letter. That would mean all property confiscated by governor's action must be returned. Right? But Terrazas did not send Jemez any letter with a copy of the president's proclamation. You heard Jemez' wife say he received a letter from the governor asking him to come to Chihuahua City and they would talk about restoration of his confiscated land." I waited for an answer.

Buck Green cleared his throat and said:

"It's hard t'believe, but it sure as hell appears that what you say could be true. If it is, then it's damn sure Torres and Terrazas are in cahoots and trying to wean away any Indian protection the cattlemen have."

🌱 🌱 🌱

AFTER Buck left for home, I called Hi-okee to me. I told him to get our five best available braves, borrow five more from the Tarahumari, and prepare to make a trip to Bisbee. I gave him a wad of currency from Mother's cache and a written order for supplies to be bought. The People were out of nearly everything. Dee-O-Det had advised me not to make the trip as my knee was still tricky; besides, there was so much for me to do at home. Hi-okee was back in one week with a full load and nothing untoward to report.

Another week passed before I finally got word that Jemez had returned. Maria and I immediately rode over to the Tarahumari rancheria. Jemez greeted us:

"Come in, I have much to tell." He led the way. "As you know by now, I was sent for by Terrazas. I took twelve men with me. I returned with but three. The others are—gone.

"On the way to Chihuahua City I stopped at Borega. Kelzel and I talked. He showed me a Presidential Proclamation direct to him, instructing the governor to restore his land. We compared notes, and decided my letter was a copy of his, except that the names were changed. Somebody had set a trap to get me to come to Chihuahua.

"There was only one way to straighten this out, since I am known to Terrazas, and that was to go and reason with him. But when I got there, his men seized me and locked me up. In the morning I was brought before Terrazas. He threatened me with a charge of treason and murder, then told me that in the near future the ears of the Tarahumari would join those of the Yaqui in front of his palace, unless I worked with him.

"While he held me in his office, my men walked in, surrounded me, and hustled me out. Everything went well until we were on the outside; then shooting broke out. My men were cut down as grain by a scythe. I grabbed a fallen gun, fought—and ran. We got on horses and were pursued by red-shirts.

"I had but three men left when we reached Kelzel's place four days later. He gave us fresh horses and we hurried home."

I asked about Kelzel and he assured me that Kelzel was ready for any of Terrazas' tricks. I told Jemez that Terrazas might offer a reward for him, but he said there'd be no takers. I told him we'd have a ranchers' meeting soon and I got his promise to attend it. Maria gave her folks a good-by hug and we left.

Strange to say, however, that dubious Presidential Proclamation was the one factor that stabilized life for a while all around the mountain country. Many rumors were flashed over the signal system—and passed along by word of mouth—followed by guessing, but the summer passed and neither Terrazas nor Torres made any threatening moves. Nonetheless the tension of not knowing what dire thing might happen was always with us.

Actually our signal system had been like a blessing from the endless sky; it kept us informed of what was going on and saved a lot of riding around, leaving us more time to "mend our fences" at home. We went on our big annual game hunt, and old Dee-O-Det got a huge buck to make more *shaman's* soup—as well as *zagosti* leaves to make *shaman's* tonic.

❦ ❦ ❦

THE year 1898 passed and the spring of 1899 found us enlarging our garden and fields. We had an ever-increasing number of mouths to feed and were doing so to everyone's satisfaction, even though we still were the Nameless Ones, or else did not exist, so far as our long-gone relatives and reservation officialdom were concerned.

One balmy spring evening Chee came loping down from Lookout Peak. He announced abruptly:

"Buck Green says another big meeting is set for tomorrow

night, and you are to bring Jemez. He wants me there, too, and Ealae, Dee-O-Det, Nadina, and your mother and Maria."

"I wonder why he wants us to bring women?"

"Simple. There is to be a party after the meeting. Dee-O-Det is to be the honored guest. You are to bring him but you are not to let him know that the party is in his honor."

"What have you and Buck been up to?"

"Nothing that you won't approve of in the end," said Chee with a sly grin.

At my cabin I told Mother and Maria that Buck was giving a party tomorrow evening in the *shaman's* honor and did not want him to know it until he introduced him. I told them they were included in the surprise party and were to wear ordinary trail clothes on the way down so that Dee-O-Det would not suspect anything, but to pack our very best to change into later.

The *shaman* came strolling over and I took the opportunity to make an off-hand offer for him to ride along with Jemez, Chee, Ealae, Mother, Maria, Nadina, and me to Rancho Verde the next day. He seemed pleased and said he would get ready

❧ ❧ ❧

MOST of my people were cultivating the fields the next day, so Chee and I had to saddle the horses for the trip. He was in a sour frame of mind. When I didn't ask why, he told me that Ealae had kicked up a fuss when he told her no children were to go; their siblings were old enough to stay home and give their parents a chance to have fun for a change, but she could not see it that way. He added he couldn't understand women.

"Why try?" I chuckled. "They can't even understand themselves."

"She won't even eat horse meat any more."

"Yeah?"

"You remember when those bandits ambushed us?"

"Yeah."

"And you had your horse shot out from under you?"

"Yeah."

"Nobody thought to save the meat. In the good old days that meat would not have been wasted."

248

I thought to myself, we *have* come a long way. The idea of eating my own horse somehow didn't seem right, though I had eaten horse meat many times and liked it. Mules were better eating, but I doubted that now anyone would eat mule meat. Finally we had the horses saddled and led them to the compound.

"Where is the pack mule?" Mother asked.

"Pack mule!" I repeated. "What pack mule?"

"The one we'll eat!" Chee snickered.

"The one to carry along just in case," Maria laughed.

"Oh, that one! Cousin Chee, go fetch a pack mule!" I had forgotten to saddle a mule to tote our extra clothing and some of the charms Dee-O-Det wanted to take. When Chee got back with the mule everybody was waiting.

"What so long him kept?" Maria wanted to know.

"Just in case," I laughed. I straddled the saddle atop my new white stallion, now named *Chelee*—actually an Apache word for horse.

Chee and Ealae rode in the lead, followed by Maria, Mother, Nadina. I rode in back, hooraying the mule led by Dee-O-Det. It was the first time in many years I had ridden at the rear and now I remembered why men who rode as rear guard of a column always had dry water bags at the end of a trip—to say nothing of red eyes and clogged noses. When Jemez joined me, we dropped farther behind.

We trotted through Chi-hua-hua's old rancheria, now one of the most serene spots in the great mountain chain. It was hard to realize that once The People lived here peacefully—only to meet with violent death from Crook's cavalry, or imprisonment. Here also sixteen of us had trapped and smashed the Yaqui raiders one cold autumn day just five years ago; and shortly afterward Taglito and I had found Buck Green near death from a Yaqui ambush down at Burnt Ranch.

Water abounded everywhere, due to recent rains, and we soon entered the Rancho Verde gate. As we rode in, I noticed by the number of horses that some of the ranchers had already arrived. Buck and Anna Green welcomed us to the meeting.

Ammon Tenny spotted us and came over to talk. Kelzel almost smiled as Maria and I exchanged greetings with him. Jemez looked up a few of his tribesmen who were working for

Buck. John Brewer and Al Bower were conspicuous by their absence. Big Jim Grey appeared to be at least two drinks up on everyone. Soon John Slaughter and his foremen, Juan Flores and Jess Fisher, arrived.

"Howdy, Niño!" Slaughter greeted me. "Had a letter from the colonel the other day. He said to say hello to you."

"Oh, Colonel Roosevelt! Say, now there *is* a man for you. How is he getting on with his war?"

"Haven't you heard? He won it! Last summer."

Buck Green called for attention. "Friends," he said, "all of you are acquainted with the facts and the reason for meeting tonight. You need no introduction to Chief Jemez; who is a trustin' man. He trusted Terrazas. I could stop here and I think you would all know what I mean, but what happened to Jemez has a double meaning."

He related the story of Jemez' arrest and escape. "Now the governor has declared Jemez and all his people outlaws and has put a price on their heads." He went on; "The treacherous attempt to hold Jemez was to use him as a hostage to force his people to come back to Chihuahua and thus leave us ranchers with less protection. Then we would be unable to pay taxes and confiscation would follow.

"A neat plot on the part of Terrazas; but we have one much better. We are going to hire all of Jemez' people to work in the mines and on the ranches. They will work under American protection and will be paid double the going wage of two-and-a-half pesos—*five* pesos for a day's work.

"Now, friends, I'm giving a dance tonight in honor of the greatest *shaman* and medicine man that ever lived. His name is Dee-O-Det. Dee-O-Det come here, I want everybody to meet you."

Looking surprised, Dee-O-Det walked over to Buck, who put an arm around the old man and said:

"Friends, here is a man who can make you have faith in yourself. If it had not been for him I would not be here today."

Dee-O-Det was dazed but happy. He just couldn't seem to understand what was happening.

At that moment somebody outside began banging the dinner triangle and just about everyone headed out to the barbecue pit. A whole beef was on the spit, and people began cutting off slabs

250

Colonel Emilio Kosterlitzky led forag-
ing Mexican forces in our area

John Horton Slaughter, one of the
American ranchers near our rancheria

Thomas Jonathan Jeffords
Owl Head Ranch, 1913.

Tom Jeffords, our good friend Taglito, was blood brother to my grandfather Cochise, my own best partner and a true friend to all Apaches. He greatly admired my mother and she returned the sentiment. He died at the age of eighty-two a year after this photograph was taken at his Owl Head Ranch. We buried him at Owl Head Butte nearby

OPPOSITE: Mike Griffith took this picture of me last year, showing that I manage to get around and do most of what I want to do

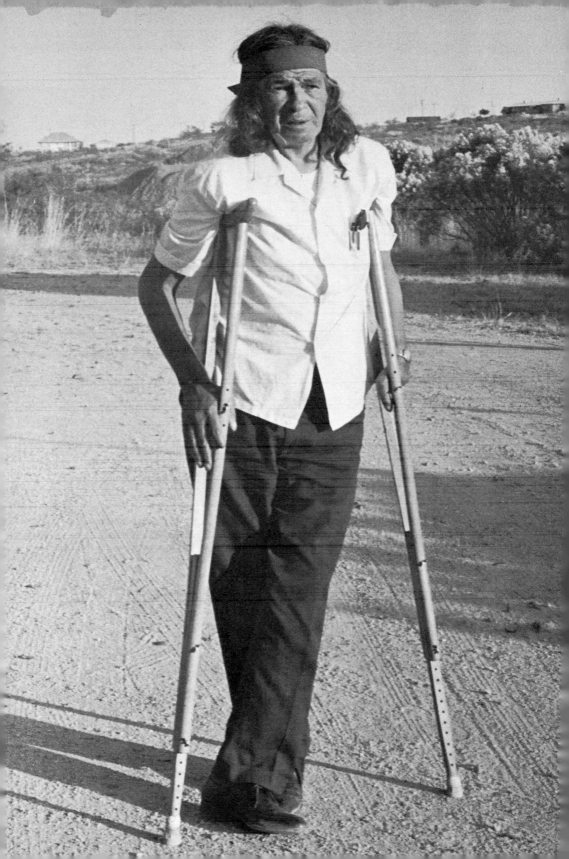

My coauthor and friend Kinney Griffith visited me last
year to talk over final arrangements for this book and his
son photographed us

to put on their tin plates; then they retired to some place where they could sit and enjoy themselves. There were barrels of wine that had been cooled in the depths of the ranch well.

And the food—it was a feast! The pinto beans had been seasoned with red chili and salt pork and baked in a huge iron pot buried in hot coals. The meat was seasoned with garlic and cloves; home-grown vegetables, such as onions, carrots, corn, and parsnips, had been cooked in the cavity of the beef. The bread had been baked in a *hornito*—a Spanish or Indian oven made of rock, its shape resembling a stoop-door wikiup. The method was to preheat the rock oven with a fire of oak wood. When hot enough, the coals were withdrawn and the dough was placed inside to bake slowly. A cattle ranch always had milk, so there was plenty of butter to go with the hot bread, and there were bowls of wild honey.

After the feast, many gathered around the wine barrels. Mother, Maria, Nadina, and I returned to the house and entered the living room, which by now had been gaily decorated and turned into a dance hall. A five-piece Gypsy band was strumming away and several couples were already dancing. Chee and Ealae were acting like newlyweds. Kasale was dancing with Anna Green. Buck Green grabbed Mother, saying:

"Come on, Niome—let's dance!"

Mother had been taught to dance by Tom Jeffords, who, when he wanted, could dance. Maria and I tried. Though I had done some dancing before, I wasn't too graceful in my new *kabuns*. The music suddenly stopped, and we heard the beat of an Indian drum. People withdrew, clearing the floor for Dee-O-Det who had leaped into his solo dance. He let out shrill yells in time with the drum as he swept into the Apache Harvest tune. He soon switched to his version of a rollicking tune that Buck Green had taught him:

> *I'll trade my shoes . . .*
> *for a bottle of booze,*
> *Nobody knows . . .*
> *how dry I am . . .*

When his act was finished he received a standing ovation, and I have never seen a prouder man. He danced with my wife, my mother, and with Nadina. Even Kelzel put on a Yaqui Deer dance, with horns and all, while Dee-O-Det chipped in with his chant.

The old guest of honor regained the center of the floor and asked the drummer to give him a beat. Then he really did a dance. I have never seen one like it, before or since. It was a kind of combination of a strutting turkey gobbler and a squirrel up a pecan tree. I got out of breath just watching him. Finally he came over where we were standing and flopped on the floor.

"How did you like that?" he asked between gulps for air.

"Much better than I could have done," I answered.

The crowd was cheering. He got up and gave me one of his rare smiles—it looked like a coyote snatching mice out of a haystack—and he took Maria by the arm and they whirled out on the floor. Afterwards we three went outside for air. Soon Kelzel came out to the barbecue pit for meat and a goblet of wine. He seemed half-drunk already. Spotting us, he came over and nodded.

"How are things at Borega?" I asked.

"Good so far," he replied slowly. "The land is good and we have a good irrigation system, but we have to pay for it by a percentage of our crops."

"That sounds like a fair arrangement."

"That is what I thought at first." Then Kelzel spoke faster. "But I found that I pay too much for the construction of the canals over a period of years. We could have built them ourselves. When we were on the Yaqui River I built an irrigation system, dam and all. They confiscated that, and gave me land on the Arros River—you saw it—and now this system costs more and is owned by a foreign company. Tell me, how are you getting along?"

"Well, I do not have any tax troubles. My land is valueless because there are no roads to take produce to market and we cannot pack it out at a profit—that is why they do not bother me. Also, they remember I helped them out in the battles of Basaranca and Tesorabi."

"Stop being so simple-minded, Niño. You are lucky the generals did not outlaw you after helping them. I have done work for them and they have outlawed me seven times. Each time I came back to my mountains and each time they made peace with me. They know they cannot fight me in my mountains any

252

more than they can fight you in yours. They run me off my land by force of arms but they cannot budge me from my mountains."

Kelzel had guzzled a lot of wine and was talkative, so I urged him on. "The provincial governors have always been their own bosses—ever since Coronado."

"We have inherited his sins." Kelzel nodded. "Those governors even defy the Federal Government. Mexico City is a long way from Chihuahua and Sonora, and Diaz has to have such men as Terrazas, Batista, de Vega, and Torres to make his government work. So what is to stop them from graft? Consider the tax system: the Federal Government demands ten percent; the State five percent but the State collects twenty-five percent and keeps fifteen of that. Death is the penalty in lieu of taxes."

Kelzel, High Chief of Mexico's most hated tribe of Indians, turned to get more wine, and Maria tugged at my sleeve. "This scares me and his talk," she whispered. "Let us away go."

People were leaving the dance floor to find places to sleep. All seemed tired and feeling the effects of too much wine. The musicians were packing up. Maria and I got our blankets and smoothed out a place to bed down. Mother and Nadina were already bedded down; Chee and Ealae were back by the barn; Dee-O-Det was sitting nearby with his head in his hands, though he shouldn't have had a headache before morning.

In the morning we were slow getting started for home, but we made it, and home we stayed. All summer long we tended our fields, and except for one trip to Bisbee and messages from our signal system, we were isolated from the outside world. The half-expected call to arms never came. We had a good harvest, and during the autumn frosts we had a great inter-tribal feast with the Tarahumari. The year 1899 faded and the only one worried was our canny old *shaman*, who said this life was too good to last.

Chapter 15

The Burning Sky

BUCK GREEN invited us to help him celebrate the Turn-of-the-Century holiday. It was to last, as he put it, from Christmas through New Year's Day, and would be the biggest shindig south of the border.

Generally, the American settlers had good cause to celebrate. So far tax troubles were tolerable. Cattle rustling had been brought to a minimum by the alert Indian cowboys employed by the white ranchers under the leadership of Buck Green. Even the red-flaggers seemed to have retired. The ranch pay-rolls were sizeable and pay was at a minimum of 100 pesos a month. The Greene Copper Mining Company of Cananea had the largest payroll in Sonora, and individuals as well as businesses depended on it.

The day before Christmas, all of us in shape to ride headed down the trail toward Rancho Verde. We arrived shortly after sunset. It was good to get down out of the wintry high country of Pa-Gotzin-Kay. There were fifty-four in our band. We found about 200 people assembled at Rancho Verde. Chief Kelzel had brought twenty; Chief Jemez had brought his family and twelve warriors. There were a few Opatas and Mexicans. I could only guess at the number of white people. The Greens were well able to host the multitude. They provided everything, only asking their guests to bring their own camping equipment.

In the big yard between the house and barns many large tables and benches surrounded barbecue pits, cooking fires, and serving tables. Some lanterns helped a full moon to light a dance patio, and a band of Sonoran Gypsies were tuning guitars, violins, and a bass fiddle. Maria and I were watching the activity when my mother came running, almost out of breath, shouting:

"My son! My son! Taglito is here!"

"Where is he, Mother?"

"Talking to Tenny and Grey!"

"He now coming is," said Maria, pointing.

The tall figure of Tom Jeffords was striding toward us. He hugged Mother, to her great delight and his own satisfaction, and thrust out both hands to grasp Maria's and mine.

"Maria! Neen-yo! It is good to see you youngsters again. And to think a new century is about to come! I never thought I'd live to see it. I won't miss this party for love nor money."

Noticing Chief Kelzel nearby, Taglito greeted him. "How's it going with you—you old pirate!"

"Hello, Mister Jeffords! Hello, Niño!" Kelzel responded with his usual exactitude when speaking in Spanish. He shook hands all around, and said, "Things in Chi-hua-hua are too good. I do not understand it—it is too quiet."

"Lots of people here seem to think the same way," Tom replied. "But there aren't many left who were here the last turn of a new century—so does it matter?"

"Oh, very well, Mister Jeffords!"

I could see that Tom was somewhat thrown off balance with the polite way Kelzel acted. I think he was expecting something different from the vicious head-hunter of northern Mexico. When Kelzel left to meet with some others, Taglito remarked:

"Polite but deadly."

"Well, he was educated in a mission school," I remarked. "He makes a better friend than he does an enemy."

Tom went on to say he had sold his silver mine at Owl Head and all the steers on his ranch, keeping only some bulls, cows, and heifers. He had hired a small family as caretakers in his absence. Mother grasped the opportunity to invite him to live with us now—permanently. He put an arm around her waist and they strolled away.

Soon they returned. Anna Green had them in tow, with Buck lagging behind. "Maria, Nadina—you and Niome come with me," said Anna. "We must discuss these men in their own light."

"Light or dark," snipped my mother, "it makes no difference with men. All the same, they are—*Los Goddammies!*"

Apparently somebody was mad at somebody. After a hearty laugh, Buck said, "Well, come on, you stinkers." Taglito and I followed him across the patio to a table where old Dee-O-Det was nursing a mug of eggnog—a luxury we could not afford. He stared at us, blankly. The tables were loaded with platters of assorted meats and bowls of other inviting victuals. Taglito and I each tried a mug of eggnog. "Come into the house when you're ready," Buck said. "I've kept the house strictly private for this shindig—except for a few. I got some good booze that I know you'll like."

"Let's go get some of that good whisky he's braggin' about," Tom said to me.

"Yeah. I don't like the sour wine he serves."

"I heard that." Buck bristled. "Yuh hombres don't know good likker—only when you're told." We headed toward the big ranch house, ducking people along the way, and when we made it, Buck began filling glasses full to the brim.

From then on it was one kind of drink after another and all I've ever been able to recall was that I woke up and saw the sun shining. I was bedded down in the yard between Taglito and Dee-O-Det, and Buck was urging us to wake up and get up. After a while we made it into the house and Buck poured us some hangover cure. He began to chuckle.

"Merry Christmas! Now, the family an' house guests will eat Christmas dinner in the house. *Sabe?* Only Tenny, Grey, Dee-O-Det, Niño, Tom, and your womenfolk. Did you bring your womenfolk, Tom?"

"No, but I will next time."

"How come you never got married, Tom?" Buck snorted.

"How do you know I'm not married?" Tom shot back.

"I *don't* know—that's why I'm asking."

"How do you like the way you're finding out?"

"Not makin' much headway, am I? Here, let me refill your glass."

The banter continued and I knew the three of us were getting drunk again. The next thing I'm sure of was being seated with our women at a big table, and there was a joyous Christmas dinner with turkey, all kinds of vegetables, pies, puddings. The turkeys were home-grown on the Tenny ranch. The party really got going. There were kegs of whisky and barrels of wine —Buck must have bought out a liquor store in Bisbee or El Paso.

The thing that sticks uppermost in my memory was the Christmas present Buck Green gave me. He gave me a beautiful, engraved "One of One Thousand" model 1873 Winchester rifle, calibre 44/40.[1]

The rifle was handy for all occasions, since I could use the shells from my belt gun in it. It was true up to 200 yards. Colt sixguns of that calibre would carry that far, but accuracy was a different story.

Maria and I gave the Greens our largest cougarskin with mounted head, and a silvertip grizzly hide that measured ten feet from nose to tail. Both pelts had been carefully tanned by our Old Ones, people who were expert in the art. Dee-O-Det gave them the mounted head of an enormous bighorn ram he had personally mounted and blessed with *hodenten.* Mother gave them a bedspread made of thousands of white moleskins.

During the week there were all sorts of contests—sack races, women's stickball, bronco-busting, trick riding. The Tarahumari put on a foot race, a contest in which they are unbeatable. We staged an Apache arrow-shooting exhibition.

New Year's Eve there was a small feast and a big dance—and, as usual, plenty to drink. Colonel William Greene and his entourage arrived. Everybody celebrated till midnight.

❦ ❦ ❦

THE next day, New Year's Day, was my contest: a rifle-shooting match for a top prize of a silver-mounted saddle. It was a black leather beauty, embossed with silver buttons, conches, and Ocho Reales coins, and had matching stirrup cover, woven-hair surcingle, and a silver-mounted bridle with Spanish bit.[2]

1. This rare model soon became a collector's item; if I had not let it get away from me, it would be worth at least $5,000 today.

2. This was the saddle mentioned earlier. Buck had ordered it for his own use, but Pablo, the old saddle maker, was ambushed by the Mexican slaves before

I had competition in this—good competition. To meet it, I got my fleet-footed Golden Bird to pace me in a brisk run around the barn area so I could get my blood circulation up to normal after the night's overindulgence with whisky.

The shooting match went as follows: to compete in the contest cost each contestant $20.00—a goodly sum in those days, but there were about thirty who parted with the entrance money to get a crack at that prize.

First came an elimination contest. To qualify we had to have a number of hits in the bull's-eye. The guns were rifles (or carbines) and the distance was 100 yards. Six of us were left for the semifinals: Tom Jeffords, Jim Grey, Kelzel, Colonel Greene, his bodyguard Ed Massey, and me.

A fresh target was marked with the shooter's name as each man took his turn, and this was then judged at the finish of the contest. Rules were set for standing or kneeling, the points counting being the number of holes within the six-inch bull's-eye.

We had to place five rapid-fire shots, as in the elimination test. I fired and got four in the bull's-eye. Massey got three in the black, the other two in the white part of the target. Green got three in the bull's-eye but they were in the outer part of the black, and the other two were in the white nearby. Taglito got only one in the black and four just on the outside. Grey and Kelzel had one or two in the bull's-eye, not enough to get them in the finals.

That narrowed the contestants down to just three: myself, Colonel Green, and Ed Massey. The rules for the finals were to stand and shoot just once. Massey took first try; he hit the white, several inches away from the bull's-eye. Green nicked the bull's-eye. I was tense but I hit the bull's-eye right in the center and was awarded the silver saddle.

Colonel Greene offered his congratulations. Delirious from having won the prize, I exclaimed, "I learned young and get much practice!"

"You should be a good shot—being old Cochise's son!"

"I am the son of his son," I corrected.

"Has Buck told you that I would like you to work for me?"

he could deliver it; the saddle was recovered by Kelzel's warriors and Kelzel gave it back to Buck—who, for some reason, never used it.

"Yes, he has. What would you like me to do?" I asked, only from curiosity.

"Well, for one thing, I would like you to be a companion, just to ride along with me wherever I go. You have a fine reputation; Tom Jeffords has spoken of you. You handle a gun better'n I do and that's what I need. I'll pay you well."

"I will think about it," I stammered.

"Think it over and give Buck your answer."

He looked at his watch and said he had to get back to Cananea. I watched him as he drove two beautiful blacks hitched to a light surrey through the gate and was gone. Like Colonel Roosevelt, there was a man whom I admired.

I looked around for Tom but he was nowhere in sight. I went into the house and found him having a drink with Buck. I was mystified as to why Taglito had made such a poor showing in the rifle contest. I respected his ability with a rifle, and I had seen him hit a quail on the wing just for the sport of it. When I started to question him, he grunted:

"Oh, shut up and drink. You won the saddle, didn't you?"

"Yeah," drawled Buck. "And I have seen Taglito shoot th' nit off'n a gnat's nut—let's have a drink."

❦ ❦ ❦

BACK at the rancheria the following evening, the *shaman* spoke of the new century's celebration. He maintained that all who were at the great celebration would always prosper because *Ihidnan* smiled on peaceful people. He said people like to have a good time, to live and let live. Tom expressed some doubts about that theory, claiming it was un-Apache when judged from the past. I made no comment but asked Tom if he was going to work for Bill Greene. Would it benefit Pa-Gotzin-Kay if I worked for Greene?

"Well," he evaded, "that new copper mine of his at Cananea sure looks promising. I stopped by Ronquillo on the way over —that's the town across the tracks from the mine—and it's mighty nice. They have company-owned stores and you can buy anything you want on credit, as long as you work for the mine. Old Bill secured a lease from General Pesquiera's widow, with the approval of Porfirio Diaz, an' he's really developing that property."

"Are you going to work for him?" I pressed.

"Yeah, I think I will, but not until later. I'll need to lease out Owl Head ranch first, if I can; kinda quiet around there. Then I'll move into one of those cabins at Ronquillo and go to work. Old Bill pays well."

"We will come and visit you, Taglito," Mother offered.

"The colonel will put you all to work, Niome," he chuckled.

He visited with us several more days, but complained about it being too cold for his old bones and left for Owl Head.

🌱 🌱 🌱

SPRING came and brought renewed rumblings. The Yaqui on the Rio Arros were again under the heel of the tyrants. Chief Kelzel once more defied the tyrants and again was driven off his land. This time, though, when he retreated, he took up his stand in the nearby mountains overlooking Borega. From there he destroyed the irrigation system by blowing up the dam he'd built on the Arros, delaying the *federalistas* long enough for his tribespeople to gain the safety of the mountains and the stock of rifles and supplies he had cached there against just such an emergency.

Governors Terrazas and Torres, working together, with the help of Federal "advisers," put 1500 *soldatos* into the field. Word was spread and every rancher armed his workers to defend lives and property. Buck Green notified Colonel Greene at Cananea that a hostile force was on the march.

When my call came, I took a force of thirty Apache and Tarahumari braves and rode for Rancho Verde. On the way I observed that Basaranca had somehow about doubled its garrison without my knowing it. I stopped at a point where I could get a good view of the town. It was swarming with uniformed red-shirts.

We rode like wild Indians for the Green ranch. It was also an armed camp. Buck was giving orders, sending out groups and scouts in different directions. Buck informed me that Eugene's family had got out of Basaranca, and he motioned me to the ranch house. I hurried to the house where Anna Green let me in and led the way to the kitchen.

"Shis-Inday!" (Hail to the chief) Eugene greeted me. "If you hadn't come soon, I was going to get you myself."

"Skeè-kizzen!" (Welcome brother) I said. He was thin, and even had his hair cut short like a *blanco. "Aco tndn-níl gon-yè?"* (What is the trouble?)

"I left Tenny's for a time, but when I went to the garrison to get my family, the soldiers grabbed me and put me in chains. They forced me to work in the powder plant all winter. Nakai was the troublemaker. My family managed to get out, and yesterday I broke away. There is a war coming and their aim is to kill all Indians—you first, as they hate you most. Yesterday they adobe-walled two Yaqui families.

"The most important thing I wanted to tell you is that they are going to pack cannons up on each of the three peaks that overlook Pa-Gotzin-Kay and blast all the Mansos off the earth."

"When are they going to do this?" I asked.

"I do not know for sure. They had just ordered me to direct the moving of the cannon. That's another reason why I left. That powder plant is an arsenal—they make the powder there for Torres and Terrazas, and store it along with the cannons. It is very dangerous. We must wear moccasins or work in bare feet. The other day while making an inspection I saw two soldiers wearing their boots. I ordered them to take their boots off and then leave. They removed them all right, but hit me on the head with them. I just can't take that any more."

Now I knew why Eugene was so nervous. He told me he was going to take his family to Cananea and work in the copper mines. If the chance came later, he would go to America—for here the Mexican bushmasters would be after him. I told him Buck was already getting a wagon ready to take him and his family to Cananea, but I asked him to reconsider and come back to Pa-Gotzin-Kay where he'd be safe. He refused, saying for his wife's sake he had adopted her Mexican ways and now believed in their God. This was a shock to me, but I was in for an even bigger one.

He informed me that as he left Basaranca he had shot and killed Major Nakai—and called him a two-faced, forked-tongue *yùdastćin* (bastard). The shot had blown his head open. Therefore, Eugene said, if he came back to us he would involve us in our own destruction. Buck called to us that the wagon was loaded and ready. He had five mounted men waiting to accompany Eugene, his wife, and two children on their trip to Cananea, and they all set off.

Having had time to reflect on what Eugene had made known to me, I burned with anger. Why, those dirty *golinki* (skunks). Brush-apes! They would kill us Apaches first, eh? My men would cut them to pieces. I began to plan.

I thought about the *shaman*, all the old men and women, the children, my wife, my mother—and my blood boiled. Those dirty murderers, treacherous as ever! They would try to pack cannon into the mountains and blast us off the earth, eh? Those cannons were no good without powder—the powder plant, that was the answer. *Atà Inday' t'n-nen-t'-to-kohi!* (Their chief thinks like a crazy man!)

I called my braves together and told them what I intended to do—blow that powder magazine. I had to figure out a way to get in, for a direct assault would be impossible with the soldiers and their bristling guns. I dispatched one man to Pa-Gotzin-Kay to alert the remaining warriors, forgetting I could have used the signal system. We were ready to ride when Buck rushed up and wanted to know where we were heading.

I told him we were going to blow up that powder arsenal. He grabbed my mount's bridle and said I couldn't get near it. Besides even if I got lucky, Torres would say the white ranchers did it just to get America involved in the war. I knew the *gusanos* were always making false claims, so that didn't bother me. All I knew was that I did not intend to stand still and wait till they blew up my rancheria—and I knew the whiteman would not wait either. Then Buck pointed out how impossible it was to drag a mountain battery up Juh's Trail.

That set my mind at ease, but not for long. It was obvious that Terrazas and Torres were up to something bad for us or they would not have all those *soldatos* at Basaranca—and some *á-nèt'j* (spy) would know the way. I got to wondering about Kelzel. How did he fit in, and how was he making out in his mountains? Buck had told me Kelzel was waiting, ready to spring a trap on any force fool enough to walk into it. Buck told me to wait there while he ran to his signal post. I was pondering all this and at the same time making sure that my men, especially the Tarahumari, understood our system of sending signals and orders.

Buck returned with a message that a regiment of red-shirts was marching to attack Kelzel from the Chihuahua side of the mountains, while the Basaranca force figured to attack his rear is a sort of pincers movement. This sounded to me as if the Mexican generals figured Kelzel would turn to attack the force from the east. If so, then this was my chance to invade Basaranca. When I told Buck of my decision, he sternly told me to remember that he had been elected commander and that I had helped to elect him.

He admitted my strategy was fine, but my tactics would get us all into trouble with the Mexican Federal Government, and that if Diaz sent troops after us, we'd be sunk. He repeated that Colonel Greene was a confidant of President Diaz and would protest if our property was damaged in any way. I knew Buck had our interests at heart, as well as his own, but I insisted I did not like or understand the look of things.

"You don't need to understand, Niño!" he said impatiently. "You just handle your Indians, and I'll handle the rest my way; and never mind that goddam powder plant—for now!"

He suggested that I make another check on the horses and saddles, the mules and their packs, for when we moved we didn't want faulty trail gear to foul us up. He was right, there was a lot to be done to get a large mobile band of Indians organized in a military manner. Finally we had to light lanterns to finish the job.

☙ ☙ ☙

SUDDENLY there was a brilliant flash that lit up the night sky, followed by rolling thunder that seemed to keep on rolling and rumbling.

As I studied the glare, it seemed to rise and fall in waves, from amber to dull red, in the southern sky. It was the wrong time of year for a thunderstorm, I knew, and the stars were out all over. The sky was clear—except where it seemed to be burning in the direction of Basaranca, twenty miles away.

Buck joined me and said harshly, "What th' hell's going on?"

We had both seen the "burning sky" many times. It was, and is, a common sight over the Sonora Desert hills and the Sierra Madre at sunset; but never had I seen it burn at night, unless above a fire.

"Buck," I said, "I think the powder plant has blown sky high!"

"You could be right, Niño, and if you are, our troubles are over for a while—I hope."

I had my doubts about that, and had a sudden feeling of depression. Now there was no more thunder and the burning sky gradually darkened above the mountainous skyline. We talked some more, then bade each other good night. I joined my warriors around their campfire. No one mentioned the thunder, but all were curious about our next move.

I got to thinking along a different line: some years before, Tom Jeffords had whittled a set of chessmen from madroña wood and taught me the game. Tom said then, "Once you learn the game, the game teaches you. It teaches you to think—think in a different way. You will find, Neen-yo, that your first thought will be analyzed. You will think: what will the result be if I do that? You will act accordingly."

Now, I could see. In my mind's eye the chessboard was there in front of me as I sat before the fire, listening to the men argue pro and con the merits of attacking Basaranca. The queen was Basaranca, who in truth could swoop down on us from any direction and capture us. Then I could see Buck's strategy. He arranged the pawns around our king so that if queen Basaranca made a move to capture a single pawn, she would fall to the beleaguered king—Kelzel. The knight on the board was Buck Green.

A rooster crowing at the first signs of dawn wakened me. There were some embers in the fireplace and by piling on dry wood I soon had a blaze. The men were getting out of their blankets, some grunting and snorting as if they didn't like it. We had got our horses attended to and made breakfast when Buck Green came out to our fire.

"Niño, I just got a message for you to think about. My men who left yesterday with the wagon say that about ten miles out on the road to Cananea, Eugene suddenly jumped out of the wagon and ran into the hills. Before they could do anything to

264

stop him, he was plum gone. You know how Apaches are that way. They took his family on in, then sent me the helio message. Thought you'd like to know."

I did some quick thinking: ten miles west—from there a man fast on his feet could cut down Lobo Canyon and be in Basaranca in a couple of hours. Good old Eugene. He often did the unexpected, but I wouldn't bet four bits he had got out alive. Buck was eyeing me so I told him I'd take a quick ride up to Pa-Gotzin-Kay and tell my people what to expect. I picked five men and told Kasale to keep the others at Buck's until I got back. We were on our way soon, and when we topped the rimrock that overlooked Basaranca, I saw where the two-stack powder plant had been only a wide black hole now remained. Around its perimeter fires were still smouldering in what was left of houses. There wasn't a *soldato* to be seen. Aside from the six of us there wasn't a living person within miles.

Chapter 16   1900-1902

Apache Anguish

WHEN we got to the rancheria I was met by Mother, Maria, and Dee-O-Det. They anxiously fired questions at me about the great thunder that shook the earth and made the sky burn, and the *shaman* wanted to know about the war. I answered their questions and calmed their fears.

When we entered our cabin Maria threw her arms around me and would not let go.

"My husban', afraid for us I am. Afraid if you to war am go, I will again never see you."

"Dear, Golden Bird. I have been to wars before and I have always been protected . . ."

"Frightened now I am, me! I not want you to war go. Send Chee, you can; he is good warrior."

"Chee has to stay here and protect the rancheria, my love. He is my subchief."

"Fight I can. Let me with you go, my Niño," she pleaded. "Once you said always wanted me with you."

"Maria, I want you with me always, but I do not want you to run the risks of war. If you were killed, I would be as nothing. I would lose my spirit without you. Just wait for me, and when I come home, I will bring you tales of how we won."

This brought a smile to her lovely golden-brown face. She began teasing me, as she often did, but I avoided her, knowing Dee-O-Det had called a council meeting and was waiting for my report. I walked to my usual place and did not need to call for silence. I told the men that what we had feared had happened, but I assured them that the war would not come to Pa-Gotzin-Kay. I said it was strange that we now had the White-Eyes on our side, yet when our ancestors lived on American soil they had fought the Americans. And now we live on Mexican soil and we fight the Mexicans.

Just then Chee rode in with word from Buck Green that at this moment Chief Kelzel was being pursued into the mountains by Mexican soldiers. Green was sending reinforcements and Kasale and our men were riding with him. Young Juh, young Chi-hua-hua, and others rode with Tenny, and many Tarahumari were with them. Buck told me to take all our warriors and ride to help the Americans. Chee also brought word from Lookout Peak that our Eugene, son of Chatto, had been seen entering Basaranca but was not seen coming out—and the powder plant was no more. I added that Nakai, too, would be seen no more.

I stepped down and the *shaman* took over and began the chant for a brave who had gone to Big Sleep. War drums began to beat. Led by Hi-okee, the warriors began a dance around the fire, asking *Usen* to give them victory in the coming battle.

Dee-O-Det handed me a sacred headband of woven eagle-breast feathers; it was the sacred charm to prevent any enemy bullet from touching me. I put on the sacred band and informed the council that our *shaman* had given us protection against the enemy in battle and he would give wisdom to Chee so that he might defend Pa-Gotzin-Kay against the enemy of The People.

The drums resumed their beating as I left and went to our fire, where Mother and Maria were glumly waiting. I told them I was not afraid of war, though I wished there were some other way. Mother said I must do what I had to do—that is always the way with men who are leaders. I told them we would win. Colonel Greene was sending men from the mines; Jim Grey was to send ammunition and rifles; and the ranchers would provide us with food. I bade Mother good night and took Maria to our cabin. I had to get up early in the morning.

Inside a fire was crackling in the fireplace. I sat down on a chair Maria had made and she sat on the floor beside me.

"My husban'." she said, "when to Buck's we went, and the silver saddle you won—how long was that?"

"Oh, that was New Year's Day."

"And before that how long were we married?"

"Oh, two, maybe three years . . ."

"How much is two maybe three?"

"You've got me puzzled, my love."

She sighed. "I know because now that all the years we married have been you and I happy have been and so afraid I was you might angry be with me. Forgotten you have that the year was 1896 when married we were." She added sadly, "And all that time I have given you no sons, me!"

I had never known her to have any moods of depression, but now I had a trying time consoling her; she finally quieted, but I had failed to bring back that golden smile. I could see her fears were like all women's fears that their men going to war would never return. It occurred to me she would be the loneliest woman on earth if I did not return, and that thought made me gulp with fear, until I remembered the *shaman's* charm . . .

Poor Golden Bird, I did not know what else to say or do, except stay home, and that would have been unthinkable. I tucked her into bed and held her close, hoping that would comfort her.

I awoke early and dressed, examined my weapons, and took care of my white stallion, Chelee, before daybreak. At breakfast everyone was quiet. Maria's eyes were red from weeping. I did my best to console her and Mother, telling them this war would last only a few days and then we would have our happy days back because our world would be free. Maria just nodded her head and tried to speak but no words would come.

Chee galloped in and for once he seemed ruffled.

"Buck just sent word that many red-shirts are on the way to attack Kelzel's flank, the left flank. They are approaching Las Chipas Canyon where it joins the Bavispe. You are to intercept them and hold them until reinforcements can get there."

Maria's voice seemed to peal out of the endless sky. "My husban', if I lost you I am, allow me with you to go—that I may died with you."

"My beloved little wife, you are very brave to want to be with me—and die with me—but I am not going to die and you cannot go with me."

"Then I will have to died alone," she sobbed.

"Mother," I pleaded, "I must hurry. Take care of Maria and

yourself. Everyone will be all right here."

I rode out with fifteen men: Hi-okee, Neo-ot-Toden, Na-Shis-Tor, Kersus, and Klan-o-Tay of my age group; Bylas, Do-meah, Half-hand, Non-Ni-No, Al-con-Chi, Achinera, Rosanto, Loco-cito, Cal-I-To, and Zin-Ley, of the younger group. We headed through the south rampart, turned east, and made for the distant red lava-strewn ridge that overlooked Las Chipas Canyon.

❦ ❦ ❦

AFTER about three hours of hard riding—possibly thirty-five kilometers—we dismounted on the southeast slope of the red ridge, turned our horses over to one man, yanked our carbines from the saddle boots, and ran to the summit and peered into a narrow valley with no cover to speak of, though there was a hedge of beavertail cactus bordering the base rock along the canyon wall. A cloud of red dust heralded the movement of mounted men; if the enemy were approaching, they were riding into our trap.

I gave the glasses to Hi-okee for a look, then pointed to a spur off to our right. I told him to take six men, get behind the cactus below that point, and wait until the *soldatos* passed his position. My signal would be a rifle shot; then he was to open up on them. If any escaped, he was to follow to where the canyon widened and we would meet him. The enemy had to pass that point to link up with the main force in the Bavispe Barranca. Hi-okee chose his men and departed for the rocky point.

We squirmed into better positions behind the top rocks and thus commanded the mouth of the Las Chipas to the limits of effective carbine range. Our position was about 100 yards above where they had to pass, and the canyon widened at that point. We waited and watched. The column of two's approached at a normal gait, and the commander was riding as though he owned the world. Slowly they shortened the distance between us. The commander waved an arm several times and the march halted, then men dismounted and some of them drank from the stream. A little too far for good carbine shooting. I knew that only the rifle I had received as a Christmas present from Buck would carry true that far.

We waited. I wanted them to hurry, yet half-hoped they would not. They hunkered down in a semicircle as if going into council. Finally they stood up and approached their horses. They tightened cinches and mounted, then continued their slow ride toward us. I was worried, having the nagging feeling that something was all wrong. The *soldatos* were now directly below us. I had a bead on that haughty commander and in a moment I would fire the signal shot. Riding two abreast, half the column had passed when I pressed the trigger. That *Godo* never knew what hit him.

Our fusillade banged out all around—and panic hit the red-shirt ranks. Men were falling, yelling, horses were neighing, and with the clangor of rifle fire, it was some time before any of them could even return our fire. Then they saw they had no targets since we were hidden behind the top rocks. About twenty of them regrouped and made a run for the cactus cover at the junction below the sharp spur. As they passed Hi-okee's band, their scattered ranks were subjected to more deadly fire.

As I moved to a position slightly higher on my rock, a distant movement behind caught the corner of my eye.

I turned and saw Maria on her white mare, riding like the wind across the red slope behind us and heading to where our horses were bunched together.

"Stay back!" I shouted. "Go back, Maria!"

Then before my horrified eyes she slid from the saddle. The white Barb swerved, bolted, and Maria's foot was caught in the stirrup. Frantic, I was up and running toward her. Then I saw her foot pull free and she collapsed on the rocky ground. I dropped beside her and raised her head and shoulders gently.

"Great *Usen!* Maria! Are you hurt?"

I heard the death rattle in her throat and saw that part of her breast was blown away. Everything seemed to go black. The anguish within me made me oblivious to all else.

I picked her up and held her in my arms—she was limp, lifeless. What was I going to do? Then I felt something jerk my headband and I heard a loud report, followed by the sound of a horse running. Through a blur I saw a red-shirt on a fleeing horse.

I must have laid her down and grabbed up my rifle, for the next thing I felt was the buck of my gun and the *soldato* tumbled from his horse. I ran to where he was lying on his side, twisting. I kicked him over on his back, shoved the muzzle of the rifle under his chin, and pulled the trigger.

The gun exploded and so did his head.

🌱 🌱 🌱

I FOUND myself again holding the lifeless body of my Golden Bird in my arms. Someone helped me to mount Chelee, and in a daze I rode the long trail back to Pa-Gotzin-Kay.

Mother, seeing me, exclaimed, "Oh, has Maria been hurt?"

I managed to say, "She has left us forever."

"The poor child! I did not even know she was gone until too late."

The *shaman* came and put a hand on my shoulder:

"It is with heavy heart that I say this—*Ihidnan* has called his child to Big Sleep."

I carried my Golden Bird to our cabin and gently laid her on the bed. The *shaman* began the ritualistic keening to light the way for an Apache spirit to the Spirit World far up there in the endless sky.

I dropped to my knees, my heart bursting. The *shaman* knelt down by Maria—he was moaning, his head moving back and forth.

"Oh, *Ihidnan!* You have taken your child and left a man with great pain. We do not ask why, but we ask that you keep her safe for all time to come." He rose, nodded to me, and left abruptly; I knew he had gone to prepare the place for her to enter the Spirit World.

Sitting on the floor, Mother was sobbing, moaning, and rocking back and forth in her grief. When I got down beside her, she took my face in her hands and I smelled the charcoal and clay. She was rubbing my face with the black ash. I saw hers was already painted with the black of mourning for our loved one.

I had not yet forced myself to admit that my Golden Bird actually was gone forever. I was still kneeling, thinking that perhaps it was a dream from which I would awaken . . .

Sometime later I heard Mother's voice as though in a dream. "My son, the *shaman* comes."

It was no dream. In a daze I placed Maria's personal possessions beside her and wrapped the blanket around her. I picked up poor Maria, the most loyal and lovable partner a man ever had, and carried her to the grave that was ready to receive her —under the cliff of the gold cave.

I climbed down into the cavern and laid her gently on the bottom. Then the *shaman* began to hand me the proper-shaped stones to build the coffin around her. I placed each one carefully, building the tomb. When the last stone was ready to be placed, I kissed her cold lips in farewell . . .

I could not do more, so the *shaman* took the stone, placed it, and I watched as he covered the stones with the soft red earth, muttering the sacred words for the departed—working as if protecting, yet hiding, his most precious thing in this world. When all was done, I stood at the foot of the tomb and talked to her silently. Words and thoughts crowded my feverish mind:

"Farewell, my Golden Bird. Farewell, my beloved. With you gone there is nothing for me here. Grieve not for our short separation. I will be with you soon. The sons and daughters not bestowed upon us here will come to us in the Spirit World. One glorious day soon again we will ride our white horses in the lands of the bright golden sands . . . and peace will be with us forevermore."

🌱 🌱 🌱

I WAS left with only one thought in mind: battle! I would get myself killed in battle, and soon, but I would take a lot of the hated Nakai-Ye with me to light the way out of this world of tears. I must have ridden poor Chelee off his feet—I don't remember. The battle line had advanced several kilometers in my absence. Someone tossed me a carbine and I was charging into battle with the setting sun on my back. I had never taken the old *Netdahe* vow, but I found myself fighting like one now —or so I was told later.

A few of the original fifty red-shirts had somehow escaped in Las Chipas and had joined up with the main force at the Bavispe crossing. The battle was going in our favor, though, and when Buck Green and his men joined the fray, it soon ended. Around the campfires that evening, and after the heat of hate within me had lessened some, I noticed only a few familiar faces were missing: Na-Shis-Tor and Neo-ot-Toden of my group, Peridot and Asa from Kasale's braves with Buck's forces.

The one thing that was a blessing for me was the Apache rule or law of never speaking a person's name, when one knew that person had gone to Big Sleep—unless in an emergency. I was too numb to feel much of anything until the white mare, running loose, caught up with us, trotted into camp, and took a place beside her brother on the picket. The pressure within me surged up then, but what could I do about it? I hunkered down near the white Barbs and must have fallen asleep, for it was daylight when Buck Green shook my shoulders. Sensing what was going on within me, he led me to a packsaddle, dug out a small whisky jug, and handed it to me.

"Get outside o' this, Niño," he said gruffly. "Then when you are ready, take your men up to Diablo and reinforce Kelzel and his men." I nodded—there was nothing to say. "Take those three pack mules along, with Pete here," he added, indicating an undersized half-Mexican. "They're loaded with cases of shells; Kelzel will need 'em. The trail leads right up Diablo Canyon—and ends there."

When I found Kelzel, he was slowly driving the Mexicans back, inflicting heavy damage. Their route lay in a southwesterly direction. When I told him I was there with my men to relieve him, that deadly *Yaqui-Yori* said he was there for the sole purpose of killing Mexicans. He had them on the run and would not stop for the devil himself. He took the ammunition load from one mule and left. I sent messengers to have ten men at a time come in to the pack mules to replenish their belts. As they were rearmed, I moved them out in pursuit of the enemy. We were not in shooting contact with the red-shirts just then; they were either retreating to regroup, or were fleeing the relentless pursuit of the Indians.[1]

Skirting the peaks of the high Sierras, we advanced until too

1. Records of this rout of the Terrazas forces by the Apache, Yaqui, and Tarahumari are buried in the State Archivos, Cuidad d'Chihuahua, but the researcher must also be a magician to get permission to unearth them. AKG.

dark to hold the trail. The next day, nearing the down-Bavispe Canyon, there was still nothing but trail to follow. But at about sundown, as they were haphazardly fording the rushing river, we caught up with a disorganized group of about 160 *soldatos de cuera* under Batista, one of Terrazas' "generals."[2] Only a few managed to escape our gunfire. I told my men to let them go— maybe they would carry a grim warning to Torres or Terrazas.

The following day we crossed the Naco-zari-Oste and pressed on. Our scouts reported that the Chihuahua forces were attempting to join us with the Sonoran forces and double back. We crossed the Rio Montezuma and now were in the grassy San Miguel Valley. We paused for half a day to give our horses and mules a chance to rest. This made us lose contact with the enemy, but I figured it was worth it. Making good time the next day, we caught up with a black-shirt column of Terrazas' Chihauhueno-Negreros. We made short shrift of them and pressed on. During the night two outrider scouts came in and said a body of the Torres-Terrazas forces was camped about fifteen kilometers to the southwest. I chose fifty warriors and we rode out before dawn to either attack the enemy in camp or to encircle them and thus prevent them joining up with Torres' troops coming from Hermosillo.

Crossing a rolling region with the rising sun at our backs, we heard distant rifle fire. A scout arrived and informed me that the Yaqui under Kelzel and Doroteo Arango[3] had performed a similiar maneuver and beat me to the quarry—which had also been reinforced during the night.

The sound of shooting now was nearer and louder and we could see blue smoke puffs from the enemy rifles. After a quick appraisal, we skirted the hill to our left, just below its crest, and gained the enemy's right flank.

My force of assorted warriors slashed through the Mexican ranks, turned, and charged back. Many Yaqui, by now dismounted, covered our movement with sharp-shooting fire, seeing targets that we mounted Indians missed in our headlong charge. I lost some men and quite a few horses. Wounded men

2. Half the peons who ever served in the Mexican Army claimed to have been generals.

3. The man later known as Francisco "Pancho" Villa by Mexicans and adopted by the Americans.

and those whose horses had been shot came running back. At my signal, Arango led a platoon of about twenty dismounted men in a quick flank movement to cut off a group of red-shirts trying to retreat down an arroyo. When that skirmish was over I saw no red-shirts, but only ten of Arango's men made it back. In the meanwhile we had reassembled most of our horses. A quick estimate revealed we had only 100 horses fit to travel but about 150 men in our combined forces.

With many men riding double we were soon on the trail of the retreating enemy, whose only chance was to link up with reinforcements at Caborca, about twenty kilometers west in the Altar Valley. A cover of black clouds rolled over us and a downpour began, cooling us but limiting our range of vision. We followed scattered trails, finding that the enemy had made it across the arboreal ridges along the wide Altar Valley. It took some time for our scouts to determine the enemy's exact route, to make sure we did not ride into a trap before our force crossed the last ridge.

We split our force—half on foot and half mounted on each side—and charged. We drew a blank; in the lowering gloom the *soldatos* had made good their escape. We bivouacked on the highest point. Our supply train eventually caught up, and the cooks prepared food for our tired and hungry men. Our doctors were busy, caring for a wide assortment of wounds.

Arango and I held a powwow. He reasoned that the enemy was more than just tired—they were shot up and running scared. They not only had our warriors pursuing them, but those of Green, Tenny, and Jemez, while the main body of Yaqui under Kelzel was closing in. After two weeks in the field, the Mexicans' losses were heavy. In the field only seven days, I knew how they must feel. For myself I didn't care—I was there to kill or be killed. Doroteo Arango and I calculated losses of men and horses and weighed the result with losses by the enemy. They had begun the campaign with 1,500 well-mounted *soldatos.* Now they were down to about 400 and, except for officers, were dismounted. They had modern weapons similiar to ours, but our advantage lay in the Indian's instinct and determination. We had been pushed beyond endurance, and it was now or never. Tomorrow, we figured, we could kill them to the last man.

"They do not seem to learn how to fight in the mountains," I remarked. "They never pick a good place to make a stand; they let themselves get caught out in the open. Torres' men can only shoot men against a 'dobe wall."

"Poor generalship," Arango said, grinning. He was good at taking advantage of another man's mistakes. "Terrazas is good only when the odds are ten to one in his favor. So, let us eat and rest—we need it. Tenny and Green and their men will advance along the west river bank in the morning and cut off the generals before Caborca. Those ranchers want to capture horses at the Mayotoreno Ranch, owned by one of Torres' rich generals."

Our cooks made a supper of hardtack, jerky, and coffee. During the night we were joined by the forces of Jemez and Kelzel. It was past midnight before everyone was fed and the horses cared for. The clouds had blown away, the sky was clear, stars were bright, and *Gotchamo* was full—and Apache red. There was blood on that moon and it seemed to wink down at me, telling me the Mexicans had also made the mistake of launching their campaign during a full-moon week! Tomorrow would be the day! Somehow I felt contented. Back at the Bavispe I had grabbed a bandolier loaded with twenty-eight shells, and there had been six in my carbine. Now I had none left and I knew I had not missed often. So I was content in a way. In the morning I would load up and have a field day. The Apache Moon had said so.

❦ ❦ ❦

AT daybreak Jemez, looking tired but not unhappy, came over to where I was standing with Kelzel and Arango. He apparently did not know about the passing of his daughter, my Maria. Now I did not mention it—it was not the right time for that.

He motioned toward my field glasses; I handed them to him and followed to a clear spot overlooking the Altar Valley. He scanned the region for a time, then quickly handed back the glasses. I looked and there in the wide open valley was a large group of men, obviously what was left of the northern Chihuahua army. Although they were about five kilometers away, it was apparent that they were preparing to move out. I waved to

Kelzel and Arango. They took quick looks, then shouted orders. In a minute our bivouac seethed with activity. A vengeful band of Indians can move fast on war trails. We rode out, deployed in an encircling formation. The ones on foot marched in a body to rendezvous at the junction of the Pitiquito farther south. They were the lucky ones—they surrounded and captured a *caballada* of nearly 200 fresh horses belonging to the Mayotoreno Ranch, killed all the *cabalgadors,* and rode on, well mounted.

Later that day our newly mounted men charged into a support regiment of Terrazas' Chihuahuenos. Kelzel proceeded to mete his special brand of justice to three generals and a half-dozen lesser officers we captured by lining them up against the river bank and shooting them on the spot. There would be no "phantom pay" for him this time, but the head of General Luna Luz would be put on his gatepost.

Governor General Luis Torres, if he was in the field at all, escaped us, as did General Joaquin Terrazas. They were slippery officers, the kind who always lead their men—in retreat.

Now they were through, at least for the time being; their fighting force of 1,500, so carefully recruited over the past several years, was now embalmed in inglorious history.[4] The dispatch wallet of Luna Luz had revealed a gold-stamped letter to Terrazas from President Porfirio Diaz saying Colonel William C. Green, an influential American, had personally protested to his friend Diaz, who in turn had issued a proclamation to Torres and Terrazas that all *revolucionarios* must surrender to the Federal forces immediately.[5]

"For you the war is over," Doroteo Arango told me the following morning. "But Kelzel and I will not know peace until death has stopped Terrazas and Torres and their evil schemes to enslave or destroy the Indians. We Yaqui are also far from sure that Diaz means what he says in his proclamations. So, adios, Niño! We Yaqui will see you again!"

"Bien suerte, mis amigos!"

I signalled to the four braves left of my band and we started

4. Also buried in the Archivos d' Indios, Cuidad d'Chihuahua.

5. President Diaz personally dispatched Colonel Emilio Kosterlitsky and his squadron of *Rurales* to enforce the order. A copy of this order is available in the Sonora State Archivos, Hermosillo. AKG.

the long ride back to the Sierra Madre. We made the return trip in five days, having been gone from Pa-Gotzin-Kay two weeks.

As I now look back all of those years to the year 1900, I know those two weeks of strenuous campaigning marked my deliverance from the trauma that had seized me when Maria was killed on that first day. With the exception of a few short pauses to eat and sleep, I had been in violent action constantly. I had worn out three horses and my clothes; I had been shot at, stabbed at, kicked at. Even now, at times, I shudder, and wake up screaming over it all.

❦ ❦ ❦

BACK in Pa-Gotzin-Kay I made a full report to the council and tried not to think of the familiar faces that were missing. When we held a victory dance—the traditional celebration for all Apache triumphs over the hated Nakai-Ye—the old spirit was lacking. The losses we had suffered in winning the war, and the sadness we all felt over the tragic loss of my wife, turned the ceremony into a dirge for the beloved departed.

Mother, Dee-O-Det, Nadina, and others were so solicitous of my welfare that they tired me. Nothing seemed right. I tried working in the fields, tending our livestock, and making signal talk with Buck from Lookout Mountain—it all galled me. A trip to Bisbee for supplies and a prolonged drunk with the old *shaman* helped a little. Somehow the summer slipped by and it was harvest time.

In the meanwhile news and rumors began drifting in over the heliograph and by word of mouth. The fact that Diaz had proclaimed the revolutionary forces out of existence had made him some powerful enemies. Terrazas and Torres were reactivating under cover. Bands of bandits began to operate on both sides of the border; cattle rustling became big business in Chihuahua and Sonora, Arizona, New Mexico, and Texas.[6]

Colonel Kosterlitsky and his *Rurales* were working overtime. On several occasions he came to the ranches to recruit addi-

6. *Gun Notches,* by Thomas A. Rynning, Captain of the Arizona Rangers, Stokes Company, New York, 1931. Also *Cap Mossman* (Arizona Rangers), by Frazier Hunt, Hastings House, New York, 1951. AKG.

tional men. Once I rode with his bunch on a cattle-theft foray. Ammon Tenny had made the charge. Ten rustlers were surrounded and caught with over 300 prime beeves. But then Diaz assigned Kosterlitsky and an elite company to recruiting duties all over the country, and soon again the cattle industry began to suffer and the herds of Torres and Terrazas began to grow.

However, the hands of time and justice seemed to be working. Porfirio Diaz, seemingly to make amends, gave new lands to Kelzel along the flats where the Arros flows into the up-Yaqui in Sonora. Kelzel seemed satisfied. The Opatas were relocated to their satisfaction; adventurous young Emiliano joined up with Jim Grey for he did not want to become a farmer. Jemez received good lands below the red hills of the down-Yaqui, and the Tarahumari who had not married into my clan moved out of Pa-Gotzin-Kay and settled down in their new home.

Before they left, however, Chief Jemez and I got together finally for a down-to-earth talk. Ordinarily a death in an Indian tribe was not of too much concern. Life always had been hard and violent, and death often came suddenly and with no regard for persons of distinction. But the sudden death of his daughter —my beloved Maria—had left both our tribes stunned. We had not wanted to talk about it.

Jemez had found out somehow, of course. Now that he was leaving, we *had* to talk about it—over a jug of good whisky. I told him how it all happened, right down to the last detail, hoping to unburden my own torment. I told him my part in the big battle with the *revolucionarios*—even though he had participated in the running battles and knew most all of what had happened. As we talked we got drunk, and drunker, and remarks were made between us. What was said I did not remember the next day—and I do not think he did either—but somehow our friendship was never the same again.

🌱 🌱 🌱

LIFE settled down to a quiet calm at Pa-Gotzin-Kay, but no one seemed very happy. All our Apache braves had been mustered out of service with the white ranchers, although some preferred to stay on for hire. One day in 1902, in early winter, Colonel William Greene, the copper mining magnate rode in. His constant companions when traveling were Ed Massey and Red Fox,[7] an Indian bodyguard. They stayed a week. Greene expressed a desire to hunt the famous Sierra Madre cougar and bighorn rams.

Four young men and I took him into the canella ledges along the up-Bavispe and he soon bagged several magnificent trophies. When they were packed and ready to return to Cananea, Greene remarked that he liked the way my men worked in his copper mines and wished he had more of them. I told him I'd see if I could get him a few more.

"Good!" he exclaimed. "Niño, I hope you will join up with me. You could move your mother, and any others you want, right down to the mine. We have good housing; and you could run back here weekends to see that things are going all right. Try it, Niño; I think you'd like it." Then he added, "Tom Jeffords is working for me now as my topside foreman, and I think he would want to board with you folks."

I was glad Mother was not within hearing as thoughts of Taglito always thrilled and excited her. We had been invited to Buck's for another New Year's party and I said I understood that he and Tom were also invited. He nodded, said they would be there, shook hands with me, and left.

That evening, seated under the *ramada* around the fire, Chee asked if I was going to work for the colonel. The question nettled me, so I told him I would like a change, but hated to leave Pa-Gotzin-Kay. Now that the country was stabilized, many of our young men and their wives had moved away. There were not many old people left, but someone must look after them. Chee quickly said he and Dee-O-Det would, reminding me that they had done so before.

Mother got up and placed some wood on the fire. It was nearly going out and I remembered that at various times I had heard both the *shaman* and Mother say that when the fire went out, it meant one would move to a new home. I called for Dee-O-Det,

7. It is interesting to note that Red Fox, who is also still living, wrote a book with a collaborator entitled *The Memoirs of Chief Red Fox,* published by McGraw Hill, New York. His home territory is the northwestern plains country. Editor.

and he came so quickly it seemed he had been waiting to be summoned.

"You wish to know if The People will approve of your going with the big colonel?" he asked.

"Do you think you and Chee can take care of the many things that need to be taken care of, if I go?"

"We have done so in the past, have we not?"

"I knew you could, but I wanted to hear you say it." I turned to Mother, "Shall I go to work for the big colonel?"

"If you go, and permit me and Nadina to go with you, I say go, my son."

"It is the will of *Usen!*" the *shaman* added, but did not go into his usual wild dance. I did not think he really wanted me to go.

Several days later Chee and Ealae, Mother and I rode down to the warmer Rancho Verde. Dee-O-Det did not accompany us, complaining that his blood had thickened this winter and he had been unable to gather enough *zagosti* leaves to make his *shaman's* tonic. Kasale, permanently stationed at Buck's ranch as our liaison, and the Green family met us with open arms on the last day of 1902. Buck lost no time pouring cups of cheer.

Colonel Green rode in at dusk with his entourage. Taglito was there and Mother was pleased. The colonel began pressing me; I turned to Buck to ask if he thought there would be any more trouble with the red-flaggers and bandits, but it was the colonel who answered my question:

"Porfirio Diaz is my firm friend and he has assured me that if any trouble starts, he will see to it that it is taken care of promptly—to my satisfaction. I pay him 100,000 pesos a year to be my friend."[8]

I did not recognize the implication at the time, but should have guessed it. Buck and Tom were noncommittal. I told Greene I would come to work for him; we shook hands on it and discussed our problems for a while. As the old year wore out and the new was born, between drinks, everyone became hilariously happy; forgetful of the past, we all agreed we lived in a good world—free of troubles.

Back at Pa-Gotzin-Kay the day after, Mother and Nadina immediately began bundling up their clothes and the things they

8. According to Tom Jeffords, the rank of "colonel" was an honorary title bestowed on Bill Greene by Porfirio Diaz in about 1893.

would not part with, but I wanted to go to bed, for there was no hurry. I asked Mother if it was Taglito that made her hurry.

"I do not wish to talk about that."

Her face turned red, but she went right on packing, and I thought it best to keep quiet on that subject. She packed as though every moment counted. I knew she did not want to leave Pa-Gotzin-Kay any more than I did; she just wanted to help me to forget the tragedy of Maria, and home associations kept it ever-present in our minds. To get out of the cabin and out of her way, I walked over to old Dee-O-Det's cabin and kicked on the door.

"Tell your mother that I am sick," he called out.

"Oh, all right!" I snapped, wondering why I ever bothered to talk with the old coot.

Chapter 17   1903-1904

Big Wikiup

ON January 7, 1903, we rode into Cananea with the warm sun directly overhead. Colonel Greene and Tom Jeffords met us at the bridge and took us across the railroad tracks to the company-owned town of Ronquillo on the west slope of Capote Hill. They led us to the biggest house in the area. It had six rooms and was completely furnished—easy chairs and all. The colonel said this was our home for as long as we wanted it; he asked Taglito to stay with us and help us get settled, then he left.

We pitched in, unloading the mules and carrying our stuff into the house. Finally Taglito and I took time out for a smoke, but Mother and Nadina kept on working. Tom told me he had been there about three months and his job was to see that all supplies were stored in the right places; he had to ride herd on a gang of twelve supply men—all Mexicans—and prevent smuggling.

When I told him I was hired just to follow the colonel around, he snorted. I had been hired as Greene's bodyguard, he said, so it was up to me to see that he lived to get around. Greene had many enemies—people called him "Bunco Bill" and threatened him. He added that I might not have to shoot anybody; quite likely my looks would scare enemies away. I expressed some surprise, as I figured Colonel Greene looked and acted like a man who could take care of himself. He admitted that Greene could, and did, up to a certain point, but he had a temper hotter than gelatin dynamite and as hard to handle. Greene was sitting on top of the world's biggest pile of copper, which he mined and sold to the world. "Copper is man's oldest metal," Tom explained, "and a lot of people try to get to him for it, one way or another, and that's where you come in."

Later that afternoon, Tom took Mother, Nadina, and me to the company store and commissary and showed us how to buy food and other needed items on account. He then took us on a tour of the production area where the roaring hoists, smelters, crushers, and other equipment of a copper-producing plant spread a mile along Capote Hill. He introduced me to many men above and below ground, and also to the office workers.

I noticed that everyone was looking me over. Perhaps it was my long Apache hair. These men were either bald or had short hair, but mine hung below my shoulders, and I still wore Indian-made leather clothes. But the colonel wanted me to look like an Apache Indian Chief!

Back at the house we entered through the kitchen, where a fire was going in the cook stove. Nadina was peeling potatoes at a huge copper sink. Mother was laying white biscuits in a copper pan which she put into the copper bakeoven. Tom and I went into the living room and I settled into what must have been the world's softest chair. A fire was crackling in the stove and the room was cozy, but the smell of food and coffee became so overpowering that I soon got restless. I headed for the kitchen, with Tom right behind me. There were individual chairs around the table—not rocks or logs as at our rancheria.

Our women brought platters heaped with steaks, fried potatoes, fried onions, hot biscuits, and also a huge copper coffeepot. We needed no urging—we ate like *lobos*. When we finished, Tom and I returned to the living room, sat down, and soon were asleep. When I woke up it was black night and I was alone. I prowled around; there were four beds in the house and I found three already occupied, so I took the one that was not. All too soon, the shift whistle awakened me; I crawled out of the world's softest bed, had a quick breakfast, and headed for the office.

Colonel Greene greeted me with "Good morning, Niño!" Then he remarked that I looked a little too wild for some people, so he was going to get me spruced up just right for this job. He was heading out the door as he talked and I followed. We walked across the tracks to the clothing store. He introduced me to Fred

Ballard, the storekeeper, and told Ballard to fix me up with a pair of those fancy boots that had come in on special order. Ballard looked me up and down, stared at my boots, and made a noise that sounded like "Hummm." He reached up on a shelf and dragged down the fanciest pair of boots I ever saw. I pulled one on, stood up, and sat right back down. Too tight. He got down another pair in the same style, and they fitted just right. Noticing my bare feet, the colonel demanded six pairs of socks; then he told Ballard to fix me up with three complete outfits of those new brown Levi-Straus clothes. He insisted on the best and added that Niño Cochise was a proud Apache chieftain who deserved the best—in everything.

The storekeeper looked at the mine owner as though he were crazy. Wordlessly he got a tape measure from a drawer and took my measurements. He laid out three pairs of Levi's new brown britches, jumpers, and three light-wool shirts, each a different color. The colonel had noticed I wore no underclothes and ordered three sets of B.V.D.'s. I had everything new but a hat.

"We don't have any good hats here," Greene growled. "Just stupid Stetsons. We'll get you a real hat in Bisbee tomorrow. Now, Niño, you run on home, change into those new duds, and then come to the office and let me look at you."

I was as happy as a child with a new toy. I had never before worn socks or underwear, and I was so eager I actually ran home to try out my new finery. The boots and socks felt all right but the underwear itched. Nadina looked me over with an approving eye. Mother was curious about the underwear. I could tell by the look in her eye that she thought the underwear was a fine thing.

I went over to the office, where the colonel said:

"Well! you look the way I thought you would, but the outfit isn't complete. Tomorrow we'll fix you up with an embossed black leather gun belt with holsters, to match the saddle you won at Buck's. Now, go back to the store and tell Ballard to give you a black vest."

Back at the store Fred Ballard said, "You look like a dude, but you need a . . ."

"Black vest," I snapped.

"That's just what I was tryin' to tell you!"

While he fitted me, he rattled on, "Mr. Greene says Stetson

hats are no good; well, I'm going to give you one, but first come here . . ." He led the way to the door. "See that red-and-white pole down there—that's Benny the Barber. Go down there and tell him to give you a haircut and a bath. Then I'll stick a Stetson on your head, and you tell Greene the hat's on me."

I hustled down to the barbershop. Benny acted as if he knew me, calling me by my full name. I sized him up, a big fat man in his late forties and getting gray and bald. I told him Ballard said to give me a bath and a haircut, but all I wanted was a bottle of that loud-smelling hair oil (bay rum) and a bath. Benny said that if he had a mop of blue-black hair like mine, he'd be so proud he'd let it grow plum down to his bellybutton. I assured him I had no intention of cutting it—Mother trimmed the ends once in a while—but I would put it up in braids after I brushed it and rubbed in the oil, following the bath. He filled a large copper bathtub in the back room. I stripped and stepped into it. Ah, warm water! Perfumed soap!

When I came out of the bathroom, Benny said I looked great and must be held in high esteem to have a position of trust with the boss. He mentioned that he, too, held such a position with the colonel—his job was to report any talk indicating trouble at the mines. I guessed Benny was a spy. I stood at his mirror, rubbed in the hair oil, and combed and brushed my hair. Then I made a braid on each side of my head. When I was done to my satisfaction, I nodded and left.

"Thank you, Mr. Cochise!" he called after me.

Mister—I had to smile. I went to the store for my new Stetson, and on to the colonel's office. No one was around so I sat down and rolled a smoke. A picture on the far wall attracted me, and I got up and went for a closer look. The wording on it said Cochise. It was a painting of my grandfather, the one made under the supervision of Taglito while he was Chiricahua Reservation Agent. So that's how he looked! No camera picture had ever been made of him. How long I stood and stared I don't know, but when someone cleared his throat, I turned around. It was Colonel Greene with his bodyguard Red Fox.[1]

"You look Jim-dandy—all except that damn gray hat. No good. I want you to have a real hat. A Davis! Take the rest of the

1. See footnote, p. 280.

day off and be ready to ride the train at the crack of dawn."

As I went out he called, "Niño!" I turned back. "Tell Jeffords to be ready to go with us in the morning." I nodded and left, walking on air. I thought to myself, I'll fool Mother and Nadina. They won't know me, so I'll knock on the door. I waited till Mother came to the door.

"Why do you knock—can you not open the door?"

"How do you like my new hat?"

"You have cut your hair!"

I took my hat off and my braids, folded up into the crown, fell to their natural place.

"Hah! You get pitcher took?"

Nadina came. "Oh! You look like Indian in store window—but you stink good!"

Since I had nothing to do and the rest of the afternoon to do it in, I decided to loaf around the house. It turned out to be one of those afternoons when the neighborhood women visited new residents. They came in droves. All were Mexicans and they chattered like Mexicans. They stared at Mother, but as Nadina was dressed like them, seemed to accept her as one of their own. I went out the back door, saddled a horse, and mounted.

I rode aimlessly up an arroyo at the foot of Capote Mountain and wound up at the south end of Ronquillo. Going by a small house, I noticed a Mexican woman who seemed to look familiar, but she avoided my gaze. There were two children playing in the yard and they waved to me as children sometimes do to a stranger. It occurred to me: that Mexican woman was the widow of Eugene. I rode about a mile down a road that seemed to lead nowhere, so I turned back but took a different route. I was in the stable, caring for our four horses and four mules when the shift whistle blew. I saw Tom walking home from work and I joined him. When I mentioned that he looked tired, he admitted it. I had been wondering why an old frontiersman like Tom did this kind of work—he wasn't pressed for money; but all I ever got out of him was that he liked to keep busy and it was too lonesome at Owl Head.

❧ ❧ ❧

THE next morning we rode the caboose of the rattling freight train to Bisbee. It was about sixty kilometers on winding track and a heap faster than a pack train. Talk was desultory, but one thing the Colonel made plain: he wanted to hire a good hoist operator and Tom was to find one even if he had to pirate a man from the Cooper Queen. When the train bumped to a stop in the Bisbee yards, we followed Greene to Goldwater's store. He not only bought me a pearl gray Davis hat[2], but two Colt .45 Peacemakers and two embossed black leather holsters with a double cartridge belt to match.

"Now you look the way I want you to look," he said. "My prestige man. Come on, now, we got work to do."

Tom headed for the Brewery Gulch pool hall where off-duty miners loafed, and I followed the colonel first to the bank of his partner, Ben Packard, then to the telegraph station, the post office, and Thomas Healy's law office. No one bothered Greene. We eventually ran into Tom at the livery stable and he reported:

"I got you a man, Bill—Frank Lavish. You remember him. I found him boozing in the Lavender Saloon. I've got him sobering up in the caboose."

"Fine! He's a good man, drunk or sober."

We rattled back to Cananea that night with Lavish in tow. We took him to our house and he slept on the floor in Tom's room. Next morning we took him to George Mitchel's office before the whistle blew. He recognized Lavish. They talked a little and Mitchel—the night boss—told Lavish to start right away at five dollars a day, a dollar higher than the going rate.

The whistle blew and he went to work; I went to the office. The Colonel said, "Good morning, Niño; come, follow me." I followed him to a big red barn in which there were ten of the glossiest, blackest horses I had ever seen.

"They're Hambletonians—I got twenty of them. The stableboy's out in the bunkhouse; go get him. His job is to hitch these two blacks to the surrey whenever I want to use it. There's a fine saddle horse, a black stud, I want you to ride with your silver saddle." He pointed. "That star-faced one there. He's a

2. Bill Greene knew hats, all right. That Davis hat lasted me many years, but I finally lost it on a bet with a young man named Newsome who beat me in a game of chess.

humdinger. Have the boy saddle him; you and I are going to take a look around these diggin's!"

I rousted out the sleeping stableboy and while he hitched up the surrey, I saddled Star-face and mounted. He was skittish—probably because I was a stranger. The Mexican lad came with the surrey, and Greene got in and put the team into a brisk gait. He kept up a sharp go-and-stop pace for several hours around the project, inspecting everything from the mules' stables on the north edge to the open-pit experiment about two miles south by La Democrata. I rode about ten paces from the surrey to keep an eye out for any strange activity—after all it was my job to see that no harm came to Colonel Greene.

Back in the office, he was soon stuffing papers into his brief-case. He seemed worried. Suddenly he slapped the briefcase shut and headed for the side door (with me at his heels), yelling for Ed Massey as he went out. Massey came and we all climbed the outside stairs to the roof of the two-level office building where the company maintained an elaborate heliograph station. A man began to "warm up" the apparatus to alert some-body far away, while Greene and Massey, talking copper production, opened the briefcase with its impressive papers.

Greene "talked" with Buck Green at the distant Rancho Verde and with Frank Mason at the Cananea Cattle Company headquarters far out across the Chivatera Hills. I watched this modern way of holding council with the subchief and the war chief when the High Chief wanted their approval on his next move. *"Mitchel thinks the lode has petered out . . . diamond drills . . . I know better . . . I want to get more . . . got to get to New York . . ."*

When it got too dark for signalling, Greene headed for his house on the hill and I was done for the day. I stopped for a quick beer at the CoppeRoom and was about halfway home when I saw Greene, alone, with his briefcase in one hand and a suitcase in the other, rushing out of his house and heading for the railroad switching yards. He climbed into an engine with steam up. After a whistle blast, the engine with two cars began to move. Another blast, and Colonel Greene was barreling to-ward Bisbee.

I thought it strange that he should go off at night without saying anything—but I'd learn! It had been a long day. I walked home. Finding the house dark, I let out an Apache war whoop. Taglito called from the kitchen, "We heard you!" He, Mother, Nadina, and Lavish were in the kitchen popping corn. Mother gave me a plate of warmed-over stew, and as I ate, I told them about the colonel. Tom had already heard a rumor that Cananea had run out of ore, and that Old Bill was trying to raise money to continue explorations without mortgaging his other properties. That was how come he was in a helluva hurry. He wanted to get refinanced.

I was eating popcorn when we heard a whistle blast and a locomotive bang up to the loading platforms. I went out on the porch for a look. I saw Greene jump off the engine cab and hustle to his office. I ran over. George Mitchel was there, and I heard Greene tell Mitchel he had forgotten the corporation stocks he intended to sell in New York. Mitchel, who owned a quarter interest in the copper mine, asked, "How in hell you goin' to sell stock when we just ran out of ore?"

"Never mind. Just pay attention to what I say. When I send you a telegram . . . Wait a minute—first you get as many carloads of ore as you can scrape up, and when you get my wire you fire up the smelters. I'll do the rest." Then he pointed to me. "You're the other thing I forgot. Get on that engine—guns and all!"

Surprised—and luckily I was still fully dressed—I followed as he ran for the engine. He called back over his shoulder, "Mitch, there's a lot of ore in Capote Mountain—*find it!*"

The whistle really blasted this time and we were on our way to New York, the colonel apparently to sell stock in a mountain of copper ore that perhaps did not exist.

❦ ❦ ❦

IN the morning, while we watched the landscape roll by as the train neared El Paso, an idea popped into Greene's head. He banged an elbow into my ribs. "Come on! We get off here!" Never a dull moment around this man.

We got off, and he rushed to a printing and engraving shop. There he had a prospectus drawn up and maps and certificates printed. The maps marked the places where copper ore was supposed to be, although there was nothing in the engineers' report stating there was ore in the areas. This nonsense required a day and a night, and then we took the Sunset Limited straight through to New York.

We took a carriage to *the* hotel—the Waldorf-Astoria—and what a heap big, no-stoop-door wikiup it was! Greene told me over a thousand people lived and worked in it. After browbeating the clerk about the rate, the colonel signed the book, "Col. W. C. Greene & N. Cochise." We got a "sweet" of three fancy rooms with a marble bathtub. Greene told me to hide my guns in the dresser as we had to watch our step here in the East, but to stay close to him at all times, and to bust anybody wide open who looked cockeyed at him. I sure had a time as he hit the high spots. First we went to an enormous store where he bought five boxes of new clothes for himself and a pearl-gray derby hat— a Davis. Then he took me to a store called Abercrombie & Fitch and bought me a long elkskin jacket, because it smelled clean and mine didn't.

By now I did not like New York. Too many big buildings, too much noise, too cold, too much smoke, and too many *Los God-dammies.* The people all seemed happy, but they weren't. They smiled only until they had grabbed your money, gold preferred, and whatever else they could gouge out of you. I followed the colonel to offices and parties and watched. He knew his way around. The men ignored me, except for furtive glances, never looking me in the eye. But not the women—they tried to corner this Apache. One slim thing, with hair the color of that of the Maid of *Holos,* tried to finger my braids, which I resented, so I told her Indians had no dandruff since they never washed their hair. She sniffed and walked away with her nose up in the air. Ugh!

Although his corporation was short of funds, the colonel splurged in New York. We were there ten days. He wined and dined his prospective investors. (I liked Mother's venison stew and Dee-O-Det's Shaman's Delight much better than baked oysters and brandy.) With his El Paso prospectus Greene was successful in capturing the interest of some very wealthy people—one, a financier named James Costello. Copper at that time was the talk of the stock market. One could usually attract those able to invest when they heard the magic word "copper."

At one champagne party (not as good as a whisky party at Buck's ranch) the colonel announced that he would haul them all free of obligation to Cananea, Mexico, in his private Pullman coach and let them see for themselves what they were privileged to put their gold into. Colonel Greene[3] had no private Pullman, but that did not stop him: he rented a Pullman and a diner and had the word *Cananea* painted in copper in huge letters on their sides. This bit of strategy was impressive and caused those who had at first demurred to accept the free ride across the continent.

At Bisbee, Arizona Territory, where the two cars were uncoupled from the Limited, he ordered his own company engineers to be "damn careful" how they hauled the big cars over the bumpy copper-company railroad to Cananea. I was at my smiling best as we started the last leg of the long journey. Knowing those last fifty kilometers would be tiring, Greene was foresighted enough to bring an extra supply of fancy liquors—and an assortment of guns so that his "city slickers" could "defend themselves should any wild Apaches appear bent on a raid."

Fears began to creep into Greene's active mind as we neared Cananea. What if Mitchel and Massey had not found any ore at all and there were no fires in the smelters? But the colonel's fears were dispelled when he saw smoke belching from the tall stacks. "Mitch must have got my wire—I sure timed this right," he said in an aside to me.

Our distinguished guests disembarked from the Pullman, the colonel assisting the ladies, especially Hetty Green (no kin of his) who seemed to be impressed with his booming industry in the Wild West and with his Apache chief as an escort! I had let my braids down and belted on my show-off guns long before we got to Bisbee.

The eastern group was fascinated with the roaring smelter, mill, and converter, and that was where the colonel led his guests. I followed along as usual. Actually the colonel himself was amazed. Here was a full-scale operation; men were bustling around and not one of them seemed to notice that there were visitors. Greene called to a workman:

"Hey! Go get Mitchel—quick!"

3. The New York *Times* had a column that called him the Copper King.

The man departed hurriedly. I caught the form of Massey, who was darting here and there, and called to him. Greene could contain himself no longer. He pulled Massey aside and demanded, "What the hell's going on here, Ed?"

"What the hell's it look like?"

George Mitchel appeared before Massey could say more. "You want to see me?" he asked with a sly grin.

"I want to know what the hell's going on here. Where did all the ore come from—this looks like a full-scale operation!"

"What the hell else could it be!"

Although the guests were watching the activity and could not hear that conversation, Greene lowered his voice to tell Mitchel to entertain the guests while Massey explained to him what had happened. I stayed with the colonel as we hurried to his office.

"What you see out there is not a bunco deal, Bill. It's the real McCoy!" said Massey in the office. "We've done found a mountain of high-grade copper ore!"

The colonel nearly choked. "For Chris-sake!" was all he could say.

"We're sittin' on a whole damn mountain of copper!"

"I knew it!" Greene finally gasped. "I knew it was there all the time. I kept telling you and Mitch to get diamond drills and go down after it."

"Yeah. All we gotta do, Bill, is dig it out," added the elated Massey.

Greene heaved a big sigh of relief as they left the office to join Mitchel and escort the guests to the Pullman, where they would be more comfortable than in the Ronquillo Hotel and where he could have a final get-together with them.[4]

I headed home. I was fed up with those eastern people. Tom Jeffords caught up with me as I crossed the tracks. I gave him a rundown on Bill Greene's performance in New York. We both were pleased with the outcome, and he remarked that Cananea

4. Bill Greene, discoverer of Cananea, man of action and intrigue, had somehow failed to arrange for advance publicity, and his wealthy eastern guests had come to Cananea, invested a heap of money in copper, and were back in Bisbee changing trains for their return trip before the Copper-Queen-related *Bisbee Review* and the *Bisbee News* (1903–1911) caught on that the Copper King had done it again. Today the Cananea Mine is still going strong. AKG.

would have no more trouble operating now, regardless of the ups and downs of copper prices here and abroad. He figured that all foremen and special duty men would get a big raise out of it. Mother called me from the kitchen window—just as if I hadn't been gone for three weeks. And me wearing my New York elkskin hunting jacket!

Next morning as Tom and I walked to the office, I remarked:

"Greene's got me guessing. I didn't do a thing in New York except follow him around like a pet raccoon. Me and my guns are just for show. Nobody even looked cockeyed at him. He doesn't need a bodyguard any more than I need a toothache. He doesn't even pack a gun himself—you know that. How come?"

"Well, it's a complicated story, Niño, but since you brought it up I'll tell you before he shows up. You remember when we were in Tombstone about ten years ago and I asked that bartender about Big Bill Greene and Judge Jim Burnett?"

"Er—yes."

Tom told the story of how, back in 1881, Burnett had dynamited Greene's irrigation dam on the San Pedro and the resulting flood had drowned Greene's oldest daughter, Helen, and another girl. Bill shot and killed the judge, but got off with a justifiable-homicide plea. Although the jury acquitted him, Bill's conscience must have bothered him, for he changed his ways, and swore off violence. Now, he didn't pack a gun any more—even though he kept on making enemies.

❦ ❦ ❦

ANYWAY, Big Bill Greene was not a loser. More months sped by, and as his copper production boomed, so did his spirits. Mine did too—they had to, just to keep up with him. I had come to admire him and felt a bond of loyalty. In the meanwhile we made another trip to New York, and this time he took Ed Massey along, too, for he knew everything about the copper business and could talk with stockholders. The colonel also leased a suite on a permanent basis in the Waldorf-Astoria and set up an office in Wall Street. The rumors were that he was now a multimillionaire.

One Monday morning in Cananea, Tom and I, not yet recovered from a hangover earned at Nadina's Saturday-night wedding to Frank Lavish, were sitting in the office doing nothing. The sounds of the colonel's brisk strides came down the boardwalk toward the office. He nodded to us, entered his private office, and slammed the door. The wedding had given me a touch of homesickness, even though I heard from Pa-Gotzin-Kay now and then and knew things were going all right there. On an impulse I asked Taglito if he would like to ride up to Pa-Gotzin-Kay with me. His old eyes brightened and he nodded. I barged into Greene's private office and said Tom and I wanted to go to Pa-Gotzin-Kay. Greene said we were due time off. Red Fox[5] and Quirt could take my place for a week. He wanted us back by then, though. Things were going too smoothly to last.

Tom and I headed back to the house. True to her early warrior's-wife training, Mother always had ready a flour sack half-full of dried beef, flour, coffee, salt, etc.—just in case. She told me to tie it to her saddle and get the horses; she ordered Tom to write a paper to leave for Nadina and Frank, who were on their honeymoon.

We took the shortest, but roughest, trail to Naco-zari Canyon and made camp for the night. Mother fixed a light supper. We sat around the fire afterwards, smoking and listening to the rain. Finally Tom stood up slowly, stretched his legs, muttered something about not being as young as he used to be, and we all rolled up in our blankets and were soon asleep in the brush lean-to we had put up.

It was still overcast but not raining as we ate breakfast. We hit the trail soon after dawn and reached the Bavispe Bend *vado* that night. The next forenoon, overlooking Basaranca, we saw the blackened area that had once held the powder plant. About an hour later on the steep climb to the rancheria of Chi-hua-hua, we were interrupted by an Apache yell:

"*Shis-Inday! Shis-Coza-Iria! Shis-Taglito!*"

"Somebody thinks you're still Chief," Taglito laughed.

It was the trail guard. We could not see him but we could hear his horse galloping through dense foliage and boulders along the trail. When we arrived, all my people, alerted, had gathered

5. See footnote, p. 280.

in one large group to greet us. Mangas-Chee began with:

"We thought you had forgotten us."

I took his hand, saying, "How could I? I have been gone only about a year. I did get lonesome, I admit. You all look all right."

"Things are quiet here," he reported. He had men out rock-scratching for yellow iron, as I had told him to do, but they had found none. He had let two men help Kasale at Rancho Verde, and two were at the Tenny ranch. And, he added with evident pride, he and the other men managed to get all the work done here at the rancheria.

Mother, still the Queen Bee, was surrounded, and she was soon telling of our house in Ronquillo and describing its modern conveniences. Tom was looking for a coffeepot, and found one. The old *shaman* was bubbly with talk of hard work in the fields and said there was plenty of grass for the livestock. He felt strong, he assured me, though sometimes sad, and invited me to have coffee with him. Taglito and Mother were faring well, so I went. Dee-O-Det began questioning me about my new life and how it fitted in with the life to come. He was one of the few Apaches who ever gave a thought to the future. I briefly described my life with the whiteman, telling only of the many good things. I added that I was going to school part-time, and then I asked:

"Ever hear from Jemez?"

"He still mourns the loss of a daughter and a son . . ."

"I am sad that I will not be able to see him. Tell him that I will always look upon him as a father."

"That is good. I will tell him. He will like that."

He spoke of the peaceful life at Pa-Gotzin-Kay and was confident that I would keep it that way. He said he'd had his doubts at times, but the spirits had counseled him many moons ago and now it had come to pass. He looked serene as he said he would rest well when he went to Big Sleep with his ancestors.

"You are not ready to go to Big Sleep yet!"

"No—I have yet much to do before I can rest."

That made me feel better, as I had thought he was leading up to telling me he was going to give up. To switch the subject, I told him that Nadina had married a whiteman and was very happy. He thought that over a moment and then he too was happy. He bounced up and went in one of his famous dances and chants. Then he sat back down, laughing, having paid tribute to a good omen.

Chee and Ealae had us over to supper. Afterwards we all went to the council fire, where I made my report of what I had been doing at Cananea. I told about my trips to New York, but did not go into detail.

All the young men wanted to learn to be copper miners. I told them if more men were needed, I would send for them, but that I could not see an Apache as a copper miner. There was much other good work besides laboring deep underground. The young women were interested in the living quarters. I described the difference between a wikiup and a whiteman's house. The men wanted to know about the rate of pay and what they could buy with a day's wages. Chee suddenly stood up and asked to be heard. I nodded.

"I almost forgot," he said quickly. "John Slaughter gave me a letter for you. I will get it." He ran to his cabin for the letter.

To my surprise, it was from the former soldier-chief, Theodore Roosevelt. He was President of the United States! It was addressed to me, over a month before, and marked to be forwarded by John Slaughter.[6] There was enclosed with my letter another addressed to the Superintendent of the Carlisle Indian School, Pennsylvania, directing him to admit Niño Cochise and three other Apaches of his choice as students. I read the letter aloud and asked the council members how many wanted to go to Carlisle and get a whiteman's education. No one responded, and after a period of silence while I thought it over, we voted not to go to Carlisle.

Later Dee-O-Det, Taglito, Chee, Mother, and I were sitting at Mother's fire under the old *ramada* sipping spiked coffee. Chee was telling about tribal affairs and of his improved signal system. He had gone to Rancho San Bernardino several weeks before. John Slaughter wanted the Manso Apaches to help find some missing cattle thought to have been taken by rustlers. Chee and his riders found over 200 head in a boulder-hidden meadow in the mysterious *Cañon de los Embudos*. Now

6. The letter said in part that his present life was not an easy one—like the life he has seen with us and hoped to see again, and that after I had followed out the instructions in the enclosed letter, I was to come and visit with him in Washington.

Slaughter wanted the dependable Mansos to help him with the roundup.

Dee-O-Det left to fetch a little whisky from his cabin. While he was gone, Chee suggested I take the *shaman* down to Cananea for a short visit; he could make do without him and the change would be good for the *shaman*. I didn't think too well of the idea, but I asked Taglito what he thought of it. He said it might be a good thing. I asked Mother if she could arrange for Dee-O-Det to stay with us for a week or so and she readily agreed. When he returned with a half-full quart bottle, I asked him if he would care to come to Cananea with us and see what he could see.

"I was about to ask if I could visit you some time."

"You will find the whiteman is not very funny. The Nakai-Ye is like us in some ways but the Pinda-Lick-O-Ye—no one resembles him but another one."

"Good; then I will look forward to this. It may be my time to learn something that I have always thought to be."

❦ ❦ ❦

WE made it back to Ronquillo four evenings later. Nadina—now Mrs. Frank Lavish—greeted us and helped to make the tired old Dee-O-Det feel at home. When Tom and I reported to the office in the morning, Colonel Greene looked up from his desk and said:

"Well, you made it—and a good thing. We've got another hoist broken down and they need a good mechanic. Tom, see what you can do. Niño, stay with me."

I followed that man of everlasting energy around all day. The Cananea copper complex was a world of noise activity, and new development—above and below ground. That's the way Greene wanted it; whenever some unit broke down, he was right there.

It was the hoist engine on number three stope that had quit. Tom and Lavish got it going by noon, but had to rob a magneto from another engine that had a broken piston. The increased activity had been hard on machinery and the stock of parts was low. Tom and Lavish stomped into the office and said they were forced to go to Bisbee and get more parts. The colonel agreed and said he'd go along with them in the morning.

When we got to Bisbee, Greene soon had yardmen loading rails and switching equipment on flatcars, and he stayed with them "to make sure the *hombres* didn't sluff off." I stayed with Greene, and Tom and Lavish went to the C.Q. warehouse distributor for compressor and engine parts. Later the four of us were in the telegraph office when a tall whiteman came in. After a jovial "Howdy, Bill!" and a "Howdy, Tom!" Greene and the tall man shook hands. Their remarks indicated a long acquaintance that also included Tom Jeffords and Frank Lavish. Greene introduced me. "Tom Rynning meet Niño Cochise—old Cochise's grandson."

Tom Rynning, Captain of the Arizona Rangers since President Theodore Roosevelt had appointed him on September 1, 1902, sized me up and made some jocular remark about it being just like Bill Greene to have the Apaches working for him. He offered to hire me away from Greene. He needed a good Apache scout south of the border. Green, always alert for the main chance, said he'd loan me to Rynning for thirty days if Rynning would guarantee me American protection south of the border.

Greene and Rynning got to arguing the point; I don't remember all that was said, but they wound up sending a telegram to Colonel Kosterlitsky at Magdalena, to be relayed to the *Rurales* headquarters at Hermosillo.[7] What was in the telegram I never found out, but the two big men obviously were in agreement. Rynning shook hands all around and left, and the four of us had a quick meal in the restaurant next door. Then we went to the freight depot and found that the ordered parts had been loaded and the engine was whistling with steam. We piled into the caboose and soon were rolling back to Cananea.

It was late when we arrived. Mother and Nadina were sitting at the kitchen table, solemn as judges, trying to play chess, when Tom, Frank, and I walked in. I didn't see old Dee-O-Det, so I asked about him.

"Oh, he returned to Pa-Gotzin-Kay," Mother replied. "He remembered he had a message to give to Jemez. He said to look for him when you saw him."

---

7. The Rangers and the *Rurales* were in full cooperation with each other.

I recalled I had asked Dee-O-Det to tell Jemez I would always look upon him as a father, and he had agreed to do so. It was just a passing remark on my part, but the old *shaman* had taken it as a command. He had forgotten about it because of our proposed trip to Cananea, and today he had suddenly remembered it. I got to thinking: an Apache will keep his word no matter what the inconvenience might be, but I doubt that a whiteman would do it.

Chapter 18   1905-1920

The Red Earth

JANUARY, 1905, came and Colonel Greene staged the kind of New Year's celebration Buck Green usually had at Rancho Verde. Buck and Kasale attended the party and during the festivities Kasale told me Dee-O-Det had arrived at Pa-Gotzin-Kay, but had ridden out almost immediately. Kasale had not heard about him since, so he must be all right.

Mother and I, however, were worried about the old *shaman;* he had left us over a month before, in midwinter, and this unexplained absence was not like him. I got a week off from the colonel and rode along with Buck and Kasale on their return trip to Rancho Verde. We parted at the Naco-zari ford and I pushed on to Carrizo Springs, knowing Dee-O-Det would not take the rough Mututi-to-Chivatera short cut if he happened to be on the way back to Cananea.

When I got to Carrizo Springs it was dark and I was tired and hungry. It was cold. I located a campsite in the madroña grove, then unsaddled and hobbled my horse where he could graze. I started a small fire and tried to make myself comfortable. I had forgotten to bring something to eat, but luckily I had nearly a full sack of Bull Durham tobacco and papers, so I could smoke and wait out the night—and think.

I had now been employed by Colonel Greene for two years, there were the trips I'd made with Tom Jeffords and Buck Green, and I'd had other associations with white people. Yet the more I was around white people, the less I understood them. I trusted Tom Jeffords and Buck Green, but no others. I did not trust Colonel Green—he was far too fast for me—and my trips to New York and elsewhere with him had shown me much of his inherent character. Yet I did admire his spirit. He got things done and he was generous; he went out of his way to help Mother and me. He had given me two substantial raises and I was saving most of my pay. I had started at $100.00 a month, now I was getting $200.00. That and what was left of my share in the gold bars stored away in the cave at Pa-Gotzin-Kay would some day buy me a tidy piece of land in Arizona, now that the Indian Laws of the Territory had been relaxed.

Yes, the whiteman is indeed strange, I thought to myself. He speaks with a forked tongue; his thoughts are erratic. White-men do not trust each other: they will do to others what they do not want done to them, and as long as they do it, it is justified —or they make it appear to be. They think that is exoneration. They are showoffs and pretenders. I do not pretend to be anything but what I am, and if they cannot stand such honesty, to hell with them!

Even Taglito seemed to think like them at times. Yet that old-timer sometimes knocked the wind out of me when pointing out my "shortcomings." Now I wished I had someone who could give me straight answers. There was only one man who could do that—my old *shaman.* I would talk with him when I found him. Sitting there alone by the fire, my thoughts ended abruptly when I heard:

"Hah! So you come to think!"

I looked up and there stood my old *shaman,* trail-worn and weary, in the firelight.

"Yes, Dee-O-Det, I have strange things to think of and I have come to find you . . . or did you find me?"

"You wish me to help you think?"

"I want you to give me answers to my problems."

The thought came to me how good it was to carry on a conversation in Apache again. I did not have the heart to berate him for being gone so long; instead I tore into the Americans and the Mexicans. I cleared my mind of everything I knew that was bad about them and all I'd heard bad about them, and omitted anything that was good.

Dee-O-Det got a faraway look in his eyes.

"Many moons ago when the Great Chies-Cochise was Chief

of The People and Nochalo was the Great *Shaman* who drew his power from the Ancient Ones who lived in The Land and who wore as charms the huge tusks of the Great Cat who has faded from the earth and is no more to be seen, he, the Great Nochalo, told Cochise he could trust the Pinda-Lick-O-Ye.

"Later, Nochalo saw he was wrong and admitted it. This was found when Cochise was no longer a great warrior . . . too many winters were on his shoulders. The trusted Pinda-Lick-O-Ye had promised him that if he stopped killing them, they would give him the land on which our people lived, and he agreed and killed no more of them.

"I am not a Great *Shaman* and I do not have the charms of the Great Cat who no longer walks the earth, but I know that what already belongs to a man cannot be given him by one who does not own it . . ."

Dee-O-Det sighed, obviously tired, then went on:

"I see you have no food. I have left meat on the fire in my camp. It is but a short distance from here . . . On the way down, some suns ago, I slew a great mossback buck and made *shaman's* soup. My pot was not large enough to hold all of him so I made it in parts. I have eaten much of him; now I need more. It is pure substance—with hide, hoofs, and horns for flavor."

I breathed a sigh of relief. This old coot had all the answers. We walked over to his camp. He had a thick mass of cooked meat in an old five-gallon can that must have previously contained oil. Knowing that he would not have any vessel for me to eat from, I found a piece of curled bark to serve as a dish. His *shaman's* soup smelled "ripe," tasted powerful, but was surprisingly good. The *shaman* ate, then rolled himself a cigaret from my Bull Durham, and pulled a burning stick from the fire to light it.

"There is much more I wish to talk about now that I feel strong again," he said. "I had to go to the new rancheria of the Tarahumari on the Yaqui Bend (a four-day ride). I took Hi-okee down there with me and performed the Apache ceremony for him to wed a Tarahumari maiden. He remained there. I delivered your message to Jemez, the Tarahumari chieftain, and his answer is that the Chiricahui and his 'son' are always welcome on his land."

"Isn't that something!" I muttered to myself.

"What did you say?"

"Have you no coffee?"

"I have some but first we must eat all of the soup so as to have a pot to boil it in."

"Have you no cups to drink from?"

"Had you, like Taglito, been with The People in the old days, you would know how to drink without cups."

I shut up but my mind was working. Old scout Taglito acted as though he had truly been born an Apache. Most of the time he thought like one. I was afraid I was beginning to think like a whiteman! I felt so ashamed that I swore to change that. After a long silence I said:

"Throw out that stuff and boil some coffee!"

"What will we do for our breakfast?"

"I do not want to talk about that."

He emptied out and rinsed the can in the nearby creek. He scooped up about a quart of water into the can, tossed two handfuls of coarsely ground coffee into the cold water, and put the can on the fire to boil. Then he hunkered down beside me.

The nostalgic Old One reminisced, going back to Chief Tulac who was the father of my grandfather, and of Tulac's rejection of the long-frocked Jesuits who came into peaceful Apacheria. He recalled legends that had been handed down through time from 1540 to 1872, the time when Chief Cochise made his last treaty with the whiteman at Treaty Rocks in the Dragoon Mountains, my grandfather's last stronghold.

The *shaman* recalled that when that peace treaty also was broken, the Great Chief was already a dying man. "This blow hastened his departure into the Spirit World, but before he went to Big Sleep he called his trusted people about him; among them his two sons, Tahza and Naiche, myself, and Taglito, who was his Blood Brother.

"The Great Chief told us that when he made the treaty and put his mark to it they gave him the land of our people to hold forever. They marked the boundary lines and said the land within was to be the Chiricahua Reservation—beyond which we could not go, and also the whiteman could not trespass thereon. They made Taglito our Agent. This was good, although

304

I did not think the white *Nant-án* would keep his word with us or with Taglito, but what else could we do? They had many soldiers, and our warriors were down to a few. Our women already had their faces painted black."

Before the Great Chief went to the Spirit World he insisted that his sons keep his treaty, even though he knew the whitemen would not keep their word. That was the greatest difference between us and the Pinda-Lick-O-Ye. The Great Cochise showed them that the Apache were men—men who would keep their word.

Dee-O-Det recalled that the Great Chief was sitting on his favorite cougarskin, placed there by Tesal-Bestinay, who went to Big Sleep shortly after him. Cochise reached out and took a handful of sand, saying:

"We are as this sand." Then, letting it sift through his fingers, he said, "The sand that is escaping—that is the Chi-hui-ca-hui who are no longer with us". Opening his hand and showing a few remaining grains of sand, he added, "These are all that are left of my people. I have failed you. So now you must study the whiteman's ways and adopt them if you are to remain a people. You can no longer fight them, but you are yet strong and can sow seed that will keep the *A-pa-chui* on the earth that was given to us by *Ihidnan.*"

I had heard all this before, but as I heard every word of it again, my questions were answered. I finally realized that we faced a people who, though now they treated us well, had strange ways and these ways had to be learned or we would perish. Many of my people would try, and fail, to accept the whiteman's ways, and I was not sure about myself. They treated me well, but why?

So engrossed were we in the telling and hearing of Apache days gone by, we had not noticed that the fire had died out. I reached over and grasped the rim of the can. It was not hot. When I brought it to my lips, the coffee was warm but it did not smell right.

"We have waited too long," I said.

"I did not want it anyway," the old *shaman* replied. "We will drink it in the morning."

He pulled a blanket around his thin shoulders and slept.

❧ ❧ ❧

WE got back to Cananea the next evening, tired and hungry. For months thereafter, the place was vibrant with noise— smelters and concentrators going full-blast day and night. It was obvious that Colonel Greene's copper-mining troubles were pretty well ironed out, although my job of guarding him remained the same.

One evening as I walked the colonel over to his house and was about to leave him, we watched the late train pull in from Bisbee and a group of eight men get off. The colonel paused, then told me he had a hunch and to stay with him. Tom Jeffords joined us but did not say anything. The strangers were walking toward headquarters by this time. We returned to the office.

"My name is Thomas Lawson," one of the men, who appeared to be the leader, said as he shook hands with the colonel. "You are William Greene, I presume?"

"Right. What can I do for you?"

"Allow me to introduce William Rockefeller; this man is Harry Rogers; and this is Abe Goldfarb. We represent Amalgamated Copper Corporation. These other men are our aides. Now, Mr. Greene, we will not take much of your time."

The colonel led the way into the conference room with me next in line. Turning to me, he said in a low voice; "This, I think, is going to be good."

He took his big chair, and I stood slightly to his left rear. I had been eyeing the visitors carefully and decided that none of them was armed. Tom took a wall chair. I folded my arms and made further appraisals. Goldfarb was a splay-footed *blanco* whose moon-round face had an oily, pallid sheen that reminded me of *Gotchamo* on a cold night. Lawson was a hard-as-nails Easterner; Rockfeller and Rogers, both baldish and fatish, looked as if their main aim in life was to corral every dollar in sight. The others were obviously just followers—the kind who always suck the hind tit when the leaders are through.

"We will come right to the point, Mr. Greene," said Lawson. "We want the controlling interest in the Cananea mines! You can name your price and there will be no quibbling."

"I am sorry, gentlemen, but Cananea is not for sale—and I own the controlling stock."

All four leaders started talking at once. They argued, shouted, and cajoled, but the colonel remained adamant.

Exasperated, and apparently beyond control, Lawson stormed on. He called Greene a stubborn horse's ass and that if he did *not* sell, they would wipe him from the face of the earth.

Tom leaped to his feet, his right hand flashing out his gun. I tensed and grasped my guns but did not draw. Greene calmly said:

"I've never shied away from a fight, from you or any other goddam Wall Streeters. Now get to hell out of here!"

The eight got to their feet and walked out quietly. I was disappointed.

"What got into you two?" Greene asked when we saw the visitors were headed back to the railroad station.

"When they said they were going to wipe you off the earth," I answered, "I thought they meant it. There were eight of them and only three of us, and you were not wearing a gun."

"How could we know whether or not they were just bluffing?" Tom said.

Colonel Greene laughed, then explained:

"Those Wall Streeters usually get what they want but when they don't, they use strong language. Their meaning is different from ours here in God's country. What they meant was that they would try to bankrupt me. But even so, have Quirt, or somebody, keep an eye on them until the train pulls out."

That night at the supper table, Tom asked, "What was going through your mind, Apache, when you almost drew your guns?"

"I was looking forward to killing a few *Los Goddammies.*"

We both had a good laugh and let it go at that.

The next day was my day off. To pass the time I was helping Tom in the storehouse when he suddenly told me he had come to the conclusion that he was too old for all these shenanigans; besides, his job was becoming more of a strain. He was going back home, take it easy, and live the rest of his days doing nothing.

I asked him if he had talked with the colonel about this and he said he would before next payday. He *was* getting old—seventy-five. I would hate to see him leave—that old frontiersman had meant a lot to me. Mother would miss him, too, but it was best for him.

❦ ❦ ❦

THE colonel was in his private office and I was in the front office, keeping an eye on things, when Tom Jeffords walked in on a hot afternoon. The sky was partly overcast, with rumblings of distant thunder. It was the fifteenth day of August, 1905.

"Man, it's sultry," Tom remarked to me. "Must be full-moon week."

"Yeah—worst part of the year."

"Old Bill's got new troubles now . . . maybe . . ."

"What's up? He hasn't said anything to me."

Tom explained he had come by the dispensary and heard Doc Hart say they had a miner who might have smallpox. He went on to explain what a smallpox epidemic could mean to a mining operation like Cananea. While we were talking, the colonel had come out behind us and overheard the conversation. He let out a roar. We followed him on the run to the dispensary, arriving just as the doctors were bringing in another sick miner. With his usual drive the colonel telegraphed Bisbee and enlisted the services of all doctors and nurses in the region. But they arrived a little too late.

The smallpox threat became an epidemic overnight. That doctors' crew worked valiantly. People who had previously had the "cowpox" vaccine were impressed as aides. Tom had been vaccinated, so had Colonel Greene and most of the white people; but few of the Mexicans and none of the Indian miners had. In spite of the hurried vaccinations and other medication, many miners died.

I never knew the over-all toll, but I know nine Apaches and fifteen Tarahumari died. I worked until I caught it and nearly died, and so did Mother. Nadina caught it and died, but old Dee-O-Det, the indestructable, was untouched. Meanwhile, the whole mining operation was shut down, and three months passed before it was back in full production.

❦ ❦ ❦

ONE chilly day in May, 1906, I was waiting in the barbershop while Benny gave the colonel a haircut, shave, and mustache trim. Whenever Greene got slicked up like this I knew he was up to something. I was reading a dog-eared *Overland Monthly* and at the same time listening to Benny jabbering away, giving Greene the latest news and rumors. When the colonel and I went outside, he told me to go home and put on old duds, then loaf around town for a while and see what was going on. He did not like what he'd been hearing and wanted first-hand information.

I did as directed and later in the pool hall, adjacent to the Club Saloon, I overheard some men talking. They were strangers, apparently Mexican of the *haiga* class. One of the trio was giving our off-duty miners a spiel, his point being that miners in America got twice the pay for the same work. This sounded like trouble. I nosed around and found that these men's names were Estaban Baca, Manuel Dregues, and the haranguer was Ricardo Flores Magon, who answered only to "Big Bill" Haywood, the American Labor agitator. Señor Magon, I was informed, also had the backing of Thomas Lawson, a big man in the United States in copper. Those *haiga* boys were shrewd operators. They operated in Ronquillo (population 15,000) where most workers lived; they bought drinks for everybody; they talked to anyone who would listen. They pointed out how miners could all walk out on strike—demanding and getting wages equal to the American miners—and there would be no trouble.

Next morning I reported to the colonel in Tom's presence all I had seen and heard. The colonel reacted like a man who had suspected as much, and he told me to keep my eyes and ears open some more. He said this was part of Lawson's plot to break him or force him into the Copper Trust. Tom figured they might belong to the I. W. W. (Industrial Workers of the World). I said I'd heard them called "wobblies" and figured they were troublemakers. The colonel busied himself with preparing telegrams. I went out and joined Tom. Soon Greene called:

"Niño! Come here!"

I hurried in and could see by the scowl on his face that he had been thinking things over, and I smelled action.

"Stick close to me. I want you to sit right there." He indicated my chair, which he had moved into a position commanding the door and the big window. "If any of those sonsabitches come in here, watch them like a hawk, and if you think they're up to no good—shoot the bastards!"

The old thrill I hadn't felt for quite a spell began to simmer. I said, "Hot damn!"

"The company will back you," Colonel Greene added. "In the first place, those 'wobblies' have no legal right to strike in the State of Sonora. They're just an upstart bunch of bastards anyway. If they pull a strike, I'll damn well break 'em!"

It was one of the few times I had seen "Cananea Bill" Greene really wild with anger. George Mitchel, Ed Massey, and Jerry Kirk came in. Massey was now general superintendent; Kirk was head of the legal department; Mitchel now was vice-president. Massey proposed we run those organizers out of town. Kirk advocated we sue them.

"I don't think they'll get very far." Mitchel shrugged. "These greaser miners are too damn lazy to do anything except what they're used to doing. As long as they have a woman to keep 'em satisfied under the belt and below the belt, they're happy. We treat 'em good, and they know it. I don't allow the foremen to work them too hard. Ten hours is all we work them. I could get eleven out of them and they wouldn't know the difference if it wasn't for the whistle."

"Well, for now," said the colonel, having cooled down a little, "we'll just sit tight and see which way the worm turns. Whatever they demand, I'll turn 'em down flat. We'll fire the miners and hire new crews—Mexico is full of men out of work. Maybe I'll import some Welshmen and Cornishmen."

The office errand boy came in with a telegram. As the colonel read it, his eyes lit up. Last time he was in New York he had ordered an automobile and it had just arrived in Bisbee by freight car. He said he'd take Massey, Mitchel, and me in the morning to get it. Tom, Red Fox, Quirt, and Mason were to stay on the job and not take anything from anybody. Obviously Greene wasn't too worried.

Early in the morning we boarded the passenger coach Greene

had recently acquired. Since this was a special occasion, all four of us were dressed up like dudes.

His "machine"—as they called automobiles in those days— was a Locomobile four-passenger phaeton. It was painted green. It had copper and brass trimmings, leather seats, and a folding top. It had *Cananea* painted on each side in copper. To start it, gasoline was squirted into four primer cups along the head of the engine by the spark plugs. The cups were opened and the gasoline drained into all four cylinders; then the magneto was "goosed." Next a hand crank in front turned the engine until a piston came to a compression position, whereupon the crank was given a quick jerk upward. If nothing happened, you repeated the operation. If you were lucky and the sixty-horsepower, four-cylinder engine didn't kick the crank back and break your arm, it started. It did on Greene's third try.

We all piled into the fateful machine and he drove first to the telegraph office, then to the post office. The automobile ran well, and people stopped and watched. The Copper King was the proudest man in Arizona Territory. I always went with him to the bank. This time I swaggered a little and clicked my heels.

We stopped at Naco on the border for a drink. Then we headed south across the low hills, on the winding dirt road from Bisbee to Cananea. To this day it has not been paved. It took two and a half hours to make the trip. With a horse it took from four to six hours, depending on the horse and how much you pushed him.

The colonel was exuberant. "Two and a half hours!" he crowed when we arrived. "Two and a half hours! I'd like to see a horse do that. Why it's faster than the goddam train!"

The car was a green beauty, but the trouble was, it frequently went sour and needed repair parts, and its pneumatic tires were always going flat. Maybe it was a lemon.

❦ ❦ ❦

BUSINESS was booming at Colonel Greene's cattle ranches [1] and the smelters at the copper mines were roaring. On the

1. Cananea Cattle Company; Chivatera-Capote Cattle Company; San Raphael Hereford Ranch—in Arizona.

surface the miners seemed happy, but on the subsurface mutterings grew louder. The I.W.W. organizers were getting a large following. Rumors of a coming strike were increasing.

One forenoon Greene and I were in his private office when through the open door I saw five well-dressed men enter the front door. Three were Americans—strangers—and the other two were Manuel Dregues and Estaban Baca, who acted as spokesman.

The colonel gave them a stony stare until Baca said they'd like to speak with him alone for a few minutes. Green drummed irritably with his knuckles on the desk. Suddenly he stood up and motioned me to follow. He went into the conference room and took the chair at the head of the table, and I took my chair at the back so as to command the entire room and door. The five followed us, and Baca came right to the point.

"Mr. Greene, we understand you pay your American help a much higher wage than you pay your Mexican help. Is there an explanation for this?"

"There is—but it's none of your goddam business!"

"We are merely trying to smooth things out, sir."

"My American help comes from the United States and their pay is the same as they were getting there. My natives get all they are worth."

"Mr. Greene!" said Baca. "We want the same wages as your American workers get for doing the same work. We want an eight-hour day, and we think it fair that you hire at least three-fourths native labor—and no Indians!"

"I'll see you in hell with your back broke!"

"We will shut you down. You won't turn a wheel!"

"My answer to your ridiculous demand is—get out of my office! And stay out, or I'll have your heads blown off!"

By now I was standing, itching for action. The Mexicans took a quick look at me and left without another word. In a couple of minutes the quitting whistle blew, although it was not yet noon.

Men began swarming from the shafts, mills, and smelters. The foremen and straw bosses trooped into the office, wanting to know what was going on—and they found out by just listening in as Colonel Greene was "burning up" the one-line telephone to Governor Joseph Kibbey of Arizona Territory, asking help of Captain Rynning and his Arizona Rangers, and then to Civil Governor Rafael Ysabel of Sonora, demanding soldiers to fight off the rebellious miners. He then fired a telegram to his friend, the President of Mexico, Porfirio Diaz, who in turn alerted Colonel Kosterlitsky of the *Rurales.*

Meanwhile the troublemakers mounted a flatcar and began haranguing the miners who were grouped around. The agitators soon had the miners really riled up. They cut the telephone and telegraph wires. They formed into a spearhead and advanced toward the headquarters office building, with a mob of several hundred following. Obviously this was mob action and we braced for an attack. Someone—it was never known who— lost his head and fired a shot into the advancing mob. At this time the miners were still without weapons. It is possible their intentions were to bargain peacefully. They retreated after the shot, but soon became angry again, and a group rushed the sawmill and set it afire; someone set off a blast in a concentrator tank at about the same time another group wrecked the main switch at the powerhouse.

The colonel had had all he could take. He dashed for the automobile, with me beside him. He set the controls, and I cranked it. For once it started on the first turn. I leaped into the tonneau as it lurched forward, engine roaring.

Greene drove toward the crowd. Someone in the forefront took a shot at us and buckshot dotted the windshield. Seeing a shotgun being leveled at us—I took a quick shot at the man and he dropped. Somone else fired back, and that bullet ricocheted off the left front fender. Then the colonel swung the heavy car into the shouting mob. A man threw a long crowbar at Greene. Ducking it, he drove the roaring machine into the milling mob, which panicked and ran in all directions.

Greene then began a quick tour around the mill area to see if any other mischief was afoot. A crowd was forming near the new concentrator so he headed straight for it, gathering speed, blowing the horn; I fired an occasional shot in the air. Those strikers sure scattered! People were now running in all directions, as disorganized as a bunch of drunks. Thinking the riot was quelled, Greene turned back to headquarters. Our office people in the meantime had armed themselves; now they climbed to the flat roof and took up positions along the parapet.

313

The "wobblies" had started new fires in several places, the largest of which were the haystacks and the barns where the pit mules were kept. The barn where Colonel Greene's thoroughbred horses were stabled remained intact, for Quirt and Mason had it well guarded, while Ed Massey and Dave Allison guarded Greene's house on La Mesita. Our Indians, all of whom remained faithful to the colonel and me, ranged the outlying districts. As twilight of the second day of rioting neared, the awful heat and smoke from the haystacks billowed overhead, forming a cloud with an amber glow that reminded me of the burning sky over Basaranca six years before.

🌿🌿🌿

INTO this inferno rode Emilio Kosterlitsky and his squadron of *Rurales* from Magdalena. Whooping and shooting, they charged into the central compound. I hadn't seen such a bunch of bushmasters[3] since the big battles with the Terrazas-Torres forces back in 1900. Their horses were dust-and-lather streaked, as were the men. Half-breeds, *zambos, mestizos* all, they had the lust to kill on their swarthy faces. All wore the crossed bandoliers and the brown rawhide jacket which was the only uniform part of their garb and marked them for what they were. Their wild charge and fierce gunfire lasted less than ten minutes. In that short time those *Rurales* killed more of their countrymen than we had in two days and one night of fighting. We had been waging a defensive battle; the *Rurales* charged in on the offensive. We were peaceful workmen; but Kosterlitsky recruited only born killers, and then trained them to kill efficiently.

Soon came wails of *"Me rindo!"* (I surrender!) and it was all over. There was a lot more to this war than I have set down here and much more than I can remember, but Kosterlitsky got the credit for forcing the surrender of the strikers, and he reluctantly issued the cease-fire order at the insistence of Rynning. The miners threw down their guns but remained under cover;

3. Reconstructed outlaws and renegades. AKG.

316

they were afraid of the infamous Russian who was the *Rurales* chieftain.

Rangers and the men from Bisbee began patrolling the area. After a quick meeting with Greene, Jeffords, Rynning, Foster, Mitchel, Massey, Kirk, Healy, Packard, and to me a *"Cómo l'va, Neen-yo?"* Kosterlitsky withdrew his men to the west edge of Ronquillo. There they were fed during the night by a crew of cooks sent over by Colonel Greene.

We had dinner at the colonel's house, with Kosterlitsky in the role of guest of honor. The next day newspaper men with Military Governor Luis Torres and Civil Governor Rafael Ysabel rode in leisurely with a battalion of State Militia. They set up patrols and posed for pictures and pretended they had won the war. Captain Tom Rynning and his Rangers had restored order at Cananea. Thoroughly beaten, the remnants of the "wobblies" had disappeared. The *Rurales* rode off toward Magdalena, and several days later the State Militia also decamped.[4] Colonel Greene organized a green-uniformed company of American guards who patrolled the six-square-mile area and kept things under control.

Over 300 men had been killed or wounded during the hectic fighting. Greene ordered the casualties buried in the abandoned test pit at La Democrata: Mexicans were placed at one end, "wobblies" at the other, and quicklime was shoveled over the bodies. Mule-drawn fresno scrapers moved earth to a depth of six feet over the bodies and the surface of the mass grave was leveled off.

About twenty-five slain Americans were sent to Bisbee for interment. Widows and children of these men were pensioned off and sent to their homes in America.

Greene then called the Mexican strike leaders together, reasoned with them, and the miners quietly went back to work at the old wage of $3.50 silver per day. The old spirit of camaraderie was lacking, however; in its place was a moody toleration.

What irritated the colonel most, I think, was the loss of his green Locomobile. It had been left standing outside the office

4. Details may be found in the Los Angeles *Times* daily articles from June 2 through 12, 1906; also in the Bisbee *Review,* and the Bisbee *News* of the period; also *Arizona History,* by James H. McClintock, S.J.Clarke Publishing Company, Chicago, 1916. AKG.

building and some time during the night of fighting it had been set on fire. In the morning only a hulk of blackened metal was left of the grand machine. He was forced to go back to horse-and-surrey days for a while.

Colonel Greene ordered a quick inventory and an audit of his financial losses. His lawyers and accountants got busy and came up with an estimate of $2,000,000. To recoup his loss he ordered twelve-hour, round-the-clock shifts for all departments, with overtime pay. He made hard-boiled Jerry Kirk smelter superintendent. Soon the Southern Pacific and the El Paso & Southwestern railroads had to increase their shipping facilities from the copper plant. Before long Cananea was mass producing ninety-seven percent pure copper blisters, and William Cornell Greene became internationally known as the Copper King.

Tom Jeffords finally retired to his ranch at Owl Head Butte in the Tortillitas. Frank Lavish quit and took a part-time job with Phelps-Dodge in Bisbee. Colonel Greene scheduled a long vacation for himself and family in New York, but before he left he gave me a leave of absence—which I sorely needed.[5] It was planting time, and after Mother and the *shaman* packed up, we left for Pa-Gotzin-Kay.

❦ ❦ ❦

HOW good it was to be back riding up the old Chi-hua-hua Trail in the canella hills and red earth, although the whiteman's world had been good to me in many ways during my Cananea sojourn. Th Mexican miners' trouble—letting themselves be talked into a disastrous strike—I did not fully understand. They had seemed happy and were hard workers, but they were not capable of thinking in the right direction, I guess. With us (at least with me) the job had not been one of money; it had been a desire to escape from the past, an urge to learn, and to keep a promise. Taglito understood, and so did Dee-O-Det and

5. Thomas Healy, attorney for Colonel W.C. Greene, and Treasurer for the Cananea Copper Corporation, kept an annual payroll ledger that showed the termination date for T. Jeffords and F. Lavish was Tuesday, April 30, 1907; for N. Cochise it was Saturday, May 18, 1907. AKG.

Mother, but they were true people. They were not the kind who were blind to realities—they knew that nothing in nature is really constant. It took some hard knocks to make me realize it.

Colonel Greene understood my background problem, and he also understood the Mexicans. As a man, it seemed to this Apache, there were two sides to the colonel. One side I liked, the other I did not understand. Both Taglito and Buck Green liked him, accepting him for what he was, and that was that. I respected their judgment. When he left for New York and said he would send word when he needed me, I was happy but made him no promises.

After we passed the north rampart, I began to see changes. First, no trail guard had challenged us. Then I noticed cattle of a different breed. There were plowed fields where formerly virgin grass grew. Although we had come back to the rancheria during the five years I had worked at Cananea—mainly for the planting and the harvest seasons—I had not noticed any changes worth a second thought. I knew, however, that some of the Old Ones had gone to Big Sleep and many young ones had gone either to the mines or ranches, or they had associated themselves with other tribes.

Now when we rode in only a few people paid attention to us. There were more Tarahumari than Apache; Jemez had moved his clans to his new lands above Yaqui Bend, but maybe some had moved back. Two Tarahumari families had built shacks close by my cabin which, happily, was as I had left it. Mother's domed wikiup seemed tired and forlorn, and Ticer's wikiup had a man, woman, and three shrill children in it. Dee-O-Det's new cabin and his weird old wikiup were as he had left them. This I could understand. It had the *shaman's* ring of sacred stones around it which no Indian dared to cross without the *shaman's* permission. Mother and I ducked into her old wikiup. From the primitive to the Waldorf-Astoria and back—I had been told the world changed, but not how much!

Soon the new people came by to pay their respects, and Chee rushed over to welcome us back home. For some reason he did not offer to shake hands and neither did I. Smiling self-confidently, he overdid the welcome-home greetings custom. Then he told us with parental pride that his two oldest sons had graduated from Anna Green's school and now could read, write, and speak English as well as she could! That, if true, would certainly show that the young Apache had great inherent talent, so I remarked that as long as there were Mansos in Mexico, those who could speak English as well as Spanish and Apache, would certainly be able to get along.

He wanted to know about the trouble in Cananea, adding that Buck had asked him to arm his warriors to help fight the Nakai-Ye, but that the trouble had blown over before his men were needed. I told him some *gusanos* had refused to work unless paid more money and they had wound up paying with their lives. Chee sneered and said *his* people would be glad to work for the regular wage—and do a better job. I noticed the "his" that had slipped in, and I began to wonder . . .

Several weeks passed before I was able to think myself back into being chieftain of what was left of the Chiricahua "Nameless Ones" who had fled from the United States in 1876. Chee was not included in that group as he was a Mimbreno and had arrived in Pa-Gotzin-Kay thirteen years later. I made a head count of my people as of this moment in 1907: ninety-one Tarahumari, eleven Opatas, but only thirty Apaches, and many had intermarried.

Mother, Dee-O-Det, and I held closed meetings until we had fully determined our course of action. We then included Chee, Kasale, who came up from Rancho Verde, and Hi-okee, who rode up from Yaqui Bend. The six of us decided to include all eleven direct descendants of the original clan, as they were inheritors.

We reopened the sacred cave, removed all the gold bars still stored there, and divided them as originally voted back in 1894. We carefully resealed the cave and made final disposition of long-stored personal properties of departed ones.

Then I ordered removal of the Tarahumari who had taken up residence in Pa-Gotzin-Kay—but had not intermarried with Apaches—to their former nearby mountain meadow. The Opatas I relocated on the old Cos-codee shelf. This made necessary a division of livestock and settlement of claims of personal properties, which brought considerable argument from Chee and the leaders of the two non-Apache clans at council meetings. But Dee-O-Det and I insisted it was best for all concerned, and it was done. Although I lost no friends, I hardly gained any in these transactions. My firm purpose was to preserve our old Apache way of life and to keep it from slipping into oblivion in my time.

🌱 🌱 🌱

CHAWN-CHISSY walked and we settled down; it was not a pleasant winter, compared with the weather we'd had down in Cananea. By the Season of Little Leaves in 1908 and spring planting, I had word three times from Colonel Greene, asking me to return to Cananea. Each time I declined—through Buck. It was my conviction—reinforced by some advice—that I must stay at Pa-Gotzin-Kay, or lose it.

A few years passed during which I kept in close touch with Cananea through visits with Buck Green and via our signal system. I learned that the colonel was getting richer, that he had joined the Catholic Church and now was praying for his enemies instead of damning them. I'd never understand the whiteman and his ways.

Within four years Greene had doubled his ore production and his holdings, and probably tripled his financial income.[6] His most perplexing problem was transportation to the West Coast. He needed better facilities to Guaymas on the Gulf of Lower California. He wangled with the American Consul, connived with officials in Mexico City, paid out huge sums in bribes, and spent even bigger sums to finance all the improvements he demanded. Tiring of this, he schemed to take over the northern third of the State of Sonora and annex it to the United States. When that didn't pan out, he tried to form the region into an

6. By summer, 1910, Greene had seven shafts and four levels with interconnecting stopes in his mountain of ore; he had seven furnaces (smelters), five stands of converters with flue-dust chambers from the mills, blowers, chemical tanks, amalgam-extraction units, improved slurry and tailing movement, an enlarged battery of hoists, larger steam shovels, new rail trackage, a new fuel source for the steam plants, an ice plant, an enlarged electrical output, an artesian well that flowed 1,500,000 gallons of fresh water a day, and a production of 800 tons of refined copper a day. The population of Ronquillo and suburbs passed 16,000, a bank had been organized, the post office enlarged, another school added.

autonomous enclave, independent of the two nations.[7]

In the summer of 1911 he ordered a pair of his matching black thoroughbreds hitched up to his surrey for his regular inspection tour. (After the Locomobile episode he had not bought another car.) Some men were talking business with him as he started to get into the surrey, and he snapped answers in the testy way that had become almost second nature to him. His foot slipped on the step and he bumped his knee. He didn't swear any more, but he was not averse to making cutting remarks. The spirited horses reared and neighed as he grabbed for the reins. He missed getting them because the Mexican stableman, whose duty it was to hand him the reins, had for some reason leaped aside.

On his second try the colonel got one rein, but the other was flapping loose. He jerked on the rein, at the same time yelling at the stableman. The excited horses swung around and bolted. The surrey smashed into a power pole beside the nearby stone fence. The surrey overturned with the colonel half in and half out between the wheels. He was thrown against the pole, and one of its spike steps snagged his chest and penetrated deeply.

He was rushed by special train to the Bisbee Hospital, and was successfully operated on (August 2, 1911), but three days later pneumonia set in and he died. Interment was in New York.

His estate was estimated at $100,000,000. George Mitchel and Ed Massey took over operation of the mines, Buck Green and Frank Mason the main ranches, Thomas Healy the registered Hereford cattle management—all on a temporary basis. Buck Green summoned me, and the result was that Mother and I moved down to Rancho Verde for a few months while he was away supervising the far-flung cattle empire and helping with legal matters in both Mexican and American probate courts.[8]

7. I think Colonel Greene was stymied when on May, 25, 1911, President Porfirio Diaz, now immensely wealthy, unexpectedly resigned and with his family sailed for Europe. Francisco I. Madero became president.

8. Records of fiscal and physical assets of the Cananea-Chivatera-Capote-Copper empire were turned over to the Cananea Central Copper Company of New York (a holding corporation) shortly after Greene's death. This did not please the new Mexican president, and so La Compañía Minera de Cananea S.A. de C.V. was formed as sole operating authority—and everyone was displeased. Later the records were returned to Cananea and were placed in the old Pesqueria Building vault.

❦ ❦ ❦

BACK at Pa-Gotzin-Kay my old *shaman* had become physically feeble and could no longer get around. One night in December, 1911, he called me to his old wikiup. He was in bed but smiled a welcome as I entered.

"My chief," he began, "it is time that I leave you and take my place by those who have gone to the Spirit World. There I will serve the Greatest Chief of them all."

I noticed that his breath had become labored, and I held up a hand to make him pause; he ignored it and spoke on in whispers:

"Chief, Pa-Gotzin-Kay is done—and so is your *shaman*. But the spirit lives. I ask that you lay me in the cave by one side of that sweet child I gave you for a wife, whose father (Jemez) is a good chief and yet has people to rule."

"So it will be, Dee-O-Det, my faithful *shaman.*" I was quivering. "Shall I call Mother . . ."

"You must not tell your mother that I am going to Big Sleep. She would tell me that I cannot go. Yet I am very tired with the weight of so many winters, so now, my chief, I go for all time . . ."

I put my arms around him and lifted him; he seemed to wilt in my arms.

Dee-O-Det was gone. I called Mother, but I kept my word and did not tell her how he had passed away. She always thought that he went in his sleep.

"My son, it is the best way to go to Big Sleep," she sobbed, "not knowing you are going. And now he is with *Ihidnan* in the Spirit World."

I am an Apache Indian. The Apache, according to the whiteman's histories, is not supposed to show or feel pain. But for the second time in the adult life of this Apache, tears flowed freely.

I prepared a place in our former gold cave near the resting place of my Golden Bird—reserving the other side for myself—and there I laid the withered remains of Dee-O-Det whom I had always loved. My *shaman*, who was not only a *shaman* but a father who advised me, helped me reach manhood, and gave me the outlook that enabled me to get along with a people I did not understand.

I laid his head to the west so that he might watch *Holos* rise, then I placed his sacred treasures beside him. As I laid the last stone over him and covered the cairn with the soft red earth, I called upon the Supreme Being to reserve a place of honor for this greatest of all Council Chiefs. I took a final look at his grave and again tears came like streams down my cheeks. How I would miss this Old One! To the best of my knowledge he had lived one hundred and eleven years.

I thought of his predictions. I could hear him saying:

"Oh, *Ihidnan!* You have taken your child (Maria) and left a man with great pain. We do not ask why, but we ask that you keep her safe—until we, too, can join her in the Spirit World . . ."

❦ ❦ ❦

PA-GOTZIN-KAY was dying, as Dee-O-Det had prophesied, and I knew it. My old people were all gone to Big Sleep and my young people were scattered. Pa-Gotzin-Kay, my mother's dream, my dream, was dying. Only my mother, Kasale, Ealae (Chee's wife), and I were left of the original Chiricahua clan. Could I stay and witness the last struggle, or could I desert the place, the land that had given me so much? I was sick at heart. The sudden realization came to me: with my *shaman* and my wife gone, my dream of a little empire where I ruled, and where my word was law, had ended. Again I heard Dee-O-Det saying:

"Those with understanding will survive the passing of Pa-Gotzin-Kay. The land does not end—only the people on it . . ."

Mother, her face black with ashes, sobbed, "He is gone forever."

"No! No, Cimá! As long as he is in the hearts and minds of his loved ones, he lives with us forever."

"You loved him, Ciyé Cochise, You loved him as you would have loved your *Citá,* had you known him."

I heard her words as though they were coming from across the canyon . . . over the mountains . . . out of the endless sky.

❦ ❦ ❦

MOTHER and I were invited to Buck's ranch for an Admission Day celebration: New Mexico had become a State on January 6, 1912; Arizona followed on February 14. We drank "bottled in bond" to their success, and visited for a few days before returning to wintry Pa-Gotzin-Kay.

Life went on in a normal kind of way, except that I took more interest in helping Ealae teach English reading and writing to our Apache siblings, and we included some neighboring Tarahumari—as many as we could handle. Our only contact with the outside world was via the signal system. Spring came and the Opatas and Tarahumari worked with us as we planted our gardens and fields. We were looking forward toward a bountiful harvest, but it did not quite turn out that way.

We had a stunning blow. Our herds of livestock suddenly became sick, and we did not know what to do about it. Before I thought to ask Buck Green for help, everyone of our cattle died. So did our goats. The same thing happened to the herds of the Tarahumari until not a cloven-hoofed animal was left alive. The plague had stricken them down within a week. When I described it to Buck, he said our cattle had foot-and-mouth disease.[9] He warned us not to come within a country mile of him or his ranch for two moons. We soon found that the local bighorn and deer herds had suffered and died of it, too; but the plague was not widespread for by nature cloven-hoofed animals did not cross the Bavispe Canyon.

For meat we went back to eating rabbits, bear, and cougar, and we hunted turkeys until there wasn't even a poult left within miles. The Tarahumari found a new way to trap moles. As a result, the bountiful crops we had dreamt about were eaten about as fast as they ripened. Only our frequent trips to Bisbee that autumn saved us from reverting completely to the primitive.

The next year, 1913, turned out to be a good year for by then Buck Green and other ranchers had restocked us. They would

9. Aphthous fever.

not accept even a pinch of gold dust for their help, but we reciprocated by keeping them supplied with free manpower to handle their ranges and fields. We did so well, in fact, that Buck and Anna and their sons took the first real vacation they'd had in over twenty years: they rode the train from Douglas back to their native Texas and stayed a month.

❦ ❦ ❦

IN our rancheria we were again holed up for the winter when a heliograph signal came from Buck saying he had a letter for me from Tom Jeffords. I happened to be on Lookout Peak on duty at the time so I asked him to read it; decoding his flashes and dashes, I gathered that Taglito said this was a good time to head down out of the high country and visit him at his low, warm Owl Head ranch. When I told Mother about the letter, she was all for the trip. She had the feeling, as I did, that Taglito quite possibly needed us.

We got ready and left, putting Chee in charge at the rancheria. We stopped overnight at Buck's Rancho Verde. Next morning we continued north, making a leisurely ride as compared with former days, and got to Owl Head in four days. Taglito greeted us in his kindly old way and told us to make ourselves at home, which we did. He did not seem quite his usual durable self, so I took over most of the chores on his small ranch. He complained that the *shaman's* tonic—*zagosti* leaves —had not been effective this winter and his blood had thickened.

We urged him to see a doctor, so he and I headed for Tucson —after promising Mother we would bring her a surprise since she said she'd stay home and mind the ranch. Tom again seemed lively and carefree. We arrived in Tucson after dark and checked into the Santa Rita Hotel; then we went into the bar and got drunk. The following morning Tom was examined by a Doctor Collins, who gave him some pills. Then we went to Ochoa's where Tom bought Mother a white silk dress, and I bought her a pair of white kid gloves. We got back to Owl Head late that night.

The next morning, February 19, 1914, Thomas Jonathan Jeffords, my grandfather's Blood Brother, my mother's great admirer, and my best partner, died while pulling on his boots at the age of eighty-two.

I got word to Tucson and the funeral was held three days later. We buried Taglito at Owl Head Butte.[10] Governor George W. P. Hunt, former territorial governors and legislators, and other old-timers attended, but Mother and I were the only Apaches there. We had painted our faces black in mourning.

After doing what we could to straighten out his tangled affairs—Taglito had kept records only in his head—we left. In Tucson we loaded our belongings and horses on the Southern Pacific and took a train ride to the Mescalero Reservation. We visited the few relatives we had there, but did not stay long, as their attitude wasn't what it used to be.[11] In due time we were back in Pa-Gotzin-Kay.

This was the year the Big War broke out in Europe. This, too, caused many changes. It was also the year I was forty years old. I had spanned the era from Cochise to the Kaiser and had very little to show for it. Mexico continued to stagger under one revolution after another—even sided in with Germany—but as long as they let us alone in Pa-Gotzin-Kay we let them alone.

Later, when Uncle Sam got into that European war early in April of 1917, we were told that America urgently needed cattle for meat, as well as horses for the artillery and cavalry. We Apaches had no livestock worth giving, but we had some manpower—men who were sharpshooters. Many of our people enlisted, but not me. I wanted nothing to do with that whiteman's war. From a military standpoint my age was against me anyway, as was my long hair which I had refused to cut short.[12] I could not go whiteman all the way.

So I rode down to Rancho Verde and Buck Green immediately made me range foreman. Kasale was general foreman but did not try to outrank me. I helped trail-herd thousands of beef cattle and saddle horses from the ranches below the border to the railroad corrals at Douglas and Bisbee, Arizona.

10. Ten years later reinterment was made in Tucson Cemetery.
11. Christian Naiche, Dorothy Naiche, Eva Geronimo, Robert Geronimo, Ramona Chi-hua-hua, James Kawaykla, Nané Juh.
12. It still hangs down over my shoulders, although it is no longer the Apache black that it used to be.

327

Mother spent her summers in the canella hills at Pa-Gotzin-Kay and winters at Rancho Verde. On each trip down we packed along a gold bar and a load of possessions to Buck's for convenience and safekeeping. Mother could no longer stand the highland cold, and she was losing weight. One autumn evening as we were sitting by our fire in front of her old wikiup, I noticed her head fall forward.

"What is it, my mother?" I asked softly.

When her voice came back like a faint call for help, I moved closer and put my arms around her shoulders—how thin they were!

"I see my old home in the Dragoon Mountains," she said softly. "The Stronghold of our Great Chief—the Stronghold of The People. I see myself as a young woman . . . your father is calling to me . . ."

She went on, recalling the past. Then she whispered, "I have had a good life, *Ciyé.* I wish . . . you will tell others some day . . . I bequeath to you, my *ciyé* . . . my good son . . ." Her voice failed.

Nod-Ah-Sti (Niome), my mother—the only real friend a man ever has—went to Big Sleep there in Pa-Gotzin-Kay in 1920 when she was seventy-two years old.

With her I buried my dreams of a land where what was left of The People could live the life they chose—and choose it for themselves with, perhaps, a little help from *Usen.*

Enju!

Epilogue

I NEVER kept records, although Tom Jeffords and Jim Ticer had urged me to do so. They also remarked that I had a good memory, so I relied on it. At Pa-Gotzin-Kay we kept time by counting the moons and the seasons, or we would ask the *shaman*. Sometimes we overlooked a season or two—sometimes we might have added one or two. It did not make any difference. It did not occur to us that others in some future time would want to know about us.

Our main problems were of today; who knows what the future holds? We were "The Nameless Ones," and I had never been dog-tagged, tattooed, or registered on a reservation, so in the whiteman's view I did not belong in history. Now I was not only an orphan but I had no close kin. Shortly after Mother's passing, Chee, Kasale, Hi-okee, and I again got together and held council meetings and made final disposition of all personal properties, each taking his share and going his separate way.

Down through the years my mother, Dee-O-Det, and I had accumulated many things, and these plus the things of others I had inherited represented a problem—as did my share of the gold. I got to thinking of Big Jim Grey, an old hand at moving "trade goods" both ways across the border. Buck Green helped me locate him. Grey was getting old but was still in business, having moved his base of operations out of Mexico and into America.

I told him what I had in mind and he said it was no problem.

He could put an elephant through a chain-link fence if the price was right. It was, and he did. With a motley crew of border men we packed all my belongings at Pa-Gotzin-Kay and Rancho Verde and eventually unpacked them and cached them in his adobe warehouse in the Camisillacabo Island district of El Paso. This "ragged shirt-tail district" was a sort of no man's land hemmed in between the river and the city with about 100 residents of dubious nationality—just the place from which to operate. Big Jim liked to get by with a minimum of contact with officialdom.

Among the many items we had packed out were: eleven bars of gold, a raw-silver bowl made for my mother by Taglito, the oil portrait of my grandfather, Chief Cochise (painted by an itinerant artist under the eagle eye of Taglito about a year after Cochise's passing); the Nakai-Ye thighbone used as a war club by Ma-T-O-Tish but not held sacred by Dee-O-Det; the silver-inlaid Mexican saddle given me by Uncle Naiche when I was a boy; the heavy silver saddle I had won as a prize at the Turn-of-the-Century party at Buck Green's Rancho Verde; and hair of the mane and tail of the white Barb stallion that had been shot out from under me near Chi-hua-hua's old rancheria. There were also two very valuable white moleskin ceremonial robes; my fancy buckskin and bighorn ceremonial outfits; one complete heliograph outfit; two telescopes; a gold watch; a fine Sibley stove made of copper; a basketful of jewelry; numerous animal skins, serapes, and blankets; not to mention the sheath knife that I used to kill the *Netdahe* Apla-Chi-Kit in Basaranca; the set of twin Colt 44/40 sixguns I carried while bodyguarding Colonel Greene; and an assortment of primitive and modern weapons accumulated through the years by the clan in Pa-Gotzin-Kay.

I dallied at Big Jim's, even considering his proposition of going into partnership with him. It was through this arrangement that I was easily able to dispose of my share of the gold bars. I received exactly $12,000 in U.S. Paper currency for them. This, along with the currency Mother and I had already saved, gave me net cash of slightly over 17,000 U.S. dollars. At no time in my life, before or since, have I had that much money. It was a small fortune. But the shifting climates of mood and age play their part in the lives of men.

Epilogue

What with the constant unrest of the people in northern Mexico, Buck Green finally got fed up, sold his Rancho Verde, and moved to Texas. Ammon Tenny had also given up in disgust, disposed of his property as best he could, and moved to Arizona. Al Bower and Jack Brewer had already quit ranching and farming in Mexico. Jim Grey, spurning the demands of a mere sentry who was seeking a bribe, was shot and slightly wounded. Put in the prison hospital at Chihuahua City for treatment, he died of neglect. This was also the year, February 15, 1922, to be exact, when John H. Slaughter died in his new home in Douglas, Arizona, where I attended his funeral.

I was not gifted with foresight like Uncle Golthlay (Geronimo) or my *shaman,* Dee-O-Det, but I saw I had better get busy and make a move before someone beat me to it. I quickly took all my properties from the adobe warehouse and, under my old pseudonym of Ramon Rodriguez, stored them in Tucson.

With my money in a belt, I headed for Hollywood, and soon fell in with Leo Carrillo, a *Godo*-Californian motion-picture star, and his crowd of fast-steppers. Then I shifted my allegiance to a Cherokee, Monte Blue, and his hard-drinking band of Indian friends. This was in the Prohibition Era—a law we delighted in breaking—and in a few years I found myself short on cash but long on experience. It seemed that I was always making mistakes. Sometimes I made the same error two, three, even four times before I caught on to the whiteman's ways. In my former years in the Sierra Madre it had been different—there I had been able to make on-the-spot decisions and they always turned out right.

I finally decided to become an actor. On the Jesse L. Lasky lot I met Apache Charley Stevens and Apache Bill Russell. Both were from Arizona and had white blood, but they looked more Indian than white. After a few snorts of bootleg whisky, Charley got me an extra's part in *Robin Hood,* starring Douglas Fairbanks—a fine man who placed Charley in every one of his pictures. Later I was an extra in a sea epic, *The Black Pirate,* also starring Douglas Fairbanks, with Charley Stevens in a supporting role. Bill Russell and I were in *Cimarron,* starring Richard Dix; and we wangled our way into *Tumbleweeds,* starring William S. Hart, and *The Big Trail,* in which Charley had a heavy role. It was John Wayne's first motion picture.

After several years of this I got restless and saw I wasn't getting anywhere. My goal was to buy some land in Arizona, but I wound up riding the Pickwick bus north to Eureka in the company of Larry Douglas, another Indian I had met in Hollywood. He too was fed up with "things" in the movie industry. He was a big Huppa, from the Modoc Reservation on the Oregon-California border. Enroute home he told me about his former job with the Hammond Lumber Company, then one of the biggest lumber producers in America. We got signed on as choker setters, but the job didn't last; there was a depression and the lumber industry sawed to a standstill.

Franklin D. Roosevelt was inaugurated on March 4, 1933, and got things moving again with the NRA program and "a pint on every hip." I owned an old Packard sedan by then and had a little money, so I headed south. The Packard quit on me in Monterey. I pushed it into a garage and when I got out of there I owned a two-year-old Chevrolet. I had about $40.00 left in my jeans. Meanwhile I had been making yearly storage payments for my relics from my Pa-Gotzin-Kay days. Paying storage fees had always griped me, so after thinking things over a week or so, I swapped the Chevrolet for a good one-ton Studebaker stake truck. I loaded all my relics into it and headed for Phoenix, where I opened a museum but soon saw it was a losing game. Phoenix was an unappreciative cowtown. The snowbirds who came there for the winter were my only customers. Then I got smart: I moved north to Montana and set up business in resort areas for the summers, then went back south for the winters. Moving around, I operated at one time or another in all eleven western states and was doing all right, especially at the State and County Fairs.

At the time Pearl Harbor was bombed I had about half my original batch of relics left, a heap of old-west items I'd traded for, and a wad of about $300.00. I put the relics back into storage in San Fernando, California, and went to work. By the time the war ended, I had been hired and fired by four different defense contractors (always on account of my long hair), but I was fat and sassy. In the meanwhile I had formed a close friendship with Rory Taylor, a half-Yakima Indian, who had been a crop duster until the war put him out of business. I had enough cash

saved up to go fifty-fifty in business with him in the Wen-
natchee country east of Seattle. We hired a former fighter pilot
and he and Taylor did the dusting while I did the promoting.
When the fighter pilot, Gib Evans, got himself killed, Taylor
insisted on making a pilot out of me!

Well, we had firm contracts and money in the bank—so why
not? This was 1947 when I was seventy-three years old, but felt
like thirty-three. You only live once! Besides, who's afraid of
anything he understands? At least I let myself believe I understood my chances. Taylor said "the odds were seventy/thirty";
what he failed to add was "not in my favor." He was a good
instructor and I was soon soloing. However, we were shortly
able to hire another ex-war pilot, Bob Peters. Then he and
Taylor got to drinking and horsing around with a couple of
blondes, and business began to fall off. I got disgusted and we
dissolved our partnership. Again I came out on the short end of
the stick.

I took off in the Swift GB-model cabin monoplane that was
my share of the split-up, intending to fly down to Eureka, California, but hadn't gone fifty miles when something went sour.
I crash-landed in a cloud that had a rocky hill in it and woke
up in the Beacon Hill Hospital in Seattle. When I left there I
was shy my left leg and half of my left hand. I hobbled to the
bus station on an artificial leg.

This was in 1950 and I felt low. I was seventy-six years old!
After all I had been through, I had to go and get myself crippled
in the whiteman's flying machine! It was the first time in my
life I felt my age. I got to wondering how many whitemen lived
past seventy. I recalled old Dee-O-Det who lived to be 111, and
others who had lived to 100—even Taglito lived and was active
for eighty-two years.

My mind seemed fuzzy when I looked back, but I was determined to go down to Eureka and see an old museum operator
acquaintance, Carl Mathiesen. Then I'd settle down in the relics game. I limped in on him and we made a bargain, with the
result that I sent to San Fernando and got my bunch of relics
out of storage. Carl had a fine house on the Eureka outskirts
along Highway 101 where the highway crossed the Eel River
and the Mad River. We staged a grand exhibit, but erratic man-
agement and a slow season made us both dissatisfied.

I told Carl I would sell out to him for $50,000. He agreed that was a fair price, but since I wanted cash, he would have to borrow some money. I gave him a one-week option for $100.00.

Fifty thousand dollars! I could just see a nice piece of land with the bright golden sand in Dragoon Springs at the entrance to Cochise Stronghold in the Dragoon Mountains—and a nice house on it.

In the meanwhile, unbeknown to me, some dealer from Phoenix, Arizona, came to town and talked to Mathiesen. Carl offered to sell him all "his" old Apache and frontier relics for $70,000. The dealer told him he would come out the next day and make an appraisal.

This was during the northern California rainy season—and when it rains there, it rains! A construction job in progress on Highway 101 had formed a temporary land-fill dam a short distance above Carl's house. That night both the Eel and the Mad Rivers overflowed their banks, dammed up behind the land fill, and then the dam gave way. Many buildings, including Carl's house with my lifelong accumulation of relics and papers, were swept downstream by the flood.

Stripped to my underwear, I managed to escape on one leg with the other one under my arm, and with a few clothes—including my pants and my wallet. I was unable to salvage more than a wheelbarrowful of my property. I offered a $200.00 reward for the recovery of my lamented wife's white moleskin, wedding-ceremony robe.

I gave up after a month of searching. I was not only lost, but forlorn. I headed for Hollywood to see if I could pick up some of the old trails there. I did, and I didn't. Too many changes had been made in the past twenty years. I found Charley Stevens was still acting in pictures, and Bill Russell was getting along by making personal appearances at social parties and club banquets.

Hollywood was making *Broken Arrow,* which was the film title of *Blood Brother,* written by Elliot Arnold, an historical novel in which my paternal grandfather, Chief Cochise, and Indian Agent Tom Jeffords (Taglito) were real-life characters from the historic past. I applied at United Artists for the chance to play the part of my grandfather, thinking there was no one left alive who was so fully qualified. The fat casting director

334

looked me up and down and spat; "Nah, ya ain't d'type!"

If he had said one more word, I'd have killed him.

I followed Bill Russell on the personal-appearance trail and rode in a few parades; then I rode off on my own, billed as an Apache Scout for a tourist agency. This, among other things, eventually galled me, although it was an easy way to make a living. One thing I detested was the way many people made a fuss over me, especially women. "Niño Cochise—grandson of the Great Apache Chief!" Ugh! Then, too, I hated the rush and smell, the noise and traffic; it seemed there were millions and millions of automobiles in southern California where there used to be only a few thousand. I had known change was inevitable, but not to this extent. I took the Greyhound bus to Tucson, back to the land of my birth—Arizona, where the skies are always blue. I was willing to settle for any piece of land near the Dragoon Mountains, with any old shack on it. What was that saying about a young man's fancies and an old man's memories?

Down through the years I had become acquainted with other men who followed diverse trails, but whenever our trails crossed we'd pause and, sometimes, have a drink. One of them was A. Kinney Griffith, who never wanted anything from me, except that I write my life story.

Some ten years or so ago, he got to pushing me hard about it. "If you don't get with it soon, you'll never make it," he maintained. I was irrevocably disenchanted with the whiteman by now, but since he was always, like Taglito, a *simpático,* I buckled down and—got with it. *Hi-dicho*—it is finished.

CO-AUTHOR'S ADDENDUM

This biographer was introduced to Niño Cochise at the funeral of pioneer John H. Slaughter in Douglas, Arizona, on February 19, 1922. Niño was, and is, the most outstanding male Indian I have ever met—before or since. He told me a little about himself at the time, and I kept in touch with him down through the years, often helping him to avoid the exploitation he faced in the whiteman's world. I followed his ups and downs in the cinema capital, through the prohibition era, the depression, his adventures as a trader, and the eventual loss of his rich legacy. His end nearly came when he tried to master the ultimate of the whiteman's world—the airplane. Crippled, he entered the life of a near-celebrity: an Apache chieftain riding in rodeo parades, wild-west shows, sporting events, political meetings, etc. Pitfalls were many. He never quit trying, but nature and physical handicaps worked against him. Some friends helped him set up Cochise Trading Post near Tombstone, and he settled down. His infirmities are such that it is almost impossible for him to move around now unaided. He doesn't look at TV much, but he enjoyed watching the astronauts walk on the moon. Today, in his upper nineties, with paradise lost, he sometimes gets a twinkle in his black eyes that seems to say, "This whiteman's world is just about what my old *shaman* said it would be."

A.K.G.

Index

Index

Index

LEGEND

1 Fort Whipple
2 Fort Mojave
3 Fort Verde
4 Fort Apache
   (White River)
5 Fort McDowell
6 Camp Goodwin
7 San Carlos Res.
   (Sibley City)
8 Fort Thomas
9 Fort Grant
10 Fort Yuma
11 Chiricahua Res.
12 Fort Bowie
13 Fort Haachuca
14 Fort Buchanan
15 Fort Bayard
16 Fort Cummings
17 Fort Seldon
18 Fort Stanton
19 Mescalero Res.
20 Fort Bliss
21 Sasabe
22 Cananea
23 San Bernardino
24 Boca Grande

TERRITORY
OF
ARIZONA

PHOENIX

COLORADO

GILA

VERDE

GILA

SANTA CRUZ

SANTA ROSA

TUC

10

21

Gulf of Californ

ALTAR

SECO

ALISOS

29

30

M

SAN MIGUEL

Cochise, Ciyé, 1874–
      The first hundred years of Niño Cochise; the untold
story of an Apache Indian chief, as told by Ciyé "Niño"
Cochise to A. Kinney Griffith. London, New York, Abelard-Schuman ₁1971₁

      346 p. illus. 24 cm. $9.95(U.S.)   B***

244854

      1. Apache Indians.   I. Griffith, A. Kinney.   II. Title.

E99.A6C57   970.3 [B]   70–157980
ISBN 0–200–71830–4   MARC

Library of Congress   71 ₁40–2₁